RELIGION AND THE SOCIAL ORDER

Volume 4 • 1994

BETWEEN SACRED AND SECULAR: RESEARCH AND THEORY ON QUASI-RELIGION

RELIGION AND
THE SOCIAL ORDER

BETWEEN SACRED AND SECULAR:
RESEARCH AND THEORY ON QUASI-RELIGION

Series Editor: **DAVID G. BROMLEY**
Department of Sociology and Anthropology
Virginia Commonwealth University

Volume Editors: **ARTHUR L. GREIL**
Division of Social Sciences
Alfred University

THOMAS ROBBINS
Rochester, Minnesota

OFFICIAL PUBLICATION OF THE
ASSOCIATION FOR THE SOCIOLOGY OF RELIGION

VOLUME 4 • 1994

 **JAI PRESS INC.**

Greenwich, Connecticut   *London, England*

jet

CONTENTS

LIST OF CONTRIBUTORS

Eileen Barker	Department of Sociology London School of Economics and Political Science
Benjamin Beit-Hallahmi	Department of Psychology University of Haifa
Lewis F. Carter	Division of Humanities and Social Sciences Washington State University
Clarke E. Cochran	Department of Political Science Texas Tech University
N.J. Demerath III	Department of Sociology University of Massachusetts
Beth A. Eck	Department of Sociology University of Virginia
Shoshanah Feher	Department of Sociology University of California, Santa Barbara
Richard K. Fenn	Princeton Theological Seminary
Arthur L. Greil	Division of Social Sciences Alfred University
Irving Hexham	Department of Religious Studies University of Calgary
James Davison Hunter	Department of Sociology University of Virginia

Meredith B. McGuire

Department of Sociology and
    Anthropology
Trinity University

Mary Jo Neitz

Department of Sociology
University of Missouri

James L. Nolan, Jr.

Department of Sociology
University of Virginia

Nikos Passas

Department of Criminal Justice
Temple University

John Steadman Rice

Department of Sociology
Boston University

Thomas Robbins

Rochester, Minnesota

Terry Schmitt

Program on Non-Profit Organizations
Yale University

Amy B. Siskind

New School of Social Research

Melinda Bollar Wagner

Department of Sociology and
    Anthropology
Radford University

Arnold S. Weiss

Los Angeles, California

INTRODUCTION:
EXPLORING THE BOUNDARIES OF THE SACRED

Arthur L. Greil and Thomas Robbins

ABSTRACT

This volume brings together a series of papers dealing with groups, organizations, and movements which appear to straddle the border between the sacred and the secular. A concern with sociological definitions of religion draws our attention to "para-religions," apparently secular phenomena which nonetheless appear to have certain religious features. A concern with folk definitions of religion focuses our attention on "quasi-religions," groups and activities which deal with the sacred but are anomalous given the American folk category of "religion." A concern with political definitions of religion leads us to examine the question of "authenticity," the process by which interest groups compete for the right to be seen as genuine religions. The papers in this volume, taken as a whole, seem to suggest that contemporary society is witnessing a rise in the number and significance of quasi-religious groups and that the boundary between the sacred and the secular is becoming increasingly blurred. As folk definitions of religion continue to evolve under the pressures of modernity and as religion increasingly becomes more controversial, the scholarly study of the boundary between the sacred and the secular becomes more important to an understanding of religion in modern societies.

Religion and the Social Order, Volume 4, pages 1-23.
Copyright © 1994 by JAI Press Inc.
All rights of reproduction in any form reserved.
ISBN: 1-55938-763-7

My religion? Well, my dear, I am a Millionaire. That is my religion.
—George Bernard Shaw,
Major Barbara (1960)

To define "religion," to say what it is, *is not possible at the start of a presentation such as this. Definition can be attempted, if at all, only at the conclusion of the study.*
—Max Weber, *The Sociology of Religion* (1963)

it is stupid to call cults like the Branch Davidians "religious." It would be more accurate to call them "personality cults." They shut out the world and subject themselves to charismatic authority figures like Koresh. But whether the religion they claim is Christian, non-Christian or New Age,...religion is just a "flag of convenience" that cults use to give themselves tax-exempt status and shelter from critics.
—Nick Coleman,
St. Paul Pioneer Press 1993)

"What we have in the environmental movement is not science but a guilt-obsessed, secular religion," says Steven Hayward, chief of research for San Francisco's Pacific Research Institute for Public Policy. "These people don't deal in evidence and research but in the advocacy of 'received truth.'"
—Christopher Byron,
New York Magazine (1992)

This volume brings together a series of papers dealing with groups, organizations, and movements which appear to straddle the border between the sacred and the secular and which have sometimes been referred to as "quasi-religions" or "para-religions." Focusing on such groups highlights the problematic nature of the task of distinguishing the religious from the nonreligious and draws our attention to some of the theoretical issues involved in defining religion. The papers in this volume, taken as a whole, seem to suggest that contemporary society is witnessing a rise in the number and significance of quasi-religious groups and that the boundary between the sacred and the secular is becoming increasingly blurred. Thus, the present volume attempts to achieve two goals simultaneously. On the one hand, it uses the analysis of quasi-religious and para-religious groups as a means of contributing to (and, we hope, transcending) the sociological debate over the definition of religion. On the other hand, it uses the analysis of quasi-religious and para-religious groups as a springboard for understanding changes in the nature of contemporary religion and the role of religion in postmodern society.

QUASI-RELIGION, PARA-RELIGION, AND THE TASK OF DEFINITION

That the boundary between the religious and the nonreligious is not easy to pinpoint is indicated by the large number of scholars who have pointed out analogies between religion and such avowedly secular enterprises as business (Bromley and Shupe 1990; Peven 1968), sport (Mathisen 1992; Novak 1976), politics (Crippin 1988; Lane 1981; O'Toole 1977; Warner 1959; Zuo 1991), therapeutic groups (Galanter 1989, 1990; Greil 1993; Greil and Rudy 1984; Rudy and Greil 1988), medicine (Frank 1963; Roth 1957; Wolf 1988), and social movements (Beyer 1992; Brinkerhoff and Jacob 1987; Hannigan 1990, 1991). There is, apparently, no institution in society which is totally without the patina of the sacred (see Greil 1993 for a general review of this literature). Perhaps the best-known literary treatment of the sacredness of the supposedly secular is George Bernard Shaw's (1960) play, *Major Barbara,* in which Barbara Undershaft—a major in the Salvation Army—tries to show her father—a munitions manufacturer—the wisdom of Christianity at the same time that he tries to convert her to his faith, Capitalism.

Another indication that the boundary between sacred and secular is problematic is the enormous difficulty sociologists have encountered in their attempts to construct a generally acceptable definition of religion. After all, one function of a definition is to demarcate instances of the phenomenon being defined from instances of apparently similar phenomena; an inability on the part of scholars to agree upon a definition of religion would seem to indicate a lack of consensus with regard to the boundaries of their subject. In this paper, we discuss three types of definitions of religion: *sociological* definitions, *folk* definitions, and *political* definitions. Each type of definition draws our attention to a different set of issues concerning the boundary between the sacred and the secular.

Sociological Definitions of Religion and the Realm of Para-Religion

Sociological definitions of religion represent attempts on the part of social scientists to delimit the phenomenon of religion as an area of scholarly investigation. The sociological literature on defining religion features a debate between those who advocate functionalist definitions and those who promote substantive definitions. Functionalist definitions of religion emphasize that the essential element in religion is the provision of an "encompassing system of meaning" (Luckmann 1967, p. 53) or the ability to "relate man to the ultimate conditions of his existence" (Yinger 1970, p. 70). Substantive definitions of religion argue that the feature that is essential in distinguishing religion from other types of human activity is its reference to the sacred, the supernatural or the "superempirical" (Robertson 1970, p. 47).

The advantage of functional definitions is that they allow us to transcend commonsense definitions of religion and to look at beliefs and practices not commonly referred to as religious but which may nonetheless resemble religious phenomena in important ways. One major disadvantage of functional definitions is that they may have the effect of so broadening the concept of religion that it becomes meaningless. An advantage of substantive definitions of religion is that they accord more closely with American folk definitions of religion—that is, with commonsense views of what a religion is. But substantive definitions are not without their critics. Some argue, for example, that to limit the "religious" to that which has a supernatural referent is to exclude from the category of "religion" belief systems such as Buddhism, some versions of which do not involve belief in a God or Gods. Others argue that the very notion of the "supernatural" implies a particular religious or cultural point of view and that, therefore, to limit the notion of "religion" to that which entails a belief in the supernatural is to establish one religious tradition as the "scientific" standard by which others are to be judged.

Greil (1993) has used the term "para-religion" to refer to phenomena which seem to share features with religious phenomena but which do not make explicit reference to a supernatural or superempirical realm. The concept of para-religion may perhaps be regarded as a compromise between functionalist definitions and substantive definitions. To use the term "para-religion" to refer to activities and organizations which involve expressions of ultimate concern or organizational dynamics similar to those of religious organizations narrowly defined, but which do not involve a belief in the supernatural or superempirical, seems preferable to engaging in interminable debates about what religion "really" is.

Thus, for example, several scholars have drawn attention to the religious aspects of certain types of businesses. Peven (1968) analyzed the use of what she called "religious revival techniques" to socialize personnel of home-party sales organizations. Bromley and Shupe (1990) have described such direct sales organizations as Amway Corporation, Herbalife International, and Mary Kay Cosmetics as having sectarian characteristics. But the similarities between business and religion are not necessarily limited to "fringe" businesses. The paper by Demerath and Schmitt (this volume), titled "Transcending Sacred and Secular: Mutual Benefits in Analyzing Religious and Nonreligious Organizations," argues that, because religious and presumably nonreligious organizations share many features in common, sociologists of religion and sociologists of organizations have much to learn from one another. For example, Demerath and Schmitt suggest that students of religion could learn much from new developments in decision making, institutional culture, and social movement organizations now taking place within the sociology of organizations. Likewise, sociologists of religion have much to tell sociologists of organization about the organizational importance of non-tangible means and goals, about the importance of symbols within organizations, and about the subtle interdependencies of leaders and followers.

Numerous scholars have highlighted the religious aspects of political institutions. O'Toole (1977) has described the processes of conversion and commitment in several political sects operating in Canada, including a Maoist group called the Internationalists and the Socialist Labor Party, followers of Daniel De Leon who wait for a Communist millennium which they regard as imminent. The Radical Sullivanian therapeutic community described by Siskind (this volume) might also be profitably described as a political sect. Siskind provides a rich, textured account of the rise and demise of the Sullivan Institute/Fourth Wall Community, a group which based its communal lifestyle on an unorthodox synthesis of psychotherapy and Marxist political analysis. Among the central tenets of "Sullivanian" ideology were an approach to psychotherapy that rejected traditional barriers between patient and therapist, a conviction as to the interpenetration of the personal and the political, and a belief in the repressive nature of traditional family and sexual relationships. While the Sullivanians would have rejected the assertion that they had any religious features whatsoever, Siskind nonetheless finds it appropriate to use such terms as "millenialism," "perfectionism," and "prophecy" in describing their beliefs and practices. Siskind concludes that communal groups will share certain features in common whether they see themselves as religious or not.

To take one last example, several writers have attempted to characterize *secularism* itself as a religious enterprise. Campbell (1972) and Budd (1977) have treated Ethical Culture and other humanist groups as analogous to religions. Hunter (1986) has examined the claims of fundamentalist groups that "secular humanism" constitutes a religion whose views have been receiving preferential treatment in the public schools. In "Is 'Nothing' Sacred?: 'Sacred' Cosmology Among the Avant-Garde" (this volume), Hunter, Nolan, and Eck interview avant-garde artists in order to outline the "sacred cosmology" that is central to the worldview of these self-proclaimed secularists who see themselves and are seen by Hunter et al. as being on the cutting edge of modernity. While this cosmology certainly differs from traditional cosmologies in its emphasis on process, relativism, and the contingent nature of truth, the authors demonstrate both the existence of a coherent worldview and the utility of analyzing that world as if it were religious.

Folk Definitions of Religion and the Realm of Quasi-Religion

As we have noted earlier, the sociological debate over the proper definition of religion has typically pitted the supporters of functionalist definitions of religion against those who support a substantive definition of religion. To use language employed by Barker in her paper, "But Is It a Genuine Religion?" (this volume), both substantive and functionalist definitions of religion are stipulative definitions, put forward by scholars for the purpose of clarifying how they intend to use the term "religion." But scholarly definitions are seldom *merely* stipulative. Scholars who argue on behalf of a particular definition of religion are usually saying more than, "This is how I will use the term religion." They are simultaneously making an assertion about the nature of social reality. Thus, proponents of substantive definitions of religion are implicitly putting forward the claim that whether or not a belief system refers to the supernatural or the superempirical is *crucial* for understanding the nature of that belief system. Proponents of functionalist definitions are implicitly arguing that whether a belief system refers to the supernatural is not as important as the role that belief system plays in individuals' lives.

Both substantive and functional definitions begin, then, with the assumption of "definitional essentialism." Proponents of both substantive and functionalist definitions assume that "religion" is a phenomenon that exists objectively in reality and that any belief or practice could be permanently labelled as being either religious or not religious if only we could agree on an acceptable definition. But, as Robertson and Robbins (forthcoming) point out, religion is not an entity but rather a *category of discourse* whose precise meaning and implications are continually being negotiated in the course of social interaction. Religion, from this perspective, is not a concrete "thing" which may be either present or absent in a society, but rather an idiom, a way of speaking about and categorizing actors' experience.

According to Robertson and Robbins, religion should be seen, not merely as a category of discourse, but as a *distinctly modern* category of discourse. In other words, the very notion of religion as an institutionally distinct sociocultural sphere is a product of modernity. In premodern society, the realm of the sacred is not clearly distinguished from the realm of the secular; rather the sacred is a relatively undifferentiated force that permeates all aspects of culture. As we shall suggest later in this paper, it may well be that an essential characteristic of religion in postmodern society is a return to the indistinct boundary between sacred and secular that characterized premodern society.

Barker's paper serves to focus our attention on the importance of paying attention to actors' own definitions of religion, to what we might call "folk definitions." Folk definitions of religion refer to the efforts of ordinary people to categorize phenomena as either religious or not religious in order to make sense out of their everyday lives. Following Douglas (1966), Barker argues that members of all societies need to create categories in order to make sense out of reality and in order to communicate to one another the sense they have made. For Douglas, drawing boundaries separating things which belong together from things which are different is necessary, but *where the line is drawn is arbitrary.* Wherever the line is drawn, there will be some phenomena that just do not fit neatly into any of the categories which have been created. Such anomalies, Douglas says, will be regarded as threatening.

"Religion" to most Americans, whether they see themselves as religious in this sense or not, has—at least until recently—referred to beliefs and practices focusing on a transcendent deity, standing above nature, controlling but not controlled by natural law. "Religion," in this view, usually centers around "churches" where people gather together to "worship" this transcendent deity, usually called "God."[1] Furthermore, in the American folk conception of religion, the denomination has come to be viewed as the "normal" institutional context in which religious activity takes place. "Proper" religions are rather circumspect in the claims they make on their adherents, demanding only a portion of adherents' commitment and accommodating to existence in a pluralist environment (Cuddihy 1978).

Is this "American folk conception of religion" in fact uniquely American, or is it, rather, a common feature of modern societies? Our sense is that most modern cultures share such essential features of the American folk category of religion as the assumption that religion involves a belief in a transcendent God and the expectation that religion will be institutionally separate from other spheres of life. Yet, the unique historical development of religion in America means that the American conception of religion constitutes a distinctive variation on the common theme. In modern America, for example, the category "religion" tends to refer more to the individual, private realm of belief than has been the case in Europe (Neusner 1988). Religion in America is increasingly thought of more as a matter of personal conscience and moral energy than a question of institutional membership or collective culture (Finke 1990; Neusner 1988; Tiryakian 1993). Finally, religion in America has, at least during the mid-twentieth century, been regarded as a relatively benign phenomenon (Cuddihy 1978).

In "But is it a Genuine Religion?," Barker suggests that sociological definitions of religion are of limited usefulness in understanding how ordinary people draw and defend the borders between what is to be accepted as a proper religion and what is not. Actors, Barker claims, often start with a priori assumptions about what groups and beliefs are under no circumstances to be allowed to count as religions and construct ad hoc definitions that exclude those groups. Barker further argues that the religions which people find most threatening are those which strike us as somewhat alien but not absolutely beyond the pale. Thus "exotic" religions may be so removed from actors' folk conceptions about religion that they are not seen as challenging actors' own beliefs. The truly threatening religions, Barker suggests, are those that are recognizable to us as religions such as our own but which are disturbingly anomalous given folk conceptions of what a religion ought to be like.

A concern with folk definitions of religion leads us to focus our attention on groups and activities which deal with the sacred but are anomalous given the American folk category of "religion." Greil (1993) has referred to such groups and activities as *quasi-religious*. Here the question is not where the phenomena in question fit in relation to sociologists' definitions of religion, but how they fit in relation to actors' *own* definitions. Most of the phenomena Greil would classify as quasi-religions would probably qualify as religions under any sociological definition of religion, whether substantive or functional, but either do not see themselves or are not seen by others as unambiguously religious.

As we will suggest later in this paper, there is evidence that quasi-religions are becoming increasingly influential on the American scene. A common feature of many contemporary social movements is that they are not easy to classify as being either sacred or secular in their focus (Beckford 1985, 1990, 1992; McGuire 1993b). Rather, these movements are "holistic," combining concerns with spirituality, health, personal growth, ecology, and social reform in ways that are not easy to sort out. Many groups dealing with the occult and with astrology could probably be classified as quasi-religions (Campbell and McIver 1987; Jorgenson and Jorgenson 1982; Melton 1985; Tiryakian 1974; Truzzi 1974) as could many groups identified with the Twelve-Step Movement (Greil and Rudy 1983, 1990; Jones 1970; Petrunik 1972; Rudy 1986; Rudy and Greil 1987, 1988; Whitley 1977) as well as some environmental groups (Beyer 1992). A characteristic of "holistic" and "New Age" groups is that they defy attempts to classify them neatly into categories.

Especially prominent among contemporary quasi-religions are healing movements (Beckford 1984; McGuire 1988, 1993a, 1993b). Many alternative healing movements are not overtly theistic or even professedly religious, but nevertheless "do appear to function as religions for many adherents—providing cosmologies, rituals, a language for the interpretation of believers' worlds, a social context for belief and practice, and a group of fellow believers" (McGuire 1993a). Like other quasi-religious movements, healing movements are often holistic, steadfastly insisting on the integration of the physical, mental, spiritual, and sometimes even the ecological aspects of healing.

One organization which can serve as an example of the quasi-religious nature of groups within the occult tradition is the Spiritual Frontiers Fellowship (SFF) (described by Wagner, this volume), which combines features of a religious organization and a therapeutic group. Members learn to solve personal problems by such means as meditation, prayer, positive thinking, spiritual formulas such as "giving" one's problem to God" or "putting it in the White Light," and making proper use of spiritual laws. The imagery employed by SFF members is the imagery of science and technology rather than the imagery traditionally associated in American culture with religion. SSF ideology exalts individualism; students are not asked to embrace a collective creed but only to use what works for them in their everyday lives. According to Wagner, SFF is functionally specialized, dealing with only a limited range of the supernatural. SFF does not require total commitment but is willing to let individuals draw spiritual resources form wherever it seems appropriate to them to do so.

According to Wagner, many of the features that make SFF anomalous with regard to the American folk conception of religion are the same features that account for the group's appeal. In Wagner's view, SFF's emphasis on individualism, its respect for the culture of science, and its embracing of the principle of autonomy combine to make it highly attractive to those who embrace a middle American lifestyle.

Another good example of a quasi-religion is to be found in Neitz's (this volume) account of Dianic and Neo-pagan witchcraft. Witches' orientation toward goddess-centered religion and their practice and advocacy of magic place them in ideological tension with most religious groups that have developed out of Western religious traditions. But what truly makes witchcraft anomalous with regard to the American folk definition of religion is its intense resistance to the formal and permanent organizational structures often associated with the term "church." In Wicca, one finds, not congregations and ecclesiastical organizations, but informal networks of people who move in and out of fluid groups which coalesce and dissolve as members' interests change. In her paper, Neitz argues that witchcraft's "deviant" organizational culture has important implications for understanding such areas of Wiccan experience as recruitment, identity, and leadership. Nietz also argues that methodology employed by the sociology of religion has been influenced by an "organizational bias" which leads sociologists to consider the congregation as the "normal organizational form" for religious entities and which limits their ability to study groups and movements with more fluid structures.

Some groups and movements which Greil (1993) would call quasi-religions clearly see themselves and present themselves to the public as religious, but most are ambiguous in their self-presentation. Alcoholics Anonymous (A.A.) and other Twelve-Step or co-dependency groups can serve as a good example here. A.A. literature and A.A. members frequently express the view that A.A. is not religious but spiritual. The heart of the A.A. program, the Twelve Steps, repeatedly mentions a "Higher Power;" however, in A.A.'s view, the "Higher Power" can indicate anything from a traditional Judeo-Christian God to the group itself. Such views allow members with extremely divergent views of God and religion to band together under one umbrella. Rice's "The Therapeutic God: Transcendence and Identity in Two Twelve-Step Quasi-Religions" (this volume) demonstrates the importance of taking the theologies of quasi-religions seriously. In his comparison of A.A. and Co-Dependents Anonymous (CoDA), Rice shows that such surface similarities as a pragmatic approach to the sacred and espousal of Twelve-Step philosophy mask deep ideological differences between the two groups. While A.A. sees individuals as personally responsible for their own moral failings, CoDA embraces a social etiology which blames oppressive family structures for people's psychological problems. Thus, Rice argues, A.A.'s message has a culturally conservative thrust while the ideological thrust of CoDa is culturally radical. For A.A., to be "cured" means to submit one's own will to the superior morality of society, while CoDA defines cure as self-liberation from collective constraint. While Rice does not try to interpret the cultural significance of this transformation of Twelve-Step ideology, it is tempting to do so. The ideological shift Rice describes may be an indication of a growing malaise within American society; alternatively, it may be an example of a maturing quasi-religion's attempt to universalize its message.

There is a natural tendency, when writing about religious, para-religious, or quasi-religious phenomena, to write as if groups are monolithic entities. We tend to assume that the question, "But is it really a religion?" has one answer for each group. In "The Hidden Truth: Astrology as Worldview," Feher (this volume) shows that this assumption is not always valid. Using data gathered from questionnaires distributed at an astrologer's conference, Feher argues that for some respondents—but not others—astrology provided a consistent overarching worldview and thus functioned as a religion. Feher's paper can then serve as a reminder of the danger of reifying the group. The point of studying the boundary between the sacred is not to place individuals, organizations, and labels on one side of the border or the other once and for all but rather to demonstrate the socially constructed nature of religious labels.

The notion of quasi-religion (and para-religion, as well) is not without its problems. One possible shortcoming of the term "quasi-religion" is that it may be seen by some as containing an implicit value judgment. Thus, calling a group a quasi-religion may be seen as delegitimizing, implying that quasi-religions are some lesser order of phenomenon that do not fully deserve to be graced with the title of "religion." Another danger inherent in using the term "quasi-religion" is the possibility that we are unnecessarily proliferating theoretical entities. Perhaps Cochran is right when he says (in "The Interface of Religion and Politics: A Normative Approach," this volume) that "to think in 'quasi' terms is to think crazily." According to Cochran, giving a name like "quasi-religion" to the boundary between two concepts, like the sacred and the secular, is to create an imaginary entity when what we really want to do is describe a relationship. All that has been accomplished, in Cochran's eyes, is that we now have two boundaries to deal with instead of only one. After all, what are we to do with the blurred conceptual territory between "religion" and "quasi-religion?" Are we to call it "quasi-quasi-religion?"

But perhaps the more important problem with the idea of "quasi-religion" is that the term implies the existence of an entity, when what we are really dealing with is a process of negotiation. We have argued that religion is best seen as a category of discourse, as a label people apply to certain phenomena in order to create and communicate categorizations of reality. If "religion" is a label rather than an entity, the outcome of a complex process of negotiation among social actors, then to use a term like "quasi-religion" is to engage in reification. What we really need is not a noun but a verb. What we want to call attention to is not a discrete set of social phenomena called "quasi-religions" but rather a social process whereby people come to agree about the range of phenomena that may appropriately be called "religious." While we recognize these problems with the term "quasi-religion," we will continue to use it in the absence of less problematic terminology.

Political Definitions of Religion and the Question of Authenticity

While Cochran rejects such notions as "quasi-religious" or "quasi-political," he nonetheless asserts strongly the interpenetration of religion and politics. According to Cochran (this volume; see also 1990), government could avoid dealing with matters central to faith and the sacred only by avoiding issues of "social regulatory policy" altogether. In what is an essentially normative argument, Cochran argues that religious voices are an important part of the democratic conversation and should by no means be excluded from the political process. A paradoxical feature of American society is that the dialogue between religion and politics must be conducted in an argot influenced by the principle of the strict separation of church and state.

It is a sociological commonplace that one important function of religion is to confer legitimacy upon the state, but just as important is the state's ability to bestow legitimacy upon or withhold it from religious groups. This introduction has relied thus far on the distinction between sociological definitions of religion and actors' definitions, but the student of religion must contend with a third type of definition of religion: the *political definition*. Political definitions of religion refer to official attributions to particular groups of the right to the "religious" label. From a political perspective, the definition of religion is not a process pursued by disinterested and dispassionate observers of the social scene but, rather, as something which is continually being *negotiated* by competing interest groups.

To be awarded the right to claim the religious label is a matter of great practical consequence in the United States. Organizations that are granted that right usually have a distinct competitive edge over organizations that are denied it. First of all, the religious designation carries with it financial advantages (Richardson 1985), including the right to solicit tax-deductible contributions, exemption from property taxes, and exemption from certain regulations dictated by civil rights and labor legislation.[2] But perhaps the most important practical reason for claiming the religious label has to do with the legitimacy conferred upon groups who can lay claim to it. Religious organizations and religious leaders are held in high esteem by many, and any organization that is successful in getting itself seen to be religious can benefit from the respectability that the label implies. This is, of course, also a major reason why opposing groups may choose to challenge an organization's claim to be religious in nature.

While this is by no means the only interesting theme in his work, Weiss provides a nice illustration of the pressure the sociopolitical environment can exert on a quasi-religious movement in his paper on *A Course in Miracles* (*ACIM*), a well-known ideology often identified with the New Age movement. While the language employed in *ACIM* appears at first glance to be the traditional language of Christianity, concepts like "God," "prayer," "heaven," and "miracles" are all given distinct, psychologized meanings. But where the ideology promoted by *ACIM* deviates most dramatically from the American folk definition of religion is in its rejection of the notion of a formal church structure. Weiss argues that *ACIM* clearly qualifies as a religion under any sociological definition of religion, whether functional or substantive. It is not clear, however that *ACIM* qualifies as a religion according to legal definitions of religion, which are often based on folk conceptions of religion. The Internal Revenue Service limits tax-exempt status to organizations which it classifies as churches according to a list of criteria based on the American folk definition of religion. Thus, the *ACIM*'s religiously based rejection of a formal religious structure may limit its ability to be recognized as a religion for some legal purposes. It seems quite plausible that the desire to receive the practical rewards of being a "religion" may push *ACIM* in a "churchly" direction.

It may be useful to think of the "cult controversy" of recent years as in part a struggle between two opposing interest groups. On the one side we have new religious movements like Scientology, ISKON, and the Unification Church claiming the privileges that go with religious status while on the other side we have the anti-cult movement trying to deny these groups access to the religious label by arguing that these groups are not really religions but rather pseudo-religions merely using the religious label as a cover-up to disguise their unsavory activities. Thus, in spite of the formal separation of church and state, the courts and other governmental bodies often find themselves in the position of having to determine which groups are entitled to enjoy the benefits of the religious label. In *Larsen v. Valente*, for example, the Unification Church asked the Supreme Court to overturn a Minnesota statute that imposed special reporting requirements for churches which receive more funds from the general public rather than from their own members (Robbins 1988). The court overturned the statute, but a procedural dissent submitted by Justices Rehnquist and O'Connor questioned whether the court had to address the Constitutional issues, as it was not clear that the Unification Church had established that it was a church and thus had standing to sue Minnesota. Anthony and Robbins (1992) have documented recent attempts to create a "brainwashing exception to the First Amendment" by those who argue that certain aspects of cult activities do not deserve the same protection generally accorded to religion.[3]

We have thus far been writing as if religion is viewed in American society as an unalloyed good and as if it is always in the interest of movements and groups to have the religious label attached to themselves. This is clearly not the case. Groups and movements sometimes have a vested interest in dodging the religious label. Conversely, opponents of certain movements or organizations may try to discredit these groups by "pinning" the religious label on them, thereby challenging their claim to have a secular, rationally based concern with a particular social issue. While being labelled "religious" may bestow a certain kind of legitimacy on an organization, being labelled "nonreligious" may bestow a different kind of legitimacy. In a society like the United States, where science and rationalistic arguments have a great deal of prestige, the religious realm is often associated with personal preference or even with unreasoned fanaticism. Therefore, people may attempt to discredit a scientific or political position by arguing that the position is not really based in rational considerations but that it is instead grounded in messianic religious zealotry. Thus, critics of the environmental movement have sometimes argued that environmentalists are really religious fanatics who falsely present their beliefs as having a rational basis. It has been for years standard practice among certain groups of intellectuals to dismiss Communism as being, not the scientific political philosophy some Marxists claim it to be, but rather a secular religion worshiping a "God that Failed" (Crossman 1952). Indeed, the messianic and redemptive qualities of Marxism may underlie its ideological vigor and appeal (Pfaff 1991).

While religions may get tax exemptions and other special considerations from government based on the free exercise clause, there are some services that government may not provide to entities identified as religions because of the Constitutional prohibition against the establishment of religion. In *Melnack v. Maharishi Mahesh Yogi*, a Federal Circuit Appeals Court ruled that, because Transcendental Meditation *is* a religion, it cannot offer instruction in the public schools. In an Alabama case, proponents of Creationism asked the court to rule that Secular Humanism is, in fact, a religion and that, therefore, its principle religious tenet, evolutionism, should not be taught in public schools (Hunter 1986).

It should be clear from the above that the American attempt to define religion politically has been shaped by the distinctive features of church-state relations in this country. The First Amendment to the Constitution, by articulating the principle of the strict separation of church and state, has, paradoxically, created a public debate over the question of what may count as "religion" (Burkholder 1974). And, as Tocqueville (1945) noted in *Democracy in America,* political issues in the United States tend to manifest themselves as juridical conflicts. Thus, the political debate over the proper definition of religion has largely taken place in the courts rather than in legislatures. There have actually been two debates rather than one. The First Amendment text on religion is divided into a Free Exercise clause and an Establishment clause, and the courts have not always used the same definition of religion in deciding Establishment cases as they have in deciding Free Exercise cases. In the latter half of the twentieth century the Supreme Court has tended to work with a broad, functionalist definition of religion in deciding Free Exercise cases and with a narrower and a bit more substantive definition in deciding Establishment cases. This has recently led to conflict over the issue of whether humanist quasi-religion is thereby being privileged (McKenzie 1991).

Our discussion of political definitions of religion leads us to conclude, with a number of other scholars, that the religion has become increasingly more controversial in recent years (Beckford 1985; Fenn 1978; Robbins and Robertson 1991; Robertson 1979; Wuthnow 1988). Whereas in the 1950s and 1960s, religion was generally seen as a relatively benign force in society, by the 1980s it had become a highly politicized topic. As Wuthnow (1988, p. 6) writes:

> On all sides American religion seems to be embroiled in controversy. Whether it be acrimonious arguments about abortion, lawsuits over religion in the public schools, questions over who is most guilty of mixing religion or politics, or discussions of America's military presence in the world, religion seems to be in the thick of it. Scarcely a statement is uttered by one religious group on the issues without another faction taking umbrage.

At the same time that religion became a more controversial subject, so too did the category "religion" become more *contestable*. It seems that in the 1950s and 1960s there was a consensus about the proper referent of the term "religion" which has since broken down.

This breakdown of consensus probably had several sources. One of these sources may have been the increasing controversiality of religion itself. Given the twentieth-century American cultural premise that religion is "good," it may have seemed natural to argue that "bad" religion was not really religion. Fenn (1978, p. 58) has linked the increasing contestability of religion on the process of secularization, which weakens the possibilities for consensus about the nature of the sacred. Finally, the rise of new religious movements exposed Americans to a number of belief systems that did not conform to the American folk conception of religion.[4]

With the increased controversiality and contestability of religion has come a change in the focus of studies of the boundary between the sacred and the secular. The recent history of concern with these issues can be seen in terms of two phases. The first phase of interest in religious boundaries peaked in the 1960s and early 1970s. American sociology (and, indeed, American culture in general) was preoccupied with political and economic issues. Religion did not appear highly controversial and topical so that the sociology of religion was more or less a "backwater" within the larger discipline. In what was perhaps an attempt to make their field seem more interesting, topical, and relevant, sociologists of religion began to emphasize broad, functional definitions of religion and to argue that more seemingly relevant phenomena, such as

Marxism, nationalism, and rock music, were essentially religious in nature. Thus, the focus of studies of religious border phenomena in this earlier phase of interest was on the realm of the para-religious.

The second phase of interest, which became prominent in the 1980s, has, ironically, been a product of the increasing topicality, controversiality, and contestability of religion. As the public has begun to ask how one can tell genuine religion from pseudo-religion, whether the Twelve-Step movement is a therapy or a "cult," whether politicized Liberation Theology is authentically religious, and so on, sociologists, too, have begun to focus more on these types of concerns. Thus, as religion has become more controversial and contestable, sociologists have begun to pay more attention to the realm of the quasi-religious.

The paper in this volume by Passas, "The Market for Gods and Services: Religion, Commerce, and Deviance," could serve as a model for case studies of quasi-religion in the era of contestability. In this piece, Passas situates the Church of Scientology (CoS) solidly within its sociopolitical context. He examines the charge made against the CoS in an effort to justify the denial of the religious status of Scientology and concludes, that while many of the charges against Scientology are valid, they do not necessarily distinguish the CoS from "real religions." Passas interprets Scientology's unorthodox practices (such as fee-for-service financial arrangements and the development of corporate ventures) as, in part, a response to a competitive disadvantage in the "religious market" the CoS shares with other new religious movements. Passas argues that Scientology's need to adapt to a hostile social environment gives rise to a self-fulfilling prophecy whereby blocked social opportunities lead new religious movements toward unorthodox economic activities which are, in turn, used to justify withholding from these groups the right to claim the religious label and to subject them to increased efforts at social control.

A concern with political definitions of religion leads us to examine the question of *authenticity*—that is, the process by which interest groups compete for the right to be seen as genuine religions. Carter's paper, titled, "The Problem of Authenticity in the Study of Religious Traditions," argues that it is possible for sociologists to study questions of authenticity without becoming bogged down in the task of evaluating the truth-claims of various groups. Authenticity has both a general and a specific dimension. The *general* dimension of authenticity has to do with the process by which groups within society pass judgment on a particular group, movement, or tradition's claim to be "religious." Thus, journalists may argue that an anti-social "cult" like the Branch Davidians cannot authentically claim to be a religion (Coleman 1993). The *specific* dimension of authenticity involves judgments made by organizations and individuals within a particular religious tradition concerning which groups or ideas can claim to be authentically part of that tradition. Thus, Jews may pass judgment on whether "Jews for Jesus" are "really" Jewish, and the Catholic Church may designate certain theological positions as heresies. Carter focuses on the specific dimension of authenticity, looking at the mechanisms by which religious traditions police themselves in order to preserve the authenticity of the tradition. He calls for the development of a descriptive study of religious "authentication" as a social process. We see this as an intellectual task well worth pursuing.

THE SIGNIFICANCE OF QUASI-RELIGION AND PARA-RELIGION

Just how widespread are para-religious and quasi-religious phenomena in the contemporary United States? As one might expect, reliable statistics on membership in quasi-religious organizations are not readily available, but impressionistic evidence presented in the papers gathered for this volume suggests that the appeal of some of these organizations is far from insignificant. Rice points out that Beattie's (1987) *Co-Dependent No More* has sold over 2,000,000 and that, in 1990, there were 2,088 weekly CoDA meetings in the United States. According to Weiss, 800,000 volumes of *A Course in Miracles* (1975) have been sold, and *ACIM* spokesperson Marianne Williamson has achieved celebrity status. Feher notes that a recent Gallop Poll has shown that as many as 25 percent of the American public claim to be believers in astrology. While Wagner makes no claim that SFF can boast large numbers of adherents, her argument that the SFF ideology fits hand in glove with some of the central traits of Middle American culture suggests that metaphysical groups are likely to have continued—and possibly growing—cultural significance.

If quasi-religious movements are, as we believe, gaining in popularity and influence within American society, this suggests that the American folk definition of religion as a body of beliefs and practices focusing on a transcendent deity, standing above nature, controlling but not controlled by natural law, is beginning to lose its hold over many people. The growing appeal of quasi-religion suggests that large numbers of people are not finding satisfaction with the transcendent worldviews offered by many of their traditional religious options and that they are increasingly conceptualizing their experiences of transcendence by means of linguistic idioms that stand outside the American folk category of religion. Likewise, people seem to be tending to give expression to their experiences of transcendence in institutional contexts that Americans have not typically thought of as religious. To put the matter perhaps too simply, the apparent increase in the incidence of quasi-religion suggests that we find ourselves in a period of cultural lag; Americans' religious behavior is changing, but conceptions of the nature of the religious seem to be trailing behind the changes in actual religious practice. It seems clear that the line between religion and non-religion is becoming harder to discern. What

is not yet clear is whether this confusion along the boundary between the sa.
and the secular is a temporary phenomenon that will last only until fo.
definitions have caught up to behavior or whether it is rather a chronic feature
of religion in the postmodern era.

Beckford (1985, 1990, 1992) argues forcefully that the latter is the case.
Beckford argues that the postmodern era is giving rise to a new form of holistic,
problem-oriented, practical spirituality. Religion, Beckford argues, is being
freed from its institutional moorings and is becoming a "free-floating resource,"
available for various uses and causes. Similar arguments are made by Bibby
(1987) and Bibby and Weaver (1985) who assert that most people who leave
traditional churches are more likely to espouse collections of diffuse "a-science
fragments" than they are to join new formal religious organizations, and by
Beit-Hallahmi (this volume) who argues that formal religious organizations
are giving way to "private salvation movements." If these authors are right
and this new form of quasi-religious spirituality is to become an integral feature
of postmodernity, then the very notion that reality can be divided into sacred
and secular spheres may become outmoded.

If we are, in fact, witnessing an important cultural trend away from the
transcendent worldview that has characterized the Judeo-Christian tradition
and toward quasi-religious and para-religious forms of religious expression,
then we must inquire about the social and cultural trends that lie behind this
transformation. Several of the papers collected here deal with this issue in a
direct and straightforward manner.

In "The Quasi-Sacred: A Theoretical Introduction" Fenn (this volume)
attributes the appeal of what he calls the "quasi-sacred" to the intertwined
trends of modernization, privatization, and secularization. Fenn argues that
modernity leads to secularization by shattering the taken-for-grantedness of
sacred institutions at the same time that it accentuates individualism and *self*-
consciousness. But while modernity leads to the desacralization of institutions,
Fenn argues, it does little to alter the psychological realities that propel the
self in search of the sacred. Thus, we see the simultaneous development of two
apparently contradictory trends: the growth of such privatized religions of the
self as CoDA, SFF, and *ACIM* and the increased tendency for individuals
to immerse themselves in such sacralized groups as "cults," corporations, and
political sects. In modernity, Fenn asserts that no claim to the sacred "can be
unqualified, long-lasting, or incontrovertible." Secularization challenges
religious definitions but does not alter those aspects of the human condition
which give rise to religion. Thus, the ebbing of the sacred gives rise, not to
the secular, but to the quasi-sacred.

In "Gendered Spirituality and Quasi-Religious Ritual," McGuire (this
volume) specifically addresses issues of gender identity, but her argument has
important implications for a general understanding of the relationship between
the problem of identity and the appeal of the quasi-religious in modernity. After

all, she argues, gender issues represent the epitome of contemporary identity concerns. McGuire asserts that, under the conditions of modernity, gendered identities must be *accomplished* rather than received as given. Because official religion tends to confirm the traditional sex roles promoted by the dominant group, confusion over gender identity is difficult to resolve within the context of established religious forms. Thus, McGuire argues that the new religions and quasi-religions of the nineteenth century—Spiritualism, Christian Science, Freemasonry, and so on—revolved around a concern about the nature of maleness and femaleness. She interprets both the contemporary Women's Spirituality Movement as well as the Men's Movement as extensions of this nineteenth-century attempt to resolve issues of gendered identity outside of the contexts that the American folk definition of religion would recognize as properly religious.

Beit-Hallahmi (this volume) continues the theme of privatism and the self raised by Fenn and McGuire in his discussion of the rise of what he calls the "private salvation movement" in Israel. For Beit-Hallahmi, private salvation includes occultism, astrology, and other magical approaches to personal and social issues. What Beit-Hallahmi finds most striking about the private salvation movement in Israel are its relative newness and the rapidity with which it has permeated Israeli cultural life. Because the Israeli case strikes him as historically unique, Beit-Hallahmi looks to unique features of Israeli society and recent history for an explanation of the Israeli "occult explosion." He traces the rise of the private salvation movement with the demoralization, exhaustion, and collective self-doubt that have come in the wake of the Yom Kippur War. While the Israeli context is certainly historically unique, a collective loss of faith in established institutions is by no means limited to Israeli society but seems, rather, to be a common effect of modernity. Thus, the Israeli case may be simply one intriguing variation on the general theme whereby modernity leads to a loss of faith in established institutions which in turn gives rise to new, individualized, ad hoc forms of spirituality.

In "Evolution: The Central Mythology of the New Age Movement," Hexham (this volume) argues that, due to modernization, Christianity has ceased to function for most people as a central mythology that gives them a coherent understanding of life. In Hexham's view, the central myth that threatens to supplant Christianity in Western societies is the myth of spiritual evolution. The underlying theme of this new mythic consciousness, Hexham argues, is the hope for an evolutionary transformation of the essential nature of humankind. Hexham is not arguing here that religion is being replaced by scientific, secular ways of thinking; rather, he is arguing that the Christian belief in a transcendent God is being replaced by a belief in the natural evolution of humans, a belief that he sees as *scientistic* rather than as truly scientific.

Parenthetically, it should be noted that the trends which these authors have attributed to modernization, secularization, and privatization are also related to the process of globalization, which has resulted in greater exposure to religious ideas outside the Judeo-Christian tradition. Many of the groups and movements discussed in this volume have been shaped by influences outside the Western religious tradition with its emphasis on religion as an institutionally distinct phenomenon focusing on a transcendent God.

Taken together, these papers strongly suggest the possibility that both the nature and social context of American religiosity are undergoing a profound transformation that may make old categories of analysis inapplicable. It may well be that the transcendent religion recognized by the American folk definition is giving rise to a new type of spirituality, of which the para-religious and quasi-religious movements discussed in this volume may serve as examples. Among the major themes in this emergent form of spirituality are holism, the sacralization of science, a concern with the practical, a preoccupation with the interpersonal, and a disdain for rigid institutional forms.

To conclude, the papers in this volume demonstrate that the study of the para-religious and the quasi-religious is not merely a parlor game suitable for the amusement of academics. Taken together, these papers constitute a call for the sociology of religion to acknowledge the study of the production of "religion" as a category of discourse as central to its mission. These papers also demonstrate that the study of para-religions and quasi-religions can provide us with a strategic vantage point from which to observe the transformation of religion in the postmodern era.

NOTES

1. Most sociological definitions of religion tend to accept implicitly this American folk conception of religion with its equation of "religion" and "transcendent religion." The very belief that it is possible to distinguish between the sacred and the secular, between the supernatural and the natural, or between the superempirical and the empirical, implictly assumes the validity of a transcendent worldview.

2. For example, if an organization is defined as a "religion," then its clergy are exempt from military service and its members can claim Conscientious Objector status more easily. If an organization is defined as a religion, its leaders can be defined as clergy and may legally marry people. An organizaion which is considered to be a religion can conduct healing and therapy practices with diminished fear of scrutiny by regulatory agencies.

3. Such controversies over religions often revolve, not around the general question of whether a given group has an unqualified right to the religious label, but rather around the issue of whether some specific aspect of an organization's activity is legitimately religious and thus protected from regulation. Thus, in the prosecution of Reverend Moon for tax evasion, the state did not argue tht the Unification Church was not a church. Instead, the question to be resolved was whether certain funds in Moon's private account were used for "religious" as opposed to "business" or "personal" purposes (Robbins 1988). In the *Hernandez* ase, the Supreme court ruled that Scientology auditing costs are not tax-deductible even though it did not question the Church of Scientology's status as a church (Passas and Castillo 1992).

4.   Many of the new religious movements would qualify as quasi-religions in that they do not fit neatly into the American folk category of "religion." Some groups, like est and other groups within the Human Potential and New Age movements, do not posit a supreme being (Stone 1976; Tipton 1982; Wallis 19850. Many groups, including TM and other meditation disciplines, de-emphasize "theological" considerations and focus primarily on spiritual practice (Bainbridge and Jackson 1981). A number of groups, such as Scientology, do not focus on communal worship, instead offiering classes on a fee-for-service basis (Bainbridge 1987; Straus 1985, 1986; Wagner 1984; Wallis 1977). Some enterprises classified as new religions scarcely qualify as organizations at all. Many devotees of occult practices are organized into informal networks of individuals which coalesce around book stores and psychic fairs (Jorgenson and Jorgenson 1982). Some very encapsulating groups, like ISKON and the Unification Church, do not conform to the American expectation that "real" religions ought to behave like denominations.

REFERENCES

Anthony, D., and T. Robbins. 1992. "Law, Social Sciences and the 'Brainwashing' Exception to the First Amendment." *Behavioral Sciences and the Law* 10: 5-29.

Bainbridge, W.S. 1987. "Science and Religion: The Case of Scientology." Pp. 59-79 in *The Future of New Religious Movements,* edited by D.G. Bromley and P.H. Hammond. Macon, GA: Mercer University Press.

Bainbridge, W.S., and D.H. Jackson. 1981. "The Rise and Decline of Transcendental Meditation." Pp. 135-158 in *The Social Impact of New Religious Movements,* edited by B.R. Wilson. New York: Rose of Sharon Press.

Beattie, M. 1987. *Codependent No More: How to Stop Controlling Others and Caring for Yourself.* New York: Harper/Hazelden.

Beckford, J.A. 1984. "Holistic Imagery and Healing in New Religions and Healing Movements." *Social Compass* 31: 259-272.

――――. 1985. *Cult Controversies: The Societal Response to the New Religious Movements.* London: Tavistock.

――――. 1990. "The Sociology of Religion and Social Problems." *Sociological Analysis* 51: 1-14.

――――. 1992. "Religion, Modernity, and Postmodernity." Pp. 11-23 in *Religion: Contemporary Issues,* edited by B.R. Wilson. London: Bellew.

Beyer, P. 1992. "The Global Environment as a Religious Issue: A Sociological Analysis." *Religion* 22: 1-19.

Bibby, R.W. 1987. *Fragmented Gods: The Poverty and Potential of Religion in Canada.* Richmond Hill, Canada: Irwin.

Bibby, R.W., and H.R. Weaver. 1985. "Cult Consumption in Canada." *Sociological Analysis* 46: 445-460.

Brinkerhoff, M.B., and J.C. Jacob. 1987. "Quasi-Religious Meaning Systems, Official Religion, and Quality of Life in an Alternative Lifestyle: A Survey from the Back-to-the-Land Movement." *Journal for the Scientific Study of Religion* 26: 63-80.

Bromley, D.G., and A. Shupe. 1990. "Rebottling the Elixir: The Gospel of Prosperity in America's Religioeconomic Corporations." Pp. 233-253 in *In Gods We Trust: New Patterns of Religious Pluralism in America,* edited by T. Robbins and D. Anthony. 2nd ed. New Brunswick, NJ: Transaction.

Budd, S. 1977. *Varieties of Unbelief: Atheists and Agnostics in English Society, 1850-1960.* London: Heinemann.

Burkholder, J.R. 1974. "The Law Knows No Heresy: Marginal Religious Movements and the Courts." Pp. 27-50 in *Religious Movements in Contemporary America,* edited by I.I. Zaretsky and M.P. Leone. Princeton: Princeton University Press.

Byron, C. 1992. "Mr. Gore's Planet: A Case of Eco-babble?" *New York Magazine,* August 3, p. 19.

Campbell, C. 1972. *Toward a Sociology of Irreligion.* London: Macmillan.

Campbell, C., and S. McIver. 1987. "Cultural Sources of Support for Contemporary Occultism." *Social Compass* 34: 41-60.

Cochran, C. 1990. *Religion in Public and Private Life.* New York: Routledge.

Coleman, N. 1993. "Despite the Divine Pretensions, Religion Just a Prop for Cults." *St. Paul Pioneer Press* (March 7): A17.

A Course in Miracles. 1975. Tiburon, CA: Foundation for Inner Peace.

Crippen, T. 1988. "Old and New Gods in the Modern World: Toward a Theory of Religious Transformation." *Social Forces* 67: 316-336.

Crossman, R., ed. 1952. *The God That Failed.* New York: Bantam.

Cuddihy, J. 1978. *No Offense: Civil Religion and Protestant Taste.* New York: Seabury.

Douglas, M. 1966. *Purity and Danger: An Analysis of the Concepts of Pollution and Taboo.* London: Routledge and Kegan Paul.

Fenn, R.K. 1978. *Toward a Theory of Secularization.* Storrs, CT: Society for the Scientific Study of Religion.

Finke, R. 1990. "Religious Deregulation: Origins and Consequences." *Journal of Church and State* 32: 501-510.

Frank, J. 1963. *Persuasion and Healing: A Comparative Study of Psychotherapy.* New York: Schocken.

Galanter, M. 1989. *Cults: Faith, Healing, and Coercion.* New York: Oxford University Press.

_____. 1990. "Cults and Zealous Self-Help Movements: A Psychiatric Perspective." *The American Journal of Psychiatry* 147: 543-551.

Greil, A.L. 1993. "Explorations along the Sacred Frontier: Notes on Para-Religions, Quasi-Religions, and Other Boundary Phenomena." Pp. 153-172 in *Religion and the Social Order,* Vol. 3, Part A., edited by D.G. Bromley and J.K. Hadden. Greenwich, CT: JAI Press.

Greil, A.L., and D.R. Rudy. 1983. "Conversion to the World View of Alcoholics Anonymous: A Refinement of Conversion Theory." *Qualitative Sociology* 6: 5-28.

_____. 1984. "Social Cocoons: Encapsulation and Identity Transforming Organizations." *Sociological Inquiry* 54: 260-278.

_____. 1990. "On the Margins of the Sacred." Pp. 219-232 in *In Gods We Trust: New Patterns of Religious Pluralism in America,* edited by T. Robbins and D. Anthony. 2nd ed. New Brunswick, NJ: Transaction.

Hannigan, J.A. 1990. "Apples and Oranges or Varieties of the Same Fruit?" *Review of Religious Research* 31: 246-258.

_____. 1991. "Social Movement Theory and the Sociology of Religion." *Sociological Analysis* 52: 311-331.

Hunter, J.D. 1986. "Humanism and Social Theory: Is Secular Humanism a Religion?" Unpublished paper.

Jones, R.K. 1970. "Sectarian Characteristics of Alcoholics Anonymous." *Sociology* 4: 181-195.

Jorgenson, D., and L. Jorgenson. 1982. "Social Meanings of the Occult." *Sociological Quarterly* 23: 373-389.

Lane, C. 1981. *The Rites of Rulers.* New York: Columbia University Press.

Luckmann, T. 1967. *The Invisible Religion: The Problem of Religion in Modern Society.* New York: MacMillan.

Mathisen, J. 1992. "From Civil Religion to Folk Religion: The Case of American Sport." Pp. 17-33 in *Sport and Religion,* edited by S.J. Hoffman. Champagne, IL: Human Kinetics.

McGuire, M.B. 1988. *Ritual Healing in Suburban America.* New Brunswick, NJ: Rutgers University Press.

———. 1993a. "Health and Healing in New Religious Movements. Pp. 139-156 in *Religion and the Social Order,* Vol. 3, Part B, edited by D.G. Bromley and J.K. Hadden. Greenwich, CT: JAI Press.

———. 1993b. "Health and Spirituality as Contemporary Concerns." *The Annals of the American Academy of Political and Social Science* 527: 144-154.

McKenzie, D. 1991. "The Supreme Court, Fundamentalist Logic, and the Term, 'Religion'." *Journal of Church and State* 32: 731-746.

Melton, J.G. 1985. "The Revival of Astrology in the United States." Pp. 279-296 in *Religious Movements: Genesis, Exodus, and Numbers,* edited by R. Stark. New York: Paragon House.

Neusner, J. 1988. "The Theological Enemies of Religious Studies." *Religion* 18: 21-36.

Novak, M. 1976. *The Joy of Sports: End Zones, Bases, Baskets, Balls, and the Consecration of the American Spirit.* New York: Basic.

O'Toole, R. 1977. *The Precipitous Path: Studies in Political Sects.* Toronto: Peter Martin.

Passas, N., and M.E. Castillo. 1992. "Scientology and its 'Clear' Business." *Behavioral Sciences and the Law* 10: 103-116.

Petrunik, M.G. 1972. "Seeing the Light: A Study of Conversion to Alcoholics Anonymous." *Journal of Voluntary Action Research* 1: 30-38.

Peven, D. 1968. "The Use of Religious Revival Techniques to Indoctrinate Personnel: The Home-Party Sales Organization." *Sociological Quarterly* 20: 97-106.

Pfaff, W. 1991. "A Secular Religion in whose Service Much Evil was Done." *Chicago Tribune,* September 1, section 4, p. 3.

Richardson, J.T. 1985. "Legal and Practical Reasons for Claiming to be a Religion." Paper presented at the annual meeting of the Society for the Scientific Study of Religion, Savannah, GA.

Robbins, T. 1988. *Cults, Converts, and Charisma.* London: Sage.

Robbins, T., and R. Robertson. 1991. "Studying Religion Today." *Religion* 21: 319-337.

Robertson, R. 1970. *The Sociological Interpretation of Religion.* New York: Schocken.

———. 1979. "Religious Movements and Modern Societies." *Sociological Analysis* 40: 297-314.

Robertson, R., and T. Robbins. Forthcoming. *Religion at the End of the 20th Century.* Oxford: Polity Press.

Roth, J. 1957. "Ritual and Magic in Control of Contagion." *American Sociological Review* 22: 310-314.

Rudy, D.R. 1986. *Becoming Alcoholic: Alcoholics Anonymous and the Reality of Alcoholism.* Carbondale: Southern Illinois University Press.

Rudy, D.R., and A.L. Greil. 1987. "Taking the Pledge: The Commitment Process in Alcoholics Anonymous." *Sociological Focus* 20: 45-59.

———. 1988. "Is Alcoholics Anonymous a Religious Organization?" *Sociological Analysis* 50: 41-51.

Shaw, G.B. 1960. *Major Barbara: Definitive Text.* Harmondsworth, England: Penguin.

Stone, D. 1976. "The Human Potential Movement." Pp. 93-115 in *The New Religious Consciousness,* edited by C. Glock and R. Bellah. Berkeley: University of California Press.

Straus, R.A. 1985. "But We Are a Religion: 'Religion' and 'Technology' in Scientology's Struggle for Legitimacy." Paper presented at the annual meeting of the Society for the Scientific Study of Religion, Savannah, GA.

———. 1986. "Scientology 'Ethics': Deviance, Identity, and Social Control in a Cult-like Social World." *Symbolic Interaction* 9: 67-82.

Tipton, S.M. 1982. *Getting Saved From the Sixties: Moral Meaning in Conversion and Cultural Change*. Berkeley: University of California Press.

Tiryakian, E. 1974. *On the Margin of the Visible*. New York: Wiley.

————. 1993. "American Religious Exceptionalism: A Reconsideration." *The Annals of the American Academy of Political and Social Science* 527: 40-54.

Tocqueville, A. 1945. *Democracy in America*. New York: Vintage.

Truzzi, M.P. 1974. "Toward a Sociology of the Occult." Pp. 628-645 in *Religious Movements in Contemporary America*, edited by I.I. Zaretsky and M.P. Leone. Princeton: Princeton University Press.

Wagner, M.B. 1984. *Metaphysics in Midwestern America*. Columbus: Ohio State University Press.

Wallis, R. 1977. *The Road to Total Freedom*. New York: Columbia University Press.

————. 1985. "The Dynamics of Change in the Human Potential Movement." Pp. 129-152 in *Religious Movements: Genesis, Exodus, and Numbers*, edited by R. Stark. New York: Paragon House.

Warner, L. 1959. *The Living and the Dead: A Study of the Symbolic Life of Americans*. New Haven, CT: Yale University Press.

Weber, M. 1963. *The Sociology of Religion*. Boston: Beacon.

Whitley, O.R. 1977. "Life with Alcoholics Anonymous: The Methodist Class Meeting as a Paradigm." *Journal of Studies on Alcohol* 38: 831-848.

Wolf, Z.R. 1988. *Nurses' Work, the Sacred and the Profane*. Philadelphia: University of Pennsylvania Press.

Wuthnow, R. 1988. *The Restructuring of American Religion: Society and Faith Since World War II*. Princeton: University of Princeton Press.

Yinger, J.M. 1970. *The Scientific Study of Religion*. New York: MacMillan.

Zuo, J. 1991. "Political Religion: The Case of the Cultural Revolution in China." *Sociological Analysis* 52: 99-110.

PART I

SECULAR RELIGIONS: THE REALM
OF PARA-RELIGION

TRANSCENDING SACRED AND SECULAR:
MUTUAL BENEFITS IN ANALYZING RELIGIOUS
AND NONRELIGIOUS ORGANIZATIONS

N.J. Demerath III and Terry Schmitt

ABSTRACT

This paper argues that research on religious and nonreligious organizations should be symbiotic rather than separated into different realms. Sacred and secular organizations are not as distinct as their past treatment would suggest; each has potentially important insights for the other. Just as every religious organization has undeniably secular aspects, so does every secular organization depend upon a certain "religious" dimension of shared beliefs and rituals. The paper begins by describing some of the debt that secular scholarship owes to religion, noting a number of critical concepts that have seeped from the study of religion to the study of social phenomena more broadly. In the reverse direction, the paper then notes several recent developments in secular organizational analysis that apply to religious institutions. Finally, to reverse direction once again, the paper offers 10 characteristic problems of religious organizations that may be generalizable to such secular counterparts as nonprofit agencies, trade unions, political movements, institutions concerned with education, health, or the military, or indeed, business corporations.

Religion and the Social Order, Volume 4, pages 27-49.
Copyright © 1994 by JAI Press Inc.
All rights of reproduction in any form reserved.
ISBN: 1-55938-763-7

For almost three-quarters of a century since the heyday of Max Weber and Emile Durkheim, the study of religion has been, at best, a peripheral focus of the social sciences. This is partly because of the putative secularization and marginalization of religion itself. It is also a function of social science's own developments—its turn toward a more quantitative epistemology, its shift to the ideological left, or, more generally, its tendency to stress structural as opposed to cultural phenomena.

But another reason for religion's displacement stems from the way in which that tiny minority of scholars concerned with religion have conceived and presented their ouvre. Most have seen religion as compelling in its own terms and have sought to understand it as a singular domain of the social, one that is conventionally and colloquially comprised of churches, sects, and cults, with all of their attendant doctrines, rituals, and polities. In viewing religion as a phenomenon unto itself, students of religion have tended to segregate themselves in the very process of segregating our subject-matter. This tendency has been a detriment both in *importing* insights to religious organizations and in *exporting* insights from religious organizations.

A different perspective on religion might facilitate both the importing and the exporting. Instead of setting religion out in the scholarly cold, it is possible to bring it closer to the social scientific hearth. Instead of asking how religious institutions and behaviors are different from all others, one can ask what is shared in common. Instead of depicting religion as something sociologically *sui generis*, one can treat religion as a dimension of social experience at virtually every level. Instead of viewing religious organizations apart from other organizations, one can explore religion's several organizational forms as strategically comparable to those of nonreligious organizations. Thus, we want to suggest both that there are "religious" dimensions to every organization, and that there are also organizational dimensions to (virtually) every religion. This reciprocity affords fertile opportunities to researchers who normally pay attention to only one of the two sets.

At this point, however, hackles will rise owing to the very term "religion." The word itself is not a sociological concept, and it is fraught with connotations of other-worldliness, overt spirituality, and pious ritual—all of which have a decidedly Christian coloration in the Western context. The term has tended to scare more secular scholars away from the "sacred" sector, and social scientists asked to treat this as an analytic dimension of the manifestly nonreligious will demur understandably. In order to benefit all of scholarship, the term needs to be rescued from its connotations so that it can be used more theoretically than theologically, more inclusively than exclusively.

As an alternative conception of religion, consider that religion is: *any mythically sustained concern for ultimate meanings coupled with a ritually reinforced sense of social belonging.* Other similar definitions drawn from the functional tradition of analyzing religion and its equivalents would do as well.

The point is that once religion is shorn of its sacerdotal, sectarian, and spiritualistic implications, it can be analytically serviceable across a wide range of social experiences. We can therefore examine the "religious" comportment of strictly secular organizations.

This paper seeks to explore "religious" behaviors with special reference to the study of organizations and social movements—whether conventionally religious, nonreligious, or more likely, a-religious. We begin with a conceptual and historical demonstration of social science's religious dimension, showing that the field is already in far greater debt to its scholars of religion than is customarily acknowledged. We then review the field of complex organizations research, in order to suggest fresh and potentially fruitful avenues with which to view religious organizations. The paper concludes by suggesting a series of characteristics of religious organizations which may apply to a greater or lesser extent across the organizational board.

A BRIEF INVENTORY OF SOCIAL SCIENCE'S INDEBTEDNESS TO RELIGION

As much as the study of religion may seem epiphenomenal to contemporary social science, it is not difficult to demonstrate the religious legacy within this generally secular discipline. This is not entirely surprising in light of the attention given to religion by two of the field's most renowned classical scholars, Weber and Durkheim. It becomes even more understandable in light of the field's sporadic use of the "culture" concept to reach under and around religion in a fumbling search for its secular equivalents—whether applied to whole societies or to specific organizations and life-worlds.

In fact, the very word "culture" is religiously impregnated and encoded. When the word is hyphenated as *cult-ure,* its relationship to religion becomes apparent (cf. Halton 1992). Nor is the relationship merely a matter of plausible (though, to our knowledge, undemonstrated) etymology; it has both theoretical and substantive thrust as well. As many would argue (e.g., Durkheim 1965 [1912]); Stark and Bainbridge 1985), cults are most likely to develop among those for whom the mainstream culture has lost its cultic draw. Lately the term "cult"—like the related "fundamentalism"—has been blurred through overuse and taken on a snide, pejorative connotation. But in its original meaning as the organizational core of a cultural innovation with compelling power, it has an applicability that has ranged far beyond religion itself. It is common now to consider such entities as political cults, drug cults, or "cults of personality"— to name but a few examples.

A number of related cultural forms and processes have religious sources of their own. Durkheim's generalized insights concerned the *relationship between social order and a "collective conscience"* which imbues society with a sense of the sacred. Originally developed in an effort to understand the "Elementary Forms of the Religious Life" (1912), the insight became a cornerstone of even secular versions of functional social science. Indeed, Durkheim himself sought to apply the basic point in the last years of his life as he worked on a secular and scientific ethic that would perform sacred functions without relying on traditionally religious forms. Moreover, Durkheim shares with Rousseau the originating honors behind the concept of *civil religion*. As reformulated and reintroduced by Robert Bellah (1967), the concept offers a classic instance in which an initially religious formulation has taken on far broader (and sometimes far more cynical) implications in the hands of secular social scientists of various stripes.

Of course, sociology's Weberian heritage offers comparable examples. Consider Weber's rebuttal to Marx concerning the circumstances under which culture and ideas may be agents and *"switchmen" of change* rather than mere consequences. This has been frequently inflated (and often overblown) into a more general theoretical principle. Meanwhile, it is worth recalling that the basic insight derived from a study of religion (cf. "The Protestant Ethic and the Spirit of Capitalism" 1958 [1904-1905]), whose subsidiary point regarding the development of *capitalism's own quasi-religious "spirit"* is often forgotten.

Max Weber is also responsible for propelling two additional concepts form the religious margins into the sociological mainstream. The first is *caste*. Essentially a product of Hindu theodicy (especially as codified for administrative purposes under the British raj), Weber used the concept as the extreme case of status by ascription. As such, it has been applied to a variety of nonreligious inequalities, including those of race and gender.

If caste is tied to tradition, Weber's second religious concept both derives from, and provides for, a break with tradition. Of course, he deployed *charisma* as one of three forms of authority or sources of legitimation for power, one that is generally a source of innovation pitted against its "traditional" and "rational-legal" rivals. Weber has noted that charisma, or the "gift of grace," is derived from early Christian vocabulary. Certainly it has become old hat in the world of organizational and movement analysis, where its religious roots are seldom noted. While we are discussing forms of authority, it is worth noting a neo-Weberian variant that was also born of religion but deserves wider application than it has received. Paul Harrison's (1959) concept of *rational-pragmatic authority* suggests a form of rational power which is based more on evolving practicality than codified legality. Harrison developed the notion while studying the polity of the American Baptist Convention, whose principled emphasis on local autonomy led it to look away from the denominational bureaucracy emerging in its midst.

Both Durkheim and Weber were concerned with religious change, and both portrayed an erosion of the sacred at the hands of the secular. While neither coined the resulting concept of *secularization,* each helped to give it historical meaning, whether in the context of turn-of-the-century France where Durkheim saw a "moral mediocrity" sometimes verging on "anomie," or during the same period in Germany where Weber sketched the "iron cage" of post-Protestant capitalism. Of course, the notion of secularization no longer refers exclusively to conventional religion. It has been applied across the sociological field wherever cultural symbols and meanings lose their urgency. It has taken with it a series of related concepts born of religion, including the processes of *privatization and voluntarism,* which refer to the way in which individuals begin to seed and cultivate their own (often hybrid) meaning systems while exercising a new freedom of affiliational choice within the markets of religious or other forms of organization.

Neither Durkheim nor Weber saw secularization as linear or irreversible. Durkheim was careful to point out that new religions would arise to fill the void, and Weber saw charisma as a source of counter movements interrupting long-term trends of rationalization. In this sense, the two provided background insights to yet another batch of religious concepts with secular application. The related terms of *revitalization, revivalism,* and *sectarianism* all refer to processes of *sacralization* in which religion is reasserted against a secularizing trend. Nowadays these concepts have considerable currency in fields far removed from religion itself, including political movements and developments in the "secular culture," if that is not an oxymoron. The related dialectical dynamic relating *church and sect* has been discerned in realms as seemingly diverse as politics, trade unions, and the sociology of knowledge (cf. Iannaccone 1988).

All of the concepts thus far reflect the rich legacy of the classical tradition of the sociology of religion. However, more recent research has also exported important insights and terminology. For example, the wide-ranging social psychological paradigm of *cognitive dissonance* originated in the Festinger, Riecken, and Schachter (1965) research on the failure of an apocalyptic prophecy to materialize in a millenerian religious cult. The work of Lofland and Richardson (1984) on *conversion processes and networks* stemmed from work on the early "Moonies" but has been applied to organizational recruitment in a range of venues, from the civil rights movement to addiction treatment programs. Ebaugh's (1977) models of *role exit* began with sociological reflections on her own exit from the ranks of the Catholic religious, but she herself has developed it in contexts ranging from the military to the matrimonial. Finally, within the economics of religion, Iannaccone (1988) has developed a *rational-choice model of habit formation* to account for patterns of religious participation; the model has subsequently been applied to other phenomena such as addiction and smoking behavior. Meanwhile, the exporting of religious concepts has led to applications of *myth and ritual in both the old and new "institutional" schools* of organizational analysis (cf. Perrow 1986;

Powell and DiMaggio 1991). Even some of the forthcoming work from the Program on Non-Profit Organizations (PONPO) on religion aspires to this kind of generalizability, including a preliminary assessment of the sources and consequences of *organizational cynicism* that was provoked by religious settings but is by no means restricted to them.

RELIGIOUSLY PERTINENT DEVELOPMENTS IN THE STUDY OF SECULAR ORGANIZATIONS

As much as religious analysis has benefitted the broader scrutiny of society, the reverse is also true. At this point we want to shift specifically to the organizational level, and begin with a brief description of several approaches to secular organizations that have particular promise for the world of denominations, churches, and even sects and cults. In fact, the field of complex organizations is so rich and diverse that a draconian concision is necessary in representing it here. We suggest that almost all classical organizational theory can be understood under the three rubrics of bureaucracy, decision making, and power. In addition, there are three more recent approaches that have special potential for religious organizations; namely, "new institutionalism," organizational culture, and the developing study of social movements.

Bureaucracy

If there is any single term that has come to dominate the study of complex organizations, it is bureaucracy, with all of its connotations of rigid inefficiencies and its presumably crabbed and constipated guru, Max Weber. Ironically, however, Weber saw bureaucracy as the very opposite of inefficient: a rationally designed tool for policy implementation in a complex world. Indeed, as Perrow (1986) has pointed out, the problems that occur in most bureaucracies arise because they are not bureaucratic enough in resisting the sorts of nonrational exceptions-to-the-rules that pave the way to organizational hell.

What most people think of as bureaucracy is an organization characterized by a hierarchy of offices, each under the control of a higher one. But this was only one of the ideal-typical characteristics that distinguished this new organizational form from the small, loose-knit, unpredictable, and capricious structures prior to the nineteenth century. Besides mere hierarchy, Weber noted that the business of the organization was conducted on a continuing basis; the hierarchy divided the labor of the whole organization into units based on the training and expertise necessary to fill the office; the duties of each office were to be governed by written rules; written files were maintained of the activities of each of the organization's units; officials in the organization received fixed salaries which were graded by rankings related to the overall hierarchical structure; the officials could not own the offices that they occupied; and the officials were to separate their official life from their private life. That all of these characteristics now seem so obvious tells us how completely we have succumbed to the "organizational revolution" involved.

Today, some 75 years after Weber's seminal work, studies of bureaucracy often begin with descriptive accounts of how an organization looks or works. It then moves on to explanatory or predictive relationships such as, "If a firm has a combination of 'A' resources, 'B' technologies of manufacture or service, and 'C' kinds of market, its organizational structure will look like 'D'." In fact, a great deal of research here begins with matters of bureaucratic form (i.e., the shape of the "organization chart"), and then moves into considerations of process and product (e.g., Meyer and Brown 1977; Blau 1969); professionalization as a possible alternative to bureaucratic organizational styles (Blau, Heydebrand, and Stauffer 1966; Hall 1968; Stinchcombe 1959; Wilensky 1964); social structure and organizational structure (Stinchcombe 1965); technical functionalism, which argues that each technology may be suited to a particular organizational structure (Burns 1971; Perrow 1967; Woodward 1971; Blau 1970; Kimberly 1976); and whole groupings of structures in interorganizational networks (Burt 1980; Benson 1975; Granovetter 1974; Baty, Evan, and Rothermel 1970; Laumann, Galaskiewicz, and Marsden 1978). The literature also includes rational-choice and economic models (e.g., Williamson [1981] argues that transaction costs between organizations will determine whether they are organized into markets or hierarchies—internally and/or externally).

Perhaps understandably, bureaucratic models had relatively little currency in traditional work on religious organizations. After all, stereotypes of corporate behemoths and covenanted churches are virtually orthogonal. More recently, however, some of these stereotypes have been unmasked, especially in the religious case. It is true that few religious institutions are formally organized in explicitly bureaucratic fashion, and the churchly tendency to rely on exogenous authority (whether divine, denominational, or laity based) may disrupt the formation of internal classic bureaucratic procedures. At the same time, there is increasing recognition that bureaucracy is no stranger to religion. Not surprisingly, the Roman Catholic Church has spawned several analyses that deal with bureaucratic matters of organizational structure (cf. Goldner, Ritti, and Ference 1977; Seidler and Meyer 1989). Harrison's (1959) account of unacknowledged bureaucracy among, of all denominations, the American Baptist Church has pointed the way to other inquiries concerning Protestant denominations (e.g., Takayama 1975; Luidens 1982; Wright 1984; Scherer 1980; Reifsnyder 1986; Iannaccone 1988), more sectarian groups (Beckford 1975), and special purpose institutions (Zald 1970). As studies of religious organization become more probing—and as the theological bloom leaves the organizational rose—we can expect more analyses in bureaucracy's structural spirit, if not its Weberian letter. This applies not just to religion's largest organizations but to some of its smallest as well, because size and bureaucracy are imperfectly correlated at best.

Decision Making

Although the study of organizational form is useful, it is also worth examining what people actually do in organizations. Most of what they do, especially at the managerial level, is make decisions. Thus, investigation into how decisions are made—and how they are affected by structural, environmental, psychological, and political influences—is also a critical strand of contemporary organizational analysis. The parent of decision-making research was Chester Barnard (1938), an early adherent of the rational choice paradigm. The basic presupposition here is that executives are rational actors making careful decisions with all the information necessary for informed choice available at their fingertips.

More recently, that assumption has come under attack from a series of scholars, most notably Herbert Simon, James March, and others associated with what has come to be known as the Carnegie School. Drawing on psychology as well as political theory, these theorists introduce the concept of "bounded rationality" as critical in understanding any manager's decisions. Their insight is that there is no such thing as full or perfect knowledge about a situation. Thus, every decision, no matter how "rational," is made within the confines, or "boundaries," of whatever information is accessible. Decision makers may know 90 percent of everything about a situation that needs a resolution, or they may know only 25 percent, but it is sure that they never know 100 percent (Simon 1976; March and Simon 1958; March 1978). Because decision makers can only be "boundedly rational" despite their resolve, the research agenda concerns the nature of those boundaries.

This line of reasoning has ultimately led to the "garbage can theory" (March and Olsen 1976) in which exogenous events, time, flow of participants, attention span of participants, the ambiguity of goals, ambiguity over the roles of participants, and the opportunities for action are all made problematic for each decision. In this model, the process of reaching a decision begins to mimic a "garbage can" into which all of these factors are tossed haphazardly, and out of which comes a decision which could very well have been different depending on what factors were extant in the garbage can at that moment. Garbage can theory predicts a chaotic process of decision making whose results are not necessarily chaotic in their own right. The scholarly payoff comes in examining which organizational settings are more or less characterized by this model.

One can hardly imagine a setting more conducive to garbage can theory than the church, but to date there are virtually no studies of religious organizations identified with this perspective. Although there are certainly analyses of religious decision making (cf. Pope 1965; Campbell and Pettigrew 1959; Demerath and Hammond 1969; Elcock 1984; Marsden 1987; Hoge et al. 1988), these have not been self-consciously related to decision making in the broader organizational literature. This is no doubt partly because individual decision making is de-emphasized in religious organizations presumably dominated by consensus, tradition, and ritual. Once again, however, stereotypes are at work. Every form of religious organization affords ample room for such decision making at virtually every level. Even if these decisions are affected by nonrational variables, this in no way sets religious practitioners apart from secular decision makers. Indeed, just as secular decision makers may be less rational than they are often depicted, religious decision makers may be more so—especially in the less priestly and sacramental rounds of the religious life.

Power

The first two classical perspectives have focused on the context of organizational behavior and the decisions made within it. The question now shifts to struggles over bending both contexts and decisions to particular advantages and interests. While organizations as a whole have interests vis-à-vis other organizations, within any given organization subgroups and individuals are often engaged in battle. It is within this realm of conflict that power and politics are at home.

In fact, this emphasis is relatively recent, and it is a response to the earlier panglossian tendency to describe organizations as cohesive teams pursuing consensual goals with the kind of maximum efficiency associated with the Weberian ideal-types. This viewpoint ignored the uses and abuses of power within the internal disputes of a closed "rational" system; it also gave little attention to an organization's external boundaries as these are revealed from more "open" and "natural" system perspectives (Scott 1987).

The concern with power has provoked research on a wide variety of topics, including professionalization as a form of worker and social control (Johnson 1972; Dougherty 1980); how external elements (often resources, but also information, institutional environment, and regulatory climate) control the shape and behavior of organizations (Zald 1978; Pfeffer and Salancik 1978; Aldrich and Pfeffer 1976; Child 1972; Thompson 1967), and the effect that organizations themselves have on their surroundings, often unintentionally (Perrow 1986; Zucker 1983; Useem 1980; Lukes 1974).

Although power disputes would appear an anathema to the image cultivated by many religious organizations, a number of scholars have begun to lead the way in exploring this dimension (cf. Hadden 1969; Wood 1981; Derr and Derr 1982; Falbo and Gaines 1987; Ammerman 1991; Demerath and Williams 1992; Chaves 1993). Yet power considerations remain somewhat alien to religious analysis, and here is a major area where studies of the sacred stand to benefit from the richly nuanced and tightly textured accounts of the secular. This is especially the case concerning the obstacles that stand between the goals and outcomes of most religious agencies. Virtually every religious institution seeks change of some sort, whether among their members or in the external environment. To ignore power factors which intrude upon their aspirations is to ignore much of the reality with which they must contend.

The New Institutionalism

One school of organizational analysis that both spans and criticizes the concerns of bureaucracy, decision making, and power is the institutional tradition. Whereas the three approaches already discussed tend to focus on how individuals operate within and exert influence upon organizations, institutionalism takes a decidedly nonindividualistic cast. In opposition to behavioristic and rational-choice models of the calculating actor, institutionalism focuses on the way organizations constrain and transcend their members, while operating within a social environment over the longer haul.

In fact, we have not one but two branches of institutionalism. The "old" is represented by Parsons (1951) and focuses on the way organizations are "infused with value" to become normative citadels exercising benign hegemony over their members. The "new," as expressed in the collection of articles by Powell and DiMaggio (1991), puts less stress on values and norms and more emphasis on scripts and routines as the secrets of organizational persistence. The concern here is how key objectives and practices become established to control an organization's internal and external activity within a broader organizational "field." Attention is also directed to how these institutionalized scenarios may be subverted in the short and long term. Such subversion may occur through structural necessity (bureaucracy), by leadership action (decision making), or by internal and external conflict (power).

This school of thought can ask bureaucratic-like descriptive questions, such as, "Why do organizations look so similar?" (DiMaggio and Powell 1983) in order to suggest the answer, "Because they all operate in the same institutional matrix of norms, values, and objectives." The school can also wonder about the power in and of organizations (Zucker 1983; Meyer and Rowan 1978) as well as styles of decision making and their effects on the norms of their environments (Meyer and Rowan 1977)—a compelling issue for such recently institutionalized norms as "management by objective," an idea which has invaded the church (cf. Smith 1980) as well as other nonprofits. It is scarcely risky to predict that the new institutionalism will be increasingly compelling to scholars of religious organizations (cf. Ebaugh 1977; Bartunek 1984).

Organizational Culture

Meanwhile, a still more recent organizational perspective cleaves even closer to the prototypic religious institution. Although beliefs and rituals have considerable currency within the institutionalist tradition, they function more as means to the end of organizational control rather than ends in themselves. This latter view is more characteristic of the "organizational culture" school (cf. Burawoy 1979; Deal and Kennedy 1982; Schein 1985; Ouchi and Wilkins 1985; Ott 1989; Frost et al. 1991; Czarniawska-Joerges 1992).

Put most pithily, this perspective seeks to adapt the broader culture concept to the narrower sphere of the organization. Just as societies have systems of meaning that are symbolically expressed and ritually reinforced, so do organizations. Just as societies depend on an often arbitrary but nonetheless potent culture for their coherence and their cohesion, so do organizations. Just as functionalists, neo-Marxists, critical theorists, deconstructionists, and post-structuralists differ about culture's various qualities and significances at the societal level, so does a new breed of analyst reflect some of the differences within organizations. Indeed, just as the study of culture writ large has produced more theoretical debates than clinching research, so has the study of culture writ smaller within organizations. After all, culture's very abstractness has discouraged many researchers drawn to the empirical concreteness of more structural perspectives. This is another case of the oft-told tale of the methodological tail wagging the theoretical dog.

In some ways, the organizational culture perspective stands to gain more than it contributes in exchange with the study of religious organizations. Hall (1984) points out that a number of critical secular organizational forms (especially in the nonprofit sector) have religious origins. If any perspective has been dominant in religion, it is the cultural. As the next section of this paper will seek to demonstrate, there is considerable insight available there for export. At the same time, religious scholars also have much to learn from grounded accounts of how culture functions within corporate, military, educational, political, and health organizations. Here we encounter less idealized conceptions of culture at work in organizational settings—a kind of critical test of culture's pertinence in circumstances not often thought of as congenial.

Social Movements

As noted in the paper's first section, here is another example in which research on secular processes is indebted to path-breaking work on sacred equivalents. To mention social movements of any sort is to take up issues of social change, and while both sacred and secular spheres have long-standing concerns with change, religion's pedigree is especially rich. Early and continuing work on the church-sect distinction and on cults has spawned a series of insights applicable to "social movements" within a range of sectors— political, economic, intellectual, artistic, and so forth. The processes that produce new organizational splinter movements (sects) or culturally innovative organizations begun anew (cults) have been replicated in a wide variety of circumstances. The same is true of the temporal dynamic by which sects may grow and become routinized into churches, only to provoke new sects in response.

In recent years, however, the study of social movements has been subject to theoretical diversification, if not outright discord. Older "value added" models (cf. Weber 1978) tended to focus on the underlying societal strains and personal grievances which gave birth to such movements, noting how charismatic leaders were matched with followers in need. But a newer strand of social movement theory argued that the search for ultimate origins was less important (and perhaps less defensible) than an analysis of proximate facilitators. This "resource mobilization" perspective (cf. McCarthy and Zald 1977) focuses on the pursuit of such scarce resources as money, members, and network contacts as the critical variables influencing a movement's course. While it is possible to argue that even founding value grievances can be subsequently "constructed" as a revisionist resource, it seems clear that the two traditions of social movement theory are not mutually exclusive. Indeed, recent work by Snow et al. (1986) and Demerath and Williams (1992) suggest grounds for a convergence. The latter's conception of "cultural power" stresses the importance of mobilizing cultural resources, and thereby completes the circle by marking a return to some of the earlier value-driven conceptions.

Most recent social movement research has concerned seemingly nonreligious groups pursuing changes in civil rights, gender relations, the environment, welfare, and so forth. But many of these movements are religious at their edges, if not their core, as noted by Wuthnow's (1988) treatment of religious "special purpose groups." Moreover, the efflorescence of religious cults beginning especially in the 1960s has also been an important research arena (cf. Lofland and Richardson 1984; Stark and Bainbridge 1985; Robbins 1988). Much the same is true of the European concern with "new religious movements" (Beckford 1989).

Meanwhile, an especially welcome development of recent years has been the tendency to break down the old dichotomy between social movements, on the one hand, and complex organizations, on the other. It is not just that movements may evolve into organizations, which can in turn spawn movements. It is rather that movements, even in their earliest stages, may depend on complex organizational resources that supplement or even substitute for the charisma of the cliches. Even more important, the most formidably rigid and rigorous complex organizational structures may generate internal social movements as either gas or cancer within the belly of the beast (cf. Zald and Berger 1978). Here Seidler and Meyer's (1989) treatment of post-Vatican II "aggiornamento" within the "lazy monopoly" of the American Catholic Church is one telling case in point; Ammerman's (1991) account of power struggles within the Southern Baptist Convention is another.

So much then for six major areas of recent theory and research on organizations. While there are certainly examples of both secular and religious applications in each area, the interchange has not been as rich as one might hope. Just as few religious scholars have fully immersed themselves in the literature on secular organizations, even fewer analysts of nonreligious organizations have bothered to sip from the religious cup.

Of course, there are myriad reasons for this mutual disinterest. As we have suggested earlier, the very word "religion" may alienate some researchers while inappropriately attracting others. There may be considerable confusion over the definition of terms common to one field but not to the other. Although both fields operate within the broad traditions of the social sciences, the study of complex organizations really begins with corporate management and administration concerns, whereas the sociology of the religious institution field grows out of a concern with the relationship of religion to society. Thus, even though the two groups of scholars may be asking very similar questions, they are framed with such different assumptions and different vocabularies as to afford little ground for cross-fertilization. The remainder of this paper seeks a bridge across this gap.

PROBLEMS OF RELIGIOUS ORGANIZATIONS WITH NONRELIGIOUS APPLICATIONS: ENTERING THE EXPORT MODE

At this point we switch the tables once again and return to a consideration of insights from religious organizations that might be exported to organizations with quite different missions and identities. Here again we argue that there is something sociologically compelling about religion which is not restricted to the conventionally religious.

Below is a list of problematic organizational scenarios that are common within religious settings but not confined to them. Most are derived from religion's self-conscious effort to confront and express a sense of the sacred, but the concept of the sacred is itself sociologically relative, and most secular ventures have sacred components which elicit similar dynamics. The idea here is to blur the line between religious and a-religious organizations without obliterating it entirely.

The problematizing tendencies to follow take the form of ideal-typical traits leading to ideal-typical dynamics. The list is neither exhaustive nor definitive;

in fact, it is offered as something of a foil in order to begin discussion rather than end it. Just as it is possible to find instances of each in many secular organizations, it is also possible to imagine exceptions within the religious field where organizational forms vary widely and are by no means confined to anyone's stereotypical notions of "church" or "congregation." Moreover, the list is intended to convey no value implications. While most of the characteristics are presented as organizational liabilities, it is also possible to see them as virtues, depending on one's assessment of the particular organization at issue. They are presented abstractly in order to span the sacred-secular divide and avoid entanglement with specific substantive cases. However, it is hoped that examples from both sectors will help to make the larger point at issue.

1. *Non-Tangible Goals.* Insofar as organizations pursue ultimate objectives which are either other-worldly, highly subjective, or plotted into the indefinite future, these goals tend to resist both operationalization and measurement. Certainly this is the case with "pursuing personal salvation" as a goal whose resulting ambiguity makes it difficult to mobilize members and sustain momentum. The result may be a problematic gap between ultimate and proximate goals (e.g., "growth" becoming the visible goal: recruiting new members, raising money, building new structures) often leaving the latter ad hoc, highly contested, and lacking in legitimacy. This may finally lead to either "goal displacement" (whereby means to ends become ends in their own right) or "goallessness" itself (Demerath and Hammond 1969), in which case the organization becomes vulnerable to processes of change, takeover, and co-optation. While these are common scenarios within religious organizations, they occur in secular settings as well. The federal poverty programs of the 1960s and 1970s have been accused of just this problem: a goal so long-term and amorphous (a "war on poverty") that the program was inevitably co-opted by its aparachniks.

2. *Non-Tangible Means.* Insofar as organizations depend on non-demonstrable and non-calculable methods (e.g., prayer or assurances based on moral merit in the religious case), the organization rests on a fundamentally a-rational basis. This may lead in turn to various forms of "means displacement" by which ends become means in their own right, and the process of goal setting takes rhetorical and substantive precedent over goal achievement. Ultimately this may lead to either a short-term emphasis on ritual for its own sake, or a long-term abandonment of faith itself. By contrast, more worldly means that become covertly critical to the organizational routine may go unacknowledged and unmonitored, as in Harrison's (1959) account of "rational-pragmatic" authority among the American Baptists. For a nonreligious case, consider how peace organizations such as the World Federalists struggled with this problem before the demise of the Soviet Union,

seeking to "change people's minds" without a programmatic plan of action. Patricia Chang has pointed out that it is often under these circumstances that organizations lose their distinctive way and tend to emulate others, helping to account for the "institutional isomorphism" that often characterizes organizational "fields" sharing this quality (DiMaggio and Powell 1983).

3. *Cultural Primacy.* Insofar as organizations give priority to symbols, doctrine, and ritual, structural factors may be treated as derivative, secondary, and potentially profane. The gap between "culture and structure" ("ought and is") may widen over time, with increased tension resulting from the lack of coordination between these different facets (cf. Chaves 1993). It is possible to identify instances of both "structural lag" as churches struggle to adapt to rapid cultural changes (e.g., in perspectives concerning the role of women) and "cultural lag" where traditional religious organizations are slow to confront changing structural circumstances (e.g., alterations in local political realities). In some instances the two types of lag may be linked in a kind of dialectical two-step organizational change; nor are these processes confined to religion. Many fine arts organizations, such as museums, symphony orchestras, and ballet companies face an emphasis on the "importance of the performance" that may come at the expense of organizational necessities. The same is true of other institutions with idealized products and idealistic professional staffs (e.g., hospitals and universities).

Finally, there are two corollaries here worth noting. The first concerns the special *burden of rectitude* experienced by organizations like churches and other nonprofits so bound to the pursuit of virtue for its own sake that they become hobbled in meeting tough organizational imperatives and making tough organizational decisions. Thus, personnel actions may be based more on compassion than on merit; budget decisions may be determined more by enthusiasm than calculation, and institutional objectives may reflect moral commitments rather than organizational capacity. In the final analysis, organizations may have to sacrifice virtue altogether on the altar of an eleventh-hour expediency. Hughes (1962) has written on the problem of "good men doing dirty work;" we are suggesting that there is often dirty work required of good organizations. A related corollary involves the general problem of conferring roles and authority on the *wrong people for the right reasons.* The difficulty is compounded when various levels of authority are nested more in form than in fact, and when an organization develops models of authority that run counter to reality (e.g., the "family model" so common within churches). Different faces of the problem are associated with Weber's "traditional" and "charismatic" authority, especially the routinized charisma of office. In such settings, the well-known disjunctions between formal and informal authority and between expressive and instrumental leadership may be exacerbated. Even more serious is the spectre of authority as an empty shell.

4. *Anti-Organizational Ideologies.* Insofar as organizations champion values of democracy, individualism, tolerance, freedom, emancipation, and unfettered inquiry, they may be acting counter to their own organizational imperatives. These often include at least a dollop of unquestioning compliance and eager zealousness. It is arguable (or at least Demerath is preparing to argue) that this has been a long-range dynamic of Liberal Protestantism, according to which it can now be described as losing the organizational battle as a result of having won the cultural war. But a similar process may be discerned within other institutions, ranging from families to universities. For instance, two politically progressive magazines (*Mother Jones* and *Ms.*) struggled through staff unionization movements, including one strike, that left both organizations struggling to reconcile ideological commitments and organizational imperatives.

5. *Constraints of Historicity.* Insofar as organizations stress continuity with the past as revealed through sacred events, sacred texts, and traditional authority, they are controlled by a definite past even as they are oriented to an indefinite future. This "institutional anchor" may produce unique processes and trajectories of organizational change. For most religious organizations, the concrete, canonized, and readily accessible manifestation of deity occupies a special place of authority to which anyone can appeal regardless of power position. For most Protestants, that authority is the Bible. For Roman Catholics, it is the traditions of the church as well as the Bible. For most Jews, it is the *Torah,* the *Talmud,* and the ongoing tradition of the faith. There are organizational strengths as well as weaknesses inherent in any organization that is so "anchored." This dilemma is illustrated by the reliance of Islam on the relatively inflexible seventh-century *Koran* which has served to motivate many adherents powerfully but has also tended to inhibit organizational and social adaptation. In a secular venue, the problem is similarly demonstrated by the inflexible dependence of both the American Communist Party and the John Birch Society on their early declarations of principles. Both major political parties in the United States suffer from a variant of this problem, and some would say the country as a whole struggles within the clutches of its Constitution. At quite a different level, business annals recall the problems introduced in the top-of-the-line Gar Wood speedboat company when it was ordered to reconfigure in order to produce a budget model. Many business corporations such as IBM still operate in the shadow of their founding icons. When organizations reach a point in which innovation itself becomes illegitimate, they are frequently cut off from important processes of adaptation. Far more cults and incipient corporations die than stabilize over time. On the other hand, this can also be the backdrop for wrenching organizational innovation, ranging from reform to revolution.

6. *Dependence of the Leaders on the Led.* Insofar as voluntary organizations require not only the compliance but the financial support of their

adherents, this may place the governors at the mercy of the governed. This is consistent with an overall tendency in recent organizational studies to shift from a formal Weberian top-down emphasis to a more processual bottom-up motif. But religious organizations offer a particularly arresting case in point. Churches overall have an unusually high ratio of donors to total donations when compared with other nonprofit organizations. While the problem is compounded within a locally autonomous "congregational" polity, it is by no means absent within the hierarchical "episcopal" model. Wherever it occurs, it may serve as an important inhibition on prophetic leadership in the service of innovation and in the midst of controversy, as studies of parish political actions have demonstrated repeatedly. To a degree that is often unrecognized, all organizations face this dilemma. Even in that most rigidly structured of organizations, the military, officers in the heat of the battle can easily find themselves dependent on the behavior, willingness, and action of enlisted personnel.

Here too, however, there is a corollary concerning any organization's entanglement with its constituency and the tendency for service organizations in particular to become dependent on the weak. Insofar as any organization has a mission toward its lowest common denominator—the young, the poor, the needy, the infirm, and the disenfranchised—its primary clientele may be in no position to reciprocate the organization's efforts, and hence will be more of a drain than a fount of organizational resources. It may also serve as an obstacle to optimal decision making on behalf of the organization itself, especially when short-range demands are pitted against long-range needs. While virtue may be its own reward according to some calculations, this is rarely true of organizational metrics. The problem is common not only among religious organizations but also among a wide range of social agencies and political movements.

7. *Taken-for-Grantedness.* Insofar as organizations become so entrenched in the broader culture that they are seen as both ubiquitous and permanent, their image may hide their vulnerability, perhaps until it is too late. This is especially a problem for voluntary service organizations whose client needs and commitments shift from primary to secondary and even tertiary. Under processes of member withdrawal, privatization, and mobility, the organization may have few chits to cash. The problem may be paradoxically compounded in the case of organizations that have cultivated images of endowment and endurance. Once the reality shifts, it may change very quickly indeed with drastic consequences. For instance, major art museums often carry indomitable reputations belied by precarious financial straights as municipal governments make drastic funding cuts. Part of the reason for this situation is that the community has taken the institution for granted for so long that there is little provision for generating new resources.

Here the corollary concerns the way in which organizations may also take themselves for granted, as in the aforementioned application of Hirschman's (1970) concept of the "lazy monopoly" to the Catholic case by Goldner et al. (1977) and Seidler and Meyer (1989). This is especially likely for religious organizations because of their traditionalism and lack of concrete measures of need and effectiveness. Inertia can be a short-term blessing but a long-term curse for any organization.

8. *Local-National Dissonance within Organizational Hierarchies.* Insofar as different organizational structures, norms, and goals exist at local versus national levels of an organization, there will be problems of coordination and control. No organization offers longer sustained experience with this dilemma than the Catholic Church. It has been especially acute of late over issues ranging from contraception and abortion to Liberation Theology and the rising numbers of de facto female priests. But if Catholicism is known for its ecclesiastical hierarchy in the short run, it must also be cited for its flexible adaptivity over the longer haul. Here church "orders" (Jesuits, Benedictines, etc.) have been especially important as outlets and sources of innovation. Meanwhile, most Protestant denominations have experienced similar problems, if on a smaller and less contested scale. This is even true of those who, like the Baptists and the United Church of Christ, nurture principles of "local church autonomy." Certainly the problem is common in nonreligious sectors. Consider the different priorities among, and communication distortions between, the assembly line and the front office, the infantry patrol and the Pentagon war room, and the political back ward and the executive office.

9. *Boundary Constraints and Community Labeling.* Insofar as an organization is perceived within a differentiated community matrix, it may be labeled in a way that is inimical to its mission. Labeling behavior applies to institutions as well as to individuals, and the labels themselves may be perniciously prophetic, especially within a broader context. Religious organizations may be especially vulnerable to such labelling because of their lack of a high profile program and highly crystallized product. To the extent to which they are perceived as peripheral, they will be assigned scripts and roles with peripheral significance. One nonreligious example might be the Junior League, in which national leadership has complained bitterly that the public's perception is 30 years out of date. But, of course, agencies and organizations may also be mislabeled in the opposite direction (i.e., as more radically activist and uncompromising than they actually are). This may have its isolating consequences. By and large, mislabeling is especially likely as a result of change—in either the organization, the community, or both. Labels can be self-defeating as well as self-fulfilling depending on their relation to an organization's own reality and resources.

10. *Cultural Power as a Political Weapon.* Insofar as any organization or political participant lacks the sort of direct structural power that characterizes political and economic contestants, it may specialize in moral appeals to influence agendas and steer discussion. This "cultural power" is a distinctive weapon in its own right, and it has become a special—but not exclusive—weapon of religious organizations and movements, some of which exert far more power than might be predicted on conventional grounds (cf. Demerath and Williams 1992). Any philanthropic or other organization known principally because it "does good," may wield this kind of power. The classic case is the cultural power used so effectively by the nonviolent movements on behalf of Indian independence and American civil rights. While religion has a clear advantage here because of its moral legitimacy and professional experience, such power is found in a variety of organizations and movements, such as the Business Roundtable in discussions of federal budgetary policy, or the long-standing anti-socialized medicine campaign of the American Medical Association. It is even used by establishment politicians themselves in order to ward off and blunt oppositional movements. It is no accident that canny politicians seek to cloak themselves in religious symbols while on the stump, even though once elected, they try to hold religion at as great a distance as possible to maximize their own political freedom.

SUMMARY

This paper offers a brief argument on behalf of conventional religion as a source of insight into seemingly nonreligious aspects of society and organizations—and vice versa. Instead of juxtaposing sacred and secular in the time-honored tradition, we have argued that each is an important dimension of the other. While the sociology of religion has been a net importer of broader social science insights and theory over the past 75 years, there is both precedent and rationale for returning to the export model which was more common in the discipline's classical period. Once shorn of its popular connotations, the term "religion" can be useful to a wide range of organizational scholarship. Rather than setting one class of phenomena apart, it can be seen as a facet of virtually all phenomena, including organizations and social movements of virtually every stripe.

The field of complex organizations is rich with insight, theory, and analytical technique. The arena of religious institutions is rich with distinctive organizational designs, special interorganizational relationships, and a large presence across the landscape of society. Religious organizations have long served as foundries of organizational forms and issues. Thus, there is immense potential for research payoff in attending to them. The field of complex organizations would be well advised to treat religious institutions more seriously, and scholars of religion would do well to study the emerging scholarship on organizations of all sorts. Thus, in offering 10 scenarios common within both religious and nonreligious organizations we hope to stimulate a sacred-secular convergence and transcendence that will profit both spheres in the grand tradition of Weber and Durkheim themselves.

ACKNOWLEDGMENT

The authors wish to thank the Lilly Endowment for support (through its grant to the Project on Religious Institutions at PONPO) for the research which led to this paper.

REFERENCES

Aldrich, H.E., and J. Pfeffer. 1976. "Environments of Organizations." *Annual Review of Sociology* 2: 70-105.

Ammerman, N. 1991. *Baptist Battles*. New Brunswick, NJ: Rutgers University Press.

Barnard, C. 1938. *The Functions of the Executive*. Cambridge, MA: Harvard University Press.

Bartunek, J.M. 1984. "Changing Interpretive Schemes and Organizational Restructuring: The Example of a Religious Order." *Administrative Science Quarterly* 29: 355-372.

Baty, G.B., W.B. Evan, and T.W. Rothermel. 1970. "Personnel Flows as Interorganizational Relations." *Administrative Science Quarterly* 16: 430-443.

Beckford, J.A. 1975. *The Trumpet of Prophecy: A Sociological Study of the Jehovah's Witnesses*. Oxford: Basil Blackwell.

_____. 1989. *Religion in Advanced Industrial Society*. London: Unwin and Hyman.

Bellah, R.N. 1967. "Civil Religion in America." *Daedalus* 96(1): 1-21.

Benson, J.K. 1975. "The Interorganizational Network as Political Economy." *Administrative Science Quarterly* 20: 229-249.

Blau, P.M. 1969. *The Dynamics of Bureaucracy: A Study of Interpersonal Relations in Two Government Agencies*. Chicago: University of Chicago Press.

_____. 1970. "A Formal Theory of Differentiation in Organizations." *American Sociological Review* 35: 201-218.

Blau, P.M., W.V. Heydebrand, and R.E. Stauffer. 1966. "The Structure of Small Bureaucracies." *American Sociological Review* 31: 179-191.

Burawoy, M. 1979. *Manufacturing Consent*. Chicago: University of Chicago Press.

Burns, T. 1971. "Mechanistic and Organismic Structures." Pp. 43-55 in *Organization Theory*, edited by D.S. Pugh. Harmondsworth, UK: Penguin.

Burt, R. 1980. "Models of Network Structure." *Annual Review of Sociology* 6: 79-141.

Campbell, E.Q., and T.F. Pettigrew. 1959. *Christians in Racial Crisis*. Washington, DC: Public Affairs Press.

Chaves, M. 1993. "Intra-Organizational Power and Internal Secularization within Protestant Denominations." *American Journal of Sociology* 99(1)(July): 1-48.

Child, J. 1972. "Organizational Structure, Environment, and Performance: The Role of Strategic Choice." *Sociology* 6: 1-22.

Czarniawska-Joerges, B. 1992. *Exploring Complex Organizations: A Cultural Perspective*. Beverly Hills, CA: Sage.

Deal, T., and A. Kennedy. 1982. *Corporate Culture: Rites and Rituals of Corporate Life*. San Francisco, CA: Jossey-Bass.

Demerath, N.J. III, and P. Hammond. 1969. *Religion in Social Context*. New York: Random House.

Demerath, N.J. III, and R.H. Williams. 1992. *A Bridging of Faiths: Religion and Politics in a New England City*. Princeton, NJ: Princeton University Press.

Derr, J.M., and C.B. Derr. 1982. "Outside the Mormon Hierarchy: Alternative Aspects of Institutional Power." *Dialogue: Journal of Mormon Thought* 15: 21-43.

DiMaggio, P.J., and W.W. Powell. 1983. "The Iron Cage Revisited: Institutional Isomorphism and Collective Rationality in Organizational Fields." *American Sociological Review* 48: 147-160.

Dougherty, K. 1980. "Professionalism as Ideology." *Socialist Review* 10: 160-175.

Durkheim, E. 1965[1912]. *The Elementary Forms of the Religious Life*. New York: Free Press.

Ebaugh, H.R.F. 1977. *Out of the Cloister: A Study of Organizational Dilemmas*. Austin: University of Texas Press.

Elcock, L.E. 1984. *Toward Strategic Management in Religious Communities*. New York: Union College.

Falbo, T., B.L. New, and M. Gaines. 1987. "Perceptions of Authority and the Power Strategies Used by Clergymen." *Journal for the Scientific Study of Religion* 26: 499-507.

Festinger, L., H.W. Riecken, Jr., and S. Schachter. 1965. *When Prophecy Fails*. New York: Harper and Row.

Frost, Peter J., L.F. Moore, M.R. Louis, C.C. Lundberg, and J. Martin, eds. 1991. *Reframing Organizational Culture*. Beverly Hills, CA: Sage.

Goldner, F.H., R.R. Ritti, and T.P. Ference. 1977. "The Production of Cynical Knowledge in Organizations." *American Journal of Sociology* 42: 539-551.

Grannovetter, M. 1974. *Getting a Job*. Cambridge, MA: Harvard University Press.

Hadden, J.K. 1969. *The Gathering Storm in the Churches*. Garden City, NY: Doubleday.

Hall, P.D. 1984. *The Organization of American Culture, 1700-1900: Private Institutions, Elites, and the Origins of American Nationality*. New York: New York University Press.

Hall, R. 1968. "Professionalization and Bureaucratization." *American Sociological Review* 33: 92-104.

Halton, E. 1992. "The Cultic Roots of Culture." Pp. 29-63 in *Theory of Culture*, edited by R. Munch and N.J. Smeltzer. Berkeley: University of California Press.

Harrison, P. 1959. *Authority and Power in the Free Church Tradition: A Social Case Study of the American Baptist Convention*. Princeton, NJ: Princeton University Press.

Hirschman, A.O. 1970. *Exit, Voice, and Loyalty: Responses to Decline in Firms, Organizations, and States*. Cambridge: Harvard University Press.

Hoge, D.R., J.W. Carroll, and F.K. Scheets. 1988. *Patterns of Parish Leadership: Cost and Effectiveness in Four Denominations*. Kansas City: Sheed and Ward.

Hughes, E.C. 1962. "Good Men and Dirty Work." *Social Problems* 40: 1-11.

Iannaccone, L.R. 1988. "A Formal Model of Church and Sect." *American Journal of Sociology* 94: S241-S268.

Johnson, T.J. 1972. *Professions and Power*. London: Macmillan.

Kimberly, J.R. 1976. "Organizational Size and the Structuralist Perspective: A Review, Critique and Proposal." *Administrative Science Quarterly* 21: 571-597.

Laumann, E.O., J. Galaskiewicz, and P.V. Marsden. 1978. "Community Structure as Interorganizational Linkages." *Annual Review of Sociology* 4: 455-484.

Lofland, J., and J.T. Richardson. 1984. "Religious Movement Organizations." Pp. 29-51 in *Research in Social Movements, Conflicts and Change*, Vol. 7, edited by L. Kriesberg. Greenwich, CT: JAI Press.

Luidens, D.A. 1982. "Bureaucratic Control in a Protestant Denomination." *Journal for the Scientific Study of Religion* 21: 163-175.

Lukes, S. 1974. *Power: A Radical View*. London: Macmillan.

March, J.G. 1978. "Bounded Rationality: Ambiguity and the Engineering of Choice." *Bell Journal of Economics* 9: 587-608.

March, J.G., and J.P. Olsen. 1976. *Ambiguity and Choice in Organizations*. Norway: Universitetsforlaget.

March, J.G., and H. Simon. 1958. *Organizations*. New York: John Wiley.

Marsden, G. 1987. *Reforming Fundamentalism*. Grand Rapids, MI: Erdmans.

McCarthy, J., and M.N. Zald. 1977. "Resource Mobilization and Social Movements: A Partial Theory." *American Journal of Sociology* 82: 1212-1241.

Meyer, J., and B. Rowan. 1977. "Institutional Organizations: Formal Structure as Myth and Ceremony." *American Journal of Sociology* 83: 340-363.

————. 1978. "The Structure of Educational Organizations." Pp. 78-109 in *Environments and Organizations,* edited by M. Meyer. San Francisco, CA: Jossey-Bass.

Meyer, M.W., and M.C. Brown. 1977. "The Process of Bureaucratization." *American Journal of Sociology* 830: 864-885.

Ott, J.S. 1989. *The Organizational Perspective*. Homewood, IL: Irwin.

Ouchi, W., and A. Wilkins. 1985. "Organizational Culture." *Annual Review of Sociology* 11: 457-483.

Parsons, T. 1951. *The Social System*. Glencoe, IL: Free Press.

Perrow, C. 1967. "A Framework for the Comparative Analysis of Organizations." *American Sociological Review* 32: 194-208.

————. 1986. *Complex Organizations*. 3rd. ed. New York: Random House.

Pfeffer, J., and G. Salancik. 1978. *The External Control of Organizations*. New York: Harper and Row.

Pope, L. 1965. *Millhands and Preachers*. 2nd ed. New Haven, CT: Yale University Press.

Powell, W.W., and P.J. DiMaggio, eds. 1991. *The New Institutionalism in Organizational Analysis*. Chicago: University of Chicago Press.

Reifsnyder, R.W. 1986. "Presbyterian Reunion, Reorganization and Expansion in the Late 19th Century." *American Presbyterians: Journal of Presbyterian History* 64: 27-38.

Robbins, T. 1988. *Cults, Converts, and Charisma*. Beverly Hills, CA: Sage.

Schein, E.F. 1985. *Organizational Culture and Leadership*. San Francisco, CA: Jossey-Bass.

Scherer, R.P., ed. 1980. *American Denominational Organization: A Sociological View*. South Pasadena, CA: William Carey Library.

Scott, W.R. 1987. *Organizations: Rational, Natural, and Open Systems*. 2nd ed. Englewood Cliffs, NJ: Prentice-Hall.

Seidler, J., and K. Meyer. 1989. *Conflict and Change in the Catholic Church*. New Brunswick, NJ: Rutgers University Press.

Simon, H.A. 1976. *Administrative Behavior: A Story of Decision-Making Processes in Administrative Organization*. 3rd ed. New York: The Free Press. (Originally published in 1947)

Smith, H.N. 1980. "Management by Objectives in the Church: Value Orientations Among Nebraska United Methodists." Unpublished dissertation, The University of Nebraska, Lincoln.

Snow, D., E.B. Rockford, Jr., S.K. Worden, and R.D. Beuford. 1986. "Frame Alignment Processes, Micromobilization, and Movement Participation." *American Sociological Review* 51: 464-481.

Stark, R., and W.S. Bainbridge. 1985. *The Future of Religion*. Berkeley: University of California Press.

Stinchcombe, A.L. 1959. "Bureaucratic and Craft Administration of Production: A Comparative Study." *Administrative Science Quarterly* 4: 168-187.

———. 1965. "Social Structure and Organizations." Pp. 142-191 in *Handbook of Organizations,* edited by J.G. March. Chicago: Rand McNally.

Takayama, K.P. 1975. "Formal Polity and Change of Structure: Denominational Assemblies." *Sociological Analysis* 36: 17-28.

Thompson, J.D. 1967. *Organizations in Action.* New York: McGraw-Hill.

Useem, M. 1980. "Corporations and the Corporate Elite." *Annual Review of Sociology* 6: 41-77.

Weber, M. 1958[1904-1905]. *The Protestant Ethic and Spirit of Capitalism.* New York: Scribner's.

———. 1978. *Economy and Society.* Berkeley: University of California Press. (Originally published in 1919)

Wilensky, H. 1964. "The Professionalization of Everyone." *American Journal of Sociology* 70: 137-158.

Williamson, O.E. 1981. "The Economics of Organization: The Transaction Cost Approach." *American Journal of Sociology* 87: 548-577.

Wood, J.R. 1981. *Leadership in Voluntary Organizations: The Controversy over School Action in Protestant Churches.* New Brunswick, NJ: Rutgers University Press.

Woodward, J. 1971. *Industrial Organization: Theory and Practice.* London: Oxford University Press.

Wright, C. 1984. "The Growth of Denominational Bureaucracies: A Neglected Aspect of American Church History." *Harvard Theological Review* 77: 177-194.

Wuthnow, R. 1988. *The Restructuring of American Religion.* Princeton: Princeton University Press.

Zald, M.N. 1970. *Organizational Change: The Political Economy of the YMCA.* Chicago: University of Chicago Press.

———. 1978. "On the Social Control of Industries." *Social Forces* 57: 79-102.

Zald, M.N., and M.A. Berger. 1978. "Social Movements in Organizations: Coup d'Etat, Insurgency, and Mass Movements." *American Journal of Sociology* 83: 823-861.

Zucker, L. 1983. "Organizations as Institutions." Pp. 1-47 in *Research in the Sociology of Organizations,* Vol. 2, edited by S. Bacharach. Greenwich, CT: JAI Press.

THE SULLIVAN INSTITUTE/ FOURTH WALL COMMUNITY:
"RADICAL" PSYCHOTHERAPY AS QUASI-RELIGION

Amy B. Siskind

ABSTRACT

This paper discusses the inception and development of the Sullivan Institute/ Fourth Wall community—a "radical" psychotherapeutic community which exhibited many characteristics that could be described as religious. The community came into existence in approximately 1957, and did not begin to disperse until the late 1980s. It was located on the Upper West Side of Manhattan, and comprised an extremely high percentage of professionals, academics, artists, writers, and musicians. The community was initially founded as an experiment in radical personality change and self-realization. Over its thirty-year life span, it evolved into an isolated authoritarian political sect with some millenarian beliefs. The basis of the community was formed by a unique type of therapeutic relationship characterized by extremes of directiveness on the part of therapists and dependency on the part of patients. Patient/members were under constant surveillance by other members and by their own therapists, who were obligated to report dissidents to the leadership. Monogamous relationships were forbidden,

Religion and the Social Order, Volume 4, pages 51-77.
ISBN: 1-55938-763-7

and procreation and child-rearing were strictly regulated. The community began to dissolve in approximately 1986, when it received notoriety due to a custody case brought by a member against his apostate wife.

INTRODUCTION

One of the singular achievements of the political and cultural movements of the 1960s was the transformation of the notion of political action from an isolated sphere of activity, practiced in political clubs and voting booths, to a way of life. The conception of the "personal as political" radically changed the forms of political activity from the time honored institutions of the campaign and the caucus to those of the march, the demonstration, and the political collective, among others. In the context of this radical shift in the conception of the political, the Sullivan Institute/Fourth Wall community came into its own. It had existed before, since approximately 1957, but only as a tiny band of psychotherapists and their patients—some of whom were already living together and engaging in relationships that breached the traditional professional boundaries between patient and therapist. Before 1970 most of these members were in their thirties and forties, but with the advent of inexpensive psychotherapy practiced by young "radical" therapists, many young people who were seeking personal growth in conjunction with a radical political perspective were attracted to the Sullivan Institute.

After the political and countercultural failures of the late 1960s, many young people retreated into what Greil and Rudy (1990) have referred to as Identity Transformation Organizations. These organizations attempted to trigger "radical shifts in world view and identity" (Greil and Rudy 1990, p. 227) among their members. Additionally, as Tipton (1982) suggests, these organizations provided a means through which young people who had "dropped out" of mainstream society could find a road that led back in, or at least a way of life that mediated between their own radical divergence from mainstream values and the society that still professed those values. The Sullivan Institute/ Fourth Wall community served this purpose for many people over its life span of approximately thirty years. Although it has rarely been written about in academic publications, the community was well-known among Manhattan's Upper West Side intelligentsia from which it sprang, and included many successful members of the artistic and academic professions. Data presented in this paper were gathered over a period of twenty years by the author and through discussions and interviews with other ex-members, as well as the writings of the founders of the community.

One fundamental issue, raised by the following discussion, is that of surveillance and social control in small communitarian groups. The ability of relatively small separatist communities to monitor and direct the lives of their members is unparalleled in mainstream society at large. The incorporation of many different aspects of life into one structure is the key factor leading to this high degree of surveillance and control. The Sullivan Institute/Fourth Wall community provided for living situations, psychotherapy, and the entire social lives of its members, even, in some cases, including jobs. While claiming to provide its members with unlimited potential for freedom and exploration in their lives, it demanded a very high degree of adherence to certain precepts and developed mechanisms for ensuring that these prescriptions were followed.

A BRIEF HISTORY OF THE SULLIVAN INSTITUTE/ FOURTH WALL COMMUNITY

In order to facilitate a better understanding of the evolution of the Sullivan Institute/Fourth Wall community I have chosen to divide its history into four periods: the formative period (1957-1970); the hedonistic period (1970-1979); the revolutionary period, (1979-1986); and the decline (1986-present), which is still occurring today.

The Formative Period

The Sullivan Institute community began as The Sullivan Institute for Research in Psychoanalysis. Named for Harry Stack Sullivan (1892-1949), one of a number of neo-Freudian revisionists that included Erich Fromm, Karen Horney, and others, it was originally founded by a student of Sullivan's—Jane Pearce, M.D., and her husband, Saul Newton. In approximately 1957, a small group of psychotherapists and their students left the William Alanson White Institute, where Sullivan had worked, and formed The Sullivan Institute for Research in Psychoanalysis. The new institute began to take on patients, and to formulate a radical conception of psychoanalysis: "Inherent in every psychological theory is an attitude about society as a whole. This orientation is expressed in definitions of mental health, insanity, normalcy, deviance, 'adjustment' and 'cure.' Most psychiatry is based on an acceptance of the established social order" (Pearce and Newton 1970, p. 1).

For Pearce and Newton, who were loosely associated with various Marxist and anthropological views regarding human cultural evolution, progress was measured in terms of interpersonal relationships. Their theory concerning the development of the individual was based on a belief that all culture is repressive, but that an evolutionary process is taking place which will eventually result in a non-repressive world culture (if humans are to survive as a species). The culmination of this evolutionary process is the Revolution, in which relationships will be radically changed and provide the basis for a new society.

While Jane Pearce was a psychiatrist who had worked closely with Sullivan at the William Alanson White Institute in New York City, Saul Newton had no formal training in psychology or psychiatry. He had been an active member of the Communist Party in the 1930s and had fought with the Abraham Lincoln Brigade in the Spanish Civil War. Together they decided to attempt the incorporation of Marxist theory with Sullivan's interpersonal theory of psychiatry.

Pearce and Newton criticized Freudian theory as "deeply pessimistic" about human nature and therefore supportive of the "capitalist establishment" (1970, p. 2), even after Marxist theory and the Russian revolution came into being (which proved, in their opinion, the viability of utopian communism). They contrast Freud with Sullivan, who stressed the importance of both interpersonal relationships in the formation of the personality, and the general sociocultural environment. According to Pearce and Newton, Sullivan believed that "hostility between people is rooted...in social frustration" (1970, p. 3). This belief is a radical departure from Freud's belief in the innate aggressive nature of human beings.

Pearce and Newton also attempted to apply Sullivan's methods of treating schizophrenic patients to patients who have had acute psychotic episodes. They use these innovations to suggest the desirability of therapeutic communities.

> [Sullivan] did extensive research into conditions that might lead to a positive outcome of an acute psychotic episode. Similar methods are being applied by many people who are trying to organize therapeutic communities. Some of the most effective of these applications ˎ can be seen in experiments in communal living. These experiments abide by the admonitions: "Hang together!" "Keep talking!" "Don't worry about eerie experiences!" "Protect against impulsive suicide!" "Maintain adequate manpower!" "Never do it alone!" (1970, p. 5).

As they accumulated patients in the late 1950s, Pearce and Newton (and their associates in the Sullivan Institute) began to experiment with an approach to psychotherapy that attempted to lower the traditional boundaries between patient and therapist. In contradiction to established ethical norms, they socialized with their patients, and encouraged their patients to meet and become intimate with each other. Over a period of approximately ten years (1959-1969), this resulted in a number of patients of Sullivan Institute therapists living together. At first patients rented summer houses together on eastern Long Island; eventually some moved together into apartments on the Upper West Side of Manhattan.

In 1963, Pearce and Newton published *Conditions of Human Growth,* which was their attempt to systematize and expand Sullivan's developmental theory. They begin by stating that social and cultural changes generated by modernity have made it necessary for human beings to learn to cooperate with each other in ways that were previously unnecessary.

> We live in a dangerous world. The technical inventions of the twentieth century have hurled us into the necessity in order to survive, of inventing hitherto unconceived social forms. Both the invention and the implementation of such forms depend on a capacity for flexibility, cooperation, and rate of change in human personality never before crucial in the history of civilization. The more we can understand about our potential for individual growth and human interaction, and about the personal illusions and resignation that impede it, the greater the chance that people can meet the challenge for their own survival (1963, p. 7).

Due to the rapidity of social change in postwar society, Pearce and Newton state that notions of personal security are harmful delusions. They state that "'Security' is a bow to the establishment. In an evolving world, there is no such thing as security.... The concept of 'security' is itself a neurotic security operation" (1970, p. 6). The implications of this statement were carried out in practice in what later became the Sullivanian community. Relationships were considered important inasmuch as they met certain immediate and developmental needs for the individual. If and when any relationship ceased to meet these needs, it could become an impediment to further growth and should be terminated.

For Pearce and Newton, the mother is the first agent of repression in life. Only those needs of the infant that she responds to will be met and become conscious; all others will be repressed. If other adults who would respond to these needs are not accessible to the child, his or her growth will be limited. They incorporated this concept into their theory, calling it the "central paranoia," which they defined as:

> [the] infant's organization of all his unfortunate experiences with ungiving nurturing figures.... In the adult, it is represented by the orientation that the goal of life is to stay alive, to seem sane at all costs, and to manage without love (1970, p. 13).

They emphasize the notion that most parents limit the interpersonal growth of their children by limiting interaction with others who are different, either culturally or in terms of economic class. Later, when children become adolescents, they are pressured to choose a career, a religion, and a mate for life before they have a chance to explore alternatives. This process reinforces cultural norms and stereotypes, often resulting in early marriage and acceptance of the interpersonal and social status quo.

In order to "grow," the individual needs experiences with others who do not share his or her background and cultural assumptions. Early marriage and childbearing prevent the young adult from having these experiences and therefore limit his or her self-conception. Pearce and Newton emphasize that "the concept of sexual fidelity or even serial monogamy, which is central to the nuclear family, is also central to the restriction of spontaneous interpersonal interaction." They also advocate the discontinuation of *pro forma* parent-child relationships after adolescence, arguing that it can be destructive to both parties because any form of obligatory behavior restricts genuine, spontaneous interaction.

The repressiveness of postwar U.S. society is used by Pearce and Newton as evidence of the need for a social and cultural revolution.

> Bobby Seale has said that the goal of the Revolution is that a man and a woman can get together on the basis of natural attraction. He understated his case. The goal is for one person and another person to be able to get together on the basis of natural attraction regardless of sex, and whether or not physical contact is involved. This is not only the goal but part of the impelling force toward revolution (1970, pp. 22-23).

They link this goal of revolution to the radical change in the organization of interpersonal life. They believe that the revolutionary process will produce the kind of human being they describe. This change includes the reorganization or elimination of the nuclear family. Pearce and Newton discuss this proposal in their scenario of the Revolution that is to come.

> The experience of mutual trust beyond the family confines challenges the priority of domestic and legal loyalties. Then, however, it is usually seen as a regrettable condition of military expediency. The usual outcome is that once the power structure is shifted, the revolutionaries tend to return to the previous family structure. This family structure now undertakes to accommodate its members to the new authorities. What we are advocating is a basic reorganization of economic, political, social, family and interpersonal priorities. If these were all oriented to meet the human needs of all—and implement a humanistic structure which could move to correct its own inherited limitations. We need a re-evaluation of all previous patterning of civilization in order to invent one that will be viable through unanticipatable technological change (1970, p. 27).

Pearce and Newton were engaged in the process of creating a community that would produce the "new individual" that they describe above. This community grew slowly throughout the 1960s, until the initiation of the Training Program at the Sullivan Institute in 1970. This program took as students young people who had little or no previous formal training in psychology and put them into private practice immediately. These younger therapists (most in their early twenties) charged a nominal fee for their services thus attracting many people who could not have afforded psychotherapy with a licensed therapist. The result was an exponential increase in the membership of the community from approximately 50-60 people to over 400. The young therapists or "trainees," as they were called, lacked any prior formal training in psychology or counseling, a factor that made it extremely difficult for them to question or critically examine any of the teachings of the Sullivan Institute faculty, thereby encouraging an increasingly authoritarian milieu within the institute.

The Hedonistic Period

A large number of the new patients and therapists were integrated into an already existing social circle and began to live together in same-sex groups, encouraged by Pearce, Newton, and the other psychotherapists who were in the Sullivan Institute. These living arrangements were often formed in consultation with the individual therapists. Men and women were discouraged from living together because it was felt that this would constrict their freedom to enter into relationships with other members of the opposite sex.

The social lives of community members were directed and regulated by the therapists and the leadership. One of the most notable precepts held by the community in terms of the conducting of daily life was that opposing monogamy, which was believed to be limiting and thereby inherently destructive to the individual's capacity for growth and change. The organization of members' social lives revolved around the "date," a block of time that could take place at any time during the day or night during which people spent time together. During this period of the group's evolution, the "date" was the basic unit of all social activity. "Dates" were categorized in various ways: as "drink" dates, "dinner" dates, "study" dates, "sleepover" dates, and even "fuck" dates (the purposes of these being obvious from their descriptions). It should be noted that the "sleepover" date entailed sharing a bed with someone of either sex for the night, and did not necessarily include sex.

The therapists advised their patients to have as many dates as possible with different people, and to pursue any activity that might interest them. At this point many different classes were taught within the community—painting, writing, dance, poetry, and so on. Members were encouraged to join these classes and to fully explore their personal potential for artistic and intellectual expression. They were also encouraged to have sex with any other member that they felt attracted to. Although it was up to individuals to seek out sex partners, it was not acceptable to only choose one person.

Furthermore, childbearing was restricted in the community to only those members who were deemed mature enough by the leadership. Even those members who were approved to have children were restricted in their choice of a parenting partner. It was not possible to simply select a mate and decide to have children together. One had to have one's choice approved by his or her therapist, who was mandated to consult with the leadership before granting approval.

As stated, during this period (1970-1979), the Sullivan Institute/Fourth Wall community expanded its membership considerably. Estimates of the total number of members are difficult to make for this time period because there was no formal organizational structure. Ex-members estimate that over 1,000 people were involved with the community at different points in its history, and approximately 400 were actually members at any one time. Membership during this period was somewhat fluid, with some people peripherally involved but not actually in therapy, and others who were in "Sullivanian" psychotherapy who were not involved with the community. This was to change radically after 1979.

Pearce and Newton incorporated the concept of a Leninist political vanguard into their practice in the Sullivanian community. Pearce and Newton, and, later, Harvey, Klein, and Moses, who were the other training analysts in the Sullivan Institute, were considered to be the most emotionally mature, and therefore the political and interpersonal vanguard of the community. Joan Harvey and Helen Moses were Newton's third and fourth wives, respectively, and Ralph Klein married Harvey after her divorce from Newton in the mid-1970s. Although the leadership were the only married couples in the community permitted to practice cohabitation, it is important to note that these were not monogamous marriages; both spouses were free to have sexual relationships with other members, and did so. The other therapists were considered to be directly below the leadership, and the patients were thought to be below the therapists in regard to their level of interpersonal growth. This belief system resulted in an elaborate and rigid hierarchy of political, social, and sexual power within the community.

It is important to note that Pearce and Newton's theory specifically eschews the rule of law that governs the secular state. In their writings, Pearce and Newton do not directly state that the members of an enlightened therapeutic community are above the law. However, their comments about the coming of the Revolution strongly suggest that they are in favor of breaking the law in the interest of destroying the established political and socioeconomic order. Certainly, their practice bore this out. Newton was known within the Sullivanian community for his penchant for threatening members with violence, and, at times, striking them. On one occasion, when something was stolen from a communal rehearsal space, he ordered a forced search of every apartment in the community. On another occasion he and Joan Harvey ordered the violent takeover and occupation of a theater that the community had leased, including physical violence and property damage. Later he organized an armed security force to protect himself and other members of the leadership. These attitudes and actions with regard to the law and the state demonstrate to what extent Pearce and Newton asserted that their morality was derived from a higher authority than that of the constitution and laws of the United States, or any other government.

The Revolutionary Period

Until the inception of The Fourth Wall Repertory Company in 1974, the Sullivan Institute community had no formal institutionalized structure other than that of the therapy. The Fourth Wall was originally formed by a few members of the community who were interested in comedic theater and who aimed some of their work toward the general public. In the summer of 1976 members of the Fourth Wall rented their own summer house and theater, apart from the rest of the Sullivan Institute community. In 1977 the leadership of the Sullivan Institute decided to take over the Fourth Wall and to redefine it exclusively as a political theater company, making membership almost mandatory for any community member. The direction was taken over by Joan Harvey, one of the four training analysts of the Sullivan Institute, and a former wife of Saul Newton. Along with the takeover, the structure of the Fourth Wall became increasingly authoritarian and paramilitaristic. The community, which numbered approximately 300 at that time, demonstrated this to the outside world by its takeover of the Truck and Warehouse Theater (noted above). While the Fourth Wall had rented this theater, the previous tenants refused to vacate the premises. Rather than going through legal channels, the order went out from the community leaders to "take over" the theater by occupying it and threatening the tenants with violence if they did not leave. Two hundred members stormed the theater, destroyed the existing tenant's stage sets, and physically attacked and removed those tenants. Two Fourth Wall members were arrested.

The next pivotal incident in the life of the community was the near meltdown of the Three Mile Island reactor in March of 1979. The leadership decided that there was a possible danger to themselves if the wind blew radioactive emissions from the plant over the New York City area. They decided that some members, notably those who were pregnant, would flee to Florida to escape this eventuality. While no formal command was issued, when the membership heard this decision, they almost unanimously decided to accompany the leaders to Florida, or to leave New York City for other locations. While in Florida, the leadership appointed a scientific committee composed of two physicists who were group members to discover exactly what was taking place at Three Mile Island. A committee was also appointed to assist members in concocting stories to tell their employers to justify their unplanned absences from work. No one outside the community was to know that the exodus had taken place. In order to avoid focusing attention upon the group, members of the community returned after one week and attempted to cover up their departure. One member, who subsequently overdosed on valium upon his return, revealed the story to a doctor, and was expelled from the community along with his friends who had accompanied him to the emergency room. These events marked the beginning of an era of increasing regimentation and separation from mainstream society for the Sullivan Institute/Fourth Wall community and catapulted the group into the anti-nuclear movement. The political concerns of the community became increasingly important at the expense of the earlier emphasis on personal growth and pleasure. Sacrifice of one's time, money, and personal preferences was increasingly required.

After the return from Florida, every member of the community was required to fill out a schedule form detailing their whereabouts and activities for 24 hours a day. An emergency communication system was devised which kept copies of all members' schedules and kept a 24-hour phone tree in operation.[1] The rationale for this practice was that because the Three Mile Island or Indian Point reactors might melt down at any moment, the members had to be ready to make their escape and therefore be available by phone or beeper at all times. Plans for disaster preparedness included the purchase of a fleet of buses for evacuating the entire community. Furthermore, a food co-op staffed entirely by community members was opened because the leadership decided that no food from contaminated areas in the country should be consumed.

As stated, at this point the Sullivan Institute/Fourth Wall community became involved in the anti-nuclear movement that had become widespread in the United States. Joan Harvey, who had become the "artistic director" of the Fourth Wall, began making a documentary about Three Mile Island which required the financial support of the entire community. Members were assessed varying amounts of "contributions" depending on their incomes as reported to their therapists. The therapeutic aspects of the group began to become less important as the political component grew. Emphasis was now placed on the impact the group could have on the outside world, most notably the anti-nuclear movement, but the general public as well. The leadership began to view themselves as serving a propaganda function in society at large, rather than simply concerning themselves with the creation of the "new man" within the confines of the community. Members were expected to sacrifice both their money and their free time to the cause. Those that refused to cooperate were either berated, threatened (often physically), or expelled.

The trend toward increasing authoritarianism continued, with Saul Newton and Joan Harvey at the top. In 1983 two important events accelerated this trend. One was the decision by the leadership directing approximately 80 members of the community to purchase a building for those members' occupancy. The building, which was in need of a gut rehabilitation, had seven floors, each of which was to be a large communal apartment. The same-sex arrangement was to be kept within apartments, so that, for example, the second floor was all women, the third floor all men, and so forth. Although members were told that they would become shareholders in the new building, in fact ownership remained in the hands of a few members designated and controlled by the leadership and no shares were ever issued. Members who resided in the building made out their checks to a corporation composed of these designated individuals, and questions about ownership were discouraged and considered to be an attack on the community.

The second significant event in the life of the community in 1983 was the advent of the AIDS restrictions. The Sullivan Institute community had known about GRID (gay-related immunodeficiency) since 1979, and had cautioned male homosexuals in the group to observe certain precautions. However, with the spread of HIV infections to the non-gay populations, it was decided that more drastic action had to be taken. The community was effectively sealed off from sexual contact with outsiders (which had been one of the predominant avenues of recruitment). Any member who had sex with a nonmember was expelled from the community. Condoms were required for all sexual contact. Members' shoes were to be removed immediately upon entering any group apartment, and hands were to be washed in a special bathroom designated the "outside" bathroom. No member was allowed to eat in a restaurant or drink in a bar. Other restrictions included wiping dogs' paws after they had been walked, and a prohibition against eating in nonmembers' houses and against travel for pleasure. Business travelers were required to disinfect their hotel rooms before using them, and to bring and cook their own food.

Some of these restrictions were relaxed when it became clear that the AIDS virus was not transmitted through casual contact. However, the restrictions against sexual contact with outsiders and regarding the use of condoms remained in place. While some part of the community's response to the AIDS epidemic was understandable, other restrictions were, in medical terms, hysterical overreactions which resulted in the increasing isolation of members and an ever-increasingly authoritarian structure within the group itself. For those who remained inside, the notion of leaving became even more difficult to imagine than before. They were convinced that the outside world was full of disease, and that they would never find friends or lovers to replace those they had in the group. In conjunction with this fear, members were often told by therapists that they would become severely depressed or suicidal if they left. Members who left the community were effectively shunned by those who remained. Members experienced an increasing sense of psychological isolation and fear in regard to the outside world. Many members reported that the idea of physical and/or psychological survival away from the group was inconceivable.

A political education committee had existed in the Sullivan Institute/Fourth Wall community since the early 1980s. Originally, the committee was chosen by the leadership, and "politics classes" were held on a voluntary basis. "House meetings" (weekly meetings of group apartment members) had taken place since the early 1970s as vehicles for addressing the organizational and interpersonal issues that came up in communal apartments. In 1984, Saul Newton decided that "house meetings" would become "politics meetings," and that every apartment group would be required to read and discuss certain books selected for them in the weekly house meetings. The first books selected dealt with the Chinese revolution, including some of Mao Tse Tung's writings, and

Fanshen by William Hinton. The practice of "going to the gate" as described in *Fanshen,* which referred to the confession of one's bourgeois past and the divestment of one's property, was applauded by the leadership as an effective means of cleansing a community of "bourgeois" thoughts and customs. The practice of criticism/self-criticism became popular within the Sullivanian community.

Simultaneously, a self-described campaign against male chauvinism was initiated by Saul Newton along these lines. The men in the community were accused of male chauvinism for refusing to sleep with certain women who had approached them. Some members were ordered to terminate romantic relationships with each other on the grounds that these relationships harmed both the individuals and the other members of the community who were deprived of their companionship.

It has been reported by some ex-members of the community that one of the precipitating factors of this phenomenon may well have been the fact that the membership of the Sullivan Institute/Fourth Wall community was skewed two to one in favor of women at that time, and that due to the AIDS restrictions, many of these women were unable to find sex partners. The refusal of male members to accede to requests for sexual relations was interpreted by the leadership as male chauvinism. It has also been pointed out that the anti-male-chauvinism campaign took place at the same time that several male members refused requests for "sleepover dates"[2] by Newton's wife, Helen Moses. The result of the campaign was that most male members felt obligated to consent to any request for sex by female members, regardless of whether or not they wished to have sex.

The Decline

There is no one particular event or time when the decline of the Sullivan Institute/Fourth Wall community can be pinpointed. The eventual demise of the group may have been predicted when the AIDS restrictions took effect, because from that time on no new members were accepted. However, it is also possible to argue that because the membership had been dwindling for many years by that time, that the decline began even earlier than 1983. In 1985, two high-ranking therapists left the community; both of these departures were experienced by members as very serious blows to the integrity of the community. They were dismissed by the leadership as defections by reactionary forces, and attempts were made to attribute the departures variously to CIA connections, to thwarted aspirations to the leadership of the community, to pecuniary motives, and to psychosis. The membership was shaken, but the ex-therapists were effectively discredited and no major upheaval took place overtly, although secretly some members were affected.

In 1986, one female member, who had been in the community for approximately fifteen years, was ordered by her therapist, Ralph Klein, to cease having any contact with her infant daughter, who was approximately two months old at that time. Previously several members had their children taken away from them. This woman had been very close to one of the two defected therapists, and called on one of them to help her flee the community with the child. The act of contacting an ex-member in this way was totally forbidden, and was already an indication that this woman was ready to defy the leadership. She hired two private detectives to help her physically seize the child, and went into hiding after accomplishing this end. As part of her strategy to maintain custody of her daughter, she went to the press. A front page article appeared in the *Village Voice* (Vol. XXXI, No. 16, April 22, 1986), and network coverage of her story resulted. This was the first time that ex-members had been willing to speak to the press, and many individuals told their versions of life within the community. A custody hearing ensued, with the judge awarding custody to the woman after members of the community were found to be illegally following ex-members in hope of locating the child, and to have surrounded the courthouse in case the child appeared in court (the plan was to snatch the child away from the mother if possible).

At approximately the same time as the custody case was initiated, other ex-members had brought legal proceedings against the leadership and management of the building that had been ostensibly purchased in their names. These ex-members were requesting that they receive compensation for their investments in the building after they had been expelled or moved out. This case was settled out of court in the plaintiffs' favor.

Due to the notoriety of the custody case, the leadership of the Sullivan Institute/Fourth Wall community were forced to reign in their tendency to prohibit certain individuals from bearing children. The result was a miniature baby boom within the community, as many members reached the end of their childbearing years. Because the leadership was no longer able to exert the same high level of control over parental decision making as it had in prior years, many new "families" were able to move away from the purview of the leaders, toward more independent lives. The negative publicity itself also affected many members. Some secretly admitted to themselves that the *Village Voice* exposé might be accurate. Saul Newton, who had been the centripetal force of the community for thirty years, became too sick to continue to exert the same degree of authority that he had in the past. Disputes broke out at the top levels of leadership which resulted in disunity. All of these factors contributed to the disintegration of the Sullivan Institute/Fourth Wall community. At the present time, some of the factions that formed during this period still exist, but in a much smaller and weaker state than ever existed during the life of the community.

THE PATIENT-THERAPIST RELATIONSHIP

The therapeutic relationship was the basic unit of the Sullivan Institute/Fourth Wall community. It was the primary vehicle for the transmission of Pearce and Newton's (and later, Harvey's) psychoanalytic theory, and the primary site of identity transformation and social control. Through the psychotherapy, entirely new identities, or self-conceptions, were fashioned for the patients. This process was crucial to the formation of a successful utopian community. Individuals came to see themselves in terms of the theory[3] which comprised the foundational belief system.

"Sullivanian" psychotherapy was different in certain critical ways from more traditional forms. The most noticeable difference was the abrogation of the professional boundaries that are usually mandated between patient and therapist, particularly in the form of extra mural relationships.[4] This practice had many interesting ramifications. Therapists received information about their patients from many sources within the community: personal contact at parties, "dates" with the patient's roommates or friends, community meetings, theater productions, communications from other therapists in the community whose patients would give them information, and so forth. In the case of the four training analysts of the Sullivan Institute, it was not unusual for them to have sexual and romantic relationships with their patients. Another unusual characteristic of the therapy was the degree to which therapists were directive with their patients. Patients were often "ordered" by their therapists to pursue a particular career, to enter into or terminate a relationship with a particular individual, to move into a particular group apartment, or to make other critical life decisions. These "orders" may have been couched in the form of advice, but if the advice was not taken, the patient could be threatened with expulsion from therapy, and from the entire community. Although some other novel therapies are equally as directive, this degree of directiveness is definitely out of the mainstream. The issue of transference,[5] a particularly difficult one in any therapeutic relationship, was also dealt with in an unconventional manner. While more traditional psychotherapies attempt to analyze the transference and to help the patient learn from it, the "Sullivanian" therapists allowed and encouraged their patients to view them as powerful, larger than life figures who had the power to give or take away happiness. In fact, this was true in the sense that any individual who alienated his or her therapist could be expelled from the community.

For many members, the primary initiation into the community began with seeking a therapist. They were referred by friends and colleagues to Sullivanian therapists. Other members became involved with the social activities of the Sullivanian community first, and were then encouraged to enter into therapy. In either case, it became necessary for any member of the community to be in therapy with one of the Sullivan Institute therapists.

The process of identity transformation in "Sullivanian" psychotherapy took place over several years. Every aspect of the patient's life was recounted, examined, and interpreted in the light of Pearce and Newton's theory. For purposes of clarity the process will be discussed in terms of four stages: the *initiatory,* the *novice,* the *participant,* and the *adept.* These stages are not necessarily formulated in the ways in which the patients and therapists themselves would have conceptualized them.

In the *initiatory* stage the major task in therapy is the taking of the patient's history. The patient starts with the earliest memory and proceeds to tell his or her life story in terms of familial and emotional life. In the context of therapy, a great deal of emphasis is placed on the potential harmful effects of certain actions of parents on their children. Memories and dreams were interpreted similarly as proof of the parents' psychological and/or physical violence.

Depending on the patient's reaction, this first stage of the therapeutic relationship may last for a longer or shorter period of time. It is usually a minimum of six months to a year. In it, the patient must come to accept the parents' malevolence. If this does not take place, the therapist tells him or her that this behavior is simply a refusal to confront the truth.

During the *novice* stage the patient is introduced to the Sullivanian community and becomes a member. There was some selectivity involved at this point in the process on the part of the therapist and the Sullivanian hierarchy; not every patient was inducted into the community. Those who showed signs of more serious mental disturbances were kept out.

In terms of the patient-therapist relationship, this stage is characterized by the therapist arriving at a diagnosis. In conformity with the stages of growth set out in *The Conditions of Human Growth,* the patient was judged to be developmentally arrested at a certain stage of development, for example, the juvenile stage (ideally ages four through eight). The act of deciding that one's mental age (in terms of interpersonal development) is eight years old was used to actively encourage the patient to think of him/herself as a person who cannot make decisions without guidance. The diagnosis was often vague; a specific developmental stage was not always specified; the patient was referred to simply as an "immature adult."

The development of same-sex relationships was stressed by the Sullivanian therapists as the most important component of "growing up." All patients who became members of the community lived in apartments (most of them in group apartments) with other members of the same sex. At the same time the practice of what could be called casual sex was encouraged; members were encouraged to seek out other members they wanted to have sex with, but not to form any exclusive and/or romantic attachments. This attitude toward sexuality shared a great deal with certain trends in the contemporary culture of the late 1950s and 1960s.

During the novice period the patient-therapist relationship becomes much stronger. The patient has acceded to the conception of the parents as the primary repressive force in his/her life, and in most cases has told the parents that he/she will no longer have any relationship with them. The emotional impact of this decision is extremely powerful; the community begins to be seen as the "rational" substitute for the family, and the therapist plays the role of house parent or counselor.

In the *participant* stage the patient becomes a full-fledged member of the Sullivanian community. He/she adopts the therapist's interpretations of her history as valid, and forms a self-image that is consonant with them. The patient-member moves into one of the communal living situations (he/she has to apply and be invited by the other residents), and is fully integrated into community life. As noted above, the content of this life was constantly changing; in the late 1960s and early 1970s, for example, it consisted of constant social interaction in the form of "dates." After 1979, group social life was dominated by the community's theater and political projects.

The interpersonal situation in the communal residences was the member's first exposure to the power of other people (other than the therapist) in the formation of a sense of self. All roommates were in therapy, and were expected to discuss "what was going on" in the living situation with their therapists. Every house member became a source of possible "feedback" to the other members. In other words, each person would see their respective therapist, tell them what their perceptions of the occurrences in the house were, and be directed by the therapist how to speak or not to speak to the other members.

Each week "house meetings" were held for the purpose of coordinating physical arrangements (food shopping, dish washing, cooking, cleaning, etc.), and of consolidating the relationships between house members. Group apartments were encouraged by their therapists to "do history," which involved each member spending one or more meetings telling the others the version of his/her history that had been constructed in therapy. This served to further consolidate the particular self-image that had been created.

The relationship between patient and therapist during the participant stage becomes increasingly focused on the integration of the patient into the community with an emphasis on relationships with other same sex members. Furthermore, the therapist becomes the arbiter of all important decisions in the patient's life. This includes professional decisions, choice of lovers, the decision to have or not have children and with whom, living situations, and even in some cases medical decisions.

At this point, the patient's identity becomes completely enmeshed with the community, to the extent that isolation from it is seen as equivalent to psychological death. The therapist stresses that the only way that the patient-member can stay mentally healthy is to stay in the community. If one leaves, they caution that suicide or psychological deterioration will follow. These cautions are exacerbated by the fact that the general attitude in the community toward outsiders is that they are primitive and unhappy people, and the outside world a cold and forbidding place.

In the participant stage, the patient-member becomes aware of a more or less clearly delineated hierarchy within the community. Status was granted for different reasons depending on the period in the evolution of the community. In the 1970-1979 period, the leadership consisted of four "training analysts," who supervised all other therapists. The next level down was that of the supervisee therapists, and then of patient-members. One gained prestige in several ways: by "dating" (having an ongoing relationship with) one of the leaders or the therapists, by moving into a living situation with leaders or therapists, by becoming a therapist, or by changing from a supervisee therapist to one of the "training analysts" for therapy. In 1978, when the Fourth Wall Repertory Company started to become the main focus of member activity, the prestige system was affected in that it became extremely prestigious to be chosen for a leading role in any of the theater productions. A new avenue of status attainment was added.

The *adept* stage was not attained by all members, and for those who did attain it, there were varying degrees to which they become "adepts." An adept is a member who has taken on (either internally or not) all the values and goals of the community, including its statements about who he/she is. He/she takes on the responsibility to move the communal life forward. In the earlier stages of the group, adepts were the leaders in their households; they confronted other members with their "problems," sometimes demanded that those who were not "changing fast enough" leave living situations, policed sexual relationships that had become too intimate, and did not tolerate any discussion that smacked of "anti-group" sentiments.

When the Fourth Wall Repertory Company became the main activity of the Sullivanian community, adepts were given high positions in the theater hierarchy, such as stage manager, director, key acting roles, costume design, and so on. These people were responsible for managing other members, in the same way that any stage manager would be. The difference was that if there were problems with a subordinate's performance of a job, they would be reported to the leadership, either directly or through one of the therapists. This could result in problems for the member outside of the theater environment, in the living situation or the therapeutic relationship.

The relationship between the adept and the therapist was usually one of "working very hard in therapy." This means that the patient is consistently concerned with "dealing with his/her problems," which can include additional discussion of historical data, possibly even a visit to the parents for the patient to "interview" them about his/her childhood. Adepts were the only members allowed to have children, although for the most part they did not choose who the other parent would be. This decision was recommended by the therapist, but in fact was made by the leadership. Some adepts were asked to become therapists themselves, others took on what were considered important responsibilities within the organizational structure of the group.

The therapeutic relationship decreased in importance during the evolution of the Sullivanian community. As the Fourth Wall Repertory Company became the focal point of community activities, the power associated with high positions in the theater company came to equal and in some cases exceed the authority of the therapists. This resulted in the demotion of several of the older therapists, who had for years enjoyed a great deal of power and prestige, and were essentially cast out of these positions. Many of them discontinued their practices and found other types of work.

The transference that had previously existed for the patient between himself or herself and the therapist came to exist between the patient-member and the leadership. The leadership in this later period consisted of the top therapists (Newton, Harvey, Klein, and Moses), and of those in high positions in the theater and film productions. The experience of the member was often that of being in therapy with the entire group. The therapy retained its importance, however, as one of the main modes of surveillance of the membership by the leadership.

In this later stage of the community's development, the production of identity was tied increasingly to one's social position within the hierarchy. This hierarchy became increasingly rigid, albeit with constant changes of personnel, as the group stopped adding new members to its ranks. Social mobility was still possible, but there were fewer routes to the top. Some members remained in lower positions. Identities became frozen; one was who the community saw them as, and it was very difficult (if not impossible) to change this image.

THE REGULATION OF SEXUALITY AND PROCREATION IN THE SULLIVAN INSTITUTE/FOURTH WALL COMMUNITY

The regulation of sexuality in the Sullivanian community was only a subset of the regulation of all intimacy. However, control of sexuality was extremely important in developing and maintaining the cohesiveness of the community. Kanter, in her study of communes and utopias, notes that the formation of strong dyadic relations is interfered with in a variety of ways.

> Two-person intimacy poses a potential threat to group cohesiveness unless it is somehow controlled or regulated by the group. Groups with any degree of identity or stability face the issue of intimacy and exclusive attachments and set limits on how much and what kinds are permissible or desirable. Exclusive two-person bonds within a larger group, particularly sexual attachments, represent competition for members' emotional energy and loyalty (Kanter 1972, p. 86).

In the Sullivanian community, sex was considered a basic human need, similar to eating or sleeping. It was not to be romanticized because it did not necessarily result in intimacy. Any notion of commitment was foolhardy because, "'[s]ecurity' is a bow to the establishment" (Pearce and Newton 1970, p. 6). There was also a theory of the "hostile integration," which was defined as "a relationship the central dynamic of which is the inhibition of growth" (Pearce and Newton 1963, p. 197). This notion was used to describe the nature of many relationships that had developed to the extent that they began to affect the participants' commitment to the community. The worst kind of hostile integration was referred to as a "marriage." "Hostile integrations" were by definition almost impossible for the persons involved to be consciously aware of. They involved a meshing of the most paranoid aspects of two people's personalities. Therefore it was necessary for the therapist or roommates to point this out.

Control of sexuality in the Sullivan Institute/Fourth Wall community centered in two particular arenas: control of procreation and control of all close relationships, including sexual ones. Although in theory, a destructive relationship did not have to involve sex, in practice it was very rare that relationships that were sanctioned did not involve sexual relations.

There were many lesbians, gay men, and bisexuals in the Sullivanian community. They remained in the minority, but were nevertheless numerically significant. Sexual experimentation was encouraged in the community, and it was not uncommon that men and women who generally considered themselves to be heterosexual engaged in lesbian or gay sex. However, all homosexuals in the community were strenuously encouraged (if not ordered) to have sexual relations with members of the opposite sex.

The ideology of the Sullivanian community regarding monogamy was explicit. As discussed earlier, monogamous relationships were believed to be essentially restrictive of both partners' personal growth. The structure of social life in the community was embodied in the concept of the "date."

Although there was no explicit limit on the number of dates a person could have in any specified period of time, if it became known that one was having sleepover dates, for example, with the same person more than once a week, this would be mentioned to other members' therapists, who in turn would inform the therapists of the individuals in question. Depending on the discretion of the leadership, those who were "caught" could be criticized and even forbidden to see each other more often.

Control of reproduction in the Sullivanian community centered around the notion that only certain individuals were mentally healthy enough to be parents. Therefore it was necessary to consult one's therapist about the decision to have children. The therapist invariably passed this information on to the leadership, where the decision was made as to whether the patient would be permitted to become a parent. If approved, the next step would be the decision as to who the patient would have the child with. The general consensus of most people in the community was that it was preferable for a child to have two parents. However, in several cases, individuals, both men and women, were allowed to either adopt or biologically produce children without a mate.

If a woman was approved to bear a child, she would first choose (with her therapist) who the father would be. It was common for couples who were planning to have children together to get married. However, marriage to another member did not imply exclusive sexual relations or cohabitation. Parents of children did not live together; they remained in their same-sex apartments and the children lived in both apartments, the mother's and the father's.

The process of conception in the Sullivanian community entailed the selection of a "sperm pool"—the men who would have sex with the aspiring mother. It was not considered necessary or healthy to wish to know who the father of one's child would be, or to choose only one man as the biological father of a child. With the help of her therapist (who was in constant communication with the leadership), the woman would choose several men who were considered discreet and cautious enough not to discuss this process with anyone else, and who were healthy enough to produce viable sperm. On the expected days of ovulation, the woman would have sex with all of these men in succession. The "sperm pool" usually, but not necessarily, included the chosen social father. (The "social father" is used here to indicate the man who had been chosen previously to be the father.) In most cases the biological father and the social father were not the same person, or if they were it was by chance.

Not only was it impossible to have an exclusive sexual relationship in the Sullivanian community, it was also impossible to decide who the biological or social father of one's child would be without the advice and direction of one's therapist. Both of these practices served to enforce allegiance to the community as a whole, rather than to any one or few individuals within it. Spousal ties and family ties have traditionally been the strongest relationships that an individual maintains throughout his or her adult life. In order to create a situation where the primary bond is with the community, it was necessary to minimize these primal relationships, to disempower them and subject them to constant surveillance. According to Pearce and Newton, these bonds were simply culturally induced means of tying an individual to his or her biological family. They could be unlearned and replaced by new patterns of behavior. One can choose one's family rather than having to settle for a biological family that is imposed. The reproductive customs of the Sullivanians served to remove the act of procreation from the direct control of the two individuals who were physically involved.

When children were born, a full-time baby-sitter was hired to care for them, whether or not the parents were working full-time. One purpose of the baby-sitter was to ensure that the parents did not exert undue influence on the child.

If the parent wanted to spend what was considered a great deal of time with his or her child, they were thought to be attempting to control the child and prevent him or her from forming close relationships with others. The baby-sitters were also used to provide information about the parents' behavior to the leadership. Each baby-sitter also had a therapist (except for some who were hired from outside the community when necessary) with whom he or she was required to discuss the behavior of the parents. If the parents were found lacking in some aspect of their relationship to the child they were told emphatically (sometimes with verbal or physical threats) that they had better listen and obey or they would lose their child.

In three known cases, women were ordered by the leadership to forfeit their children to some other member of the community. They had been deemed unfit mothers and, therefore, it was in the best interests of the child that a new parent be appointed. Two of the three accepted this decision and gave up their children; the third fled the Sullivanian group with her child. In many other cases, parents were told by their therapists to restrict the time they spent with their children, keeping it to a bare minimum.

Control over procreation and child-rearing served to minimize the formation of strong dyadic relationships. Mothers were prohibited from spending any considerable time with their children, and the choosing of a mother and father was the task of the community, not a personal matter. The necessity of obtaining approval in order to have children also served to diminish the sense of individual autonomy.

Sexual power was used in very specific ways in the community. The four leaders, two men and two women, each had their favorites among the membership at any specific time. Saul Newton was notorious for expecting any woman he found desirable to perform fellatio with him. Cooks, baby-sitters, patients, and any other women who might have reason to be in his house were pressed into service. A negative response to Newton's request could harm the chosen person in terms of her social standing in the community hierarchy. Those women who became Newton's favorites could expect increased social prestige. Some cultivated these relationships consciously because they saw them as a means to attainment of certain goals, such as childbearing or coveted positions in the theater or in the Sullivan Institute.

Joan Harvey, who had been Newton's wife after he divorced Jane Pearce, was also able to use the sexual power that her position had conferred upon her. She had a series of favorites, always younger men, and usually her patients.

Ralph Klein, who married Joan Harvey after her marriage to Newton ended, was the other male in the leadership of the community. Although he also had a group of women who he selected on the basis of their sexual attractiveness to him as his "dates," he was not quite as imperious as Newton in his expectations. However, he was also known for his attraction to young girls, and is alleged to have engaged in sexual acts with several under age individuals over the thirty-year life of the community.

Helen Moses, Saul Newton's fourth wife, had protégés among the male members of the community. These men were under constant scrutiny from Newton, and if they did anything to displease Moses, they were threatened with loss of their membership or of their positions of status.

Among the membership, sexual power could be exerted by some members attempting to move up in the hierarchy by having sexual relationships with the leaders, as discussed above. Sex among people of the same rank in the community was less connected to power concerns, although the requirement that every member have multiple sexual partners made it necessary to find partners. Failure to do this resulted in loss of prestige and possible criticism by one's therapist. The more partners one had among the desirable members, the more one's personal social standing improved.

It should be noted that some aspects of this discussion also apply to people who were "dating" each other without having sexual relationships. In other words, if one was dating a member who had a high social standing, one's own position was also improved, regardless of whether or not the relationship was sexual. Nevertheless, sexual attractiveness did remain an important means of improving one's rank.

CONCLUSION

An article about the Sullivan Institute/Fourth Wall community in a volume subtitled *Between Sacred and Secular: Research and Theory on Quasi-Religion* carries with it a certain degree of irony. The members of the community would have been horrified to see themselves depicted as in any way associated with religion. This brings us to the question of Greil and Rudy's article on quasi-religions, which proposes a subjectivist definition of religion, stating that "quasi-religions" are organizations which either see themselves, or are seen by others as "sort of" religious (1990, p. 221). In purely subjectivist terms, the "Sullivanians" are not religious because they do not identify themselves as religious. However, if a functionalist definition of religion is used, the community meets certain criteria. The elements of the "Sullivanian" beliefs and practices that could be viewed in this way are: (1) transcendence—the transcendent nature of the precepts of this community were centered upon two aspects of its doctrine: perfectionism and millenialism. Its perfectionism consisted in the belief that within the community a new kind of human being was being produced—an individual no longer bound by the fears and limitations that plague the rest of humanity. These "new" men and women would be the vanguard of a new, revolutionary society. The Revolution itself is also a transcendent notion. The Marxian idea that at some point in the future all the destructive aspects of society will disappear, and that a totally classless and egalitarian society will exist is certainly both utopian and transcendent. The millennial beliefs are detailed below; (2) the notion of the members of the community as part of an "elect" or "chosen people" that will lead the way to perfection; (3) the apocalyptic nature of some of the beliefs, such as the threat of nuclear annihilation and the threat of AIDS; (4) the requirement that members suspend their logical facilities and simply put their faith in the decisions of the leadership; (5) the existence of apostates and heretics who, when summarily expelled (or when they left on their own) from the community, were treated as nonpersons by the membership; (6) the belief in absolute good and evil—the leadership and the children were considered to be free from all aggressive and destructive impulses, the membership were "seekers," and the outside world was completely evil (or at least "unsaved"); and (7) the emphasis on confession in the form of revelations made to one's therapist. Therefore, whether or not one would choose to label the Sullivan Institute/Fourth Wall community as quasi-religious, it certainly shares many characteristics with other religious and quasi-religious entities.

Although the leadership of the Sullivan Institute/Fourth Wall community claimed to be guided by rational and scientific principles, any serious and persistent questioning of these principles led to derision, demotion in the hierarchy, and possibly expulsion. There was no room for debate among equals about the precepts or the practices of the group. After the Three Mile Island incident in 1979, it became the practice of the leadership to call general meetings whenever a major policy change or addition was to take place. These meetings were pseudo-democratic, with an open vote held on any major decision. In practice, however, the votes were always unanimously in favor of any proposal the leadership made. There was one exception to this when a member actually voted against a leadership proposal and was expelled from the community by specific order of Saul Newton. The refusal to allow for the possibility that an individual could leave the community for positive or neutral reasons also bears some similarity to the belief held by members of religious denominations or sects that those who choose to leave the fold will be damned, or at the very least will not be saved.

Although some scholars define religion as belief in a transcendent being, the belief in a transcendent society can also be viewed as religious. The difference in the case of the "Sullivanians" is that those religions that believe in transcendent beings usually view those beings as perfect, and themselves as flawed and imperfect. In the Sullivan Institute/Fourth Wall community, the leaders viewed *themselves* as perfect, and other members of the community as striving for their perfection. This belief is not unheard of in religious groups—as, for example, the Oneida Perfectionists of the mid-nineteenth century have demonstrated.

Belief in the prophetic or exemplary nature of one's life or one's community is a characteristic of many messianic belief systems. The Sullivan Institute/ Fourth Wall community viewed themselves as the beginning of a new society that would eventually replace the old by producing more intelligent and emotionally mature human beings capable of teaching the rest of society how to conduct their lives. This belief system was evident in the superiority with which members looked upon the rest of society. During the earlier periods of the evolution of the community, active recruitment and conversion was attempted by members (and was only halted when the AIDS restrictions made socializing with outsiders almost impossible).

Apocalyptic or millenarian thinking became increasingly predominant over the years. In the formative and hedonistic periods, it was limited to the belief that individuals who left the community would perish without the life-sustaining powers of the therapy and the group. Later, when the Three Mile Island accident took place, the leadership put forth the view that the world was headed for nuclear destruction unless it could be stopped by the anti-nuclear movement. There were clumsy and aggressive attempts on the part of the leaders to assume the leadership of that national movement, but these were met with resistance and defeat by other activist groups. The AIDS restrictions did not result in overt predictions of doom, but the actions of the leadership in instituting these rules showed a level of hysterical fear that went beyond the necessary health precautions. The Sullivan Institute/ Fourth Wall community underwent a transition in the late 1970s from a post-millennial group with its focus on the "new man," to a pre-millennial group that was more concerned with preventing the immanent destruction of the planet. This transition was also evident in the eventual deemphasizing of personal growth and fulfillment as a goal of the community. The survival and success of the community itself became the overriding goal; individual needs were to be subsumed by that goal.

The use of psychotherapy as a form of surveillance and social control has striking parallels to the use of confession in medieval and early modern Catholicism, and to confessional practices in other communitarian groups. These parallels are detailed in Michel Foucault's *History of Sexuality* (1978) and relate to his discussions of the technologies of the self. Foucault points out that Western society is the first to believe that in order to be free, we must first confess the truth of our inner selves. In Catholic confession in the pre-modern period, it was considered necessary to provide the confessor with every detail of one's transgressions. It was not enough to simply admit that one had sinned; part of the process of being saved was the recounting of the content of the sin. Later, the Catholic Church decided that it was not necessary to obtain a detailed description of any particular sin, but this was after the point where it had relinquished the strict control over its members' lives that it had in the earlier periods. In the Sullivan Institute/ Fourth Wall community, however, the psychotherapy served not only to set the patient on the correct path to happiness, but also to aid in the process of identity transformation. Through the therapeutic process, the patient learned to view her or himself in a completely different manner than before.

It can be argued that this transformation actually was no more than a role being played by the patient-member (Balch 1980; Goffman 1961), that some members were capable of taking on the new self as a mask over the old, but in any case the presentation of self to the outside world changed a great deal.

Rather than attempting to determine whether or not the "Sullivanians" are a quasi-religious group, it might be more productive to view them as a communitarian group that shares the characteristics of all communitarian groups, whether religious or not. Most communitarian groups in the United States have been religious, but the period beginning in the late 1960s saw the inception of many nonreligious communities. (In the early part of the twentieth century there were also anarchist communes that were nonreligious, but they did not share the authoritarian bent of most other groups of this nature, and consequently most were very short-lived) (see Noyes [1860]1961; Nordhoff [1875]1965; Oved 1988). The Sullivan Institute/Fourth Wall community shares many characteristics with religious communities, such as the Rajneesh in Oregon, the nineteenth century Oneida community, and the Children of God, but it also bears strong similarities to nonreligious (or quasi-religious) groups such as the Democratic Worker's Party, Synanon, and Lifespring.

Perhaps the question of quasi-religions, and of the clash between functionalist and substantive definitions of religion in general, can be illuminated by Weberian theory. For Weber, the notion of the separation of the spheres of life (i.e., economic, political, esthetic, erotic, and intellectual) was the defining feature of modernity. After the medieval period in Europe, when religion pervaded every sphere of life, science arose to challenge its hegemony, and the industrial revolution eventually resulted in a separate economic sphere. Weber (1930) argues that the coming into existence of Protestantism facilitated the development of capitalism, and therefore of modern Western society. The "elect" were those who had succeeded in the material world, so wealth was equated with virtue. As rationalization proceeds, however, the "iron cage" of bureaucracy results in a loss of meaning for even the most successful members of society. Although many people still use religion to provide this meaning, for some the rational, scientific aspects of life have become too pervasive to allow this. They seek to assuage their need for a cohesive meaning in life through seemingly rational belief systems. The rationality is belied, however, by the faith required of believers. They also attempt to re-create the idealized life of traditional societies where there was no separation of the spheres. While belief in a transcendent being may no longer be possible for many people, there is still a desperate need for meaning and, therefore, transcendence in some form. Modern society has failed to provide this for several classes of people, including those who it has benefited the most through education and material success. The Sullivan Institute/Fourth Wall community was an attempt to create a truly rational society, but also to fill a spiritual hole that has come to exist in an increasingly rationalized, bureaucratic society. In this sense it meets the criteria of both the functionalist and the substantive definitions of religion.

Robbins and Anthony (1990) allude to this phenomena in their discussion of "civil-religion sects." They hypothesize that the "broken covenant" that Bellah (1975) refers to has engendered attempts to repair itself by creating self-contained and morally "pure" societies (p. 483). These communities must remain outside of the mainstream of U.S. society in order to maintain their purity, and they hope to become the beacons of light in the darkness that engulfs mainstream society. In this sense, the Sullivan Institute/Fourth Wall community qualifies as a civil-religion sect. They also attempted to connect moral precepts with political action, aiming to create a revolutionary society that would eventually replace the corrupt and antiquated one that they believed most members of U.S. society live in.

Additionally, as Tipton (1982) points out, the historical period in which this community came into existence was one in which the lack of spiritual meaning and moral consensus had crystallized for a generation of young Americans. The religions of their parents seemed hollow and hypocritical; the political establishment was corrupt and cynical, and the material success that had been achieved by a large proportion of the population did not provide the happiness that had been hoped for. The movements of the 1960s had failed to provide lasting solutions to this fundamental problem. In this context, the Sullivan Institute/Fourth Wall community provided answers that enabled disillusioned participants in the New Left and the counterculture to begin again in a more systematic way. However, the internal logic of communitarian groups requires that they maintain a strong tension between themselves and the world outside. In order to do this, authoritarian measures are required, or the communities fail. The perfect society inside the boundaries of the community became more restrictive than the imperfect one outside.

ACKNOWLEDGMENTS

I would like to thank the anonymous authors of "A Short History of the Sullivans: A Record by Ex-Members" for their help with the history section of this paper.

NOTES

1.   A phone tree is an organization whereby one member is contacted and asked to contact several other members, thereby facilitating speedy communication of messages.

2.   In this case, it is a euphemism for a request for sexual relations.

3.   It should be noted here that Pearce and Newton's psychoanalytic theory had both ideological and theological components which will be discussed later.

4.   In other words, patients who became part of the Sullivan Institute community often had a certain amount of contact with their therapists outside of the therapists' offices.

5.   Transference is defined in psychotherapeutic terms as the transferring onto the therapist by the patient of feelings that he/she has had for other significant adults in his/her life, notably the parents. More traditional therapies attempt to point out to the patient that this phenomena is, in fact, taking place, and then to benefit from it by delving into the patient's feelings about the parents.

REFERENCES

Balch, R. 1980. "Looking Behind the Scenes in a Religious Cult." *Sociological Analysis* 41: 137-143.

Bellah, R. 1975. *The Broken Covenant.* New York: Seabury.

Conason, J., and E. McGarrahan. 1986. "Escape from Utopia." *Village Voice* XXXI(16) (April 22).

Foucault, M. 1978. *The History of Sexuality,* Vol. 1: *An Introduction.* New York: Random House.

Goffman, E. 1961. *Asylums: Essays on the Social Situation of Mental Patients and Other Inmates.* New York: Anchor Books.

Greil, A.L., and D.R. Rudy. 1990. "On the Margins of the Sacred." Pp. 219-232 in *In Gods We Trust: New Patterns of Religious Pluralism,* edited by T. Robbins and D. Anthony. New Brunswick, NJ: Transaction.

Kanter, R. 1972. *Commitment and Community: Communes and Utopias in Sociological Perspective.* Cambridge, MA: Harvard University Press.

Nordhoff, C. [1875] 1965. *The Communistic Societies of the United States.* New York: Schocken.

Noyes, J.H. [1860] 1961. *History of American Socialisms.* New York: Hillary House.

Oved, I. 1988. *Two Hundred years of American Communes.* New Brunswick, NJ: Transaction.

Pearce, J., and S. Newton. 1963. *Conditions of Human Growth.* New York: The Citadel Press.

_____. 1970. "Establishment Psychiatry—and a Radical Alternative." Unpublished paper, the Sullivan Institute for Research in Psychoanalysis, New York.

Robbins, T., and D. Anthony. 1990. "Civil Religion and Recent American Religious Ferment." Pp. 475-502 in *In Gods We Trust: New Patterns of Religious Pluralism in America,* edited by T. Robbins and D. Anthony. New Brunswick, NJ: Transaction.

Tipton, S.M. 1982. *Getting Saved from the Sixties: Moral Meaning in Conversion and Cultural Change.* Berkeley: University of California Press.

Weber, M. 1930. *The Protestant Ethic and the Spirit of Capitalism.* London: George Allen and Unwin.

IS "NOTHING" SACRED?:
"SACRED" COSMOLOGY AMONG
THE AVANT-GARDE

James Davison Hunter, James L. Nolan, Jr.,
and Beth A. Eck

ABSTRACT

This paper considers the worldviews of a diverse sample of avant-garde artists in the contemporary art world. From in-depth interviews with twelve such artists, we learn that, in a Durkheimian sense, their conspicuously postmodern cosmology contains a strong element of the "sacred." The substance of this sacred realm represents a departure from historical approaches to art. For these artists, the very nature of art is fluid, mutable, socially engaged, relentlessly critical, interactive, and open to varying interpretation. At the heart of the cosmology is a self-consciously constructionist view of reality, a disdain for anything that binds or inhibits free expression and a moral commitment to change society. When asked about the purpose, direction, or goal of change, though, these artists emphatically resist any identification with or allegiance to a guiding telos. The artist's *raison d'être* rests upon a normative insistence about the absence of a telos, which in turn becomes the functional telos. In this sense, "nothing" does come to represent the sacred for the avant-garde artist.

Religion and the Social Order, Volume 4, pages 79-94.
Copyright © 1994 by JAI Press Inc.
All rights of reproduction in any form reserved.
ISBN: 1-55938-763-7

Man will rather make the void his purpose than be void of purpose.
—Nietzsche (1967, 3rd essay, secs. 1, 28)

The increasing secularity of public culture in advanced societies raises important questions about the *nature* of secular ideas and commitments and their *capacity* to act as a cultural glue holding against the centrifugal tendencies of modern life. Emile Durkheim anticipated this problem as early as 1912 in the publication of his last major treatise, *Les Formes élementaires de la vie religieuse* (1912). The two most plausible secular possibilities to traditional faith in his view were "the cult of science" and "the cult of the individual"—ideologies deriving from twin intellectual impulses of the continental Enlightenment.[1] Durkheim, in the tradition of Comte, favored the former but he was deeply nervous, all the same, about the ability of either science or individualism to provide a common culture strong and coherent enough to keep an increasingly fragmented society together. It was an important, if not portentous, effort. But the questions remain pregnant with possibility.

Durkheim's speculation is significant for many reasons, but first because he defied both the conservative's fallacy that equates secularism with simple negation (e.g., "amoral," "a-religious," "a-spiritual," etc.) and the liberal fallacy that equates secularism with neutrality. He understood that secularity in the modern world was content-laden. But what is the nature of secular ideals and beliefs? More to the point, what is sacred about the secular?

In this paper we explore these questions in the context of an inquiry into the world of avant-garde art, and, in particular, the ideals and beliefs of avant-garde artists. There are two reasons for choosing this world as our case study of advanced secularism: one historical, the other sociological. The first is that well before Durkheim, aesthetics was proposed by the urban intellectual classes as the true alternative to traditional faith. The second is that most cultural change in the West has been downward: what has begun as experimentation within the aristocratic and upper-moneyed classes has tended to become in time the established moral code of the common people. Working in the realm of high culture production, and (more often than not) patronized by the upper echelon, avant-garde artists can be understood as an important sector within a vanguard of secular elites. By virtue of their social location and cultural vocation, they are carriers of a normative agenda that promises to influence, if not fundamentally define, major strands of American popular culture. It is, then, to the "sacred realm" of the avant-garde, and to the theology of its "priesthood" that we turn.

FROM IMITATION TO AUTONOMY

The potency of art, as every civilization has recognized, resides in its capacity to influence the mind and shape the passions. Objects of art invariably contain stories—stories of struggle, heroism, achievement, and tragedy as well as of life in bucolic tranquility. They also contain messages—messages of hope, encouragement, condemnation, and moral rebuke. It is for these reasons that the portrayal of events of sacred moment and ideals of noble purpose can inspire the human spirit. Likewise, the depiction of contradiction, irony, and the unexpected can jar as well as enlarge the imagination. Either way and in all ways, art invariably holds the potential of stirring the soul.

In the past, art in all of this potency was first a form of address to some kind of ultimate authority—artifacts representing a sacred order within a mundane social order. This is as true for primitive societies as it has been in Western civilization. Art, more often than not, was a *reflection* of a loftier truth, a more perfect beauty, of things eternal. Art could not so much embody those truths, that beauty, that immortality; its inspiration, rather, lay primarily in its ability to point the way to them. Art was reflective, or perhaps better, illustrative. A twelfth-century bishop expressed this role well in his high praise of the work of one artist in the church's employ: "Adorning the ceiling and walls with varied work and diverse colors, you have in some way exposed to the eyes of the faithful the Paradise of God, decorated with innumerable flowers. You have succeeded in letting the Creator be praised in creation and in showing God to be admirable in his work" (Barzun 1974, p. 32). There are several things noteworthy about this statement. At the most basic level, the artist, himself, was patronized by the church. He was literally its servant. But he was also a servant to a higher moral vision. One also thinks, in this regard, of Haydn who wore servant's clothing as he composed—as a symbolic gesture of his obedience to a higher vision; or Bach whose compositions were always signed "To the greater glory of God." But as this bishop also implied, art had a pedagogic function, instructing people in sacred cosmology. In all of these ways, art (and the artist) served the sacred cosmology and the religious and political institutions surrounding it. But by the same token, the ideals of sacred cosmology inspired and sustained aesthetic endeavor.

Modernity, however, effectively supplanted this simple correspondence, irretrievably altering the nature and form of address contained within the arts. What happened in the arts, though, was a natural outcome of challenges that were much deeper and more pervasive in the public culture of European civilization. The rationalism and skepticism of the Enlightenment and the materialism of industrial capitalism together challenged and undermined the very heart of traditional religious authority and popular piety. What would fill the vacuum in the yearning for an integrated understanding of human experience?

Rousseau was only the first to point to nature as a surrogate for the older faiths. The ideals of a transcendent beauty and harmony argued to exist in the natural (or primitive) condition of man and nature provided a totalistic and even more universalistic alternative to the older beliefs. Indeed, in nature, one could find *true* religion, for here was faith free of superstition; a higher ideal that would compliment rather than contradict reason. Such a faith had the added virtue of serving equally well the modern Romanticist and the political revolutionary—both of whom were abundant in the decades following the Enlightenment.

In this setting art continued (at first) to strive toward imitation: now, though, it was attempting to imitate the ideals contained in nature. But something much deeper and more significant had occurred that had laid the foundation for what would eventually stimulate a further transformation of art. Bound by creeds, art was little more than a decoration of ideals defined by *other* authorities; divorced from the creeds, art could now emerge as the interpreter of ideals defined by artists themselves. Constrained by the creeds, art could only be a reflection of a higher revelation; freed from these constraints, art could emerge as revelation itself.

In this slow but profound transformation, art not only gained its autonomy from the institutions and ideals that once sustained it, but in time it could offer—not just nature—but *itself* as an autonomous substitute for traditional religion. Indeed, for those whom the old religions had lost their hold, aesthetics would become "the gateway to the realm of spirit." It is in this cultural context that Walter Scott could pronounce the love of the great masters to be "a religion or...nothing;" that Goethe, Schiller, Kant and Hegel could link art with the divine; and that Hemingway and others could link art with immortality. It is not these literary figures alone. Observers have long noted that the worship of art has become the ultimate belief of the unbeliever; that our art museums have become sanctuaries for agnostics.[2] As Regis Debray (1992) has said, "the religion of art proposes to be the first global religion. To recompose what has been decomposed, this religion embraces all gods, all styles, all civilizations."

In this same transformation, however, one can find the foundation of the contemporary avant-garde. Severed from transcendent religion, the isolation of aesthetics increased. No longer a reflection of creation, but creation itself, it was inevitable that art would become an enterprise set *over against* a social and political establishment still to be shaped by transcendent faiths. To the extent that the social order was still bound by such conventions, the artist would come to assume the mantle of the prophet, the revealer of hidden truths, one who sees what ordinary people cannot. In popular cant, the task of the avant-garde artist was to "shock the bourgeoisie." But from here it would be a short step to subverting the bourgeoisie and the social order that it maintained.

The foundations of autonomy, cultural criticism, and alternative vision were firmly established by the end of the nineteenth century. Most avant-garde art in the twentieth century, then, has been an intensification of processes established long ago. As avant-garde artists themselves acknowledge, the "forms" of artistic expression have all been exhausted.

THE WORLD OF THE AVANT-GARDE

Yet certainly it is premature to conclude of art, as Barzun (1974, p. 32) has, that "there is nothing left to do except declare [its] bankruptcy." The institution and the individual avant-garde artists remain strategic and powerful carriers of a broader cultural vision that eventually will have (if it has not already) broad resonance in the larger social order. What are the contours of their worldview? What do they hold sacred, if anything at all?

To explore these matters we interviewed twelve avant-garde artists—six men and six women. They ranged between 40 and 64 years of age, with three of the twelve being over 60. Although disinclined to identify themselves with a single medium, it became possible in the course of the interviews to associate the individual artists with at least an emphasis in terms of the type of medium with which they were most familiar. As such, our sample included one poet, two sculptors, an architect, a craftsperson (working primarily with wood and metal), a performing artist, two photographers, a multi-media artist, and three environmental artists. Most of the artists themselves were more comfortable describing their work as installation or conceptual art, rather than with defining it exclusively within the boundaries of a single medium.

Just how "avant-garde" are these artists? One artist oversaw a parade in New York City where sanitation trucks proceeded down the route in synchronized fashion. Another constructs visual metaphors like watermelons to challenge society's stereotypical views of African-American women. Another artist, on the basis of previous work along this line, proposes a "postmodern" national park to allow public viewing of military bombing sites in Nevada. Another has produced an installation piece portraying various perspectives on the controversy over public funding for the arts. Included are pornographic pictures and a written message from a member of Jesse Helms' staff. A New York-based environmental artist collaborates with scientists to create plants and new technology that remove heavy metals from contaminated soil. He is involved, as he claims, in sculpting an ecological system. Another constructs multi-media type installations which include photo paintings, prints and drawings of swastikas, and other symbols to criticize Hitler's Nazi Regime.

Not surprisingly, the largest percentage of the artists we interviewed work out of urban areas. About one-half live and work out of the New York City area—five in all; two in Manhattan and three in Harlem. Four are from California—three from Southern California and one from the San Francisco Bay Area. One finds her residence in Chicago, another in Baltimore, and another in the Charlotte, North Carolina area. The sample was also racially and ethnically diverse. It included an Asian, four African-Americans, and seven caucasians. The majority of the latter were ethnically Jewish, a character trait they acknowledged as being significant to the content of their work.

All have received a notable level of prominence in their respective areas—some internationally and almost all on a national level. Collectively they have been the recipients of numerous awards. A majority have received National Endowment for the Arts (NEA) grants, several have sat on NEA panels, and one was, in fact, the first Policy Panel Chair for Visual Arts for the Endowment. Several have published books and still others have been sponsored by such elite art institutions as the Ronald Feldman galleries. Their works have been featured in scores of publications both within and outside of the art world. For example, one of the most respected periodicals in the art community, *Art Magazine,* recently ran a story on four of the artists with whom we spoke, describing them as "pioneers" in "activist" art. With respect to the mainstream media, discussion of their works have appeared in such places as the *New York Times, The Washington Post,* the *Wall Street Journal, U.S. News and World Report,* and the *Philadelphia Inquirer,* to name only a few.

COSMOLOGY

To describe the disposition of these individuals as "cosmopolitan" would be a fairly serious understatement. Their cosmology is, at the least, post-Christian and postmodern as well. Yet the remarkable consistency we observed in their attitudes does not draw from a conversation with professional intellectuals at the cutting edge of philosophy or literary criticism. Indeed, only one or two we spoke to mentioned the names of postmodern theorists. Our sense was that these artists had varying levels of familiarity with the names Foucault, Derrida, Lyotard, or DeMan, and the ideas advanced by these theorists. Yet, the tapestry of their worldview seems to be woven naturally from the fabric of their participation in a community of like-minded artists, a community whose cultural identity is shaped, in large part, by its particular social location.

Metaphysics

At the heart of their cosmology is a view of reality that is self-consciously *constructionist* and *discursive*: there is no reality except that which we will into existence through symbolic expression. "We are all being written," one artist summarized somewhat cryptically, "and we are hallowers and we are being hallowed." While this constructed and discursive understanding extends to "reality" generally, it is especially reflected in their musings about art—what it is and how it functions.

Consider how art itself is defined. "We see art as process," claimed one artist, "and process as being even with the artifact, even with the pieces that we create. They [the objects they create] are still unfinished." The fluid nature of constructed reality, and of art in particular, was captured by a California-based photographer when he stated that "by the time art gets to the museums and gets to the larger public media it is already dead.... As soon as it becomes institutionalized you can be sure that there is a new generation challenging it and striving to move beyond it." In his view, this was as it should be. This perspective is fully consistent with Adler's (1990, p. 1378) portrayal of postmodern artists, who, as she explains, believe that the very nature of art is to "call into question any definition that we ascribe to it. As soon as we set up a boundary, an artist will violate it because that is what artists do." The artists we spoke with shared this basic sentiment, favoring more fluid understandings of the nature of art. As one explained, "I define art as an activity that changes moment to moment dependent on what the individual happens to be intending and experiencing." She holds that her work "is a way of having a conversation with somebody else." Conversation is never static but on-going and processual.

This view of art makes comprehensible the claim made by an architect from New York City that his works could only be understood as "interactive and active. They are not meant to be looked at so much as to be engaged." A California-based artist made the same point when he claimed that the "major goal" of his work is to make his art "very interactive." In fact, one of his installation pieces exhibited in Boston provided a place for people to respond to his art display. Half the exhibition was designated as a "kind of uncurated free space for people to respond with their own art." An African-American poet working in New York City took this "interactive" perspective of art one step further. When asked whether she ever stepped back to observe the interaction between her art and those who come to observe it, she claimed that such a pose would be almost impossible. Besides, she said, "we artists don't privilege ourselves that way. We also are participants.... We too are all on the journey." So, even artists are continually engaged in a dialogue with the artifacts that they create because art itself is less object than it is process, more reality construct*ing* than reality construct*ed*.

In this it is essential to emphasize the proactive nature of the artistic enterprise. A New York-based artist, whose work involves close collaboration with scientists and architects, expressed this well when he described art as a "catalytic structure—something that serves as a platform for creating things to be discussed or to be created or to be denied or to be readdressed." An environmental artist living in San Diego argued similarly that "art, great art, whether it be visual or verbal or auditory, has the power to evoke a change of consciousness, a sense of altered consciousness." Another spoke similarly of art's capacity to "make changes in the discourse"—to "change the conversation about a place." Still another put it even more succinctly—"art," he stated flatly, "is about transformation and enlightenment."

In this endeavor the medium in which artistic expression takes form is of far less importance than the communicative purpose that the art is supposed to serve. The subservience of a medium to the social message conveyed was captured well by an installation artist in Santa Barbara who entered the art world through the genre of photography, but is now involved in a wide range of artistic expressions. Said he, "if it turns out someday that it will be more effective for me in a given situation to make objects rather than installations, I could do that. If it turns out that in a given situation that I need to get better at personal narrative and discussing subjectivity, I could do that. Once, when I needed to incorporate video into the work, I just learned how to do video. So you know, whatever is needed. I don't really define myself anymore as a photographer or a sculptor or anything. It is whatever works at this point"— works to further the social agenda defined by the artist.

The view that artistic medium is merely a device used to influence social reality is not idiosyncratic either but, from what we gathered, institutionalized as well. This same artist who currently teaches art at the university level claimed that in the program in which he instructs, the objective is not "to crank out painters or photographers or sculptors, but instead to create artists who are well-educated and who see their work as aimed toward more content concerns.... The medium or the technique," he asserted, "is just a tool." This fits with the overall philosophy of art education promoted at his university. As he put it, we are not simply concerned with "getting people to develop a facility in the use of the tool, but to change the definition of facility itself to include *social* purpose."

One artist, whose work has focused on uncovering the destructive impact of U.S. military activities in the desert regions of America's west, was reflective about the changes in the art world that led to this emphasis on art as an initiator of socially constructed change in this way. "Art," he said of the modernist period, "used to be for its own sake. Artists [in this period] held the notion that art was an independent, self-contained practice in the world that didn't need to be responsive, at least overtly, to what was going on in the world. There has been a dramatic shift as we approach the year 2,000 to making art that is more relevant, more responsive, and a more powerful player in the larger culture." Others agreed, speaking disdainfully of art that fails to influence the larger social, political, and economic world as "extremely one-dimensional." This avant-garde attitude toward more representational and less socially interactive art reminds one of Stevens' (1993) comparison between the Biennial in New York City and the Susan Rothenberg retrospective in Washington, DC, where artists in the former dismissed the "painting qua painting [of the latter] as irrelevant to contemporary culture," emphasizing instead the important role of the artist to critically engage "the moral, philosophical and political struggles of his society."

To this end, the artists we spoke to generally aspired to make their work—as one put it—"relentlessly critical." "The best art," as another asserted, "has played a role of providing a critique of society." "The impulse to make art is basically a critical impulse," explained another. Art serves to "challenge our biases and our value systems and everything. All art," he concluded, "serves a political function of one form or another."

Moral Obligation

This understanding of reality—as constructed—and of art's capacity to alter reality, implies a special moral burden to contribute to the shaping of reality through one's work. "Artists," one New York artist asserted, "not only have a power but also a responsibility to create our world." The responsibility and power artists have derives from the special perspective they possess. Said one, "artists spend a great deal of time working, not just with their hands but with their heads. They are capable of taking in a great deal of social and cultural information. As such they can provide a barometer of the health of a society." For these reasons, as another put it, artists are specially placed "to create a whole vision for a world to live in." The "vision," as she held, begins with the individual artist. The language in which this vision is articulated does not remain private, however, but "becomes a whole language for the whole public, that is received by the whole public and inhabited by the public.... that is what the artist can do." Most of the artists we spoke to felt this obligation deeply if not uniformly. It took expression in their musings about their own particular work.

Consider, for example, the views of an artist whose "conceptual designs" of river banks and water sheds have been displayed in locations all around the world, including France, Germany, and Sri Lanka. "What we hope to accomplish," he said, "is a change in the conversation.... Often we can make changes in the discourse. We can change the conversation about a place. We can change some of the people's ideas of the metaphors of structure with which they view the place. And if we interject new ideas, new senses, new perceptions, new metaphors, we can change behavior. *And since we hold...the realities of social construction,* we try to change some of the constructs that underlie people's understanding."

A visual artist echoed the same sentiment in more simple terms. As she told us, her work is successful if people respond to her art by saying, "Hey, I never thought of it that way!"

The obligation to "change the conversation" is not only assumed by the artist, but is something that the artist endeavors to extend to others, particularly those who normally would not have a voice. Like the others we just heard, a California-based artist whose "unusual public art" finds its expression in "site-specific and community-specific installation" pieces sees his role as "trying to figure out a way to make art a more important part of the discourse around social experience." Art, he said, "should play a central role in articulating social reality to people." But he also stated that his "overarching agenda is creating opportunities for public interaction that empower people, and that provide an opportunity for people to contribute to on-going debates about social reality." From his perspective "the larger project...is the resuscitation of the public sphere.... Most of us don't really have access to public space. So, part of my overarching agenda is creating opportunities for public interaction that do empower people and that do provide an opportunity for people to contribute to ongoing debates about social reality."

These artists are, as they say, "working for change," and hope that others after engaging their work will "go home thinking, staying open, expanding." All "want to know how they can help things to change."

Being

Another theme that emerged from our conversations with these artists concerned the sanctity of life. "I do believe that life is holy," says one. "Life is sacred," says another. "Life is the sacred domain," says a third. The sentiment is voiced again and again. Their affirmation of life and place, it became clear, was not unrelated to their understanding of reality as socially constructed.

The link, it would seem, is "expression." Expression, for these artists, is the measure of our being-existence. To express oneself is to participate in the creation of reality, a process coterminous with life itself. Conversely, not to express oneself is not to exist—in all, a curious repackaging of the Cartesian formula.

It is also "expression" that provides the common link between themselves (as artists) and others in the social world. "Art," explains one visual and performance artist, "is merely a way of getting out stuff within yourself. And lots of people do it. A lot of people don't consider themselves artists but they make art.... think of the one who bakes a cake. From their meager self and some eggs and some flour come something that brings such joy and satisfaction and pleasure to people." Because art—as all productive work—is "an expression of someone's soul," as another framed it, the more personal the form of expression, the more profound life is being lived. One artist says as much: "I would say the value of the work is higher, the more personal it gets."

It is the organic connection between life (as subjectively experienced) and expression (as the public voicing of experience) that explains the emphasis all of these artists put on the *freedom* of expression. It is an analog to the freedom of being. "Art's themes are basically those of freedom," insisted the poet with whom we spoke. This is why she and the group of artists with which she works use glass as much as they do in their work. "Glass," she explained, "is a kind of metaphor for water which is itself a metaphor for freedom." Other artists agreed; to them ultimately "freedom is sacred."

A gauge of how important the freedom to express oneself is was reflected in the comments of the multi-media artist with whom we spoke. She categorically refuses to allow anyone to tamper with her work. "I must be true to myself and that inner core," she said. For this reason she would rather forfeit opportunities of exhibition than to allow anyone to rearrange or to show only excerpts of her work. This freedom is also measured by a tolerance for aesthetic expression that many find repugnant. The African-American performance artist who addresses the stereotypes of black women in her work claimed that "if there was an exhibit of racist but good art, even though it had a racist theme, I'd want to see it."

These artists also typically use the level of freedom for expression—*ipso facto,* for self-invention—as a gauge for how much freedom generally exists in society as a whole. "And everybody has the right to express their vision of the world," claimed a New York environmental artist concerned with making public the social relevance of garbage and waste collection. That is why too, every possible artistic expression should be allowed, for it "expresses ... individual desires and individual ways of seeing the world."

This is also why, as the poet put it, "censorship is such a thorn." When limits are placed on speech, either within or outside the art world, "people's expression of their soul is being censored." Those who oppose freedom of expression, explained another, "don't want this human voice let loose in the world." To be silent or to be silenced, therefore, is to deny being. This is why artists say, as the "garbage" artist expressed it, "we don't keep our mouth shut," and why, too, artists must be "vocal" about things with which they disagree because "that is what it means to be free human beings." Thus, art's critical impulse is directed toward those things which impose "barriers against our freedom." Put more bluntly, "only if we understand our freedom then we can understand our power."

A Question of Ends

At the end of the day, art itself provides the metaphor. The painter stands before a canvass with brushes and paints. The canvass is blank and it is up to the one standing before it to paint the landscape that she envisions. In the artists' cosmology, reality itself is created on the canvass of our life together and while every individual makes a contribution to the creation of social reality, aesthetic activity itself, as they see it, is a key component to shaping that reality. The freedom of the artist to paint what she will is a metaphor of the freedom we must all have in constructing the life of our own choosing. It is not a stretch to say, in a Durkheimian vein, that works of aesthetic expression are symbolic representations—the totems—of these sacred ideals.

There is more to say about sacred cosmology among the avant-garde, however. The theme was echoed again and again in the words they spoke to us: in art, as in life, we can "redefine ourselves and our times and our values;" as another put it, "it is the human being and humanity as a whole that is being transformed through conversation." The critical question, at this point is, "to what end?" Is there a *telos,* in their understanding, to which their efforts to redefine "the conversation," the world, and themselves leads? Is there an ideal to which the human being and humanity, in toto, is being transformed? If there were all the freedom possible for people to express themselves, to invent themselves, what would be the point?

In traditional Christianity and Judaism, the answer to these questions is rather simple: in the words of Moses, "to fear the Lord your God, to conform to all his ways, to love him and to serve him with all your heart and soul" (Deuteronomy 10:12). In other traditional faiths, the *telos is similar. But among the avant-garde artists we interviewed, we quickly learned that there is no point.*

One artist we spoke to was infuriated that we even posed the question. With great irritation, he explained to us that he was "a process human being."

> Let us say I point to such an end or goal, and then you publish, ah, there is the end. That is a load of bologna. That is not how things work. What is the end of entropy? Entropy is the outcome of a long set of processes. What is the goal of the ecology? The goal of ecology is genetically driven and has something to do with the energies available. What is the purpose of prairie grass? Prairie grass would cover the whole earth if something didn't stop it. So, when you pose a goal oriented question, I think you bespeak a misunderstanding of existence itself!

If to make certain we understood just how stupid we were, he repeated his judgment: "Again," he said, "I fault you for asking such a question—it bespeaks a deep naiveté on your part!"

The installation artist concerned with governmental mistreatment of the west's desert ecology was less defensive, but no less emphatic: "my personal belief," he said, "is that there is no ultimate end. There is no ultimate goal there. It is a process. It is a constantly changing, evolving thing that never gets fixed, that there is no end goal, either God at the end of the tunnel or some sort of fixed set of values or rules to live by that will make everybody happy." He continued, claiming that ends imply fixed points of reference and that this way of understanding the world was all wrong. Another artist insisted that if any ideas or ideals were sacred, it was because of what he called their "breathability." "These ideas stay around so that other people can reform them and recategorize them and use them and believe them or rebuke them." Still another simply said, "what end?—the end is constantly changing."

We posed the question in a slightly different way to the New York-based environmental artist, asking if there was a "good" to which art ultimately speaks. He began by rejecting the term itself. "I don't think one can work with dichotomies like 'good' or 'bad'," he explained. "Things are more relative than that. Things are constantly shifting. It's that shifting that we [artists and society generally] are surfing on."

If many of the artists were emphatic in rejecting publicly definable "ends" or "goods" to which art (and life generally) should be directed, others communicated much the same message but through the language of reticence. "The very notion of a 'universal public good' or 'an end to which artists should strive' makes me nervous," said one. "I'm not presumptuous enough to believe that I understand what public goods are," said another. From still another, "I don't think anybody in their right mind can clearly define that. Of course, I think what I am doing has a public good, but I guarantee there are other people that would really challenge that. There is no way to get consensus on things like that. Such 'ends' are just too subjective."

In sum, the artists spoke of their own work as a quest "for further understanding," a "pursuit of new areas" of meaning, an "exploration" of new avenues of dialogue, and so on. These may be "very disturbing" and "uncomfortable" to people, and may often undermine "old values and mythologies." The process, however, as they claimed "ultimately liberating." But the rhetoric is contentless. This is the point that these artists were leading us to. Change itself is sacred. Transformation is its own end. The canvass, as it were, remains blank.

What of the Profane?

This is why the very question of a *telos* was, to many, such an affront. It was a violation of this fundamental, totemic principle.

This insight allows for a new perspective on contemporary controversies relating to the arts. One would imagine, from journalistic accounts, that avant-garde artists view traditional faiths and the institutions that represent them as the enemy of all they hold dear. Was this not the point of the photograph, "Piss Christ," the film, "The Last Temptation of Christ," and other provocative works with religious themes? Conservatives interpreted these works as fundamentally subversive to traditional faiths.

Perhaps some artists do hold a basic hostility to matters religious. But for the artists we spoke to, the dominant attitude toward traditional religion was indifference, not hostility. Not one artist expressly mentioned God and/or the church as a regressive force in society or to the world of art. As one put it, "I wouldn't be willing to make a broad statement that says the church prohibits artistic expression. I just couldn't say that all Catholics, for instance, were against art. I don't think that's the case." This kind of recognition without animosity was typical. Said another, "It is fine to have many different religions. And I think that the divine is smart enough to work it all out." Several artists even claimed that their religious orientations played significantly in their work.

For example, one told us that she was "raised in a Pentecostal church," had a "very strict background," but that she "used it as a ladder every day to walk up one step closer to an enlightenment." Said she, "I'm in no way putting down religion, but it exists just as other things in life exist. People don't live in church. They leave church and they use its ideas."

For all of the indifference (even warmth for some) toward traditional religion, we know at the same time there exists a visceral and passionate hatred toward censorship and anything else that would restrict the expression of self. What is "profane" in this post-Enlightenment cosmology is not so much traditional faith and its institutions, but rather the normative assumptions that makes the very idea of a church—a community defined by restraints, fixed ends, boundaries of right and wrong—possible in the first place. Their indifference to the "church" and its moral order, we would contend, is a tacit recognition of the declining power of this institution. Indeed, if traditional faiths still retained power to define public life, indifference would likely be replaced by animosity. The critique of the avant-garde, then, cuts deeper than an aversion to the church and its defenders. The artists we spoke to were sincere in this. Rather, their aversion is to the very idea of fixed ends, boundaries, constraints—not the particular institutional manifestation in which they happen to take form. One artist alluded to this reality when he reflected that "any institution you touch is going to be, at some point, participating in enslavement."

IS "NOTHING" SACRED?

We can recognize differences in emphasis and perspective among individual artists. Yet for all the talk about how everyone's view of this world is unique, one can discern certain common ideals held by artists themselves. Moreover, one would insist that their worldview comports with that of the average person-in-the-street in many ways. The culture of the avant-garde, thus, is not entirely its own. Still, there are distinct attitudes and ideals found among artists which are not only central to community identity but which are nonnegotiable as well. These ideals do indeed have a "sacred" quality about them.

Surely we have only scratched the surface of this "sacred" cosmology. For example, we have not yet fully explored the meaning of the self, autonomy, and community in their worldview. Even so, at this point, we understand a little better a crucial component of it. We understand a bit better what Barzun (1974, p. 7) means when he says art, though a public institution, is "an institution that has no theory; that has no coherent thought…as to its aim or *raison d'être.*" Barzun is pointing to what the artists themselves acknowledge as art's lack of a guiding *telos.*

It is in this sense that Nietzsche's insight is provocative. The passion artists express in defending such notions as freedom, choice, expression, change, and the like betrays the venerable, if not sacrosanct, status they accord these ideals. Yet, as we have seen, "nothing" guides choice; no "higher" good inspires freedom or freedom of expression; no "standard" of progress exists to ground their views of change. Freedom, expression, choice, and change exist in their own right and need no compelling justification. To paraphrase the melancholy philosopher quoted in the epigraph of this paper, there is no *telos* so the void becomes, in practical effect, their *telos*. The *equal* passion many express in rejecting any ideals that would ground, inspire, or guide art (or life) is one measure of this,[3] leaving one to postulate, as did Adler, that for the avant-garde artist "[p]erhaps the only standard left is to defy all standards" (1990, p. 1378). In brief, then, avant-garde art leads us on an expedition beyond the borders of normative order. The expedition is prompted by the zeal and insistence and even urgency of a missionary, but there is no guide, no map, no destination.

It is important to recall, at this point, the social and political dimension of the artist's perspective. Artists not only recognize the power of art to criticize and change, they also feel a moral obligation to use this power to change society. "The ultimate we are hoping for," said one, "is the transformation of the individual" and then society—but again, the question is, "to what?" The investment of public monies into avant-garde art points to ways in which this social perspective has been embraced by public policy (see, e.g., Fox 1991).

But, in the end, just how influential are these artists and their "sacred" cosmology? To what extent do they portend changes in popular culture? The answers are difficult to gauge. To the degree that these post-Enlightenment ideals *do* permeate popular social life, one can rightly wonder, as Durkheim did, if there is any cultural adhesive here at all. Or do these ideals and commitments reflect a significant if not dramatic movement toward what the great French social philosopher called *anomie*? Here again, the questions remain pregnant with possibility.

NOTES

1. These were, of course, the positivist (deriving from the work of Comte and the like) and the romanticist (deriving from the work of Rousseau, Voltaire, Kant, etc.).

2. Debray (1992) has noted on the European continent, that as there has been a decline in the percentage committed to Sunday worship, there has been an increase among those who pay for admissions to great art exhibits. This is true in some regards in the United States as well. Here, annual attendance at art museums has increased from 200 million in 1965 to 500 million today.

3. Interestingly, it is this "groundlessness" that is the defining characteristic of Jean-Francois Lyotard's definition of paganism.

REFERENCES

Adler, A. 1990. "Post-Modern Art and the Death of Obscenity Law." *The Yale Law Journal* 90: 1359-1378.

Barzun, J. 1974. *The Use and Abuse of Art*. Princeton: Princeton University Press.

Debray, R. 1992. "Universal Art: The Desperate Religion." *New Perspectives Quarterly* 9: 35-41.

Durkheim, E. 1912. *The Elementary Forms of the Religious Life*. Paris: Alcan.

Fox, C. 1991. "Art's New Wave." *The Atlanta Journal*, August 4, pp. N1-N5.

Nietzsche, F.W. 1967. *On the Genealogy of Morals*, translated by W. Kaufmann and R.J. Hollingdale, Edited by W. Kaufmann. New York: Vintage.

Stevens, Mk. 1993. "Brushes with Art." *The New Republic* 17: 36-42.

PART II

AMBIGUOUS BOUNDARIES:
THE REALM OF QUASI-RELIGION

BUT IS IT A GENUINE RELIGION?

Eileen Barker

ABSTRACT

Social scientists distinguish between stipulative concepts (which they use as tools) and reportive definitions (the contents and uses of which form part of their study). Drawing on the work of Mary Douglas, illustrations are offered of the ways in which the combination of the necessity and arbitrariness of boundaries allows people to juggle with concepts so that particular values and/or interests may be furthered. An underlying theme running through the paper is concerned with epistemology and the sociology of knowledge in that it reminds sociologists that they can claim no special expertise in drawing society's conceptual boundaries and that they should resist the temptation to collaborate with those who offer them the opportunity to pronounce with Platonic certainty on what is "really" religion.

Some social structures can tolerate anomaly and deal with it constructively, while others are rigid in their classifications. This difference is probably the most important subject on which sociological research can focus.

We have tried to demystify all cosmologies to peer past the purity filter and see ourselves as things in nature. The exercise ought to give an exhilarating sense of freedom. But instead we are faced with dilemmas (Douglas 1975, p. 227).

Religion and the Social Order, Volume 4, pages 97-109.
Copyright © 1994 by JAI Press Inc.
All rights of reproduction in any form reserved.
ISBN: 1-55938-763-7

When is a religion not a religion? When it is a quasi-religion? When it is convenient to divorce that which we ourselves have joined together?

A word is an arbitrary symbol which is given meaning by human beings. When we indicate what a word means we are either *reporting* what others mean by the word, or we are *stipulating* what *we* are going to mean by it (Hospers 1956, pp. 32-33). Reportive definitions are part of the data of sociology and are *more or less accurate* reports of what the people who are being studied mean by (or how they use) a particular concept. Stipulative definitions are among the methodological tools of sociologists—they can be *more or less useful* (rather than more or less true). When, like Humpty Dumpty, we say a thing means such and such, that's it. It might be a bit confusing for others if I were to say that, for me, "religion" means eating icecream on the beach; but if that is how I wish to define religion, that is up to me. I am not making a statement about reality or even about what anyone else means by religion, I am just stipulating how I intend to use the concept.

More seriously, we are used to Weber's concept of the Ideal Type as a heuristic—that is, as an analytical tool which we can use for comparative purposes (Weber 1949, section II). No claim is made that the ideal type is ideal in any evaluative sense, and most social scientists would accept the distinction, articulated by Nagel (1961, pp. 492-493), between characterizing and appraising value judgments. Characterizing value judgments are evaluations that a given characteristic is in some degree present (or absent) in a given instance; appraising value judgments are evaluations claiming that some envisaged or actual state of affairs is worthy of approval or disapproval. Social science is frequently concerned with characterizing value judgments in order to construct the tools (such as ideal types) with which it describes social reality; but it is not concerned with the construction of appraising value judgments about the reality it describes and seeks to understand and explain.

To illustrate this difference: the boundary that we might draw to distinguish between a person's being anemic or not anemic, or above or below "the poverty line," may well reflect our values as to what we take to be a significant or critical cut-off point between "good/bad" or "acceptable/not acceptable" for a group or individual; but once the line is drawn (and it is made clear exactly where it lies), then there should be no room for appraising whether or not a person *ought* to be placed one side or the other—that is now a question of fact. *Where* we draw the line is arbitrary in the sense that there is no "out-there" necessity to say that someone with X percent of hemoglobin is anemic and someone with $X - 1$ percent is not, or that an income of $50.00 per week puts someone below the poverty line, while an income of $51.00 per week does not—where the line is drawn is more or less useful according to our interests and/or values; but the *allocation* of someone to a position above or below the relevant line, once it has been drawn, is not arbitrary, it is an empirically testable truth—or falsehood.

Furthermore, social science makes no claim that the ideal type represents reality; it is, indeed, at pains to point out that the ideal type is extremely unlikely to be found in the real world. Social reality is not described *directly* by the means of the ideal type. It is we, not any out-there reality, who are responsible for the construction of the type. We draw the ideal type with clear, "ideal" lines so that we can describe by comparing, say, two or more bureaucracies with the type in order to compare the bureaucracies themselves by highlighting at what points they are similar and at what points they are dissimilar.

Alternatively, we may use the ideal type to compare a single phenomenon with itself over time. If we decide that there is less "religion" at time Y than there was at time X, then we may say that secularization is occurring. We should, however, remember that if we define (or operationalize) religion in one way (e.g., by church-attendance statistics) we may get an answer to our question about the existence of secularization which differs significantly from the answer we would get if we were to define religion another way (e.g., that which makes life meaningful).

But while out-there reality does not *dictate* the content of the ideal type, it might *suggest* it. While it makes no sense to talk of the truth or falsity of an ideal type, it does make sense to talk about its usefulness. If the type bears no recognizable resemblance to whatever it is we wish to study, then it is not a very helpful tool. Thus, social scientists are (usually) aware of the more or less useful *choices* that are made in the production of their stipulative definitions.

So far as reportive definitions are concerned, the logic of the sociology of knowledge assumes that knowledge is, in some sense, relative to the society in which it is known; it presupposes, furthermore, that there is no Platonic essentialism or universalism in the concepts that are used by the people it studies. There is no absolute, unchanging, perfect "justice," "good," "woman"— or "religion." The concepts that a linguistic community uses in its discourse make sense because they have been taught to the members of the community and, were they inhabiting another community, they would not only use different sounds, they would also cut up and order the world in different ways.

This leads us to Mary Douglas and the way in which she has taken up the Kantian epistemological problem (of sorting out the relative merits of empiricism and rationalism) that Durkheim (1915) had turned into a sociological problem in his *The Elementary Forms of the Religious Life*. In *Purity and Danger,* Douglas (1966) asks why it is that certain things are considered dangerous and taboo and why what is considered dangerous or taboo in one society is not necessarily considered so in another society. Why, for example, do Jews not eat pork? She rejects ad hoc explanations and searches instead for a universal explanation that will explain concepts of danger, dirt, and taboo in all societies. The answer with which she comes up is stark in its simplicity: dirt is matter out of place.

Using the Old Testament as her starting point, Douglas' argument goes roughly along the following lines: all societies need to have a means of communicating with each other. Members of a society—members of the human race—need to make sense of the manifest flux of experience. They need to *order* reality—"in order to" create and control reality. Categories must exist in which we can place the social and physical phenomena that appear to us. A society might, for example, cut the world up into living and nonliving phenomena. It may then divide living things into plants and animals, and then divide the latter into animals of the water, the land, and the air, and so on. But what, Douglas asks, if the society finds something which crosses one of its distinguishing boundaries? Amphibians span the boundary between animals of the land and animals of the water. What does the society "do" with such anomalies which are, Douglas argues, endangering not only the taxonomic system but presenting a potential threat to the entire fabric of society? They are dangerous; they must be dealt with.

Douglas gives several examples of things that cross conceptual boundaries and how these are dealt with by a society: how, for example, they are to be avoided as that which is polluting or taboo; how they might be relabelled— the Nuer define monstrous births as baby hippopotamuses accidentally born to humans, so they are gently laid in the river where they belong. Alternatively, the power of the boundary crosser may be harnessed—it may be held in awe and worshipped as an object most sacred and powerful. Such, Douglas tells us, has been the case in the Belgian Congo where the Lele worship the pangolin or scaly ant-eater—a taxonomic rag-bag which has scales like a fish yet climbs trees, which is more like an egg-laying lizard than a mammal yet suckles its young, and which—unlike other small mammals—bears its young singly.

Douglas also points out the enormous difference that moving a boundary can make to a society and how control of where the boundaries lie is power indeed. Consider, for example, the difference it could make to a society if it were to change the age at which a "boy" becomes a "man" (and is thereby able to vote or to marry or to die for his country) from, say, 13 to 18, or from 21 to 18. There is no fixed time that "nature" insists upon, and the change in social status is more likely to be marked by a religiously sanctioned *rite de passage,* or by a socially determined law of the land, than by an individual's arrival at physical puberty.

The basic assumption is that conceptual boundaries—the separation of those things that "go together" from those that "are separate"—*are necessary* for a society to operate; but *where* the boundaries are drawn is, to a greater or lesser extent, *arbitrary*. I would like to suggest that recognizing this combination of necessity and arbitrariness may help us to understand the social *functioning* of some reportive definitions of religion.

Thousands of words have been written on the subject of stipulative definitions of religion. One popular distinction drawn by social scientists is that between substantive definitions that define what religion *is*, and functional definitions which emphasize what religion *does* (McGuire 1992, pp. 9-15). For some purposes one definition is useful: for other purposes another definition may help us to understand better the social context within which religion is accepted, rejected, and/or changed.

Surprisingly little has, however, been written by sociologists of religion about the definitions of religion that the members of a society or group whom they are studying employ, or of the uses (and, perhaps, misuses) to which these definitions may be put. Like sociologists, most people would produce a substantive definition (e.g., belief in a supernatural being or force) or, perhaps less frequently, a functional definition (e.g., a set of beliefs and practices which, like Christianity, Marxism, or nationalism, bind a social group together); and, like sociologists, most people—especially legislators and those administering the law—would be unlikely to include an appraising value judgment *as part of their overt definition.* That is, they would claim that their definition of religion was unaffected by whether or not they approved of, agreed with, or liked the institutions and individuals espousing a belief in a supernatural being or force—or whatever. Nonetheless, it is possible to observe that people may (at least on occasions when values or interests are concerned) want implicitly to confine the use of the term "religion" to "religion-that-I-approve of." I would like to suggest, furthermore, that there are a number of ways in which we might understand more, not only about their concepts of religion but also about the values and interests of a society's members, and the struggles for power within a society, if we were to look at the uses made of the concept—or, indeed, of a number of other concepts. In this paper, space permits no more than a few preliminary observations which I shall illustrate by drawing mainly from my research into new religious movements (NRMs).

My first observation comes from over six years' experience of running INFORM (Information Network Focus On Religious Movements), a charity that I set up with the support of the British government and mainstream churches in order to provide information about the new religious movements that is as objective, balanced, and up-to-date as possible (Barker 1989). Inquirers who telephone the office frequently want to know whether a particular movement is "a genuine religion." If asked what they mean by a genuine religion, they may well answer by asking "Well, is it like the Moonies?"

In such circumstances, it is pointless to ask "in what way like the Moonies?" What the inquirers are really asking is not whether the movement in question has a belief in God, nor whether, if it has a belief in God, its beliefs are anything like those of the Unification Church. Nor are they even asking whether the movement's practices are like those of the Unification Church. The real question is: is the movement respectable (like the Church of England, perhaps) or is it one of those that the media would classify as a cult—and, therefore, something that is *not* respectable—and, therefore, "a bad thing?" Exactly *what* makes a movement bad seems, so far as such inquirers are concerned, to be something to be investigated only *after* it has been decided whether it falls into the "cult" or "genuine-religion" category—and the boundary between these two categories is, very often, seen in Platonic, absolute, unchanging, nonnegotiable terms, with very little, if any, notion of what the actual content of either category might be.

The point that I am trying to make is that there is a sense in which the categories are used to provide an a priori appraising value judgment which will let the inquirer know whether or not the movement is good or bad—despite the fact that it sounds, even to the inquirer, that the inquiry is for purely factual information. Furthermore, if the inquirer *is* questioned about what s/he means by true/false, good/bad, or genuine/not genuine, it is quite possible that some very strange bed-fellows would be found on either side of the divide—reflecting not one whit the socially prescribed conventional wisdom that defines "religion."

Mrs. R., an academic historian, has a son who had joined the Unification Church. During the course of her conversation with me, she expressed irritation that I had called the movement a new religion rather than a cult. I explained that, first, "new religious movement" was a term frequently used by sociologists of religion and that I was a sociologist of religion; second, the term "cult" was used in a special, technical way in the sociology of religion and that, according to at least some of these definitions, the Unification Church was not a cult; and, third, in popular parlance the term "cult" had come to be associated with evaluative overtones of a negative kind and that, although I certainly disagreed with certain aspects of the Unification Church and would even go so far as to say that I disapproved of others, I felt it was unhelpful to include automatically a negative evaluation of a movement when one was trying to describe its beliefs and practices; surely, I asked, it was more helpful for the evaluation to follow from such information?

Mrs. R.'s response was that, be that as it may, it was just as bad to give an aura of respectability to the movement by calling it a religion when it was no such thing. I protested that merely calling a movement a religion did not, for me at any rate, mean that it was either good or bad, but just that it had certain characteristics.

"But it's *not* a religion," Mrs. R. insisted.

"The members believe in God," I ventured. (I hoped she would not confuse matters by bringing up the fact that the Raëlians refer to themselves as an atheistic religion).

There followed a fairly lengthy discussion during which I challenged Mrs. R. to produce a definition—any definition—of religion which would exclude the Unification Church. She could not, so she changed her tactic: "It's not really a religion—it's a political organization; and it's Big Business."

> "Yes, but surely that doesn't stop it from also being a religion? Does the Roman Catholic Church cease being a religion when it becomes involved in politics or owns property, businesses and shares?" (I knew Mrs. R. to be a Catholic.)

> "That's not the point. Of course the Catholic Church is still a religion. The point is that the Moonies are not a proper religion—it's not true, all that junk about Eve having sex with Satan and Jesus being meant to marry and not saving the world."

> "Do you believe in the tenets of Islam?"

> "Of course not!"

> "Is Islam a religion?"

> "Yes, but it's not like the Unification Church—it's a genuine religion."

> "What's the difference?"

> "Well, it's been around for years and has millions of followers."

> "If the Unification Church had been around a bit longer and it managed to get a few million more believers, would that make it a religion?"

> "Heaven forbid! No!"

> "So, what would make the Unification Church a religion?"

> "Nothing would. It's rotten to the core."

Mrs. R. had made her point. She did not want the Unification Church defined as a religion even if it complied with all the criteria that made other religions "real" religions. The fact that there is a Unification theology which is centred around a strong belief in God and which has its own cosmology, theodicy, eschatology, soteriology, Christology, and Biblically based interpretation of history was of no account. The fact that other traditions could still be called religions even if they were also engaged in financial and political actions and even if their beliefs were not necessarily those accepted by Mrs. R., was irrelevant, as was the possibility that the Unification Church might continue to survive over a specified period of time—despite the fact that these criteria were used as weapons in the argument that Unificationism was not a real religion. In the final analysis, Mrs. R.'s definition, or, rather, her shifting definitions of religion, were dependent on her evaluation of the movement. It would seem, as a matter of fact, to be impossible not only for Mrs. R., but also for many others, to conceive of a "bad" religion, despite the fact that they themselves would assume that they were defining religion in a perfectly dispassionate way.

It should not, however, be thought that "religion" necessarily has a positive evaluation for everyone in the same society, even when they are of the same class or occupation as Mrs. R. There are plenty of people for whom the term "religion" has decidedly negative overtones; for them, "religion" conjures up a picture of an institutionalized, rather dead thing that has little to do with spirituality. Indeed, it is not difficult to find professed Christians who will insist that they do not belong to a religion because they do not want to be associated with the dreariness and/or hypocrisy that they associate with the concept. They do not want to be associated with "a bad thing" any more than Mrs. R. wanted the Unification Church to be associated with "a good thing."

But a penchant to turn concepts overtly relying on a characterizing value judgment into a concept covertly incorporating appraising value judgments is not the only way in which the concept of religion can be "used." There are some eminently understandable secular reasons why the boundary defining what is or is not a religion may be redrawn and used in a contradictory manner according to whether or not the definer has an interest in ensuring that a particular movement falls inside or outside the category. The apparent sleight of hand can, again, work in either direction. I was talking to a university chaplain one day.

> "We can't call the Hare Krishna a religion," he confessed.

> "Are 'ordinary' Hindus a religion?," I asked.

> "Oh yes, of course," he answered. "But they've already got a room." I must have looked decidedly nonplussed because he went on to explain, "It's a University rule that each religion should have a room, but there just aren't enough rooms to go round if all these new cults were to claim to be a religion. We'd have to start sharing, and you can see how that would lead to all sorts of problems." Somewhat naïvely, I suggested that it might be easier to modify the University rules than to redefine the Krishna devotees as members of a non-religion. "Oh, but that would be religious discrimination!" he protested.

As in the case of Mrs. R., it was clearly easier for the liberally minded chaplain to have the language, rather than himself, discriminate against the Krishna movement—and, if necessary, he and his equally liberal-minded colleagues from other mainstream traditions would have to ensure that the language carefully differentiated between those "real" religions that had already got a room, and other organizations which could not be called religions.

Not merely room allocations, but literally millions of dollars may hang in the balance, depending on whether or not the label "religion" is officially (legally) sanctioned. In such cases, the importance of the *religious* label rests, perhaps ironically, on its socially determined *secular* concomitants. There are, for example, considerable economic advantages to be gained in several countries by being defined as a religion for purposes of tax exemption—but there are also some disadvantages in being defined as a religion in a country wanting to preserve a strong division between church and state.

Unlike the Unification Church or ISKCON, the Church of Scientology is not obviously a religion—at least according to some of the more popular substantive definitions which rely on there being a belief in a deity (and which could, thereby, exclude at least some forms of Buddhism). Wilson (1989) lists twenty different characteristics, some, but not all, of which, he argues, would have to be present for a movement to qualify as a religion. He found eleven of these clearly present in Scientology, five clearly absent, and the presence of the remaining four characteristics arguable. And Scientology has won court cases in Australia and the United States to the effect that it is a religion and thereby eligible for tax concessions (*High Court of Australia* 1983; Internal Revenue Service 1993).

Conversely, the Science of Creative Intelligence, better known as Transcendental Meditation (TM), has strong connections with Hinduism which might suggest that it is more eligible for the label of religion than is the Church of Scientology. Not surprisingly, the movement is anxious that its meditation techniques should be as widely taught as possible, but the First Amendment of the United States Constitution is interpreted as meaning that no religion can be taught in the public schools. TM has fought—and lost—a case in the courts in which it claimed *not* to be a religion. The opinion stated that the teaching of TM in New Jersey public schools is a violation of the U.S. Constitution and is, therefore, prohibited (Scott 1978, pp. 5-6).

An illustration of a more subtle way in which the use of the term "religion" may have political overtones can be taken from an Inter-faith meeting to which I was invited. The meeting was concerned primarily with the British blasphemy laws in the light of "the Salman Rushdie affair," and the rights of the Muslim minority to have respect for their religion protected on an equal footing with the rights of the Church of England's members having their sensibilities protected. An eminent lawyer (whose track record in protecting the rights of minorities, even "cults," has been impeccable) made a statement to the effect that the Press Council had not included *religious* discrimination in the list of offenses that the media might commit, and that this had been done on purely pragmatic grounds as, had they used the term religion, they might then have been unable to exclude bodies such as the Moonies and the Church of Scientology. Those poor Americans had, he added, got into such trouble with their First Amendment.

It was not a public meeting and perhaps it is unfair to report the lawyer's statement; certainly, when challenged, he rephrased his argument more carefully. A point to be noted is, however, that, before he had begun speaking, he had (albeit half jokingly) made a statement to the effect that he would be careful about what he was to say because of the presence of some (very liberal) members of (the very liberal) press; *yet* he had apparently still felt secure in that (very liberal) setting about expressing prejudice related to the concept of religion which could be assumed to be understood as unexceptionable and, presumably, pass unquestioned.

Furthermore, when an argument was made about defending the *rights* of unpopular religions, this was heard by a (very liberal) bishop as a defense of the beliefs and/or practices of such religions. It took some time to explain that to express a belief that the members of *all* religions should be treated the same *in so far as the criterion for treating them in that way is that they are members of a religion* is *not* to say that certain *practices* should not be lauded *or* condemned, *whatever* the religious belief.

The point of this story is to illustrate how people who would undoubtedly fight for the principle that the law should apply equally to all may, nonetheless, be juggling with boundaries, definitions, and the usage of certain concepts, such as religion, in order to ensure that, despite their stated criteria of a just and universally applicable law, the law does *not* apply equally to all.

My last story is drawn from a conference attended by charming, middle-aged-to-elderly, middle-to-upper-class gentlefolk in an elegant resort in the South of England. I was sharing a platform with an anthropologically minded artist who talked about and showed slides describing the art of the Borneo headhunters. The slides were indeed impressive, and the audience oozed benevolent enthusiasm for the primitive artists. My talk was about science and religion and all went well until question time, when I happened to mention that the Unification Church was one of the new religions which believed that it had unified science and religion. A tension filled the room.

> "You mean the Moonies?" I was asked.
>
> "Yes," I answered.
>
> Unease, consternation then hostility seeped (or, more accurately perhaps, flooded) into the room.
>
> "They're wicked—evil—they should be banned," a thousand genteel voices seemed to hiss at me.
>
> I invited my audience to elaborate. "What's the matter with them?," I asked.
>
> The reply was instant and it was greeted with furious nods of approval: "They're not Christian!"

Why was it that the headhunters, who by no conceivable stretch of the imagination could be described as Christian, could appear to this group of Christians to be so infinitely preferable to the Unification Church which based its theology on a particular, albeit somewhat unorthodox, interpretation of the Old and New Testaments and which, in public at any rate, proclaimed itself to be Christian—and whose official name was, moreover, the Holy Spirit Association for the Unification of World Christianity?

Then I thought about Mary Douglas. It was clear that the headhunters did not threaten any boundaries; the very fact that there was no way that they could be considered Christian made them quite safe as objects of admiration; they belonged to another world; they were, quite unambiguously, beyond the pale. The Unification Church, on the other hand, was staking out a claim on the boundary perimeter. It claimed to know how to interpret Holy Scripture.

In an area where there was a lack of obvious empirical refutation available, the Reverend Sun Myung Moon—a *Korean* of all things—was claiming that his was not only a possible, but a superior, interpretation of the Christian heritage. The boundary of what might be included under the rubric of "Christianity" was being renegotiated. And to cap it all, young, middle-class Westerners were accepting Moon's redefinition of the boundary.

The threat of the Unificationists and the lack of threat of the Borneo headhunters becomes understandable in the light of Douglas' observation about the importance of those in positions of relative power needing to protect boundaries. The Unification Church was matter out of place; it was dirt; it was pollution, taboo. It threatened a boundary that defined not only the identity of the individual members of my audience, but also the stability of the society to which they belonged. It did not matter that the Borneo artists were not Christian, that they collected their enemies' heads in an admittedly rather uncivilized fashion—it was, rather, *because* of the very fact that they were "rather uncivilised" that their art could be appreciated as art in itself, uncluttered by other characteristics or attributes that might blur important distinctions between them and us. On the other hand, the claim to Christianity *did* threaten to blur an important boundary between them (Korean heretics) and us (the upholders of the British heritage).

The point here is that it was important that, rather than answering my question with an explanation such as "we don't accept their interpretation of the meaning of the life of Jesus," Unificationism had to be defined as non-Christian if it were to be completely clear not only to me but, particularly, to them that anyone calling themselves a Christian would not indulge in behavior such as engaging in mass wedding ceremonies or the belief that a Korean is the Lord of the Second Advent. No one in that room, or in most other places, would be likely to think that a "real" Christian *could* indulge in head-hunting; the empirical assumption that "Christians do not head-hunt" was never in question. However, the empirical statement "Christians don't have mass weddings or believe that a Korean is the Lord of the Second Advent" would be questioned if one relied on a definition of Christians as, say, people who believe that Jesus was sent by God to save the world—a definition that could include Unificationists and, thus, allow one to make the statement that "*some* Christians *do* believe that a Korean is the Lord of the Second Advent"—

or whatever Unification belief or practice the audience found offensive or threatening.

As part of a strategy not dissimilar to that illustrated in my earlier examples, it was important for the genteel audience that the language should automatically exclude Unificationism from Christianity, rather than have alien beliefs and practices becoming recognized as part of a category to which they themselves belonged and, thus, potentially encroaching on something which constituted a cherished part of their individual and social identity and status.

Let us return briefly to the remarks that I made at the beginning of this paper. The sociologist tries, even if s/he cannot always be successful, to describe, classify, understand, and explain what is going on in the world that we study in as objective, value-free a manner as possible. We may, presumably most of us do, believe in value-*relevance*—that what we *choose* to study should be of some use, according to the values that we share with at least some of our fellow members of society. But that is precisely *why* we need to be as objective and balanced as possible in our presentation of data. We also need to be aware of the ways in which what we say and write is understood by those who listen to or read our conclusions.

We know that members of our society are quite likely to espouse a Platonic conception of concepts. We know that they are quite likely to do so at the same time as they juggle with the boundaries that they are quite likely to believe are neither necessary to construct nor arbitrary in their construction—they are obvious, taken-for-granted givens. Most people do not spend hours considering the contents of categories nor do they spend time considering the importance for themselves or for their society of the delineation of boundaries. Nonetheless, it does seem that at some level they are cognizant of such social realities and their negotiability, and, to mix metaphors, of the stakes that are implicit in the stakes. Stretching one metaphor a bit further, the argument is that people with vested interests will not sit on the conceptual or the proverbial fence and let others move it while they sit.

But there is a further twist to the story. Sociologists of religion are now being inveigled, in a number of ways, into collaborating in the battles of the boundaries. Our fellow citizens, the people whom we study—our data—are now asking us, in the courts, in the popular press, on radio, on television, and in private conversation to pronounce *as sociologists of religion* on what is genuine "religion," what is quasi-religion, what is real "Christianity" or whatever. It is not the task of social science to draw the boundaries that society should use. Society's categories may overlap with those that social scientists use as tools; but society's concepts and sociologists' concepts do not have the same ontological status. The latter are used to study the former. Social science has no special competence to decide what *ought*, by definition, to go with what and what ought to be rent asunder. Its expertise, such as it is, lies in discovering what *does, as a matter of empirical fact,* go with what.

Not only in the interests of basic human rights, but also in the interest of the basic integrity of social science, sociologists of religion should not be party to a practice in which "religion" is overtly defined in one (characterizing) way, but covertly (appraisingly) defined in terms of those whom we like and those whom we do not like so that laws and mores applying expressly to "religion" are applied only to "religions-of-which-we-approve," while religions-of-which-we-do-not-approve are defined as "non-religions"—or, indeed, vice versa.

In other words, social scientists may be able to tell others whether a particular movement is or is not a religion *if* they tell us what they mean by a religion. We may be able to tell them about the beliefs and the practices of the movement. We may be able to tell them who is likely to join, and what the consequences of their joining may be for themselves and for others. We can try to discover how one phenomenon, described by a concept (such as religion) may vary in the presence of other, *independently defined,* phenomena. We can illuminate the unintended consequences of drawing boundaries one way rather than another; we can point out inconsistencies in the use of definitions; we can recognize and perhaps make recognizable to others the varieties of uses to which concepts and boundaries are put—and quite a few other things.

But we cannot, as sociologists of religion, allow ourselves to be lured into drawing the boundaries that society will use. We cannot, as sociologists of religion, judge whether or not a particular movement is "a genuine religion" without knowing what those who are asking for our judgment mean by the terms genuine and religion. To pretend otherwise *might,* perhaps paradoxically, be to deny ourselves the right, as sociologists of religion, plausibly to make a distinction between what we want to call real or genuine social science and what we might want to call quasi- or pseudo-social science.

REFERENCES

Barker, E. 1989. *New Religious Movements: A Practical Introduction.* London: HMSO.

Douglas, M. 1966. *Purity and Danger: An Analysis of the Concepts of Pollution and Taboo.* London: Routledge and Kegan Paul.

————. 1975. *Implicit Meanings: Essays in Anthropology.* London: Routledge and Kegan Paul.

Durkheim, E. 1915. *The Elementary Forms of the Religious Life.* London: Allen and Unwin.

High Court of Australia. 1983. *The Church of the New Faith* [Scientology] v. *The Commissioner for Payroll Tax,* 27 October.

Hospers, J. 1956. *An Introduction to Philosophical Analysis.* London: Routledge and Kegan Paul.

Internal Revenue Service. 1993. Letter fro the Department of the Treasury, Reference no. E:EO:R:2 to Church of Scientology International, October 1.

McGuire, M. 1992. *Religion: The Social Context.* 3rd ed. Belmont, CA: Wadsworth.

Nagel, E. 1961. *The Structure of Science: Problems in the Logic of Scientific Explanation.* London: Routledge and Kegan Paul.

Scott, R.D. 1978. *Transcendental Misconceptions.* San Diego: Beta.

Weber, M. 1949. *The Methodology of the Social Sciences,* translated and edited by E. Shils and H.A. Finch. New York: Free Press.

Wilson, B. 1989. *The Social Dimensions of Sectarianism.* Oxford: Oxford University Press.

METAPHYSICS:

"A PRACTICAL RELIGIOUS PHILOSOPHY"

Melinda Bollar Wagner

ABSTRACT

Adherents of the various groups that make up the American metaphysical movement label metaphysics a "practical religious philosophy." Data regarding two of these groups, Spiritual Frontiers Fellowship (SFF) and the Association for Research and Enlightenment (ARE), demonstrate that this practical nature extends to the associations' efforts to solve the quotidian problems of their devotees. However, their therapy is practiced in a spiritual idiom; the vocabulary used is not the same as that used by groups identified as "counseling" or "support" groups. On the other hand, the spiritual core of the organizations is not reflected in church-like institutions. This ambiguity qualifies the metaphysical groups for the label of quasi-religions, existing on the frontier between the sacred and the secular. It is argued that, by creating a secular/sacred, therapeutic/religious amalgam, the metaphysical groups have adapted themselves to middle-class American culture.

Religion and the Social Order, Volume 4, pages 111-125.

What kind of gathering is this? Eight casually dressed people, aged 30 to 66, sit in a circle at 7:00 on a Wednesday evening, having come from a variety of white- and blue-collar jobs.

> Jenny: The lesson tonight is "Hate or Misguided Love."

In an around-the-room fashion, the participants answer the questions, "where do negative emotions come from and how do they manifest themselves?" The homework for this lesson is to identify a fault each wished to be rid of, and to think of the positive thing to put in its place.

> Jenny: What is the fault you chose for your homework, and what are you doing about it? Grace, what's yours?
>
> Grace: My fault is that I don't relax enough. I am either going like Hades, or sound asleep. I'm trying to take time to relax, when I come home from work. And my ceramics class is very relaxing.
>
> Jenny: Good. David?
>
> David: Procrastination is my biggest fault. I was going to class Tuesday, and I thought I'd be five minutes early. Just as I went to shave, I got three phone calls. I was five minutes late to class.
>
> Jenny: Were they important calls?
>
> David: No.
>
> Jenny: If a person is calling for a reason, if they're blue or something, I don't mind talking. But some people just have nothing else to do, and I call those nuisance calls. What's your fault, Laura?
>
> Laura: My fault is that I don't always spend money wisely. I'm working on it, trying to keep better track of where it goes. But I just can't be stingy. I send money to a friend who's out of work—no use hoarding it. When I begin thinking about money, thinking "Where will it come from?" then I get some from here and there.
>
> Jenny: ...it's a good thing I don't have to worry about money. I'm not at all concerned with the material side of life. What have you been working on, Jean?
>
> Jean: My fault is that I tell my husband all the bad things that happen to me, and that's all I tell him. I should tell him the good, as well as the bad. I've been doing that, I even made a list of good things to tell him....
>
> Jenny: What about you Beverly?

Beverly reports that her fault is not telling John, her husband, when one of the migraine headaches that plague her strikes.

> Beverly: I finally told John I had a headache on Friday night. He finished dinner for me, and everyone helped with the jobs around the house. I used some medication. I don't like to take medication, and John

doesn't like for me to, but I didn't want to be in bed all day Saturday. And I got better. I don't know why, but it just kills me to tell him I have a headache.

John: Then that makes it worse.

Beverly: Yes, I think it helps to tell him.

Jenny: Sara?

Sara: I asked my family to choose a fault. It took my husband about ten minutes to come out with it. He said I get my defenses—my armor—up too often. I worked on it. I knew when I did it. He told me, too. I'm making progress.

Jenny: That's a step in the right direction. All of you should continue to work on it until it's no longer a problem. What are you working on, Dan?

Dan: My problem is traffic. I am impatient with other drivers.

Sara: Dan, you should have heard what Louise said about your driving on the way over here.

Louise: I guess that's one of my faults. In the car, I want him to go where I tell him to go.

Dan: She backseat drives!

Louise: The thing I've been working on is not to be critical of others, and to avoid forming first opinions.

John: That can be a problem. There was a kid in the plant I thought had his thumb up his tail and his head in the clouds. I was going to tell him. Then one day he walked away with a white cane. He was doing filing and deburring. I told the other supervisor about it. I would have really felt terrible if I had chewed him out.

David: But Louise, you have the opportunity to make judgments because of the people who work around you.

Louise: That's true. For example, there's a rule that no relatives can work in the same department. A girl lied to get a job. She denied she was a sister of another cashier. I was training her, and she told me. I thought this was pretty bad, that she lied on the application. But later I recommended her for a place in the office, when the boss asked me, because she had been a good worker and was smart.

Jenny: I don't think it should make any difference if they are relatives.

Louise: Well, there is a theft problem with employees, and it's often relatives.

Jenny: You have to know when to judge, and when not.

Louise: Well, we're not here to judge people.

Jenny: My fault is that I'm too available. I've been relegating things. It's working. This helps where my family is concerned. They don't get enough attention.

This could be a meeting of a support group, or a therapy group, or it could be part of a counseling session. Let me fill in the scene with some deleted items of context.

Partway through the lesson, as participants tell whether they feel they are mostly positive or mostly negative, Jenny, the leader (called "facilitator" to emphasize that she is not to be seen as an authority figure), says, "there are very few things in life which cannot be changed," and adds:

> Jenny: In the beginning we were all perfect. And we can be again. It's a matter of becoming aware of that divine inner self, that spark that's within all of us. I can always say, "I love the God within that person." Even if I am angered by what he is doing, I can love that part of him that's part of God, because that's part of me, too.

When Laura explains that when she gives money away, "then I get some from here and there," Jenny notes:

> Jenny: Yes, you get what you give. It's a natural law. You have to give to receive. When you give, you should expect something in return. A vessel can only fill up so far, then something must be taken out.
>
> David: You may not get money in return.
>
> Jenny: Right. You might get a bargain here or there, things like that.

Dan reports that he has a way of dealing with his impatience with traffic, and Jenny agrees that it is a good idea.

> Dan: By saying the word "God," I preempt my anger, and have some control over the other drivers.
>
> Jenny: Saying the word "God" raises your vibrations. There's more a oneness with everyone around you, more harmony. Saying the word "God" raises a negative emotion into a mental state which says, "wait a minute."

Louise explained that one of her problems is "getting negative at work," and she told her solution:

> Louise: I say, "Change me or change the condition." If I have problems with someone, I always say, "God, change me. Help me as well as the other person." I've prayed to God for guidance to help me understand a neighbor's situation. And sewing calms me.

John is advised to "Put a Light around" his troublesome boss. The Pure White Light of the Christ is a manifestation of God's love. It can be used for protection or to improve a situation. It is thought that the White Light vibrates at a high frequency. Anything negative vibrates at a lower rate of frequency, and cannot penetrate the force field set up by the White Light. To put the Light around oneself or someone else, it is necessary only to visualize it "like a spotlight" or "like a fog" surrounding you or the other person. If you think and believe the Light is around someone, then it is. And indeed, John reports that he has been trying to use the Light:

> John: I've been putting my boss in the Light. I tend to give things to God, then I take them back again. I take over from God. I should give it to Him and leave it (e.g., Wagner 1983a, 1983b, 1984).

In continuing to work on these problems, the book used by the study group, *Know Yourself*, advised:

> During meditation each day visualize yourself breathing in the desired quality and breathing out the fault. If you are good at visualizing, literally pump yourself full of God's love and let the overflow push away the unwanted negative fault.... This will be a great aid in helping to change our old patterns. Use the energy of God's love, rather than our own negative feelings, to renew our positive energy. The keynote is patience (e.g., Hayes 1971, p. 30; Wagner 1983a, 1983b, 1984).

These elements of description which fill out the scene make it clear that if this is therapy, it is therapy in a spiritual idiom. The vocabulary used by this assembly is different from that used by a group which would identify itself as a "counseling," "support," or "therapy" group. The solutions for problems are both spiritual ("Put it in the Light") and prosaic ("sewing calms me"). An analysis of one year's worth of these weekly meetings showed that 62 percent of the solutions offered were spiritual in nature. They were the same types of solutions described here—becoming more aware of the divine inner self, following spiritual laws, thinking affirmative thoughts, praying, using spiritual formulas, and meditating. In another 13 percent of the cases, a spiritual solution was joined to a conventional one ($N = 436$ solutions discussed) (Wagner 1983a).

Even the decor of the living room where the small party meets displays spiritual scenery. On one wall are two pictures of Christ, one with a peaceful expression, the other pained, bearing a crown of thorns and drops of blood. Beside a bookcase full of religious and psychic literature is a large string-picture of the four-armed Hindu god Shiva. Very small round pictures of the Roman Catholic stigmatics Padre Pio and Sister Rosa Ferron hang on the side of the bookcase. A table between two chairs has the shape of an elephant with an Indian howdah on its back. A gold-colored cobra statue coils on top of the television. In the corner stands a three-foot-high black Buddha, holding a candle in one outstretched hand. Arranged on the fireplace mantle are candles, a Confucius figurine, a bronze bust of an American Indian, a figure of a tree, a madonna, and a crystal ball (Wagner 1983a).

This is a Spiritual Frontiers Fellowship (SFF) study group. Spiritual Frontiers, the Association for Research and Enlightenment (ARE),[1] and many others, such as Spiritualism, Theosophy, Christian Science, the Unity School of Christianity, Astara, and several New Thought groups that are loosely organized into the International New Thought Alliance, are part of the American metaphysical movement (Judah 1967).[2]

ARE THEY RELIGIONS?

Commonsense notions of religion include a belief in the supernatural, and some kind of (usually collective) expression of that belief. For social scientists, definitions of religion abound. As just one example, Durkheim ([1912]1961) gave us the distinction between the sacred and the profane, and delineated sacred activities as either religion or magic. Religion is collective; it has a church. Magic is individual; it has a clientele. Weber ([1922]1963) added that magic was a set of ad hoc specific, instrumental acts to produce tangible results in this world. For these theorists, religion was a higher, integrative force. Anthropologist Bronislaw Malinowski made a similar distinction in 1931, the year of ARE's founding. To illustrate it, he wrote of Christian Science, another metaphysical organization:

> The main function of Christian Science is the thinking away of illness and decay; its metaphysics are very strongly pragmatic and utilitarian, and its ritual is essentially a means to the end of health and happiness.

Malinowski (1931) thought that the "remedies and blessings" offered by Christian Science "shade invariably into magic," and added, "it is very difficult to discover where common sense ends and where magic begins." Just so, in all of these attempts at dichotomizing—at discerning what is and what is not religion—metaphysics comes up a hybrid. This ambiguity qualifies the metaphysical groups for the label of quasi-religions, existing on the border between the sacred and the secular.[3]

A goal of these essays is to explore how the adherents themselves are identifying and using quasi-religions. Adherents define metaphysics as a "practical religious philosophy." They wish to relate spiritual and psychic phenomena to everyday life.

The practical, therapeutic aspect of the groups and their meetings, highlighted in our opening description, is just one of several characteristics that render metaphysics particularly adapted to today's middle American culture. These characteristics include individualism, a scholarly cultural style, an attempt to align with science, organizational functional specialization, and an acceptance of the lifestyles devotees bring with them. Let us begin the discussion of these characteristics by harking back to practicality.

METAPHYSICS IS A PRACTICAL RELIGIOUS PHILOSOPHY

Indeed, as Malinowski noted long ago, the metaphysical groups do offer practical means to quotidian ends. This practical function is, to be sure, set in the context of a search for meaning, or "spiritual growth," the product of which is defined as an ever-increasing awareness of one's divine inner self. But the practical problem-solving function is much in evidence in both ARE and SFF.

The amount of time spent on personal problems in the study groups demonstrates that dealing with problems is a major interest of the participants. Study group meetings of both associations include these activities: an inspirational reading, reports of personal experiences, a lesson, meditation, and a healing ritual. The reports of personal experiences, essentially discussions of personal problems, in SFF are called "psychic and spiritual experiences of the week;" in ARE they are labelled application of the week's "discipline." This portion of the meetings takes 33 percent to 70 percent of the total meeting time of two hours (ARE) or three hours (SFF). During this time, the eight to twelve members of the group discuss problems in their relationships with people at work, family, in-laws, neighbors or friends, and difficulties with depression, anxiety, self-doubt, guilt, hostility, irritation, and "negative thoughts." They describe worries over family members' troubles, economic problems, and concerns about work they have to do or decisions they need to make. They receive solutions from the leader and other group members.

In addition, another quarter of the study group meeting time is spent on a "lesson" which often has practical problem-solving themes. Lessons had titles such as "Selfishness and Selflessness," "The Art of Relating," "Self-Doubt," and "Depression."

Likewise, the content of SFF and ARE regional and national meetings show the metaphysicians' desire to "make spiritual and psychic phenomena practical and related to everyday living." SFF workshops have titles such as "Developing a Prosperity Consciousness," "Creative Resolution of Conflict in You, Your Family, Your Group," "Dreams: A Tool for Problem Solving and Spiritual Growth," and "Integrating the Mystical Experiences of Meditation in Daily Living." ARE Congress themes include: "Practical Approaches to a Balanced Life" and "The Power of Attitudes."

A content analysis of titles of 308 lectures and workshops presented at SFF national and regional activities (six national retreats, two national conferences, two regional retreats, and eighteen monthly regional meetings) showed that about one-third obviously dealt with improvement in interpersonal relationships or emotional or physical health.[4]

INDIVIDUALISM IS REFLECTED
IN IDEOLOGY AND STRUCTURE

Many observers have described the social character of Americans as bent toward individualism (Bellah et al. 1985; Hsu 1972; Marsella 1985; Tocqueville [1835-1840]1969; Wagner 1990). Luckmann (1967, p. 97) described a sense of individual autonomy which arose due to the evolutionary shift from all-encompassing, kin-based traditional social structures, to functionally specialized modern ones. A "private sphere" emerged "from the interstices of the social structure that resulted from institutional segmentation." Meaning-giving has moved into this private sphere, the most extreme example being the private religion-of-one, "Sheilaism," that Bellah et al. (1985) discovered.

The goal, epistemology, and organizational structure of the metaphysical societies all reflect individualism and celebrate the American sense of individual autonomy.[5] The purpose of the SFF study groups is to allow individuals to achieve "spiritual growth," defined as an ever-increasing realization of the divine inner self. Along the way to this goal, members are presented a potpourri of methods and concepts, borrowed from a myriad of religious and psychological strains. They pick and choose among these, relying on personal experience as the guide to truth. Individual exegesis is highly prized within the groups. Belief in the god within oneself—the only belief metaphysical adherents could be said to have as a core—provides a rationale for individual exegesis. The strongly held creedlessness of the metaphysical religions requires individual exegesis. The structure of Spiritual Frontiers Fellowship encourages individual exegesis: SFF has loose membership requirements that allow participants to search for their truths where they may; the fellowship is nonhierarchical in organizational form and anti-authoritarian in its style of leadership.

As I further describe ARE and SFF, I will discuss cultural alternatives—other ways these organizations could operate. In so doing, I am not implying that they *should* be operating in any other way. I am merely stating some alternatives to show what "might be," and thus to throw into relief "what is," to further clarify the choices that metaphysicians make as they create the cultures of their quasi-religions.

THE CULTURAL STYLE IS ACADEMIC AND SCIENTISTIC

The cultural style of metaphysical groups is often academic and scholarly in vocabulary and look. The ARE name itself reflects this scholarly tone: The Association for *Research* and Enlightenment. ARE's goal is stated as follows: "A.R.E., a non-profit, benevolent organization, was established July 7, 1931, to preserve, study and present the Edgar Cayce clairvoyant readings."

A brochure advertising an annual Congress describes what will go on there. Listen to the way the activities are described: "As more and more data of a concrete and practical nature are brought together through cross-indexing and extracting, it is possible to bring them to our members through lectures, classes, discussions and experiments." The Congress was to include: classes, panel forums, group discussions, experiments in extra-sensory perception, and a special research project.

It sounds like college. It does not sound like church. It does not sound like a church retreat. And it does not sound like an encounter group, (although if you go to a meeting, you will be greeted with "warm fuzzy" hugs).

Spiritual Frontiers Fellowship's statement of *Principles, Purposes, and Program* makes it clear that it wishes to be allied with science. SFF supports a Research Committee. Both ARE and SFF have lending libraries. Both review books in their scholarly looking periodicals.

Other aspects of the philosophy, social organization, and rhetoric of the metaphysical associations savor of academia and science. The metaphysical participants are called students, and the groups are classes. It is not beliefs that are discussed in the classes, but theories, concepts, or ideas (the theory of reincarnation, for example). When the classes end, the students graduate.

A teacher of metaphysical classes said metaphysics was concerned not with the "supernatural," which is forever scientifically inexplicable, but with the "supernormal," which is amenable to eventual scientific explanation, though it is not yet fully understood by science. He taught that there are physiological and neurological (and thus scientific) explanations for psychic phenomena. This search for "spiritual laws"—seen as another set of natural laws that have not yet been discovered by science—is basic to the seekers' assurance that metaphysics is a scientific religious philosophy. An example of joining science and religion was a meditation given at an SFF leadership conference entitled, "The Laser Beam of God's Love."

But even more fundamental to the definition of metaphysics as a "scientific religious philosophy" than these scientific sounding beliefs is the metaphysical epistemology. The metaphysical methodology for finding truth—relying on personal experience—is equated with scientific thought. That is, metaphysical students withhold faith until the facts of their own personal experience are in; this is considered akin to the scientific method (see Swatos 1990 concerning this aspect of spiritualism, another branch of metaphysics).

McGuire (1988, pp. 145, 151) notes that this cultural style characterized the "psychic and occult healing" groups that she observed. Speakers at lectures used scientific terminology and statistics to support their positions and borrowed images from technology to explain their theories of healing. For example, a healer said, "I take the stand that emotional situations will cause perturbances in the energy field which makes up your consciousness in the same way that it will cause disturbances in your soma, in your body tissues." Others used words such as "emits," "zaps," "plugs in," "electrified," and "magnetic forces."

> At their meetings, which were called classes, numerous participants brought tape recorders; others took notes studiously. When interviewed, many adherents proudly pointed out their extensive collections of lecture tapes. Organizing sessions as lectures, locating them in libraries or classrooms, encouraging other aspects of classroom behavior (e.g., note-taking, recommended readings, raised hands for the question-answer period), all promote the larger definition of the situation: this is not religious ritual but rather the learning of important knowledge. The classroom environment is considered "safe"—not weird—and acquiring knowledge is valued in this culture (McGuire 1988, p. 134).

Now, as to whether these experiments and research projects would satisfy a scientist's methodological rigor, that is another matter. It has been suggested that "scientism," rather than "science," characterizes the metaphysical groups (see Wagner 1983a). Nevertheless, the concern for science and the scientific and academic vocabulary and tone, show a linking up with the concerns of the surrounding culture—a desire to be the "establishment" of the occult (see Marty 1970 regarding the "occult establishment").

LEADERS REFLECT THE ACADEMIC CULTURAL STYLE

Unlike many spiritual organizations, the organizational structure of these groups is democratic; the leadership of these two groups is elected. When elections are called for, Nominating Committees make it clear that they wish leaders to project a dignified and scholarly image. The ARE Bulletin sometimes carries pictures of the "newly elected members of the ARE Board of Trustees." They tend to show middle-aged white males, wearing coats and ties and looking very upstanding. (Moving down the organizational structure to regional organizations and local study groups, female leadership becomes more likely.)

The "visiting lecturers and teachers" scheduled for ARE summer events at Virginia Beach were introduced this way: Under the picture of a middle-aged white man with very short hair, clad in a coat and tie, was this caption:

> Prof. F_____ has his Bachelor's Degree in Economics, his Master of Arts in French, and is completing his Doctorate in Philosophy, all at the University of Virginia. He has studied at the Sorbonne under a Fulbright Fellowship. He is Associate Professor in Philosophy at the College of William and Mary in Williamsburg, and acting head of the Dept. He will lecture on "The Philosophical Implications of Life and Death" in the LIFE BEYOND DEATH session, July 25-31st.

In SFF brochures, too, the credentials of workshop leaders and lecturers include college degrees, symbols of professional success, and a long list of metaphysical group memberships. An SFF Retreat leader was described as:

Dr. D_____, a prominent architect in C_____, a member of the Executive Council of SFF, is a longtime student of the paranormal... He is a member of the Institute of Noetic Sciences, A.R.E., Fellowship of Spiritual Understanding, ESP Associates, Academy of Parapsychology and Medicine, author of articles on architecture, individual liberty, and paranormal subjects, and popular workshop leader.

Think of the alternatives. Leaders could be labelled something besides *lecturers* and *teachers,* to begin with. They could be introduced to the readers by their psychic abilities, or by their experiences in spiritual growth. But the use of academic credentials is a reflection of the fact that what is important in the establishment of America is important in the establishment of the occult.

FUNCTIONAL SPECIALIZATION IS REFLECTED IN THE SOCIAL STRUCTURE

Still another way these two metaphysical organizations reflect American society is that they have become functionally specialized, just as the remainder of society's institutions have increasingly done. Functional specialization of societal institutions was made possible several thousand years ago by the discovery of agriculture. Agriculture created the "farmer" who could produce a surplus, and all sorts of "nonfarmers" who could now, for the first time, devote full time to tasks other than food-getting. Institutional specialization was accelerated by industrialization.

Likewise, some of the metaphysical groups are specialized in that they "deal with only a limited range of the supernatural. To fulfill the whole range of human requirements, it is necessary to seek membership in complementary groups" (Zaretsky and Leone 1974, p. xxv, point 9). Spiritual Frontiers Fellowship did not want to replace church for the devotees, but to supplement it.[6] Thus, SFF meetings were held on weekday evenings, with no activities scheduled for Sunday mornings. SFF and ARE have few activities for the entire family. For weddings and funerals, members must go to mainline churches or to a Spiritualist church.[7]

The metaphysical groups do not require a singular loyalty to any one group. The metaphysical philosophy, with its emphasis on creedlessness and individual experience as the arbiter of truth, is quite ecumenical, and allows for—indeed, encourages—participation in several metaphysical groups simultaneously. In the midwestern area where I did my participant observation, SFF and ARE had many members in common. The leaders, especially, joined more than one group. The two associations were thought to complement each other in various ways. ARE publishes more books and lessons than does SFF. SFF concentrates more on the psychic than does ARE, whereas ARE has a highly developed program of dream interpretation, lacking in SFF. A major concern for SFF is healing, and of course this is of great concern to ARE as well, since Edgar Cayce's records are concerned with physical healing (the "health readings"), as well as the implications of past lives and reincarnation (the "life readings"). But several SFF members felt that ARE's stand on healing was complicated by a belief that healing may disturb karmic responsibilities. These metaphysicians gained information on the psychic and healing from SFF and information on dreams from ARE.

SACKCLOTH IS NOT REQUIRED

The beliefs espoused by the metaphysical adherents do, to be sure, mark them as different from the American mainstream. But these beliefs are carried inside bodies that are leading quite ordinary *behavioral* lives. Neither ARE nor SFF require that their adherents come away from the American establishment in order to join the occult establishment. To these groups come people who want to improve themselves—who want to fill the void left by the feeling that "there must be something more to life"—but who do not want to make major changes in their lifestyles. Johnson (1981) makes the point that these groups do not advocate societal change; Bird (1983) says that they do not encourage moral responsibility.

Although metaphysical students do report notable changes in identity and sense of well-being, life-rending changes in lifestyle and physical comforts need not be made. Vegetarianism, celibacy, and refutation of material goods are not required. A spiritually mature person is not a saint or a monk; he is a success at his job and on good terms with his neighbors. This spiritual community also does not burden its followers with demands for their money or their time. The only support fellow travelers on the path to spiritual growth require is spiritual support.

Thus, ARE and SFF do not reject the values that "middle Americans" bring into the group with them. Instead, their beliefs, rituals, and structure epitomize and legitimate the individual autonomy which is so valued in American culture. These groups do not require their adherents to remove themselves from the mainstream of American society. Indeed, their acquired spiritual power and enhanced sense of self are meant to help them improve their positions in that society.

CONCLUSION

Metaphysical groups offer within their eclectic mix of ideas a philosophy that offers answers to the great questions of life and death and solutions for quotidian problems. They offer both a genuine search for meaning and practical ways of dispelling guilt or dealing with hypertension and drinking. Answers to life's grandest philosophical questions can be found in the metaphysical milieu. But so can solutions for life's most mundane irritations— headaches, backaches, little sons who will not take naps. Indeed, the study groups offered ways of curtailing the hostility aroused by the "toothpaste tube squeezed in the middle," ways of alleviating physical pain, and things to do for things we can do nothing about.

These answers are given in the context of a philosophy and structure that reflects, rather than opposes, American culture. The ontology apotheosizes individualism and autonomy. The epistemology reaches out toward the scientific way of knowing. The required behaviors fit comfortably inside a middle American lifestyle.

NOTES

1. At first, the ARE organization was the auspices for Edgar Cayce's clairvoyant readings which he gave nearly daily to people seeking help and advice. After Cayce's death in 1945, the records of his readings became the focus for the Association for Research and Enlightenment's work. He left behind records of over 14,000 readings given for more than 8,000 people over a period of 43 years (Melton 1986, 1987; Pastor 1974).

2. Spiritual Frontiers Fellowship, founded in 1956 in Illinois, had 8,000 members at its peak in the mid-1970s and today has about 4,000. The Association for Research and Enlightenment, founded in Virginia in 1931, claims a membership of between 50,000 and 100,000 members. The current figures for Spiritual Frontiers Fellowship were obtained from a regional area chapter leader in the Midwest, and corroborated by the national office on September 18, 1990, and September 25, 1990. The ARE national headquarters will not release membership figures, nor data on the number of regional councils or local study groups. The ARE membership office indicated that 50,000-100,000 members would be correct, depending on the exact year. They said "we say in our literature that we have 100,000 members by now." The number of study groups is impossible to know, they said, because groups re-affiliate (with the national office) or not, every year, and groups consolidate or fission. They would not say how many study groups are affiliated with the national office at present. Likewise, they said they had "no idea" how many council organizations were extant now, or in the past.

It should be noted, however, that the loose social structures of metaphysical organizations allow adherents to attend group functions without becoming members. In these organizations, where participation without affiliation is possible—for both members and study groups—it is understandable that "membership" figures are somewhat difficult to assess.

Also, these groups have had impacts beyond their membership. A recent Gallup poll showed that although only one-fourth of a nationwide sample had heard of "New Age," as many as 50 percent espoused belief in some of the New Age beliefs, such as extrasensory perception; one-third believed in mental telepathy; one-fourth believed in astrology (Associated Press 1992).

3. See also Johnson (1981, p. 52) who says that the New Religious movements are "preoccupied with health and personal effectiveness." Long (1983, pp. 145, 152-155) says that groups like these (and many other religious entities) have adopted a program of "medical magic applied to the everyday life problems of individuals." But "it is not pure magic" in Weber's sense. It "combines elements" of magic, religion, and secular medicine. To Long, "medical magic exemplifies the secularization of religion," but at the same time, it "involves a serious and rather systematic effort

to resacralize the world." He asserts, too, that medical magic's "combination of sacred and secular gives religion unique adaptive fitness for advanced society. Its secularity makes it plausible to modern individuals as a response to their troubled existence, and its sacredness makes that response more powerful to them than mundane expertise alone." Wilson (1990, pp. 274, 284, 288) says that "religion in this [modern] period becomes instrumental in a way which characterizes magic, although with an apparently more scientific mode of explanation." He posits these characteristics of modern religions: "they reflect concern with subjective, psychic well-being rather than with positive otherworldly objectivity"; they are "more likely to endorse the hedonistic values of society as legitimate goals," to "reflect the degree of rationalization that obtains in the wider society," thus to "emphasize reason," and to draw "assumptions, style, and methodologies" from science.

4. This analysis of titles probably underestimates the pragmatism of these activities because esoteric titles sometimes hid a pragmatic orientation that came to light when further description was available. For example, the description of a workshop titled "The Fourth Dimension" said "Inspiration as to how you can use your full range of consciousness to accomplish your goals and purposes—stimulation of self-confidence through recognition of who you are and why you are here."

5. This is, of course, an exaggeration. As Luckmann (1967, p. 97) notes, "the sense of autonomy which characterizes the typical person in modern society" is "somewhat illusory." Modern man is freer than primitives, who have fewer choices. But he is not infinitely free because he is still a part of larger systems. Everything he is "free" to do may not be adaptive for his own survival. "Although men are metabolically separate from one another, and although consciousness is individual, men are not self-sufficient and their autonomy is relative and slight. Men are parts of larger systems upon which their continued existence is contingent" (Rappaport 1976, p. 93).

6. At the *national* level the stated goals of SFF and ARE are different. Spiritual Frontiers Fellowship wants to bring the churches to an appreciation of psychic phenomena, as well as to promote individual spiritual growth. ARE's goals include research to trace the efficacy of Edgar Cayce's readings, as well as enlightenment, or aiding spiritual growth. But, at the *grass-roots* level, the goals of the national leaders hold little sway; the metaphysical groups serve as a religion surrogate for their members. National SFF is concerned that the leaders be churchgoers, but the grass-roots members do not go to church; they go to metaphysical meetings instead. While I was doing participant observation in SFF study groups, a colleague was doing the same in ARE study groups. These study groups were nearly interchangeable. The primary goal of the members, as shown by many measures, was to get practical help for everyday living, and to add "meaning" to their lives.

7. Exceptions to this are the Unity School of Christianity, the Divine Science Church, and Spiritualist churches, who do tend to have Sunday services and pastors who perform life crisis rites.

REFERENCES

Associated Press. 1992. "'New Age' Ideas Cross Boundaries of the Movement." *Roanoke Times and World-News,* February 8.

Bellah, R.N., R. Madsen, W.M. Sullivan, A. Swidler, and S.M. Tipton. 1985. *Habits of the Heart: Individualism and Commitment in American Life.* New York: Harper and Row.

Bird, F. 1983. "The Pursuit of Innocence: New Religious Movements and Moral Accountability." Pp. 54-69 in *Religion and Religiosity in America,* edited by J.K. Hadden and T.E. Long. New York: Crossroads.

Durkheim, E. [1912] 1961. *The Elementary Forms of the Religious Life,* translated by J.W. Swain. New York: Collier Books.

Hayes, P. 1971. *Know Yourself.* Miami, FL: Patricia Hayes.

Hsu, F.L.K. 1972. "American Core Values and National Character." Pp. 51-66 in *Psychological Anthropology,* edited by F.L.K. Hsu. Cambridge, MA: Schenkman.

Johnson, B. 1981. "A Sociological Perspective on the New Religions." Pp. 51-66 in *In Gods we Trust: New Patterns of Religious Pluralism in America,* edited by T. Robbins and D. Anthony. New Brunswick, NJ: Transaction.

Judah, J.S. 1967. *The History and Philosophy of the Metaphysical Movements in America.* Philadelphia: Westminster.

Long, T.E. 1983. "Religion and Therapeutic Action: From Healing Power to Medical Magic." Pp. 141-156 in *Religion and Religiosity in America,* edited by J.K. Hadden and T.E. Long. New York: Crossroads.

Luckmann, T. 1967. *The Invisible Religion: The Problem of Religion in Modern Society.* New York: Macmillan.

Malinowski, B. 1931. "Culture." *Encyclopedia of the Social Sciences,* Vol. 4, pp. 621-646.

Marsella, A.J. 1985. "Cultures, Self, and Mental Disorder." Pp. 281-307 in *Culture and Self,* edited by A.J. Marsella, G. DeVos, and F.L.K. Hsu. New York: Tavistock.

Marty, M. 1970. "The Occult Establishment." *Social Research* 37: 212-230.

McGuire, M.B. 1988. *Ritual Healing in Suburban America.* New Brunswick, NJ: Rutgers University Press.

Melton, J.G. 1986. *Biographical Dictionary of American Cult and Sect Leaders.* New York: Garland.

————. 1987. *The Encyclopedia of American Religions.* 2nd ed. Detroit: Gale.

Pastor, J.F. 1974. "The Edgar Cayce Records: Their Philosophy, Their Use, and Their Effect." Unpublished paper, Anthropology Department, University of Michigan.

Rappaport, R.A. 1976. "Liturgies and Lies." *International Yearbook of Sociology and Religion* 10: 75-104.

Swatos, W.H., Jr. 1990. "Spiritualism as a Religion of Science." *Social Compass* 37: 471-482.

Tocqueville, A. de. [1835-1840] 1969. *Democracy in America,* translated by G. Lawrence, edited by J. P. Mayer. New York: Doubleday.

Wagner, M.B. 1983a. *Metaphysics in Midwestern America.* Columbus: Ohio State University Press.

————. 1983b. "Spiritual Frontiers Fellowship." Pp. 45-62 in *Alternatives to American Mainline Churches,* edited by J.H. Fichter. New York: Rose of Sharon Press.

————. 1984. "Metaphysics in Midwestern America." *Journal of Popular Culture* 17: 131-140.

————. 1990. *God's Schools: Choice and Compromise in American Society.* New Brunswick, NJ: Rutgers University Press.

Weber, M. [1922] 1963. *The Sociology of Religion,* translated by E. Fischoff. Boston: Beacon Press.

Wilson, B.R. 1990. *The Social Dimensions of Sectarianism: Sects and New Religious Movements in Contemporary Society.* Oxford: Clarendon Press.

Zaretsky, I.I., and M.P. Leone. 1974. *Religious Movements in Contemporary America.* Princeton, NJ: Princeton University Press.

QUASI-RELIGIONS AND CULTURAL MOVEMENTS:
CONTEMPORARY WITCHCRAFT
AS A CHURCHLESS RELIGION

Mary Jo Neitz

ABSTRACT

This paper examines quasi-religions as cultural movements with beliefs and practices defined as spiritual at their core, but lacking the structure of conventional religions and religious movement organizations. Although such loosely bounded networks face problems in mobilizing participants and maintaining the movement, cultural movements play a crucial part in cultural change. Through examining one particular movement—Wicca, or contemporary witchcraft—this paper explores how people develop and maintain contact within a cultural movement's networks and how they define and defend boundaries both among themselves and in reference to outsiders. I will examine briefly some of the ways that individuals become part of Wicca, the contrasting meanings of initiation among two branches of Wicca—Dianic (women only) and Neopagan (men and women) witches—and how the linkages that develop between

Religion and the Social Order, Volume 4, pages 127-149.
Copyright © 1994 by JAI Press Inc.
All rights of reproduction in any form reserved.
ISBN: 1-55938-763-7

individuals facilitate the movement of symbols and practices. I also discuss some of the difficulties articulated by leaders and members related to the lack of structure and the internal pressures for more conventional churchly forms. I show that structurelessness has different meanings for different Wiccan traditions. On the basis of examining rituals, origin stories, and individuals' narratives, I argue that the different meanings are rooted in gendered experiences.

In the research on both social and religious movements, there is a new focus on movements as contexts for symbolic expressions and for practices through which meanings in modern society are contested and negotiated. European sociologists working on the New Social Movements claim that in post-industrial societies we need to shift our analysis from political movements to one that encompasses cultural movements (Touraine 1985; Offe 1985; Melucci 1985). Arguing that "contemporary social conflicts are not just political, since they affect the system's cultural production," Melucci suggests that the new social movements or movement areas are "increasingly autonomous" from political systems (1985, pp. 798-799). These scholars argue that while militant activity occasionally occurs in these new social movements, it is the on-going personal involvement in an alternative culture that is central to participation. In the sociology of religion as well there is new attention to religion as a "cultural resource" that can be "a vehicle of change, challenge, or conservation" (Beckford 1989, p. 170). Indeed, Beckford suggests that as the ties between religion and "natural communities" become further attenuated, it "may be better to conceptualize religion as a cultural resource than as a social institution" (1989, p. 171). One of the advantages of the "quasi-religion" formulation (Greil and Rudy 1990) is that it highlights the degree to which cultural negotiations occur not just in ecclesiastical bodies but also in the everyday practices of ordinary members.

Of concern for this paper are quasi-religions with beliefs and practices defined as spiritual at the core, but which lack the structure of conventional religions and religious movement organizations. Although "cultural movements" made up of loosely bounded networks can be crucial to cultural change, they face problems in mobilizing participants and maintaining the movement. I explore here some of the structural forms existing in these loosely organized contexts, how people develop and maintain contact within a cultural movement's networks, and how they define and defend boundaries both among themselves and in reference to outsiders.

The processes of central importance in movements of cultural transformation differ from those stressed by social scientists who study organizations or social movements. Movements aimed at changing cultural values or individual practices (e.g., the animal rights movement or vegetarianism) can be contrasted with more traditional social movements. In cultural movements much of the activity is accomplished when individuals act as "carriers" of changed values and behaviors across different contexts and settings (Gusfield 1981; Fine and Kleinman 1983). The new social movements and increasing salience of identity politics (e.g., Phelan 1989; Taylor and Whittier 1992) may be attributed to the increasing privatization of American society (Robbins and Bromley 1992), but this does not mean that these movements are necessarily more individualistic than older social and religious movements that emphasized transcendent deities or had more formal organization. Rather, we are just beginning to specify the social processes through which movements of cultural transformation work.

Gusfield's (1981) notion of a "fluid" perspective for studying social movements is especially suited for movements of cultural transformation. In contrast with a "linear perspective," a fluid perspective is not limited to the study of organizations and associations; it may be used to examine diffuse processes and collections of movements, the changing of meanings, and the transformations of values. Gusfield's fluid perspective is useful for analyzing social and cultural change because it makes the ties between movements and the ways individuals move from movement to movement central to his research agenda. The fact that individuals carry with them the symbols and practices of a social movement, sometimes even when they are not active in an organization, has implications for cultural transformation at both the public and private level: as Gusfield suggests, we can begin to understand how the nature of public discourse shifts when what had been unthinkable becomes taken for granted (Gusfield 1981, pp. 325-326).[1]

Gusfield's approach helps us to capture the personal and cultural changes which are the focus of many contemporary religious and cultural movements, including those we might designate as "quasi-religions." His notion of "carrying over" shifts the analysis of social movement success from the stability of organizational structures to the diffusion of symbols throughout a culture. His concept of "carrying on" suggests the conceptualization, developed below, of initiation as the transformation of the self.

In this paper these ideas about cultural movements are explored in the context of examining one particular cultural movement—Wicca, or contemporary witchcraft. I will examine briefly some of the ways that individuals become part of Wicca, the contrasting meanings of initiation among two branches of Wicca—Dianic and Neopagan witches, and how the linkages that develop between individuals facilitate the movement of symbols and practices. I also discuss some of the difficulties articulated by leaders and members related to the lack of structure and the internal pressures for more conventional churchly forms. In attempting to understand the latter, it becomes clear that structurelessness has different meanings for different Wiccan traditions. On the basis of examining rituals, origin stories, and individuals' narratives I argue that these different meanings are rooted in gendered experiences.

CONTEMPORARY WITCHCRAFT AS A QUASI-RELIGION

Contemporary witchcraft encompasses a broad spectrum of nature- and goddess-oriented beliefs and practices. Although groups (circles or covens) exist, they tend to be small and fluid; the meaningful collectivities are permeable, loosely structured, overlapping networks of individuals. Witches' beliefs and rituals are at variance with those of the dominant culture, but they believe society to be on the cusp of a cultural and social shift of which they themselves are the forerunners. They can thus clearly be classified as movements of cultural transformation (Neitz 1990b). Within this broad spectrum my work contrasts "Dianic" witches, who see themselves as feminist and meet in women-only circles, with "Neopagan" witches, who are loosely based in Gardnerian tradition and meet in heterosexual groups (Adler 1986; Neitz 1990a).[2]

While witches see themselves as engaged in a spiritual practice, many reject applying the word "religion" to their activities. Some explicitly identify witchcraft as "the old religion" (of pre-Christian Europe), but for others the idea of religion connotes forms of organization that are anathema. The emerging category of "quasi-religion" fits them well: they are not organized in ways traditionally associated with religion.

Wiccans view themselves as resisting organization. The basic unit is a circle or coven, often composed of fewer than ten people and lasting less than two years. An experienced priest and/or priestess may lead the circle. Disputes frequently cause groups to split, and relations between groups are likely to be based in personal ties among individuals who trained with the same teachers, or between teachers and their students. Since the mid-1970s there have been a number of attempts to create organizations linking covens. These larger organizations provide ways of making contacts and sharing information. However, they have had very limited success in terms of either creating a resource base or defining a common set of rules that member covens agree will govern their activities (Adler 1986, pp. 99-107). Such organizations exercise very limited control over member covens, and only a small portion of covens belong to them (Neitz 1992). Adler's description of the craft as decentralized with autonomous covens continues to apply today (1986, p. 99). The relative absence of traditional forms of organization requires a new, more fluid perspective on the relation between structure and process in movements of transformation.

The current witchcraft revival can be traced to Gerald Gardner in England in the 1940s. Gardner claimed to have been initiated in 1939 into one of the few covens in the British Isles that had lasted through the centuries. He saw himself as reviving Britain's ancient religion. Gardner's witchcraft is a nature religion oriented to the Goddess of birth and rebirth and her consort, the Lord of the forests. Although Gardner's claim to have been initiated into the last remaining Wiccan coven has been challenged, he did draw together a group of people and develop an attractive and coherent set of rituals. At first Wicca grew through a line of initiates, but after the repeal of anti-witchcraft laws in England in 1951, Gardner published a series of books that presented his version of witchcraft to a wider audience (e.g., Gardner 1955, 1959). Kelly (1983) and Adler (1986, pp. 80-86) argue that the basic form of ritual used by witches today originated with Gardner. It is he who put in place the sequence of steps: casting a circle, consecrating participants, calling the spirits of the four directions, invoking deities, raising group energy, working spells, sharing a ceremonial meal, and unwinding the circle. Dianic Wicca emerged out of the feminist movement in the late 1960s. It departs from the traditions I am calling here Neopagan or neo-Gardnerian witchcraft, most significantly in recognizing only female deities and practicing within exclusively female groups, but it too follows this basic ritual form set forth by Gardner.[3]

Neopagans and Dianics alike see themselves as distinct from "religions" where a "congregation" follows the lead of a "pastor." They see all initiated witches as co-participants who work together to bring forth the magic in a performance of ritual. Rather than congregational or ecclesiastic organizations, one finds among Wiccans networks of individuals who move in and out of formally constituted groups (circles or covens), which, however, tend to coalesce and dissolve, while the individuals continue to be hooked together through formal and informal networks. They share a community, but it is not based on residential propinquity nor on membership in a common association.

The next sections explore how individuals are recruited into the movement and come to identify themselves as members through participating in initiation rituals.

CARRYING OVER: MOVEMENT THROUGH ALTERNATIVE CULTURE

In comparison with evangelical Christians or the Moonies, Wicca has no explicit strategy for recruitment of individuals into the movement. It is a matter of principle (and a point of pride) for many Wiccans that they do not proselytize. However, for support and for new members Wicca depends on a cultural milieu that includes alternative healing practices, social movements (especially parts of the ecological and feminist movements), various spiritual practices, and fantasy role playing games. This alternative cultural milieu provides an environment within which Wiccan symbols and practices defuse. Individuals in this environment become aware of Wicca, and some become witches themselves.

One of the common ways for individuals to begin to explore witchcraft is through taking a class. Classes are offered by practicing witches through community alternative schools, local bookstores, and various spiritual growth centers. The topics may be oriented toward practice (e.g., "Herbal Magic," "Introduction to the Tarot") or they may be more historical (e.g., "Goddesses of Ancient Greece"). They may be general (e.g., "Beginning Magic") or specific (e.g., "Healing the Third Chaktra"). When some individuals move from studying about magic to a desire to practice it, a circle may form among participants in a class. Or, individuals may make contacts in a class with a teacher or a priestess that lead to greater involvement. The teacher may start a circle or agree to admit the individual into an established group.

One of the best known of the early feminist Witches' circles, Ursa Maior, began as a class. Deborah Bender, one of the original members, tells about the start of the group:

> We all started together as members of a cooperative class on women's spirituality, and the people who lasted out the class and decided to continue meeting became the group. And, we met like weekly for about a year and a half. Some of the women were more leaders than others, but everyone was a full participating member, and we did everything by consensus. But some of us foresaw that over time, you know, people's interests would change and, they might want to drop out or become less active, and we wanted to bring new people in. But we couldn't get consensus over how or when to introduce new people because we had, by then, a really tight unit that knew each other really well. So what in fact finally happened is that by the time we finally got an agreement to open it up, we were already running out of steam (fieldnotes, September 1986).

The women of Ursa Maior began with a class on ancient goddesses, offered through a local "free school" in the 1970s. Through readings and discussions, they began to know and trust each other, and, at the same time, began to wonder if they could put into practice some of the things they were reading about in their study group. Soon they were inventing rituals.

Other groups began as support groups. The following woman talks about initiating such a group:

> Every time I went to Michigan [Women's Music Festival] I loved it, and every time I came home again I felt like I was going to die. Because I didn't have that support at home, and it was really hard, and it hurts. And so about three or four years ago I put up posters and I said that I wanted to start a spirituality group.... It was as a support group around issues of women's spirituality. So what happened is that a group of women came together, and we agreed on what we wanted to do together.... Twenty-five women said they were interested, and eight women showed up, and it turned out to be a core of five women that met for two years (fieldnotes, September 1986).

This woman did not use the word witch in her posters but rather called for a Women's Spirituality support group. However, unlike the women who began Ursa Maior, described in the previous quote, she and the other women who formed the core of the group knew that they were interested in learning to practice magic from the beginning of the group.

Yet both circles began with individuals who had a relative lack of experience and who gained experience together through participating in the group itself. Another way that circles are formed is through training by a pre-existing coven.

In the following example, the speakers describe their coven as "birthed from another coven." The other coven was officially closed to new members yet felt some responsibility to offer a service to its community. The speakers talk about their own introduction to witchcraft as well as how they have set up the boundaries of their own group:

> What they did, they put on a summer solstice celebration and the handbills were out, and it was in the bookstore and everybody knew about it. So we went to the summer solstice celebration, and there were 50 or 60 women. There were all types. Then they had a map of the city and they said, if you're interested then write your name and address down... Then people in that group facilitated people getting together to talk.
>
> We went through this process with this other closed coven where we had like visitors' passes... We were allowed to attend everything...as long as we would contact them. And there were particular people in the coven that had issues with new people coming in, so we always had to call the people we knew had issues with it to make sure that it was okay. Anyway, we continued like that for about four months, and eventually some other women did come together, and we decided to join them.
>
> We have a cohesive group now and we have developed a lot. And our first responsibility is to ourselves.... We have set up three levels of meetings. We have meetings that are absolutely closed, where we are discussing coven business that is really private. We have meetings that are semi-open for women who are interested in our group and have expressed an interest in perhaps joining. And then major open things like the major holidays like solstice and that kind of thing. And we are just going to wait until those women say, "we are interested in joining"[4] (fieldnotes, September 1986).

This somewhat more formal system whereby an existing group trains new members who then break off and form their own group is more common among Neopagans than among Dianics. However, some Dianic groups, like the one discussed above, adopt parts of it.

In these three descriptions of group formation we also learn about the community ties that nourish the development of such groups. All the speakers, as well as other Dianic women, consider themselves to be active feminists, and are participants in the larger women's community. They also participate in alternative institutions such as the free schools. The feminist bookstore is an important institution in the women's community and in Dianic networks. It is the place where potential participants can find books, and often jewelry and other symbols such as cards and bumper stickers, that identify participants to one another. It is also the place where announcements are posted, helping individuals to find others with similar interests. In an important way Dianic witches' circles are intertwined with the women's community: the broader cultural milieu provides structure both in terms of material resources and cultural norms. Focusing on groups—the circles and covens—would miss much of what the culture is about.

For example, the second speaker begins with a reference to the Michigan Women's Music Festival held yearly in August. This represents a specific kind of tie. In the first place the festival is run by and for lesbians and is the major cultural and social event on the national lesbian calendar. So when the second speaker says she needs support, it is not only support for being a witch, but also for being a lesbian. Second, the Michigan festival draws women from all over the United States as well as from other countries. It is a nodal point in the lesbian feminist network, and has been central in the transmission of goddess spirituality through lesbian and feminist cultures.

We can now see what "carrying over" means in this context. Consider the following example which generalizes the experiences of many of the Dianics with whom I spoke. A lesbian goes to the Michigan festival where, along with a truly bewildering variety of sights and sounds, she sees Z Budapest bless the festival from the stage, hears references to the goddess in some of the songs, sees jewelry with goddess symbols for sale in the crafts area, and walks by a place where a mass of women are becoming "initiated" as witches. She goes home. At her local feminist bookstore she sees some of the same symbols, and notices an announcement for a local solstice celebration. A lesbian friend, who has attended other rituals, suggests that they attend. She finds the ritual intriguing and asks where she can learn more. There is a class offered through the YWCA where she took a class on bike repair for women the previous year. She enrolls in a class on "Goddesses in Everywoman." At the end of the class she is interested in joining a group. She thinks she may be a witch. She is ready for initiation. She has come to this point through her embeddedness in a national lesbian network and her contacts with local feminist and alternative culture institutions.

This description has focused on processes for Dianics, but similar processes exist for other witches. There are social worlds in addition to women's spirituality that overlap with Neopaganism. Gatherings sponsored by the Society for Creative Anachronism, science fiction readers, and fantasy game players are all places where an individual may encounter witches with their symbols and expressive forms. New Age bookstores serve a variety of countercultural populations and provide spaces for people to meet. Of course, just as not all feminists are witches, only a small portion of those who play dungeons and dragons or attend science fiction conventions are witches. But the important point is that Wiccans' density in these networks is great compared to what one might find in more mainstream locations, and the symbols of Wicca are reinforced within these groups, so that some recruitment of individuals does occur. The concept of carrying over emphasizes the cultural aspects of participation in social and cultural movements. In this way it is different from other perspectives that focus on recruitment or mobilization. Rather than emphasizing how social movement organizations recruit individuals to be members, this formulation suggests that we consider how ideas and symbols move through (or among) networks and organizations, carried by individuals, some of whom may not be committed members of any one group.

CARRYING ON: INITIATION
AND THE TRANSFORMATION OF THE SELF

Whereas I use Gusfield's notion of "carrying over" as referring to contact and the sharing of symbols among networks and organizations, I use "carrying on" to refer to the transformation of the self. Participants learn (sometimes in an organizational context) new practices, forms of expression, even rules for discourse. They come to think about the world in new terms and to see themselves in new ways. The ways that Dianic witches think about initiation reveal something of the dynamics of Dianic witchcraft as a cultural movement closely allied with radical feminism. Again this formulation emphasizes that the identity transformation does not depend on continued participation in a religious organization. In the analysis of initiation we also can see more clearly how Dianic witchcraft differs from Neopagan witchcraft, where initiation practices more clearly delineate the relation between a person and a group.

Among traditional Neopagans, initiation signals the acceptance of the individual into a culture of co-celebrants. Yet, it is always the case that some are "more equal" than others, and unlike Dianics, Gardnerian and neo-Gardnerian groups formally recognize differences in knowledge and experience by offering first, second, and third degree initiation. Neopagan Wiccan initiations enact a symbolic death and rebirth: "In the Wiccan rite, this process is symbolized by the binding and blindfolding, the challenge, the accepted ordeal, the final removal of the bonds and blindfolding, and the anointing for a new life" (Farrar and Farrar 1981, p. 10).[5] The initiation occurs "a year and a day" after entry into the coven. In Gardnerian and neo-Gardnerian covens (such as the Farrars'), where sex polarity is considered important for working magic, a man initiates women, and a woman initiates men. In addition, only a second or third degree witch can initiate. In other traditions (such as

Starhawk's fairie tradition) the initiation is conducted by the group as a whole, and the sexual polarity is less central (Starhawk 1979).

Initiations to the second and third degrees occur after some time has passed. Esoteric knowledge must be learned and skills demonstrated. Additional degrees indicate increased mastery of skills and the possibility of greater responsibility. Increased magical abilities and psychic powers are symbolized by specific elements in the rituals (see Farrar and Farrar 1981, pp. 21-39). The second degree initiation gives the right to be high priestess or priest in one's own coven, but still under the authority of a third degree priestess. After attaining third degree initiation, a person may lead a completely autonomous coven. Second and third degree witches who remain in the coven of their high priestess may constitute a council of elders.

For Dianic witches, "initiation" has a very different meaning because it places importance on the participant recognizing her own power. The Dianic conception of initiation symbolizes the women's striving for autonomy. For Dianics, being a witch is connected to being a woman and being self-conscious about one's power. Some Dianics have argued to me that, seen this way, they cannot imagine that another person—and especially not a male—could confer the status of witch upon a woman. They argue that one is a witch by right of birth.[6]

This interpretation is consistent with the WITCH documents distributed within the women's movement in the late 1960s and widely anthologized, including publication in *Sisterhood is Powerful*. The excerpt below clearly locates the power of the witch within the person.

> WITCH is an all-woman Everything. It's theater, revolution, magic, terror, joy, garlic flowers, spells. It's an awareness that witches and gypsies were the original guerrillas and resistance fighters against oppression—particularly the oppression of women—down through the ages... There is no "joining" WITCH. If you are a women and dare to look within yourself, you are a Witch. You make your own rules. You are free and beautiful. You can be invisible or evident in how you choose to make your witch-self known. You can form your own Coven of sister Witches (thirteen is a cozy number for a group) and do your own actions.
>
> You are a Witch by saying aloud, "I am a Witch" three times, and *thinking about that*. You are a Witch by being female, untamed, angry, joyous, and immortal (Morgan 1970, pp. 539-540).

In the Dianic context becoming a witch is a matter of self-recognition— a woman acknowledging herself as a witch. Witches within the feminist movement have not been entirely comfortable with the notion that all that is necessary is to say that you are a witch three times, but they do view initiation as self-transformation.[7] It is also a matter of identifying with a history of power and persecution. Contemporary witches identify with the midwives and healers, practitioners of the old religion, who were burned during the witchcraft persecutions. When one is told that "rebellion is a sin of witchcraft" (a quote from the Bible—I Samuel, 15:23), then identifying oneself as a witch can be identified with seeing oneself as a rebellious woman (Morgan 1970, p. 539). In Dianic circles, the same phrase is used to describe acknowledging publicly that one is a witch as is used to talk about acknowledging that one is a lesbian: one "comes out" as a witch. In both cases the use implies recognition of the identity by self and the sharing of that identity with others, although it does not mean that others need to validate the identity.

My respondents confirm the importance of self-initiation in their talk:

> I am self-initiated. That was the most powerful moment in my life. It was a wonderful thing to be able to do that for myself. It was the beginning of the rest of my life... But I would like to declare myself in front of the group.

Another woman described her experience:

> I was self-initiated... I said it three times, and I decided if I could print it on the computer that would do it. I "said it, manifest it, and declared it" when I typed it out and put it on the wall. But it changed everything for me.

Becoming a witch for these women involves a change in values, a new sense of the political and moral order. But it also involves a changed sense of where one is located in relation to the moral and political order. Many witches described becoming a witch as coming to see themselves as empowered—as individuals whose actions could have significance in the world—rather than as pawns or victims.

Initiation for Dianics is not tied to membership in a particular group, although it is supported by membership in a group of like-minded individuals, as is indicated by this woman:

> I have a political commitment... Your political commitment might be very different from mine, but I suspect that we would have some of the same struggles in the outside world. That we came back together in a closed group we would appreciate being able to get in balance again. Although the thing we were working on didn't have a thing to do with each other.

A Dianic's acknowledgment of herself as a witch is supported by her participation in a circle with other women who have a similar identification. She carries this transformed self-understanding with her, and it has ramifications for her actions as she "carries on" with life activities.

For both Neopagan and Dianic witches, initiation has a critical symbolic value. These rituals effectively define participation in the cultural movement, and the analysis here has attempted to highlight how expressive rituals affirm the transformation of the self and the carrying over of new meanings through the countercultural milieu somewhat independent of organizational participation. However, their ideology of "churchlessness," implicit in the initiation rituals, contains an understanding of "leaderlessness" at odds with the movement's needs for some degree of on-going organization. Some long-time participants in both traditions are now arguing for establishing more churchly forms of organization.

TENSIONS WITHIN A CHURCHLESS RELIGION: THE PROBLEMS OF LEADERSHIP

The definition of what it means to be a witch, symbolized in the process of initiation, makes the nature of both leading and following ambiguous. There is ambiguity in how leaders are designated and what rights and responsibilities they have. There is no clear understanding of obligations of followers. Also, churchlessness—especially the lack of structure and physical spaces—makes it difficult for individuals to transfer membership when they move from one community to another. Churchlessness is associated with marginality of a very practical nature, as when Wiccan rituals are not listed in the local telephone book or the weekend newspaper's roster of church services. Even when a newcomer locates a group, finding out whether the newcomer's knowledge and experience match the group's can be difficult.

Among Neopagans there is an emerging discourse about developing ways to establish "credentials" for both members and followers beyond the personal lineages of teachers and their students. Among some Wiccans there is even talk about establishing congregational forms.[8]

The assumption of both neo-Gardnerian and Dianic witchcraft is that all participants are priests or priestesses, that is, all initiated members of a circle have both the capability and the responsibility to share in performing the ritual and creating the magic. Wiccan circles generally do not have leaders who pastor the congregation and receive respect and financial support in return. Even among Neopagan groups that follow Gardnerian ideas of hierarchy—those which initiate into second and third degrees, with only third degree recipients allowed to split off and form their own independent covens—reject the notion of a paid clergy. Believing that money should not be a barrier to acquiring the secret knowledge, many witches adhere to norms that prohibit charging for performing rituals or initiations.[9]

Yet witches, in their circles, interacting with other witches within their communities, and as part of a national cultural movement, have leaders, even if—in theory—they have no "professional clergy." Some of these leaders are "media stars," people who made reputations through their writing. Some of them have received publicity through reports in the national press; other writers are mainly known among Neopagans. Others are local teachers, diviners, and ritualists. The roles of "leader" and "follower" in this churchless religion must be continually negotiated.

Both leaders and nonleaders express their frustrations with a system in which roles are not clearly defined for either. Both recognize that individuals within the movement have different levels of expertise and ability across a wide spectrum of activities. Both talk about how the performance of religious activities is hindered by the problems that the movement has in training followers and recognizing leaders.

Among both Dianics and Neopagans the more experienced witches often feel that their efforts on behalf of the movement go largely unrecognized. This is in part due to the lack of specification about what constitutes a leader. In an article on the women's movement of the 1970s, Jo Freeman described what she calls "the tyranny of structurelessness." Freeman observed that a movement which claims it has no leaders gives up the processes which empower leaders and foster their responsibility to the group. She also noted that, when the movement receives some attention in the public eye, the media will choose spokespeople for the movement even when the movement denies that such people exist. When individuals become public spokespeople for a movement under those conditions, the movement has virtually no control over what they say (Freeman 1972). The churchlessness of Wicca has fostered both of these problems for both Dianics and Neopagans.

Organizations at the grass-roots level rarely participate in choosing leaders for the movement. Recognition, both within the movement and—to an even greater degree—by the national media, tends to go to witches who are easily accessible, either because they have published books on witchcraft or because they are founders or leaders of a visible, national organization, such as one of the Wiccan networks.[10] These writers and activists often have a good deal of ability as well as dedication to the movement; nonetheless, the processes through which they become designated as leaders is strikingly different from those of movements with more formal organizational structures.

The kinds of people who are most likely to be publicly accessible and to be chosen as media stars are also different from the ritual leaders and teachers— the "high priestesses"—who are more usual leaders within Neopagan Wicca, which continues to promote the model of witchcraft as a highly secretive, quasi-underground association. The problem of defining the role of the leader is complicated by the traditional norm of secrecy which supports a complex, but largely unacknowledged, division of labor with national leaders whose reputations can be based on publications and attention from the mass media, and local leaders who lead ritual, teach, and do divining.

One solution currently being debated is to move toward congregationalism. This would entail a break with the norms of secrecy of the past (although becoming a public "Wiccan church" would be self-chosen). A few groups now have public spaces—sanctuaries or temples—with regularly performed publicly announced rituals and clergy who are at least partly financially supported by the "congregation." Leaders who argue for this change claim that they meet people who are not interested in becoming magical adepts themselves (the traditional Wiccan priestesses and priests) but would like to be able to celebrate seasonal holidays—such as winter and summer solstices—with a non-Christian, nature-based, spiritually charged ritual. This demand may create the opportunity for Wiccan leaders of various sorts to become more like paid clergy, and in a few places Wiccan "churches" have emerged with some congregational characteristics.[11]

Still, only a few can support themselves entirely on the basis of such activities. Those for whom Wicca is a primary source of income are likely to supplement their income through doing psychic readings or healings, through their writing, or through the contributions of members of a national network. Any consensus regarding concerns about standardized training and credentials seems far in the future.

STRUCTURELESSNESS AND THE RELEVANCE OF GENDER

Compared to conventional religions, both Dianic and Neopagan Wicca appear churchless. Yet their resistance to more churchly forms has somewhat different sources. Dianic commitment to nonhierarchical forms is rooted in radical feminism. Although Neopagans also value a nearly anarchic freedom from constraining rules and structures, they continue to reflect the origins of Gardnerian practices in secret societies. The two traditions draw on different narratives about their origins, and reflect different ideas about the goals of a spiritual journey, differences, I will argue, that are rooted in gendered experiences. These women's spiritual journeys represent an emancipatory movement toward autonomy in the context of a world they see dominated by patriarchal structures. The neo-Gardnerian rituals, based largely in the nineteenth-century male secret societies, represent learning discipline and mastering gnostic wisdom through submission to a group which views itself as outside of the dominant culture.[12]

While practices requiring the discipline and submission of an individual's will are common to spiritual journeys, these practices seem particularly designed to encourage spiritual growth in males, whose early socialization fosters the development of independence. Consider, for example, the prototypical Christian saint: a young man blessed with wealth and intelligence living a life of indulgence who changes his ways, gives up earthly pleasures, and submits to divine will. We can see in this a kind of balance to a life previously characterized by excesses in the other direction. For women, however, these same sorts of spiritual practices do not offer an opportunity to become a more balanced human being by countering their gendered socialization.[13] The socialization of women (and other subordinate groups) has tended to encourage the development of relational and connected ways of experiencing the world (Chodorow 1978; Gilligan 1982; Keller 1986). Goddess symbols and rituals ask that women learn to exercise willfulness. In the words of feminist theologian Carol Christ, the goddess symbolism offers "a positive evaluation of will" so that a woman is encouraged to "know her will and believe that her will is valid and to believe that her will can be achieved in the world" (1987, pp. 127-128). Women who have been socialized to be connected and relational come to the practice of witchcraft to learn how to be autonomous. This gives structurelessness a different meaning for Dianics and requires somewhat different forms than we observe for Neopagans.

WOMEN AND RESISTANCE TO MALE DOMINATION

In the emerging women's spirituality movement rituals and narratives focus on the empowerment of women. This is not an exclusive focus, and in fact there is some tension between ideals of leaderless groups and the attraction of the charismatic leader.

The notion that a "real priestess" has special powers that enable her to counsel and heal and teach, as well as to lead inspiring rituals, runs against the egalitarian notion that each woman in the group is a priestess who shares skills with other women. In a few cases, the first model works for a group: small circles or covens achieve ways of working together that members find psychologically supportive and spiritually sustaining without anyone taking a dominate role. Yet leaders who emerge in the Wiccan community or the national movement feel they are measured by both standards. They claim they get criticized for exercising any special talents because that demonstrates their separateness from others and violates the norms of equality. Yet they feel they are also expected to possess special spiritual qualities that will produce rituals that achieve the desired results. Few women leaders feel that they get the recognition they deserve for whatever it is that they do, either from the followers or from other priestesses.

For some leaders the lack of recognition for their role leads to ambivalence about asserting their own authority. Dianic Wiccans may be reluctant to endorse the authority of leaders because of factors specific to their experiences as women. Because it is new for women to have power—especially in a religious context—they feel reluctant to give their power over to any leader. While women accede that they may be willing to choose to let a leader make a decision in a specific situation, the idea of giving a role or person authority in an on-going sense makes many participants uneasy. One woman said to me, "We also don't want to give up our power. Because it is so new."

Some women who are new to Dianic witchcraft talk about not only needing to learn new practices but having to recover from the damage done to them by patriarchy. A nationally known priestess told me in an interview:

> Good leadership is necessary. However, if the energy is not put out by people in the circle no amount of drama, leadership—calisthenics, standing on your head—can do it. Because I have done it: I have tried in a circle of women who were very shy, very new, very cautious, and unwilling to put it out and risk anything.... So I would say that one of the things that holds us back is shyness. And caution, and damage from the patriarchy. That's why I think we have to be kind to each other about it. 'Cause we are—damaged. Two year olds don't have the problem we've got. The tools—they haven't been kicked out of them yet.... It's a healing process to go through to even be able to participate in ritual.

Part of role of the follower, then, is to overcome these inhibitions that prevent the individual from participating freely in rituals. Followers also agree that they lack knowledge and training. However, the Dianic women have an investment in structurelessness at this time. The resistance to structure is consistent with their understandings of male domination of women, and their personal search for autonomy relative to the structures of domination.

MEN AND SECRET SOCIETIES

Those who have attempted to track the origins of Gardner's rituals have found a diverse array of sources, including occult groups and secret societies such as the Golden Dawn, Rosicrucians, and Masons. Initiation into witchcraft is initiation into a secret society, and the form of the organization itself constitutes a significant part of the meaning of membership for individuals. In initiation rites of "death and rebirth" one is reborn into the community of witches, but, in the fascination with secrecy itself, many Neopagan traditions are closer to the nineteenth century Freemasons than to the feminist witches described above.

In his analysis of secret societies, Simmel noted the attraction of secrecy independent of its content. In Simmel's analysis, the pressures toward individuation in modern societies constitute a source of the pleasure of participation in a secret society. The dynamics of inclusion and exclusion mean that being initiated to the secret society from which outsiders are excluded intensifies the identification of initiates with the group.

In a series of observations on religious secret societies Simmel noted that ritual is often the most secret aspect:

> Under its characteristic categories, the secret society must seek to create a sort of life totality. For this reason, it builds round its sharply emphasized purposive content a system of

formulas like a body round a soul, and places both alike under the protection of secrecy ([1908]1950, p. 359).

Simmel argues that the secrecy itself is essential to the ability of the rituals to make claims on individuals. It creates "a sort of counter image to the official world, to which it places itself in contrast" (p. 360). References to aspects of initiation which cannot be spoken about enhance some Neopagans' feelings of belonging to a special countercultural movement.

Some witches argue that secrecy serves a valuable function among contemporary witches in protecting witches against discrimination and even persecution. I have heard accounts of witches who lost leases on rental property, and I know of witches who fear that their jobs would be endangered if their employers knew that they were witches. A parent's being a witch can be raised as evidence against her in child custody cases. In some Wiccan communities revealing the identity of members is grounds for expulsion. Yet, it is also the case that the secrecy is important for its own sake, both regarding who is a member and regarding what witches do. There are still those within the Neopagan community who are outraged about the publication of rituals by witches (and social scientists), because the availability of the rituals in published forms diminishes the effectiveness for initiates.[14]

Moving toward the congregational model will require a more public presence, something that may be most possible for those witches who are self-supporting and for whom being publicly identified as a witch has advantages as well as disadvantages. The use of "craft names" to disguise their true identity is a device that many public witches currently use to maintain a separate noncraft identity.[15] This may become more widespread.

Without feminist discourse as an ideological base, Neopaganism more closely resembles the secret societies analyzed by Simmel in which the tensions between anarchy and order are paramount. Simmel argued that "every secret society contains a measure of *freedom,* which the structure of the society at large does not have" ([1908]1950, p. 360). He suggested that "[t]he secret society...lives in an area to which the norms of the environment do not extend.... The essence of the secret society is autonomy sometimes approaching anarchy" (pp. 360-361). Ritual creates order, although it is an order that, as in the example of nakedness, may signify freedom in so far as it is opposed to the order of the larger society.

In this context, the resilience of Gardner's story of the origins of twentieth-century Wicca is of interest. Revisionists now contend that Gardner did not encounter the last remaining Wiccan coven in the British Isles, as he claimed, but the attractiveness of tracing roots to an origin in a secret magical coven remains. It is somewhat diluted in current accounts: Gardner's authorship of the rituals is acknowledged, but revisionists accept the existence of "survivals" of an "ancient pagan religion," and witches continue to speculate about the identity of the old woman who initiated Gardner into her secret coven. Gardner's story promotes feelings of exclusivity, and, as Simmel argued, the practice of secrecy gives members the feeling of being "outside of society." The elaborate initiation rituals, however, provide a sense of order.

These pleasures of secrecy undoubtedly draw certain people into Wicca. For Neopagans, the pressures toward congregationalism conflict with the pleasures of secrecy currently celebrated in their origin story and their rituals. Dianic ideology, on the other hand, celebrates openness: Dianics believe that empowerment is accessible to any woman who chooses to acknowledge the powers she has within herself. This feminist rhetoric of empowerment is inconsistent with the narrative of the secret society that is central to Gardnerian and neo-Gardnerian Wicca. The aspects of Wicca that make the quasi-religion designation appropriate—its churchlessness and leaderlessness—manifest different ritual and narrative forms in the all-female groups than in heterosexual groups. These, in turn, reflect differences in the meaning of being a witch for Dianics and Neopagans.

QUASI-RELIGIONS AND CULTURAL MOVEMENTS

An emphasis on cultural change is particularly appropriate for looking at many current religious movements which take as central concerns personal and cultural transformation. Writers since the 1960s have studied the new religions in terms of how they solve problems of meaning and identity, partly because many of the new religions have in common a focus on the therapeutic transformation of the self. Sociologists, even when studying religious meaning, have tended to do so within identifiable organizations, including religious movement organizations (e.g., Lofland and Richardson 1984; for a review of this literature, see Robbins 1988). That meant that less "organized" religious traditions, such as the Wiccans, tended to be ignored.[16] Among witches the degree of commitment required and the degree to which adherents constitute a closed group vary greatly. The witches appear elusive in part because formal groups tend to be unstable. However, often the formal group is not the meaningful unit for generating and sustaining either personal transformation or cultural change.

This points to another problem with the linear bias that confines us to organizations: researchers usually evaluate a movement in terms of organizational success (Gusfield 1981, pp. 324-325). Yet some contemporary movements are *cultural* movements whose goals are *cultural* change.[17] Indeed, to the degree that religious participation and membership is now more frequently voluntary, religion's capacity for symbolic expression plays a more central part in the choices that people make (Beckford 1989). In examining the impact of Neopagan movements, it might be appropriate to look for changes in the general culture, for example, changes in images of the deity or changes in the ways that we talk about the natural world, the cycles of the seasons, humans' relationship to nature, and even the meaning of the human body.

Seen in terms of a cultural movement, the short life span of most Wiccan circles hardly seems like the appropriate measure of the movement. Nor does it seem appropriate to label behaviors such as self-initiation as another sign of individualism in American culture. The "structurelessness" of the movement offers a challenge to the dominant culture. (Dianics in addition challenge the hierarchy within Gardnerian witchcraft.) Yet we are likely to miss these processes of cultural change if we concentrate on the group as the unit of analysis.

Cultural phenomena often transcend the boundaries of any one group. Cultural transmission and cultural change is facilitated by the movement of transformed individuals through social networks.[18] Rather than being a problem (as it is from the perspective of the organization), the fluidity of these quasi-religions actually enhances the exchange of ideas and symbols. Indeed, to the extent that groups are tightly bounded, cultural change may be less likely.[19]

Even when organized groups do exist (as in witches' circles and covens), they may not be the theoretically appropriate unit for study when one is concerned with cultural phenomena. Nor will the process of cultural transformation be understood through looking primarily at individuals: without limiting ourselves to the groups as the unit of analysis, we need to observe how ideas and symbols are formed and given shape in social contexts ranging from relatively stable organizations to effervescent gatherings. The questions become questions of how individuals carry ideas and symbols throughout their networks, how the ideas and symbols change meaning in different organizational contexts, how the ideas are reflected in the lives of the individuals who carry them. Beckford (1984) made a similar argument when he suggested we examine what affinities exist between the beliefs of movement participants and the values and concerns of other groups in the dominant culture.

As the editors suggest in their introduction to this volume, quasi-religions can be seen as forms of discourse. This implies that we need to attend to what kinds of stories these people tell about themselves and about the exemplars of their culture. We need to ask: How are these stories embodied in myths and rituals? What sorts of rhetorics are employed to create the narratives that individuals find evocative and convincing? And how do people use these narratives to make connections between themselves and others who share their discourse?

In this paper I have tried to sketch how looking at origin stories, rituals, and personal narratives can inform our understanding of contemporary witchcraft. The relative lack of structure, which is the problem of concern from an organizational standpoint, is no longer to the point when we look at witchcraft as a cultural movement. I have suggested that the processes of carrying on and carrying over help us to see individuals as carriers of expressive symbols through a cultural milieu that extends beyond any one organization, in fact considerably beyond witchcraft itself. In looking at the narratives that Dianics and Neopagans tell, we can begin to understand the different meanings of structurelessness in each context and to account for the differences in the forms that it takes. Within these cultural movements, at this point in time, the narratives are primarily rooted in gendered experience. Gerald Gardner's story with its understanding of initiation is still central for the Neopagan conceptions of the transformation of the self. Some modern feminists, coming out of a different set of cultural currents, are telling their own story with Dianic Wiccan rituals and symbols.

ACKNOWLEDGMENTS

Many people have read various drafts of this paper. I am grateful to Miriam Goldman, Peter Hall, Adair Lummis, Jim McCartney, Peter Mueser, Jim Spickard, and Judy Wittner as well as the editors of this volume for their comments. This research has been supported by grants from the Research Council of the University of Missouri, the Society for the Scientific Study of Religion, and the American Council of Learned Societies.

NOTES

1. It is this process to which Gusfield is referring when he says that social movements are reflexive. According to Gusfield, "I might even say that a social movement occurs when people are conscious that a movement is occurring.... The awareness of change is itself a second step in the production of change" (1981, p. 326).

2. I have been involved in fieldwork in two geographic areas, one in the midwest and the other in the Rocky Mountain states. I have participated in rituals, festivals, and workshops as well as in the routine day-to-day activities of the office of a Wiccan Network organization. I have also interviewed witches in both communities, as well as nationally known authors and leaders from both coasts. In both geographic areas, I have sought out Dianic witches as well as heterosexual Neopagans.

3. The principle of coven autonomy has led to a wide range of beliefs and practices included under the umbrella of Neopaganism. This makes it difficult to generalize. For an overview, see Adler (1986). For a discussion of relations between Neopagans and Dianic Wicca, see Neitz (1990a).

4. In the last line, the speaker is distinguishing her group from the traditional craft rule that stipulates initiation occurring "a year and a day" after beginning to attend rituals. Disregard for this rule is one of several ways that Dianic circles differ from traditional craft covens. This will be explored in greater detail below.

5. Many Neopagans consider it a serious violation to reveal the secrets of initiation or other rituals. In acknowledgment of these preferences, I have chosen in this paper to quote from published

sources when I want to refer to these rituals. *The Witches Bible,* by Janet and Stewart Farrar (1981), is regarded as having the most complete and most accurate versions of Gardnerian and Alexandrian rituals (Adler 1986, p. 547).

6. Some feminist witches also feel a need for a ritual to bind the individual to the group. Their understanding of what is needed is similar to Starhawk's description of initiation in *The Spiral Dance:* "In the Craft, it marks acceptance into a coven and a deep personal commitment to the Goddess. It is a gift of power and love that conveners give each other" (1979, p. 160). Several Dianic priestesses with whom I spoke suggested it might be useful to have some ceremony that bonds the individual to the group even if that ceremony was not initiation per se.

7. Some of the radical feminist witches who self-initiated in the late 1960s later sought out more traditional covens in order to learn what the tradition could teach about ritual and magic (Morgan 1978). In addition, Z Budapest, a founder of Dianic Wicca, claims to be a traditional witch initiated by her mother into the "old religion" of Hungary.

8. I first heard the term "congregationalism" used by witches at Dragonfest of Colorado in 1987, where a number of elders had gotten together a panel of long-time members of their community to debate the topic at a festival workshop.

9. My sources vary on exactly what is prohibited. One example, however, is the Covenant of the Goddess code of ethics which forbids charging money for initiates to learn the craft (Adler 1986, p. 105).

10. These groups usually publish newspapers as well as maintaining directories and sponsoring activities that link individuals and groups with one another.

11. The idea of congregationalism is not completely new, however. In his book *What Witches Do,* Stewart Farrar quotes Alex Sanders, founder of the Alexandrian branch of Wicca, as saying, "We don't want a religion of priests and priestesses—we want one of priests, priestesses, and congregations: first degree initiates, outsiders in to watch, outsiders who can come and talk" (1983, p. 44). Farrar describes Sanders' own coven as a "training coven," seeing such a mix of people as providing an opportunity for many people to learn about Wicca, but not as a context in which serious witches can practice their art.

12. Although women also participate in these rituals, Gardner's inspiration and narrative were largely based in nineteenth century male secret societies. These societies were astonishingly widespread in the late nineteenth century: Carnes (1989, pp. 3, 89) reports estimates of from 15-40 percent of American men belonging to secret societies at the turn of the century, with lodges outnumbering churches in major cities (see also McGuire, this volume).

13. For other ways that Christian symbols of the deity meet male spiritual needs and inhibit the experience of transcendence for women, see Jacobs (1989, pp. 87-88).

14. Simmel would no doubt have been interested in the practice of doing rituals "skyclad," or naked. Nakedness dramatizes the paradox of exclusion and inclusion, and is connected to the secrecy. In our society some level of trust among a group of people is usually necessary for nakedness: those among whom one would be naked is usually a relatively exclusive group. Nakedness also necessitates extra care to keep outsiders away.

15. For feminists, however, the ideology is one that celebrates open access to magical empowerment. Among lesbian witches, the identity of lesbian may be more protected than that of witch.

16. Eileen Barker notes that, "Numerous occult, pagan, and Witchcraft movements are known to exist...but, like the tribal and folk based religions that have emerged around the world..., these have received comparatively little attention as new religious movements from the sociologists of religion" (1985, p. 41).

17. Beckford (1984) suggests a similar approach to healing movements (see also McGuire 1988).

18. Another example of this can be seen in the research on the volunteers from the Mississippi Freedom Summer (McAdam 1988). Many of the women among the volunteers have a history

of moving from participation in the civil rights movement to the feminist movement, carrying with them certain values and practices and elaborating on them over time in various contexts.

19. In a recent article arguing that part of the social significance of the New Religious Movements comes from their contribution as "laboratories for social experimentation," Robbins and Bromley suggest that highly organized new religious movements may be less suited for survival than movements such as Wicca (1992, p. 3).

REFERENCES

Adler, M. 1986. *Drawing Down the Moon.* Revised ed. Boston: Beacon.
Barker, E. 1985. "New Religious Movements: Yet Another Great Awakening?" Pp. 35-57 in *The Sacred in a Secular Age,* edited by P. Hammond. Berkeley: The University of California Press.
Beckford, J. 1984. "Holistic Imagery and Ethics in New Religious and Healing Movements." *Social Compass* 31: 259-272.
_____. 1989. *Religion in Advanced Industrial Society.* London: Unwin and Hyman.
Carnes, M. 1989. *Secret Ritual and Manhood in Victorian America.* New Haven, CT: Yale University Press.
Christ, C. 1987. *The Laughter of Aphrodite.* San Francisco: Harper and Row.
Chodorow, N. 1978. *The Reproduction of Mothering.* Berkeley, CA: University of California Press.
Farrar, J., and S. Farrar. 1981. *The Witches Bible Complete.* New York, NY: Magickal Childe Publishing.
Farrar, S. 1983. *What Witches Do.* Rev. ed. Custer, WA: Phoenix Press.
Fine, G.A., and S. Kleinman. 1983. "Network, and Meaning: An Interactionist Approach to Structure." *Symbolic Interaction* 6: 97-110.
Freeman, J. 1972. "The Tyranny of Structurelessness." Pp. 285-299 in *Radical Feminism,* edited by A. Koedt, E. Levine, and A. Rapone. New York: Quadrangle Books.
Gardner, G. 1955. *Witchcraft Today.* New York: Citadel Press.
_____. 1959. *The Meaning of Witchcraft.* New York: Samuel Weiser.
Gilligan, C. 1982. *In a Different Voice: Psychological Theory and Women's Development.* Cambridge, MA: Harvard University Press.
Greil, A.L., and D. Rudy. 1990. "On the Margins of the Sacred." Pp. 219-233 in *In Gods We Trust,* edited by T. Robbins and D. Anthony. 2nd ed. New Brunswick, NJ: Transaction Press.
Gusfield, J. 1981. "Social Movements and Social Change: Perspectives of Linearity and Fluidity." Pp. 317-339 in *Social Movements, Conflict and Change,* Vol. 4, edited by L. Kreisberg. Greenwich, CT: JAI Press.
Jacobs, J. 1989. "The Effects of Ritual Healing on Female Victims of Abuse: A Study of Empowerment and Transformation." *Sociological Analysis* 50: 265-279.
Keller, C. 1986. *From A Broken Web: Separation, Sexism and the Self.* Boston: Beacon Press.
Kelly, A. 1983. "Inventing Witchcraft." Unpublished manuscript in the collection of the Institute for the Study of American Religion, Santa Barbara, CA.
Lofland, J. with J. Richardson. 1985. "Religious Movement Organizations." Pp. 179-200 in *Protest,* by J. Lofland. New Brunswick, NJ: Transaction Press.
McAdam, D. 1988. *Freedom Summer.* New York: Oxford University Press.
McGuire, M. 1988. *Ritual Healing in Suburban America.* New Brunswick, NJ: Rutgers University Press.
Melucci, A. 1985. "The Symbolic Challenge of Contemporary Social Movements." *Social Research* 52(4): 789-816.

Morgan, R., ed. 1970. *Sisterhood Is Powerful.* New York: Random House.

———. 1978. *Going Too Far.* New York: Random House.

Neitz, M.J. 1990a. "In Goddess We Trust." Pp. 353-372 in *In Gods We Trust,* edited by T. Robbins and D. Anthony. 2nd ed. New Brunswick, NJ: Transaction.

———. 1990b. "Studying Religion in the Eighties." Pp. 90-118 in *Symbolic Interaction and Cultural Studies,* edited by H. Becker and M. McCall. Chicago: University of Chicago Press.

———. 1992. "Defining and Sanctioning Sexual Deviance in Contemporary Witchcraft." Paper presented at the meetings of the Society for the Scientific Study of Religion, Pittsburgh, PA.

Offe, C. 1985. "New Social Movements: Challenging the Boundaries of Institutional Politics." *Social Research* 52(4): 817-868.

Phelan, S. 1989. *Identity Politics: Lesbian Feminism and the Limits of Community.* Philadelphia: Temple University Press.

Robbins, T. 1988. *Cults, Converts and Charisma.* London: Sage.

Robbins, T., and D. Bromley. 1992. "Social Experimentation and the Significance of American New Religion." Pp. 1-28 in *Research in the Social Scientific Study of Religion,* Vol. 4, edited by M. Lynn and D. Moberg. Greenwich, CT: JAI Press.

Simmel, G. [1908] 1950. *The Sociology of Georg Simmel.* New York: The Free Press.

Starhawk. 1979. *The Spiral Dance.* San Francisco: Harper and Row.

Taylor, V. and N. Whittier. 1992. "Collective Identity in Social Movement Communities: Lesbian Feminist Mobilization." Pp. 104-129 in *Frontiers of Social Movement Theory,* edited by A. Morris and C. McClung Mueller. New Haven, CT: Yale University Press.

Touraine, A. 1985. "An Introduction to the Sutdy of Social Movements." *Social Research* 52(4): 749-787.

THE THERAPEUTIC GOD:
TRANSCENDENCE AND IDENTITY IN
TWO TWELVE-STEP QUASI-RELIGIONS

John Steadman Rice

ABSTRACT

Previous research on quasi-religions has emphasized a variety of distinctive characteristics that such organizations have in common. This paper, comparing Co-Dependents Anonymous with Alcoholics Anonymous, argues that a full understanding of quasi-religions requires close attention to the differences among them, as well; of particular importance are variations in the groups' therapeutic orientations. Although both groups superficially hold to identical philosophies, practices, and conceptions of the sacred, they differ markedly in their beliefs about the causes of, and hence the solutions to, people's problems. Both promise to make their members' lives better, but what each means by that engenders radically different conceptions of the sacred and has no less radically different social implications.

Religion and the Social Order, Volume 4, pages 151-164.
Copyright © 1994 by JAI Press Inc.
All rights of reproduction in any form reserved.
ISBN: 1-55938-763-7

Recent years have seen the proliferation of a variety of self-help groups that have adopted the twelve-step philosophy, argot, and organizational structure of Alcoholics Anonymous (A.A.) in order to address a panoply of life problems. Like A.A., such groups as Gamblers Anonymous, Overeaters Anonymous, Emotions Anonymous, Sex and Love Addicts Anonymous, Spenders Anonymous, and Shoplifters Anonymous demonstrate characteristically quasi-religious qualities such as ambiguous conceptions of the sacred, highly permeable boundaries between sacred and secular, tolerance for a wide diversity of religious beliefs and expressions, and a pragmatic therapeutic orientation.

This paper will focus on the relationship between therapeutic orientation and conceptions of the sacred. As has been noted, in quasi-religions, "the goal of presenting revealed truth...is subordinated to the goal of helping people to make their lives better" (Greil and Rudy 1990, p. 226). If sacred or spiritual themes are a reflection of the overarching therapeutic vision of the group, then it is essential to examine what each group means by the "better life" it promises converts. These larger therapeutic purposes shape not only the members' conceptions of the sacred, but also their identities and the way that they structure their relationships to the world beyond the group. I will compare the therapeutic orientations and sacred conceptions of Alcoholics Anonymous with Co-Dependents Anonymous (CoDA) to show that the status of the sacred in twelve-step quasi-religions is a function of the groups' overarching understanding of "cure," or, in the relevant argot, "recovery."

A BRIEF HISTORY OF "CO-DEPENDENCY"

In its first manifestation, the term "co-dependency" was more or less synonymous with "co-alcoholism," an older word referring to the psychological woes suffered by those intimately connected to an alcoholic. In particular, the wives of alcoholics were said to become primarily concerned with covering-up for their husbands' problems on the job, with the neighbors, and in the community. The assumption was that these preoccupations bred a spate of personal and interpersonal troubles both for the wives themselves and for their children, while at the same time ostensibly "enabling" alcoholics to avoid the full consequences of their actions.[1]

With the rise of the addiction treatment industry in the late 1970s (Weisner 1983; Weisner and Room 1984; Fillmore and Kelso 1986; Rice 1989, 1992a, 1992b), alcoholism was subsumed beneath the general rubric of "chemical dependency." Reflecting this change, "co-alcoholism" began to be referred to as "co-dependency." But there is much more than just a change of terminology involved in the current usage. Since the mid-1980s, a small group of advocates have argued that co-dependency is not a set of problems restricted to addicts' significant others but is itself a disease which may, they aver, be the underlying cause of all addictions (see Bradshaw 1988, 1989, 1990; Beattie 1987, 1989; Schaef 1986, 1987, 1990; Subby 1987; Whitfield 1986; and Wegscheider-Cruse 1984, 1985). The root problem co-dependents are said to share is a lack of self-worth, and this is believed, logically enough, to reflect the underlying absence of any coherent sense of self. Co-dependency theorists contend that these characteristics manifest themselves in all harmful behaviors over which the person can be reasonably construed to be "powerless."

Although this conceptual framework may well be conceptually murky, as any number of critics have observed (see, for example, Rieff 1991; Kaminer 1990; Kristol 1990; Gomberg 1989), the evidence suggests that many people find this newer point of view convincing regardless of loose conceptualizations or theoretical carelessness. Beattie's *Co-Dependent No More* (1987) spent 154 weeks on *Publishers Weekly's* best-selling trade paperback list, eventually selling well over 2,000,000 copies. Bradshaw's successes are equally noteworthy. *His Homecoming: Reclaiming and Championing Your Inner Child* (1990) was not only a top ten best-selling hardback nonfiction title for all of 1991, but was also the basis for a public television (PBS) special, aired on December 2 and 8, 1990, for six hours each day. The program is still being re-broadcast, frequently during PBS's fundraising telethons. Bradshaw's earlier books (*Bradshaw On: The Family* [1988] and *Healing the Shame That Binds You* [1989])—both of which were also the basis for PBS specials—have each sold over 800,000 copies.

These media successes are only part of the story. As noted at the outset, the concept of co-dependency has taken on institutional form, as well. According to the Co-Dependents Anonymous (CoDA) International Service Office, as of July 1990, there were 2,088 weekly CoDA meetings in the United States and 64 international meetings; this, after less than five years in existence. In short, the evidence suggests that co-dependency has quickly become a significant cultural phenomenon.

TWELVE-STEP SPIRITUALITY

Co-dependency's advocates, all of whom are Anonymous program enthusiasts (if eschewing anonymity themselves) and recovering alcoholics and addicts employed in the addiction treatment industry, insist that "the core of our addictive behavior is spiritual death. Co-dependence is a spiritual problem" (Bradshaw 1988, p. 226). This formulation points to C.G. Jung's influence on the twelve-step conception of spirituality.

In his attempts to treat a chronic alcohol abuser named "Roland H.," Jung had met with little success through conventional therapeutic approaches. He did, however, offer his patient a suggestion that proved pivotal in the natural history of the twelve-step movement. A letter to Jung from Bill Wilson, one of the co-founders of Alcoholics Anonymous, explains that significance.[2]

> First of all, you frankly told him [Roland H.] of his hopelessness, so far as any further medical or psychiatric treatment might be concerned. This candid and humble statement of yours was beyond doubt the first foundation stone upon which our society [A.A.] has been built.... When he asked you if there was any hope, you told him that there might be, provided he could become the subject of a spiritual or religious experience—in short, a genuine conversion.... You recommended that he place himself in a religious atmosphere and hope for the best (*Parabola* 1987, p. 68).

These convictions have assumed a central place in A.A. philosophy and folklore. The assumptions are that conventional treatment modalities are "hopeless," and, as the first two A.A. steps counsel newcomers, because alcoholics are "powerless" over their actions, only the intervention of "a power greater than ourselves [can] restore us to sanity." Roland H.'s experience is taken as testimonial to the accuracy of Jung's speculations.

Apparently acting on Jung's advice, Roland went on to join the Oxford Group, an evangelical precursor to A.A. based on the principles of "self-survey, confession, restitution, and the giving of oneself in service to others" (*Parabola* 1987, pp. 68-69).[3] In the latter capacity, he took up the mantle of helping other alcoholics. Among those he tried to help was a man named "Edwin T.," who, in turn, tried to aid Bill Wilson in his own struggles with alcohol. Wilson reports that he was inspired by Edwin T.'s ministrations, but simultaneously depressed by his own prospects. Indeed,

> [s]oon after [Edwin] left me, I became even more depressed. In utter despair, I cried out, "If there be a God, will He show Himself." There immediately came to me an illumination of enormous impact and dimension.... My release from the alcohol obsession was immediate [and] [i]n the wake of my spiritual experience there came a vision of a society of alcoholics, each identifying with and transmitting his experiences to the next—chain-style (*Parabola* 1987, p. 70).

Wilson's "vision" became Alcoholics Anonymous, and he traced its origins back to Jung, to whom A.A. owed "a tremendous benefaction" (*Parabola* 1987, p. 70).

Jung's response to Wilson further suggests his influence on the A.A. philosophy, and, presumably, upon A.A.'s recent spate of imitators. Jung explained that Roland H.'s:

> craving for alcohol was the equivalent, on a low level, of the spiritual thirst of our being for wholeness; expressed in medieval language: the union with God.

Jung continued,

> I am strongly convinced that the evil principle prevailing in the world leads the unrecognized spiritual need into perdition if it is not counter-acted by real religious insight or by the

protective wall of human community. An ordinary man, not protected by an action from above and isolated in society, cannot resist the power of evil.... You see, "alcohol" in Latin is *spiritus,* and you use the same word for the highest religious experience as well as for the most depraving poison. The helpful formula therefore is: *spiritus contra spirituum* (*Parabola* 1987, p. 71).

For Jung, as his allusion to "unrecognized spiritual need" suggests, humans are instinctively spiritual beings, driven by a "thirst...[for] union with God." As such, specific conceptions of deity or a set of conventionalized icons are unnecessary; indeed, as Jung saw it, the church, by attempting to regularize the spiritual instinct, rationalizes and thus destroys or perverts it. What matters is the recognition and expression of our putatively innate spirituality (see, for example, Jung 1963; see also Rieff 1987, especially chapter 5).

The Jungian perspective is at work in both A.A.'s and CoDA's conception of the sacred. For example, the "Big Book"—A.A.'s "bible"—assures potential converts that a highly personalized conception of God will more than suffice for purposes of recovery: "we did not need to consider another's conception of God. Our own conception, however inadequate, was sufficient to make the approach and to effect a contact with Him" (Alcoholics Anonymous 1976, p. 46). Reflecting Jung's faith in an instinctual human spirituality, the same A.A. text observes that:

Deep down in every man, woman, and child, is the idea of God. It may be obscured by calamity, by pomp, by worship of other things, but in some form or other it is there.... We finally saw that faith in some kind of God was a part of our make-up.... We found the Great Reality deep down within us. In the last analysis, it is only there that He may be found (1976, p. 55).

By all appearances, Co-Dependents Anonymous has simply redirected A.A.'s twelve-step philosophy toward the redress of a different set of problems. CoDA instructs its members that:

one day at a time, we could "act as if" we had a Higher Power whether we actually believed in this Power or not. Because we were members of a Twelve-Step program, the form of this Power was left to each of us to discover. For some of us, a Higher Power was unconditional love; for others, this Power was divine intelligence. Our "Power Greater" might have been nature, an image of an ocean, river, or tree. Some of us chose our home group of Co-Dependents Anonymous. For others, this Power was the thought of limitless space or simply the words, "my Higher Power."[4]

There is little in CoDA's version of spirituality that might frighten away agnostics, or threaten lingering denominational or dogmatic loyalties, little to limit the pool of possible converts or obstruct the transcendental underpinnings to identity-transformation (Greil and Rudy 1984; Rudy and Greil 1989). Jung's view also renders spirituality an instrument of psychological well-being, and, in both CoDA and A.A., spirituality is an instrumental, rather than a terminal, construct. Connection with one's Higher Power promises a better life in the here and now—for alcoholics, sobriety; for co-dependents, better relationships; for both, "serenity." Thus, A.A. assuages agnostic converts with the assurance that:

> As soon as we were able to lay aside prejudice and express even a willingness to believe in a Power greater than ourselves, *we commenced to get results,* even though it was impossible for any of us to fully define or comprehend that Power, which is God.... [The] men and women [in A.A.] are strikingly agreed ... that *since they have come to believe in a Power greater than themselves,* to take a certain attitude toward that Power, and to do certain simple things, *there has been a revolutionary change in their way of living and thinking* (Alcoholics Anonymous 1976, pp. 46, 50, emphasis mine).

Reflecting an identically pragmatic spirit, CoDA instructs converts that:

> we came to believe by attending meetings and listening [to other CoDA members talk about their lives]. We heard others as they described a relationship with a Higher Power. *We noticed that those who maintained a regular connection with this Power experienced what we sought—RECOVERY....* The point was, that in the beginning of our time in CoDA, we became willing to entertain the possibility there was Something that could do for us what we could not do for ourselves. We were free to use any of these ideas of a Higher Power. We could borrow someone else's idea and try it for awhile *to see if it worked for us.*[5]

Characteristic features of quasi-religions exist in equal parts in both the original philosophy and its imitator. Yet, as suggested, to let the matter rest here would be to hold a false sense of the two organizations' comparability. Although sacred conceptions serve an instrumental, therapeutic purpose for the members of both groups, the meaning of "cure" in CoDA is dramatically different than it is in Alcoholics Anonymous.

CAUSALITY AND CURE IN A.A.

Conceptions of cure flow logically from conceptions of cause, and there are significant differences between A.A.'s and CoDA's causal models. In A.A., the presence of disease is inferred from alcoholics' recurrent violation of existing normative standards: the addiction itself, while never adequately explained etiologically, is spoken of as a "predisposition," an "allergy," or, reflecting more recent enthusiasms, as a genetic defect. Efforts to trace one's drinking problems to social causes are frowned upon, and viewed as a symptom of the disease itself; in the argot, the search for a social etiology is referred to as one version of "stinkin' thinkin'."

For most of us, self-justification was the maker of excuses; excuses, of course, for drinking, and for all kinds of crazy and damaging conduct. We had made the invention of alibis a fine art. We had to drink because times were hard or times were good. We had to drink because at home we were smothered with love or got none at all.... We thought "conditions" drove us to drink, and...*[i]t never occurred to us that we needed to change ourselves to meet conditions, whatever they were* (Alcoholics Anonymous 1985, p. 47, emphasis mine).

Also reflecting the unassailable status assigned to culture, A.A. encourages members to focus upon the damage done *by* the addiction, *to* drinkers and their family, friends, coworkers, and employers. This emphasis is dominant throughout A.A.'s major texts (1976, 1985).

If our tempers are consistently bad, we arouse anger in others. If we lie or cheat, we deprive others not only of their worldly goods, but of their emotional security and peace of mind.... If our sex conduct is selfish, we may excite jealousy, misery, and a strong desire to retaliate in kind. Such gross misbehavior is not by any means a full catalogue of the harms we do.... Suppose that in our family lives we happen to be miserly, irresponsible, callous or cold. Suppose that we are irritable, critical, impatient and humorless.... Such a roster of harms done others...could be extended almost indefinitely. When we take such personality traits as these into shop, office, and the society of our fellows, they can do damage almost as extensive as that we have caused at home (Alcoholics Anonymous 1985, pp. 80, 81).

The causal focus is mirrored in the goals of recovery. A.A. members are to make restitution and to adapt to the existing body of normative demands. In recovery, they:

no longer strive to dominate or rule those about us in order to gain self-importance. We no longer seek fame and honor in order to be praised.... Service, gladly rendered, obligations squarely met, troubles well accepted or solved with God's help, the knowledge that at home or in the world outside we are partners in a common effort..., these are the permanent and legitimate satisfactions of right living for which no amount of pomp and circumstance, no heap of material possessions, could possibly be substitutes (Alcoholics Anonymous 1985, p. 124).

A.A.'s disciplined regimen of restitution and reconnection with the existing social world frames recovery in culturally conservative terms: adaptation to existing normative expectations is synonymous with "progress in recovery."

A NEW THEORY OF ADDICTION: CAUSALITY IN CODA

Members of Co-Dependents Anonymous are guided by a new theory of addiction grounded in a directly opposed interpretation of the significance of their social milieu. CoDA converts are encouraged to understand the root cause of their adult travails in terms of a social etiology. They are advised that they suffer from "an emotional, psychological, and behavioral condition that develops as a result of...prolonged exposure to a set of oppressive rules—which prevent open expression of feelings as well as the direct discussion of personal and interpersonal problems" (Subby 1987, pp. 26-27). All co-dependency theorists agree, moreover, that this "condition" is "born of the rules of the family" and other socializing institutions (Subby 1987, p. 27). Another advocate insists that:

> the family, the school, and the church...teach us to think what we are told to think, feel what we are told to feel, see what we are told to see, and know what we are told to know. This is cultural co-dependence training (Schaef 1986, p. 45).

For John Bradshaw, perhaps the most well-known co-dependency theorist, existing social institutions operate according to the "poisonous pedagogy," a set of cultural rules that "glorify obedience, orderliness, logic, rationality, power, and male supremacy." What is more, "many of our religious institutions offer authoritarian support for these [rules]. Our schools reinforce them. Our legal system reinforces them"; they *are carried by family systems, by our schools, our churches, and our government. They are a core belief of the modern 'consensus reality'"* (1988, pp. 8, 187). Co-dependents, then, are the products of socialization at the hands of not only the "dysfunctional family," but of a "dysfunctional culture."

CoDA's emphasis on childhood experience and the socialization process plainly diverges from A.A.'s pragmatic and reparative agenda. A.A. members do survey the wreckage of their pasts, but such retrospectives are constrained by the therapeutic philosophy's emphasis on the damage the disease brings to an entire social milieu. CoDA members, by contrast, are counseled that their problems stem from the damage done *to* them, *by* others, and, although the analogy may strain credulity among any but the faithful, childhood repression is said to result in an "addiction," an inability to control conduct as an adult.

CoDA members understand themselves and their problems according to this basic formula. Gina, for example, explained to her fellow CoDA members that:

> I was born thirty-one years ago to an emotionally unavailable father and a hypercritical mother. As a little girl, I wasn't particularly attractive and I was small, so I got picked on a lot. It wasn't that there was a lot of substance abuse in my family, because there wasn't. There was an incredibly rigid set of standards and an incredibly critical set of parents who drummed it into me that there was really nothing that I could do that was okay.[6]

"Rigidity" and "critical standards" are stock themes in CoDA members' recitations. Because Gina was expected to strictly adhere to rules and standards, her parents "did not love her for who she really was," as the argot has it, and she causally links her actions as an adult with those childhood experiences.

> When I first came to CoDA, the extent of my relationships was the two minute, two days, two months type. What I did was, I'd go out to a bar and I'd pick up a guy or I'd let myself be picked up and then we'd have a "relationship" [using her fingers as quotation marks]—but that was never a question, really, because I had no self-esteem...so I had to latch onto the guy...however long that lasted. And I was hurting, but that was really the only way that I knew to get out of the pain I was in.

Engaging in behaviors that do not work, fail to deliver happiness, or result in unhappiness is the CoDA equivalent to A.A.'s concept of unmanageability. In the same analogic mode, Gina's observation that having "to latch onto the guy...was never a question, really," because "that was really the only way that I knew to get out of the pain," is CoDA argot for the concept of powerlessness. She is operating with the logic, and using the language, of Alcoholics Anonymous. But the ultimate etiological responsibility for her "addiction" to relationships lies with the "dysfunctional culture's" rules for child-rearing. Her parents, as the "carriers" of those ostensibly illness-causing rules, were merely doing what was expected of them.

In sum, this new theory of "addictions" reverses A.A.'s understanding of the relationship between addicts and their social world. A.A. members are advised that they have offended, and while those offenses are said to be the result of an addiction, recovering alcoholics must nonetheless atone for the wrongs they have done. The understanding of cure derived from these views is culturally conservative; its measure, successful adaptation to the status quo. CoDA members, conversely, have been offended, and while this also may have resulted in behavior harmful to others, and while co-dependents, too, are instructed to atone for any harms they may have caused, the understanding of cure is culturally "radical." The path to recovery in CoDA is blazed with converts' emancipation from cultural expectations for conduct.

CURE IN CODA

Not surprisingly, CoDA members are sometimes confused by the use of A.A.'s language and methods to accomplish fundamentally opposed therapeutic purposes. Dan aptly summarizes the nature of this confusion.

> I just want to share something that's been bothering me quite a bit about CoDA. Don't get me wrong, I love this program, but there's been one part of the program that I've been having the hardest time with. Okay, we get the steps from A.A., right? And, I know they've had a lot of success helping people and all, but they're a program for helping drunks, you know? People that have hurt other people a lot. And I just have a hard time with the eighth step—this idea that we're supposed to make amends to other people for the harm we've done to them. I think that's inappropriate. It's like we're saying [he affects a deliberately whiny voice], "oh, it's okay that you dumped on me," but it's not okay, you know. And I just have a real hard time with this idea that we're supposed to say "it's okay," when

what we want to be saying and ought to say is, "fuck you, man, you treated me like dog crap, and that just isn't right." So, I guess all I'm really saying is that I figured out that that step really has to mean that we make amends to ourselves for letting people walk all over us like that.

The problem, of course, is that although both A.A. and CoDA converts follow the Twelve Steps, a recovery from co-dependency cannot mean what recovery has traditionally meant for twelve-step members. As Dan suggests, if one's problems are believed to be the result of childhood victimization it makes little sense to make amends to the victimizers. Yet, this is precisely what a literal fidelity to A.A.'s steps would require.

Although Dan was evidently unaware of it, CoDA recognizes the need for a reinterpretation of A.A.'s philosophy. The eighth step to which he referred requires converts to make "a list of all people we had harmed and [become] willing to make amends to them all." A CoDA brochure instructs recovering co-dependents that on the list of people they had harmed, "Our name came first and the reason was obvious. We had been the least able to escape from our own co-dependence, and therefore, in most cases, we received the greatest injuries."[7]

The same reinterpretive necessity informs CoDA's official line on the ninth step, which exhorts members to make "direct amends to such people [on the amends list] wherever possible, except when to do so would injure them or others."

> We had waited years for someone, anyone to make amends to us. Step nine brought us to our moment of truth. It asked us to take that particular action ourselves.... Because our own name was first on the list of amends..., the question before us was this: How would I like amends to be made to me? Would a simple, "I'm sorry," suffice? The answer was "no." What most of us wanted in the way of amends from another was to have that person acknowledge his or her part in harming us.[8]

Because of the new theory of addiction's causal model, cure must be defined in terms of the self's liberation from collective constraint. As Subby remarks, "in order to get free, we must stop trying to build up our own self-worth through the caretaking of others," and begin to focus on "the things that really count, e.g., self-respect, self-esteem, self-worth, and self-love" (1987, pp. 40, 23). Bradshaw agrees, instructing his readers and viewers that "all true love begins with self-love," and achieving this entails saying "'I love myself. I will accept myself unconditionally'... out loud and often" (1988, pp. 45, 170, 158). Expanding on this premise, Bradshaw explains,

> I can remember vividly the first time I truly accepted and loved myself unconditionally. It was awesome! I later read a book by Gay Hendricks where he talked about the same thing. (See *Learning to Love Yourself* by Gay Hendricks.) He described how he would confront people in his workshops with the simple statement, "Will you love yourself for that?" ... at first ... I was taken aback. Surely there are things that we do that are unworthy of love. As Gay went on and on, asking the person if he could love himself no matter

what he did or didn't do, I remember [sic] that our love needs to be for who we are, not for what we do. You are lovable, period... Understanding the distinction between being and doing is one of the great learnings of my life (1988, pp. 158, 160).

Whatever else one may make of these observations, the contrast with the conventional A.A. view could be no more apparent. The contrast is also evident in CoDA members' descriptions of their recovery from co-dependency. Julie, for example, reported that:

I'm now to the point where I can honestly say I'm having a love affair with myself, and that's because of this program. I don't feel a lot of shame about things anymore. I'm enough. Every day, I'm enough. And there's so much freedom in that. Now, because of CoDA, I know that I can wear what I want, and do what I want, and if that bothers somebody that's not my problem. It's their problem and they can do whatever they need to do to take care of it.

Although employing the same vocabulary, following identical rituals, and using the same means to accomplish their purposes, converts to these two groups arrive at fundamentally contradictory conceptions of recovery. In CoDA the individual is assigned unquestioned priority; in A.A., that priority is assigned to the larger sociocultural context. Each group's conception of the sacred reflects these larger therapeutic orientations.

TRANSCENDENCE AND IDENTITY: THE FACES OF GOD

Although both A.A. and CoDA draw from the same Jungian well-spring, assuring their charges that no institutional or collective conception of spirituality is necessary and that none will be imposed, there is a collective understanding of what constitutes psychological well-being. In both groups, converts speak of following God's plan for them, assuming that the Higher Power will reveal the appropriate course of action in any given situation, but although each member's Higher Power may be idiosyncratic, the nature of that power's guidance is constrained by the group's therapeutic vision. God's plan for A.A. members bears an uncanny resemblance to conventional society's plans for them.

For CoDA, in sharp contrast, American culture is the cause of psychological sickness rather than the standard for psychological well-being; as such, CoDA's God has a different face. Ken tells a story about his God that illustrates this point well.[9] His CoDA sponsor asked him to describe his Higher Power, and Ken described:

the Old Testament God, the one that I was scared of, [scared] that if I did it wrong I was going to go to hell. [My sponsor] said, "would you like a new god?" I said yeah. And [my sponsor] asked me to "describe him. What would you like?" And I said, I'd like a God that's accessible, that's merciful, one that's available, one that's there for me, one that I don't have to look up to but I can look at; one who walks with me rather in front of me, or behind me trying to push me; one that genuinely loved me; one that would not judge me, or shame me, or lead me to believe that I was less than, or not important. And my sponsor said, "you got it, it's yours."

The God Ken describes is the product of a fundamentally different set of truth rules than those that undergird the A.A. philosophy. Both groups invoke the religious principle of becoming more what God intended, but, as Ken's remarks illustrate, the CoDA God's intentions perfectly mirror what the members want. The operative therapeutic principle, here, is "unconditional love," which, as Ken suggests, is "genuine love." The God that inhabits this system of truth loves people just the way they are; as Bradshaw's earlier comments suggested, "you are lovable, period." Thus, CoDA assures converts that "a faith in a Higher Power becomes a faith in me, and...my recovery lies in being true to myself and to my Higher Power."[10]

This position rests, as do all systems of therapeutic truth, upon a set of assumptions about human nature and culture. We have already seen that culture, in the new theory of addiction, is the source of sickness. But that assumption can only tell half the story. The subsequent conclusion that people must therefore be liberated from cultural demands depends on the additional assumption that people are innately benign, loving, and gentle—indeed, god-like creatures. When these two assumptions are joined in a single system of truth, culture acts exclusively in an etiological capacity; it only makes people sick.

Also as we have already seen, A.A. holds the opposite view of culture as the standard for right action. Deviations from that standard are symptoms of sickness. Although A.A. does not explicitly say so, this view assumes that behaving in accordance with social and cultural requirements is simultaneously abiding by God's plan.

The nature of the sacred in CoDA and A.A. is a function of the group's overarching system of therapeutic truth and the governing conception of cure. This has important implications for the link between quasi-religions' goal of identity-transformation and the theme of transcendence by which that transformation is to be facilitated. The shape of the new identity depends not only on transcendence but on what is to be transcended. In the truth system of Co-Dependents Anonymous, converts must transcend culture. A.A., on the other hand, demands the transcendence of a "diseased" self, and the existence of that disease is deduced from the violation of sociocultural norms. Sociologically, the implications of membership in one or the other group could not be more different, but for both, the identity born of conversion and transcendence will be more in accordance with God's ultimate plan. The nature of that plan, and of God, is contingent on therapeutic definitions of truth.

ACKNOWLEDGMENT

An earlier draft of this paper was presented to the Society for the Scientific Study of Religion, November 6, 1992, Washington, D.C. I thank the participants of the special session on quasi-religions at those meetings for their helpful comments—in particular, Arthur L. Greil, Thomas Robbins, Randolph Atkins, and Daniel Stuhlsatz.

NOTES

1. When the concept of co-alcoholism was first articulated, it was still assumed that men became alcoholics and that women did not.

2. Wilson to Jung, January 23, 1961: The correspondence between these men was reprinted in the May 1987 issue of *Parabola*. To simplify, I have here opted simply to cite that journal. *The A.A. Grapevine,* Alcoholics Anonymous' monthly magazine, holds the original copyright for Wilson's correspondence. Jung's letters can be found in his collected *Letters* (1975).

3. These Oxford Group principles are now embodied in, respectively, A.A.'s fourth, fifth, eight, ninth, and twelfth steps.

4. This quote is taken from an official CoDA brochure designed to explain and interpret the second step for new members (Phoenix: Co-Dependents Anonymous, Inc. 1989). CoDA offers a brochure for each of the twelve steps; all have been adapted (from similar A.A. pamphlets) for CoDA use with permission of Alcoholics Anonymous World Services, Inc. The same reference will apply to all subsequet citations of CoDA brochures.

5. Taken from the CoDA brochure on the second step; upper-case in original, emphasis mine.

6. Unless otherwise attributed, all quotes from CoDA members have been taken from my own field notes. From the spring of 1990 through the fall of 1991, I attended a total of twenty CoDA meetings in various locations across the United States, including the greater Los Angeles, Boston, and Omaha metropolitan areas (five, six, and six meetings, respectively), central Virginia (one), and central New Jersey (two). See Rice (1992a) for a more complete description of this research.

7. Taken from the CoDA brochure on the eighth step.

8. Taken from the CoDA brochure on the ninth step.

9. Taken from a cassette recording of Ken's comments to a gathering of fellow co-dependents at the First Annual Mid-Atlantic CoDA Conference, May 20, 1989. The tape is sold by the Co-Dependents Anonymous International Service Office in Scottsdale, Arizona.

10. Taken from the CoDA brochure on the third step.

REFERENCES

Alcoholics Anonymous. 1976. *Alcoholics Anonymous: The Story of How Many Thousands of Men and Women Have Recovered From Alcoholism.* New York: Alcoholics Anonymous World Services.

———. 1985. *Twelve Steps and Twelve Traditions.* New York: Alcoholics Anonymous World Services.

Beattie, M. 1987. *Codependent No More: How to Stop Controlling Others and Start Caring For Yourself.* New York: Harper/Hazelden.

———. 1989. *Beyond Codependency and Getting Better All The Time.* New York: Harper/Hazelden.

Bradshaw, J. 1988. *Bradshaw On: The Family.* Deerfield Beach, FL: Health Communications.

———. 1989. *Healing the Shame That Binds You.* Deerfield Beach, FL: Health

Communications.

_____. 1990. *Homecoming: Reclaiming and Championing Your Inner Child.* New York: Bantam.

Fillmore, K.M., and D. Kelso. 1986. "Coercion into Alcoholism Treatment: Meanings for the Disease Concept of Alcoholism." Monograph #B299. Alcohol Research Group, Berkeley.

Gomberg, E.L. 1989. "On Terms Used and Abused: The Concept of 'Co-dependency'." *Drugs and Society: Current Issues in Alcohol and Drug Studies* 3: 114-132.

Greil, A.L., and D.R. Rudy. 1984. "Social Cocoons: Encapsulation and Identity Transforming Organizations." *Sociological Inquiry* 54: 260-278.

_____. 1990 "On the Margins of the Sacred." Pp. 219-232 in *In Gods We Trust,* edited by T. Robbins and D. Anthony. New Brunswick, NJ: Transaction.

Jung, C.G. 1963. *Memories, Dreams, Reflections.* New York: Pantheon.

_____. 1975. *Letters,* Vol. 2., translated by R.F.C. Hull, edited by G. Adler and A. Jaffe. Princeton, NJ: Princeton University Press.

Kaminer, W. 1990. "Chances Are, You're Co-Dependent, Too." *New York Times Book Review,* February 11, pp. 1, 26-27.

Kristol, E. 1990. "Declarations of Codependence: People Who Need People are the Sickliest People in the World—And That's Just For Starters." *The American Spectator* (June): 21-23.

Parabola. 1987. "Spiritus Contra Spirituum: The Bill Wilson/C.G. Jung Letters." 12(May): 68-71.

Rice, J.S. 1989 "'A Power Greater Than Ourselves': The Commodification of Alcoholism." Master's thesis, University of Nebraska at Omaha.

_____. 1992a. "A Disease of One's Own: Psychotherapy, Addiction, and the Emergence of 'Co-Dependency'." Doctoral dissertation, University of Virginia.

_____. 1992b. "Discursive Formation, Life Stories, and the Emergence of 'Co-Dependency': 'Power/Knowledge' and the Search for Identity." *Sociological Quarterly* 33: 337-364.

Rieff, D. 1991. "Victims All? Recovery, Co-Dependency, and the Art of Blaming Somebody Else." *Harper's,* October, pp. 49-56.

Rieff, P. 1987. *The Triumph of the Therapeutic: Uses of Faith After Freud.* 2nd ed. Chicago: University of Chicago Press.

Rudy, D.R., and A.L. Greil. 1989. "Is Alcoholics Anonymous a Religious Organization?: Meditations on Marginality." *Sociological Analysis* 50: 41-51.

Schaef, A.W. 1986. *Co-Dependence: Misunderstood, Mistreated.* New York: Harper and Row.

_____. 1987. *When Society Becomes an Addict.* New York: Harper and Row.

_____. 1990. *Escape From Intimacy—Untangling the "Love" Addictions: Sex, Romance, Relationships.* New York: Harper and Row.

Subby, R. 1987. *Lost in the Shuffle: The Co-Dependent Reality.* Deerfield Beach, FL: Health Communications.

Wegscheider-Cruse, S. 1984. "Co-Dependency: The Therapeutic Void." Pp. 1-4 in *Co-Dependency: An Emerging Issue.* Deerfield Beach, FL: Health Communications.

_____. 1985. *Choicemaking: For Co-dependents, Adult Children and Spirituality Seekers.* Deerfield Beach, FL: Health Communications.

Weisner, C.M. 1983. "The Alcohol Treatment Systems and Social Control: A Study in Institutional Change." *Journal of Drug Issues* (Winter): 117-133.

Weisner, C.M., and R. Room. 1984. "Financing and Ideology in Alcohol Treatment." *Social Problems* 32: 167-184.

Whitfield, C. 1986. *Healing the Child Within.* Baltimore: The Research Group.

THE HIDDEN TRUTH:
ASTROLOGY AS WORLDVIEW

Shoshanah Feher

ABSTRACT

The longevity of the current revival of the occult forces one to stop and ask what this movement is all about. Focusing on astrology as an esoteric movement which has maintained its momentum over the past two decades, I have asked: How does astrology fit into the lives of its adherents? The focus of this study is on adherents to astrology who attended an astrology conference. Drawing on Stark and Bainbridge's typology of cults, this paper suggests that those astrologers who are very involved in astrology are part of a larger community concerned with finding a spiritual path. As members of this larger community, the respondents in this study give meaning to the world in a new way, a way that is different from that of traditional Western religions. In trying to understand themselves better, they have found in astrology a tool that facilitates the actualization of their spirituality.

INTRODUCTION

Talk about being an Aries, having one's moon in Virgo, or having a lot of fire in one's chart is reminiscent of flower children and pickup lines in bars

Religion and the Social Order, Volume 4, pages 165-177.
ISBN: 1-55938-763-7

during the 1970s. Indeed, it was in the 1970s that interest in astrology heightened. An ancient art,[1] astrology became very popular in the United States as part of the occult revival in the 1960s and 1970s (Melton 1985; Wuthnow 1976) and continues to be a part of American culture in the 1990s.[2] The persistence of astrology is shown clearly in Gallup poll findings. In 1976, 22 percent of the population "believed" in astrology (Stark and Bainbridge 1985). By 1978 the figure was up to 29 percent (Gallup Poll Survey 1978), and in 1990 25 percent of the U.S. public "believed" in astrology (Gallup and Newport 1990).[3] Despite the high percentage of adherents to astrology, its recent revival has received little attention from social scientists (Marty 1970; Truzzi 1972; Tiryakian 1974; Greeley 1974). This paper addresses a simple, but crucial, question: What role does astrology play in the lives of its adherents?

My focus is primarily on those astrologers who are actively interested in astrology—those whose investment goes beyond a casual reading of a newspaper astrology column. The numbers reported by Gallup (see also Stark and Bainbridge 1985; Wuthnow 1976) reflect the general public's interest in astrology at all levels, but they do not tell us what proportion of the public are serious-minded astrologers.[4] The majority of those interested in astrology are interested in it at a superficial level; they read astrology columns in newspapers and magazines without knowledge of the mechanics of astrology (Truzzi 1972). Scholars have termed this popular astrology of the mass media "mass astrology" (Fischler 1974). A much smaller percentage of adherents are interested in the component of astrology that is speculative and philosophical, known as "learned astrology" (Fischler 1974). These adherents read the astrological literature and are able to cast their own horoscopes. For them, astrology is a means by which to establish their identity and give meaning to the world (Truzzi 1972).

This categorization of astrology into "mass astrology" and "learned astrology" loosely coincides with Stark and Bainbridge's (1985) typology of cults, which identifies three different types of cults: audience cults, client cults, and cult movements. The most loosely structured of the three cult types are audience cults. This type of cult has little organization; in the case of astrology, the activity of the members occurs mostly through the mass media—newspaper or magazine horoscopes.

The client cult is slightly more organized. The relationship between a member of a client cult and the leader tends to be similar to that of a therapist/patient or consultant/client relationship. Client cults offer organization to the members who provide services, but not to those who receive them. In the case of astrology, this means that there is an organization of those producing and interpreting the charts. Also, when horoscopes are not generic (as in a newspaper) but are specifically produced for the client, a close relationship arises between the astrologer and the client.

A cult becomes a cult movement when members attend cult sessions regularly. Generally, the members of this type of cult are intensely committed to the group and are therefore in tension with the rest of society. Unlike the two other types of cults, cult movements are *religions* and are therefore able to provide answers to fundamental questions about the meaning of life. Organized in the form of a cult movement, astrology moves beyond the consultant/client relationship to one in which all adherents can and do produce and interpret horoscopes themselves. These adherents of astrology are not satisfied with simplistic interpretations of the horoscope. Instead, they seek deep answers to existential questions.

Stark and Bainbridge (1985) argue that astrology is limited to being an audience cult or a client cult. They note that an audience cult, through its use of the mass media, reaches the largest audience and becomes a form of entertainment. In contrast, client cult astrologers are more likely to "believe" in astrology rather than view it as entertainment. The possibility of astrology being a cult movement is not mentioned by Stark and Bainbridge (1985). They do not address the possibility that astrology may have a philosophical aspect (Fischler 1974) or that it may provide identity and meaning for some adherents (Truzzi 1972). It is my contention that astrology cannot be relegated to one or two cult "types," but rather that astrology runs the gamut of the three, depending on an individual's investment and involvement in the craft. People use astrology in different ways and, accordingly, there is variation in how meaningful and central astrology is in individuals' lives.

In this paper I will examine the role played by astrology in the life of its active adherents in the light of the three cult types described, and, also, as a function of the adherent's investment and involvement in the craft.

DATA

The data on which this paper is based were collected using standard survey techniques. The questionnaire used in collecting the data was tested at a regional astrology conference, the Saturn/Neptune Conference, held in San Diego, California in March 1989. Fifty-three of the 120 attending the conference completed the preliminary questionnaire. The results of the pretest questionnaires, as well as personal conversations with some respondents, led to a more sophisticated instrument.

The final questionnaire was distributed at the United Astrologer's Congress in New Orleans, Louisiana, 1989 (UAC'89). UAC'89 attracted people of every level of expertise in astrology from all over the world. The conference was organized by three of the four professional astrology groups in the country, the International Society for Astrological Research (ISAR), the Association for Astrological Networking (AFAN), and the National Council for Geocosmic

Research (NCGR). It was the second such conference; the first took place in 1986.

Questionnaires were distributed to all 600 attendees, 383 of whom completed and returned the survey. The final questionnaire consisted of 40 closed-ended questions, several of which had multiple parts. It included questions on a range of topics, such as: level of involvement in astrology, demographic characteristics, and the nature of the astrological services they provide or seek.

To supplement the survey data, I conducted personal interviews with several astrologers. No systematic selection process was used; rather, those interviewed were chosen by their availability and willingness to participate.[5] These interviews helped to flesh out areas that were limited by the questionnaire and to develop a qualitative understanding of the role of astrology in the respondent's lives.

Clearly, the respondents in this study are a select group; they represent those with sufficient interest in astrology to attend an astrology conference. Therefore, while these data may not be generalizable to the population at large, this study offers insights regarding the meaning of astrology in the lives of some of its adherents.

RESULTS

I present my findings in three sections. In the first two I address the basic questions: (1) whether, for UAC'89 respondents, astrology constitutes a worldview; and (2) whether, for these respondents, the degree of their involvement and the level of investment affects the role that astrology plays in their lives. In the third section, I let the respondents in the study speak in their own voices, in order to clarify and enrich the quantitative data.

If Stark and Bainbridge are correct in their assessment of who practices astrology, the UAC'89 respondents would use astrology as purely a leisure time activity, not affecting their worldview. On the other hand, if there are astrologers for whom astrology is a cult movement, astrology would be part of a larger system of meaning that helps comprise their worldview. This, as I will show, is the case.

Astrology as a Worldview

To determine whether astrology is a worldview and provides a meaning system, it is necessary to describe the kinds of organizational links that bind astrology adherents into a social network. As Stark and Bainbridge (1985) argue, a high density of linkages is evidence of a developed cult movement. My first step will be to describe how astrology is viewed by UAC'89 attendees. I will then turn to a discussion of these adherents' organizational links and social networks.

UAC'89 respondents were asked if they consider astrology to be a science, an occult movement, a healing art, or a psychological tool.[6] Ninety-eight percent of the respondents believe astrology to be a psychological tool, 89 percent believe it to be a healing art, and 82 percent think of it as a science. It is interesting that the respondents are almost evenly divided over their view of astrology as occult: 41 percent claim it is occult and 59 percent disagree. This may represent a genuine disagreement, on the other hand, it may signify that the term "occult" has acquired nebulous and negative connotations and that, as a result, some people may be hesitant to apply the label "occult" to what they do.

As mentioned earlier, examining whether astrology has organizational links and social networks is critical because it has implications for classification within the Stark and Bainbridge typology; the more linkages, the more it qualifies as a cult movement. Because organizational links in the astrological community seem to be virtually nonexistent, astrology appears to fall into Stark and Bainbridge's categories of client or audience cult. It is not that there are no astrological organizations; indeed, there are four national organizations. However, none offers *an* ideology that unites all astrology adherents. Meetings occur relatively infrequently (regional and/or national meetings are held about once a year). As noted earlier, UAC is an effort of three of the four organizations and has met three times to date (in 1986, 1989, and 1992).

Another indicator of social networks is the extent of shared linkages to other movements and activities. To this end, I examine responses to questions dealing with shared links to other movements and other activities which are not necessarily a part of astrology. In response to these questions, 77 percent of the respondents consider themselves a part of the New Age Movement, and many are involved in other esoteric practices.[7] Over 50 percent of the respondents are interested in either meditation, metaphysics, eastern philosophy, or reincarnation; and 40 percent of the respondents indicated a high interest in either clairvoyance, telepathy, tarot, or past life regression. Twenty-one percent of the respondents professionally practice at least one of the twenty esoteric teachings listed in the questionnaire (e.g., tarot, crystals, and meditation). One of my informants uses an analogy to a plumber to better explain this involvement in other teachings. He asks: "Does the plumber have a tool box?" and answers:

> Of course. You see, these are tools and it may be that a person's capacity may only allow them to come to master a few of those tools, or it may be that they master quite a number of them. I don't know that you need so many, but certainly there are a few different ones that you need.

In other words, astrology is one way of understanding the world and it can be used in conjunction with other esoteric "tools." This overlap of "tools" is a concept found in other movements. For example, it is similar to witchcraft, in that magicians situate their craft within the New Age while also engaging in such practices as tarot, meditation, and astrology (Lurhman 1989). Indeed, according to Greeley (1974), this should not come as a surprise. He argues that the occult provides people with meaning and community. As Geertz (Greeley 1974, p. 298) asserts, occultism gives its adherents a "picture of the way things in sheer actuality are—a concept of nature, of self, and of society" and as such helps adherents formulate a worldview.

Another indicator of social integration is the degree to which those involved in astrology are surrounded by like-minded persons. Thirty-seven percent of the respondents say that their four closest friends consult astrologers, while only 12 percent of the respondents report having no friends who consult astrologers. Friendships with people who are seriously involved in astrology—indicated by whether they read or have read astrological charts—are somewhat rarer. Twenty percent of the respondents report that all four of their four closest friends read charts while 24 percent of the respondents have no friends reading charts. The remaining respondents have some friends who consult and/or read charts.

These findings suggest that astrology may not form a sharply bounded community in and of itself. For those UAC respondents who are very interested in astrology, social networks are apparent; their friends consult other astrologers and read horoscopes. These respondents seem to form what Bellah et al. (1985) call a "lifestyle enclave" that involves the private sphere and brings together those who are socially, economically, or culturally similar. More important for the purpose at hand, UAC'89 respondents seem to "seek lifestyle enclaves to find the self-expression missing from the rest of their lives" (Bellah et al. 1985, p. 75). While the astrological community may not have sharp boundaries, it does seem to be a community of nebulous or permeable boundaries. In this way, UAC astrologers are like those involved in other occult movements in as much as they are part of a larger community which involves many esoteric teachings (Luhrman 1989; Jorgensen and Jorgensen 1982).

Involvement and Investment in Astrology

Does cult type depend on the degree to which a participant is involved in astrology? In other words, is astrology as a worldview dependent on the respondent's involvement? To measure degree of involvement among astrology adherents, I created a three-item index of involvement. The items included: (1) whether persons consider themselves astrologers or clients, (2) the percentage of the respondent's income deriving from astrology, and (3) whether or not they generate horoscopes (i.e., "charts"). These variables were chosen because they reflect how invested the respondents are in astrology. One point was given for each positive answer: if the individual is an astrologer, if over 50 percent of his/her income comes from astrology, and if he/she generate charts.

Table 1. Regression Estimating Level of Involvement
in Astrology Among UAC'89 Respondents[8]

Variables	Full Model Betas
Constant	1.508
Marginality Measures	
Children	0.070
Income	-0.025
Nonwhite	-0.326
Female	-0.158
Age	-0.006
Education	-0.015
Unmarried	-0.039
Job stability	0.035
Lonely	-0.161
View of Astrology Measures	
Healing art	0.301
Psychological tool	-0.394
Occult	-0.372**
Science	-0.358*
Worldview Measures	
Other teachings	0.438**
Friends consult	0.156**
Friends read	0.018
New Age	0.023
R^2	0.221
N	198
Standard Error	0.887
F	2.998***

Notes: * $p < 0.05$; ** $p < 0.01$; *** $p < 0.001$

Coding Scheme for Regression Analysis

Marginality Measures:
  Children: 0; 1; 2; 3; 4; 5 or more children
  Income: 1, under $10,000; 2, $11,000-20,000; 3, $21,000-30,000; 4, $31,000-40,000; 5, $41,000-60,000; 6,
    $61,000-80,000; 7, over $80,000
  Nonwhite: 0, White; 1, Nonwhite
  Female: 0, Male; 1, Female
  Age: in actual years (range is from 13 to 84)
  Education: 1, some high school or less; 2, completed high school; 3, vocational school; 4, some college; 5,
    graduated from college; 6, graduate degree
  Unmarried: 0, Married; 1, Unmarried
  Job Stability: 0, Unstable job; 1, Job Stability
  Lonely: 0, Not Lonely; 1, Lonely
Whether Astrology is Viewed as a(n):
  Healing Art: 0, no; 1, yes
  Psychological Tool; 0, no; 1, yes
  Occult: 0, yes; 1, no
  Science: 0, yes; 1, no
Worldview Measures:
  [Practice] Other Teachings: 0, no; 1, yes
  [How many of 4 closest] Friends Consult [other astrologers]: 0-4
  [How many of 4 closest] Friends Read [or have read charts]: 0-4
  [Consider self part of] New Age: 0, no; 1, yes

Using regression analysis, I discovered that the sizeable effects of certain demographic factors decreased significantly when controlling for worldview and how astrology is perceived. Demographic variables included: how many children the respondent had (0 to 5 or more), the respondent's family income (coded in 7 increments), ethnicity, gender, marital situation, job stability, or loneliness (all coded as dummy variables). These had no effect; nor did the respondent's age (continuous variable ranging from 13 to 84) or education (discrete variable ranging from 1 to 6). The following set of measures determines whether level of involvement affects how the respondents view astrology. These variables are measures of whether the respondents regard astrology as a(n): healing art, a psychological tool, occult, and/or a science (all coded 0, 1). The next set of variables are those that measure whether astrology provides the UAC'89 respondents with a worldview. These variables include: whether they practice other esoteric teachings, whether they consider themselves part of the New Age movement (both coded as dummy variables), how many of their four closest friends consult other astrologers, and read, or have read, horoscopes (coded 0 to 4).

The most significant predictor in the involvement model is whether the respondents professionally practice any other esoteric teachings. Also affecting level of involvement is whether the respondents' friends consult astrologers, and whether the respondents themselves view astrology as either a science or occult. I found that those respondents who are most likely to be highly involved in astrology practice esoteric teachings for money, have friends who consult astrologers, and do not consider astrology to be occult or a science.

These findings suggest that for the UAC'89 participants who are highly involved in astrology, astrology qualifies as a worldview. These respondents participate in social networking, have friends who consult astrologers, and consider astrology to be important in creating social meaning. This supports the notion that the more they are involved in astrology, the more adherents are likely to fit into the cult movement category of Stark and Bainbridge's (1985) typology.

The Astrologer Speaks

The findings discussed suggest that, for some, astrology is but a part of a larger ideology involving many teachings, that gives meaning to life. The esoteric teachings in which respondents profess the most interest—meditation, metaphysics, and reincarnation—are practices that endeavor to provide an understanding of the world. Central to this understanding is the idea of oneness. One astrologer, Brian, explained:

> You know, it's like in a sense to see, to begin to live life as a part of the whole...
> The whole energy is moving, the whole energy of mankind is moving towards

this [unification] and not this separation. Before there was both, they were moving out of the space of separation into the wholeness.

These highly involved people do not believe astrology needs to be legitimized or scientifically justified. For example, Harvey states, "people [astrologers] have got to get away from justifying astrology,…to stop trying to prove anything. I mean nobody's running around trying to prove that gravity works." For those who are highly involved, astrology becomes something that "works" and hence needs no other justification. At this level of involvement, the "less importance it [astrology] seems to have as an allegedly scientific device for prediction, and the more it represents a general metaphysical worldview for its adherents" (Truzzi 1975, p. 909).

Some respondents tend to ask existential questions and find their answers within, or with the help of, astrology. Brian, a respondent who began practicing astrology in the early 1970s, has been involved with a variety of spritualities over the years, from Krishnamurti to "saffron robes" to "black coats" (as he referred to his involvement with Bhagwan Rajneesh and Hasidism). But he kept coming back to astrology—"it seemed to have something to it." This "something" is answers to questions about the world and ourselves:

> So the question always was, who are we? You know, for me, who am I? What am I? You know, by Hillel, "if I'm not for myself, who will be? If I'm not for others, what am I? And if not now, when?" So I used to think about that a lot. And the question was always: who am I? Then it became: what am I? And it was all tied up with what's going on and astrology seemed to offer some kind of [answer]…

Similarly, Gary, a practicing psychologist who has been interested in astrology since 1973, talks about astrology as "hidden truth." He says that through the years, and through his career, he was able to "develop [a] belief system that gives expression to these hidden truths." Finally, Harvey, a retired businessman who was selling crystals at the conference, believes that we are all looking for the same answers. We all:

> have the same questions… You know, why am I here? What am I doing? What does it mean to be alive?… You could say that the astrologer uses a different way to approach that question.

From this perspective, astrology is a tool to find the answer to these questions; a tool unlike Christian Fundamentalism, which is very authoritarian and "gives" the answers, and a tool unlike psychoanalysis, which takes a very long time. Harvey says that, unlike these other techniques, astrology is a tool that quickens the pace without having someone give you the answers.

Janet is a young woman who works in a publishing house and who had to scrimp and save to be able to afford the expense of the conference. She currently lives in New York and has been interested in astrology since the early 1980s. For her, astrology is part of her "inner belief." Her family, primarily her mother, believes that astrology is a hobby of Janet's and that Janet still holds "that [Catholic] belief system" that she was raised with. Because her mother "does not want to hear any differently," Janet cannot tell her that astrology is not a hobby and that Janet's belief system is informed by astrology and reincarnation.

These informants use astrology as a way of answering existential questions. For two of the respondents just described, astrology is a belief system. For the other two, astrology is a tool which enables them to answer their existential questions. All of them ask questions, and all of them have found answers to varying degrees.

For many UAC'89 participants, astrology is the basis for a community with a particular worldview. The respondents are not searching among teachings, but rather use astrology as one way of understanding within their larger knowledge system. As Brian put it,

> I needed a different kind of knowledge and I didn't know how to get it. I didn't even know that I needed it, you know, and I found that through being…all these different people, a guy named Geoffery Hodson, Krishnamurti, Muktandanda and Rajneesh, and that's something that's totally separate in a sense from astrology but, there's a way to use the [incorporate] astrological chart.

This approach also explains why astrology is considered by the respondents to be both a healing art and a psychological tool; both can be used in conjunction with other teachings and are part of a larger framework for understanding the world.

This finding does not support Stark and Bainbridge's discussion of astrology as only an audience or client cult. On the contrary, the results of the UAC'89 survey serve to demonstrate that astrology can function as a cult movement. Indeed, while low on organizational linkages, it is perhaps *because* it is open-ended organizationally that astrology has been able to blend with other movements, qualifying it as a cult movement. It is undoubtedly true that the majority of those interested in astrology use it in a manner consistent with Stark and Bainbridge's description (Wuthnow 1976). However, I have demonstrated that, for some, astrology provides social and philosophical links that allow them to address existential questions.

Possibly the most striking finding of this study is that many people are not only interested in astrology but rather use it as one tool in their spiritual quest. The astrologers I talked to are on such a spiritual quest; they are continuously trying to understand themselves better and are engaged in an esoteric quest while trying to find a practical approach to the admonition "know yourself" (Harvey). The underlying thread in the quest is one of oneness with the universe, "as above, so below" (Gary). Harvey takes this idea further when he uses the analogy of the hologram to explain his vision of the world: "We are like a little piece of the hologram, and we are a model of the whole universe." In each piece of the hologram, he explains, you can see the picture of the whole hologram. For these astrologers, astrology becomes the tool to be used in "knowing oneself," a process termed transformation, development process, or transpersonal approach (Harvey, Gary, Brian). For some, like Janet, astrology is,

> just an interest of mine, esoteric, metaphysics, metaphysical types of things. I'm searching for an outward manifestation of how I feel inside, you know? So I'm searching.

This concept of self-knowledge is considered absolutely necessary in other occult movements. For example, witchcraft has been described as a psychological technique that enables one to acquire self-knowledge (Luhrman 1989). For some, astrology serves as a "vocabulary" to describe what they were aware of but previously could not describe (Gary). Astrology is one of many different tangible forms of the spiritual quest.

CONCLUSION

The longevity of the current revival of the occult forces one to stop and ask what this movement is all about. Taking a look at astrology, one of these esoteric movements which has maintained its momentum over the past two decades, I have asked: how does astrology fit into the lives of its adherents?

In this paper, I have presented results from an international astrology conference. Using Stark and Bainbridge's framework, I suggest that among UAC'89 respondents, astrology seems to be a lifestyle enclave. This differs from Stark and Bainbridge's findings, which fit astrology within the audience cult or client cult categories of their typology. Astrologers who are very involved in astrology, like those who attended UAC'89, are likely to integrate astrology into their lives in a way not captured by Stark and Bainbridge's audience and client cult categories. I therefore suggest that, for those adherents who show significant investment and involvement, astrology can also be classified as a cult movement. Clearly, not all those interested in astrology fall into the cult movement category; in fact most probably do not. However, the findings presented in this paper suggest that, in understanding the adherents of astrology and in conducting future studies, this third option must be taken into consideration.

For UAC'89 respondents, astrology seems to be but a part of a larger community. The concern of the larger community is to find a spiritual path, to give meaning to the world in a new way, a way that is different from traditional Western religions. In better trying to understand themselves, they have found ways to actualize their spirituality. Many seem to use multiple esoteric techniques to achieve this end, with astrology being yet another tool in this quest.

ACKNOWLEDGMENTS

I would like to thank all those who were instrumental in the development of this work. I am particularly grateful to Phillip Hammond, Roger Friedland, Michael Delucchi, Val Jenness, Elsa Feher, Naomi Abrahams, Armand Mauss, and John Sutton. Fundamental to this project were all those who attended both the San Diego and New Orleans astrology congresses. Not only would data collection have been impossible without them, but, thanks to countless conversations, I was able to better understand the world of astrology. Finally, I would like to thank the Institute for the Study of American Religion for providing the funding for this work.

NOTES

1. Astrology has historically held a role of importance. In the sixteenth century, astrology and astronomy were one and the same; for example, court astronomers determined auspicious days. However, the paths diverged, and, during the Enlightenment, astronomy joined the ranks of the sciences and astrology was relegated to the occult.

2. Astrology, and the occult in general, have had a place among North Americans for centuries. Melton has written that interest in astrology in the 1960s and 1970s did not "emerge out of a cultural discontinuity or a massive importation of ideas...but it signalled a sudden spurt in the growth rate of a movement htat has been gaining momentum for many decades" (Melton 1985, p. 294).

3. Unfortunately, Gallup did not inquire about people's interest in astrology prior to 1976, thus making it difficult to assess exactly how popular astrology was in the 1950s and 1960s.

4. While many (e.g., Gallup and Newport 1990) discuss adherents' belief in astrology, in this paper I refer to adherents' interest. Belief seems to me to be a clumsy descriptor in this case, although presumably both concepts measure the same relatoinship.

5. In this paper, interviewees are referred to by fictional names.

6. These answers were not treated as mutually exclusive on the questionnaire.

7. The New Age movement emphasizes, among other things, that a spiritual transformation will occur after which people will be better aware that we are one with the natural world (Lucas 1989). The same emphasis is evident among astrologers.

8. Superscripts indicate statistical significance.

REFERENCES

Bellah, R., R. Madsen, W. Sullivan, A. Swidler, and S. Tipton. 1985. *Habits of the Heart*. Berkeley: University of California Press.

Fischler, C. 1974. "Astrology and French Society." Pp. 281-315 in *On the Margin of the Visible*, edited by E. Tiryakian. New York: Wiley.

Gallup, G., and F. Newport. 1990. "Belief in Psychic and Paranormal Phenomena Widespread Among Americans." *The Gallup Poll Monthly* 229: 35-45.

Gallup Poll Survey. 1978. "Surprising Number of Americans Believe in Paranormal Phenomena," June 15.

Greeley, A. 1974. "Implications for the Sociology of Religion." Pp. 295-302 in *On the Margin of the Visible,* edited by E. Tiryakian. New York: Wiley.

Jorgensen, D., and L. Jorgensen. 1982. "Social Meanings of the Occult." *Sociological Quarterly* 23: 373-389.

Lucas, P. 1989. "The New Age Movement and the Pentecostal/Charismatic Revival: Distinct Yet Parallel Phases of a Fourth Great Awakening?" Paper presented at the annual meeting of the American Academy of Religion, Anaheim, CA.

Luhrman, T. 1989. *Persuasions of the Witch's Craft: Ritual Magic and Witchcraft in Present Day England.* Cambridge, MA: Harvard University Press.

Marty, M. 1970. "The Occult Establishment." *Social Research* 37: 212-230.

Melton, G. 1985. "The Revival of Astrology in the United States." Pp. 279-296 in *Religious Movements: Genesis, Exodus and Numbers,* edited by R. Stark. New York: Paragon House.

_____. 1989. Director of the Institute for the Study of American Religion. Private communication.

Stark, R., and W.S. Bainbridge. 1985. *The Future of Religion.* Berkeley: University of California Press.

Tiryakian, E. 1974. "Toward a Sociology of Esoteric Culture." Pp. 257-280 in *On the Margin of the Visible,* edited by E. Tiryakian. New York: Wiley.

Truzzi, M. 1972. "Toward a Sociology of the Occult." Pp. 628-645 in *Religious Movements in Contemporary America,* edited by I. Zaretsky and M.P. Leone. Princeton, NJ: Princeton University Press.

_____. 1975. "Astrology as Popular Culture." *Journal of Popular Culture* 8: 906-911.

Wuthnow, R. 1976. "Astrology and Marginality." *Journal for the Scientific Study of Religion* 15: 157-168.

PART III

THE POLITICS OF RELIGIOUS DEFINITIONS

THE INTERFACE OF RELIGION
AND POLITICS:
A NORMATIVE APPROACH

Clarke E. Cochran

ABSTRACT

This paper argues against the notion of politics as quasi-religion, though it does not reject the value of thinking of religion and politics together. Rather, religion and politics should be thought of as separate social spheres connected by tension between their respective purposes. The tension between them refers to their different trajectories; religion's is toward transcendence and righteousness; politics' is toward compromise. This argument is illustrated by policy conflicts over abortion, capital punishment, war, "family values," and other contemporary political issues.

To think in "quasi" terms is to think crazily, at least from the perspective of a political philosopher. Philosophy is about drawing distinctions, clear distinctions being the condition of clear thinking. Political philosophers like sharp borders around their notions: moral rights distinct from legal rights; freedom and liberty; justice as recognition of difference, but *relevant* differences. Relevant to what, precisely?

Religion and the Social Order, Volume 4, pages 181-196.
ISBN: 1-55938-763-7

From this perspective, talking about quasi-religion is of questionable utility. To do so is likely to confuse the distinctions between religion and whatever other phenomenon is argued to take on religious coloration. This is particularly the case when it comes to politics and religion. If some political phenomena can be quasi-religious (or some religions quasi-political), why bother with the distinction between the religious and the political?

Yet to reject "quasi" thinking is not to deny an essential bearing of religion on politics (and vice versa). Nor is it to regard them as radically separate. If concepts really were distinct, philosophy would be an easy job. Oakeshott once said in a famous introduction to Hobbes' *Leviathan*: "Political philosophy... is the consideration of the relation between politics and eternity.... We may, then enquire of any political philosophy... whether the gift of politics to mankind is, in principle, the gift of salvation itself, or whether it is something less, and if the latter, what relation it bears to salvation" (Oakeshott 1946, p. lxiv). I argue here that the most fruitful way of looking at that bearing is from the perspective of border tensions.

To consider the relation between politics and eternity seems particularly important in America, "a nation by intention and by ideas," as Os Guinness has put it (Hunter and Guinness 1990, p. 9). America has always existed as a nation seeking and celebrating common vision. As Chesterton pointed out, America is a "nation with the soul of a church" (Mead 1975). We seek a common ideal, a public philosophy, and discover that religious symbols (e.g., kingdom of God, city on a hill, and liberation) may shape the vision most effectively (Hunter and Guinness 1990, pp. 9-10).

This very language of vision, national soul, and common purpose does suggest that the political system, at least its most potent symbol-generating parts, is quasi-religious. That suggestion is a matter of great fear for many liberals, who pledge their allegiance to strict separation of church and state. Yet the suggestion generates hope in many on the religious right, for whom a God-infused national public life is the only hope for America. I argue that both are wrong. Religion linked to politics is neither the danger nor the salvation that these camps fear. But I argue further that, although the religion and politics links are real and indeed valuable, to conceive of political phenomena as *quasi-religious* or religious phenomena as *quasi-political* is not the most productive conceptualization. Religion and politics do have separate identities and separate purposes; therefore, "quasi" language obscures their distinctness. However, because politics in the democratic mode is a conversation among different voices, the voice of religion may enter the conversation. Or, in terms of the border image used frequently in this paper, because democratic discourse requires an open border and free trade in ideas, religious ideas, symbols, and images are a permitted, indeed needed, part of the continuing dialogue.[1]

BOUNDARIES ARE NOT QUASI

To get a visual representation of what I mean by referring to borders and boundaries, but also to interaction, think of the Okeephenokee Swamp, located on the border of Georgia and Florida.[2] The swamp's extension across the border does not deny the separate existences of Georgia and Florida, though the swamp makes it difficult to establish a clear boundary between them. Moreover, administration of the swamp may require the states' frequent cooperation. Nevertheless, though it must frequently work with Florida on swamp-related matters, Georgia is not quasi-Florida.

Now think of religion and politics as the two states of our example, and of democratic discourse as the Okeephenokee Swamp. Such discourse crosses into areas of concern to religion and, of course, into strictly governmental matters. The borders become blurred, and religious voices enter the dialogue, sometimes even into cooperative administration, but also into conflict, just as Georgia and Florida do not always see eye-to-eye on the Okeephenokee. Again, the idea of *quasi*-religion or *quasi*-politics is not the most helpful in clarifying the boundary issues. The real problem with the concept of quasi-religion is that an imaginary entity is being created, when what we really want to do is describe a relationship. Creating the new entity would at the same time create *two* boundaries where before there was one.

Religion's contribution to democratic discourse is to suggest to the sensitive participant in culture just what is at stake in border controversies between public and private life. Culture is first of all public; its beliefs, customs, traditions, stories, and emotions are the common possession of citizens who need share no significant private life.

Because religion suggests that culture is not divine (at most, it is the direct creation of the divine), religion more directly than other systems of value insinuates the tension between culture and something higher than culture. Although religion is linked to culture and frequently coopted by it, religions with reflective traditions (most prominently Islam, Hinduism, Christianity, Buddhism, and Judaism) emphatically suggest tension with culture. The inherent dynamic of religion's orientation to a transcendent source of being, independent of human control, opens the path toward cultural conflict. As much as culture takes upon itself divine color, it cannot hide its human roots.

Although the tension between the divine and the mundane sometimes manifests itself as stress between private and public life, the individual person, where the competing attractions of culture and the sacred intersect, is the locus of tension. The unique perspective of religion reveals the person as a field of cross-cutting tensions between the divine and culture in private and public life.

Because it influences moral virtue and individual well-being, therefore, religion can powerfully assist the state by inculcating and nourishing a moral foundation for culture. Yet this role is easily misunderstood and often converted into either theocracy or civil religion. Here is where the strict separationists, who desire complete autonomy of politics from religion, make their strongest case. The conversion of religious participation into either theocracy or civil religion is dangerous to democratic freedom. This danger, for example, lies behind recent separationist arguments against education vouchers (Doerr and Menendez 1991, pp. 132-137). Nationalism in Yugoslavia and fundamentalism in the Middle East provide the most potent examples of the danger.

The liberal tradition, therefore, argues for the privatization of religion, enforced by strict institutional boundaries and an active border patrol. Strong rights are one way to maintain this privatization. Religious freedom is defended by separationists, as long as the churches do not try to impinge on other rights areas: speech, artistic expression, sexual behavior, political opinions, and the like. But, as Glendon (1991, pp. 85ff, 109-144) argues, the strongly individualistic rights tradition in America depends on the idea of a "nation of strangers," creates the erroneous impression that law and morality are separate, and makes it impossible to think clearly about the contemporary war over the family and children.

Moreover, Hammond (1991, p. 121) argues persuasively that privatization of religion, even where possible, does not at all entail the privatization of the sacred. The flawed attempt to carve out a purely scientifically grounded "brainwashing" exception to first amendment religious freedom protections also demonstrates the futility of drawing clear and impenetrable borders between religion and politics (Anthony and Robbins 1992).

Although I have stressed the intersection of religion and public life, religion, nevertheless, fundamentally reminds us of the limits of politics and of the nonequivalence of politics and public life. Because religion intends transcendence, it relativizes and thereby limits all other spheres of activity, including politics. Religion points to a sovereignty beyond state sovereignty (Berger 1988). In the American tradition, for example, the Bible has reminded us "that public spirit will always be opposed by private interest," that law and coercion must supplement public virtue and participation, and that "the larger the political society, the greater the tension between body and spirit, private feelings and public duties" (McWilliams 1984, p. 19).

The distinctive contribution of religion to public and private life, to individuals and to culture is to refer them to what is beyond politics. The following pages discuss some of these things beyond politics—sin, evil, and death—and how they appear on the border between public and private life.

This reference beyond politics constitutes a challenge to political discourse to look beyond its natural preoccupation with interests and compromise. Indeed, it is this challenge that is religion's distinctive contribution to political discourse; yet politics also has a contribution to make in challenging the pretensions of religion.

THE POLITICS OF SIN

A persistent delusion in contemporary culture, an emanation of the "therapeutic society" described by Rieff (1968), makes obsolete sin and evil, and therefore guilt. The delusion pervades the contention that education and counseling, plus appropriate doses of technology and money, can cure major social and psychic ills. AIDS, teenage pregnancy, urban decay, drug abuse, joblessness and homelessness, crime, and racial and sexual discrimination could be cured or greatly alleviated if at-risk persons could only receive appropriate education and compassionate counseling and if enough money and high technology were devoted to solutions. Or so it is said.

The heated arguments over AIDS and sex education curricula in public schools illustrate quite well the utter impossibility of separating religion and politics, of keeping public language clear of sacred imagery and symbol. The public language of government, as it has been drawn into the sex business by AIDS and high rates of teenage pregnancy, is the language of "safe sex." But what does sex education involve but the question of how, when, and with whom to engage in sexual intercourse? These questions are the age-old business of parents, poets, and priests. Sexual intercourse involves personal identity, trust, loyalty, intimacy, dependence, and a whole host of other qualities deeply connected to the sacred. It is utterly delusional to think that government institutions, such as public schools and health clinics, can discuss these matters in a "neutral," nonreligious language of "safe sex."

This delusion cuts across the public/private boundary, involving weight loss fads, psychological nostrums, and self-help books as well as public programs. By labelling as delusions such approaches to social and personal problems, I do not contend that education, counseling, technology, and material resources are irrelevant. Rather, I insist that we need to acknowledge, privately and publicly, the role of intention, personal character, and fundamental life choices in creating and perpetuating what are as much evils as ills. Attacking them requires methods suitable to combatting sin as well as the methods for fighting ignorance, psychic disturbances, and lack of material resources.

I do not argue that all religions stimulate the sense of sin or that they do so in the same ways or to the same degree. But certainly Judaism, Islam, Christianity, Hinduism, and Buddhism recognize the deep roots of sin in the orientations of the human heart, and they contain stories explaining its origin, accounts of how to resist it, and rituals and disciplines for cleansing the soul.[3] Some methods are more passive than active, but the point is that private sin is recognized, as are its public consequences, and that public sin is also recognized with its private consequences. These religions discern not only "moral man and immoral society" (Niebuhr 1932), but also the reverse.

Guilt effectively links public and private life. To acknowledge guilt is to make contact with a world outside one's own delusions. Guilt ties the agent to the world through admission of the consequences of choice. Those without a properly proportioned sense of guilt (not those burdened by generalized guilt and a sense of worthlessness) lack firm connection to the world. They float through it like jellyfish on the tide, taking their nutrients, heedless of their victims.

What is true of individual guilt holds for nations and other public bodies. Religious sensitivity to guilt can call the public, especially politics, to awareness of responsibility and to illusions of innocence or grandeur. Such constitutes the public role of religious prophets. The prophet as public critic parallels the priest in the private world. (It is dangerous to reverse the two roles. The priest in public underwrites the regime; the prophet in private becomes a cynic.)[4]

Because religion has a special link to guilt and sin, the public, through the state, may profitably use religious institutions to address public problems, such as crime and drug abuse, that admit guilt and shame. It should not do so by making them matters of public sin, or by calling upon religion directly in the definition of crimes, or by turning the struggle against crime or drug addiction into "quasi-religious" crusades. Rather, the proper role of religion lies in rehabilitation efforts, service to victims of crime and drug abuse, and preventative education programs. Such efforts so directly concern both political society and churches that they cross the religion and politics border. I have specifically in mind public employment of chaplains in prisons, youth detention centers, and drug abuse treatment programs, as well as public funding of religious (on the same basis as nonreligious) youth programs, detoxification and recovery programs, counseling centers, half-way houses, and literacy and job training.

FEAR OF DEATH

If the public, especially political, significance of religion for the sense of sin is crucial, the importance of religion in the face of death is doubly so. Evil may be accounted for, and even dismissed, in a variety of ways, but death is more difficult to deny.[5] Religion and death, however, are most commonly associated with private life. Individuals face death alone or with their families, and they deal privately or in small groups with their fears. Religion, for believers, involves the encounter with death, but what relevance is that to politics?

Public life and death are not unacquainted. Think of the public funerals of heads of state or major public figures such as Gandhi, John and Robert Kennedy, and Martin Luther King, Jr. These are occasions, heavily laden with religious and political symbolism, in which the public ritually and collectively confronts death. Even more pointedly, think of the significance of the public display of Lenin's corpse and of the political crises in Argentina occasioned by disputes over the embalmed body of Eva Peron.

These illustrations pale, however, before the fact, not simply that polities hold the power of life and death, but that they claim legitimately to hold it. In the modern world at least, only the political order is allowed, legitimately, to take life through capital punishment and to wage war. This latter involves not simply ordering citizens to risk their lives, but also to take life. Moreover, polities have the responsibility to ensure that citizens are guarded as much as possible against the threat of death from starvation, drought, disease, and natural disaster, and their efforts to do so sometimes threaten the lives of citizens of other polities.

This insight into the links between death, politics, and religion deepens earlier points about morality and sin. Reflections on public and private life apart from religion could help explain the importance of character and virtue and even motivate citizens toward them, but what about death? How, apart from religion, do they motivate a person to die?[6] Religion does deal with the private and public meanings of death, so every society, every public order, must have a religious component of some sort, for every society must deal with both dimensions of death. Natural reason and political history need, in the face of death, sacred history and supernatural religion; hence, the excitement and the risk of religion and politics. They seek to instruct us in death.

OBJECTIONS

It might be objected that this argument is merely a subtle rationalization of the utility of religion to politics, of the social benefit of quasi-religious politics. Religion is useful because it provides a way to justify a regime's life-taking. My response is twofold. First, I have not yet said anything about *how* religion must interact with politics. Some ways of interaction certainly do improperly make religion the servant of politics; the tensional, border model of religion and politics does not. Second, I reject civil religion's reduction of religion to utility.

Another objection to my position cites the quasi-religious features of nationalism and totalitarian ideologies which undermine the proper distinctions between religion and politics by seeking to obliterate the border altogether. Ultimately, the power of life and death needs legitimation, which pseudo- (or quasi-) religious ideologies seek to provide. Replacing the sacred with the trans-human value of the nation, history, the race, or a utopia, they seek to justify death in the present in the name of these values. The horrible costs in human life and dignity are only too well-known. Witness "ethnic cleansing" in the name of national identity. The desire of ideologies to become substitute religions is nowhere more powerful than in the encounter with death. The political role of religion might be justified for no other reason than to guard against totalitarianism. Yet religion itself has been put to the service of justifying totalitarian and authoritarian death regimes. This service usually takes the form of theocracy or an oppressive civil religion.

Even nontotalitarian ideologies can possess these same features. Feminism, liberation theology, environmentalism (on the left), as well as capitalism, libertarianism, and the religious right (on the right) often have proponents who might safely be described as Eric Hoffer's "true believers." In light of the ideological politics of "public interest groups" on the left and right in the United States and in Europe, Lowi (1988) modified his influential classification of public policy types. He even goes so far as to use quasi-religious terms to designate new category types (sin, civic virtue, and moral government) reflecting radical ideological politics. Such groups take absolute moral stands on policy issues, refusing to enter the politics of compromise.

Hunter's (1991) description of the "culture wars" in America exemplifies well the religious crusading spirit at the heart of ideological conflict, as well as the important role of religious groups on the front lines. What makes the battle so intense, Hunter argues, is that its outcome will establish who possesses the moral authority to determine "how we will order our lives together" and the very "meaning of America" (1991, pp. 34, 50-52). These kinds of phenomena make the study of religion difficult today, for even the boundaries of religion and social science itself become blurred (Robbins and Robertson 1991). What I wish to establish is not why and how the border between religion and politics has become blurred in America, such that we are able to speculate about the existence of political quasi-religions. Hunter and others have done that work. What I want to establish is that, *properly distinguished,* religion and politics must not be thought of as the same; that is, my argument is primarily normative. Religion and politics should interact, not as civil religion or theocracy, as in nationalism and totalitarian ideologies, but across a border that recognizes their distinctness and the essential tensions between their purposes. What Neuhaus and Quade (Quade 1982, pp. vii-x, 1-2) say about Christianity should be said about all religions. When they identify themselves with a particular political order or allow themselves to become means, even to good ends, they betray their true identity.

Religion confronts politics in matters central to the identity of each. Such matters are particularly prominent in public policy today. They are issues of what Tatalovich and Daynes (1988) call "social regulatory policy" (abortion, school prayer, sex education, affirmative action, homosexual rights, prostitution, women's rights, capital punishment, crime and gun control, patriotism, immigration, and multiculturalism). The only way that government could deal with such issues *without* touching principles central to faith and the sacred would be *not* to deal with them at all; that is, to adopt the libertarian, *laissez-faire* position! Even this "solution," however, is not viable. First, it would please neither the political left nor the political right. Second, religious groups would consider nonaction on many of these issues in fact to be a government decision deeply affecting their adherents and the kind of society in which they live.

RELIGION AND POLITICS IN TENSION

The kind of interaction that I am advocating has become even more necessary (and more possible, despite the dangers) in recent decades. As Wuthnow (1988, pp. 71-131) has argued, the declining importance of denominationalism and the growth of "special purpose groups" within churches have radically altered the old relationships among churches and their relationship with government. Moreover, the entry of government into formerly sacred areas of life described above has forced religions to respond (Cochran, Perkins, and Havens 1987).[7] Moreover, and paradoxically, the interactions between church and state will necessarily grow, even as religion becomes more "privatized"; that is, as social structural differentiation defines as secular more and more matters formerly religious. The churches, in being true to their own self-understanding, then will have to deal with facts and issues now defined as "secular!"[8]

Two (or more) forces pulling in different directions define a tension. Sometimes stress holds things together as, for example, with a rubber band. But sometimes it causes things to break apart, as when a spring snaps from being wound too tightly. To understand the religion/politics tension, we must define the directions in which each pulls. We must also show how tension between them permits each to work better.[9]

Religion brings politics to awareness of the highest, lowest, and most mysterious features of life, especially of the lofty and the mysterious. Politics, better acquainted with the lowest, brings religious passion and self-assurance to awareness of the middle ground between the highest and the lowest; that is, it teaches religion the necessity and the art of compromise. "Our mistakes of understanding will be less frequent and less disastrous if we escape the illusion that politics is ever anything more than the pursuit of intimations; a conversation, not an argument" (Oakeshott 1962, p. 125).

Religion pulls toward the transcendent, toward principles, virtues, ideals, and perfection. Unrestrained by tension this religious dynamic produces fanaticism. Religious passion finds it difficult to compromise, to acknowledge how striving after perfection founders on human weakness. Politics, however, demands compromise, for the key fact of politics, especially of participatory public life, lies in confrontation with the ideas and the interests of others, with the mosaic of human frailty and plurality.

Just as religion would avoid compromise, politics would avoid righteousness. Politics pulls toward the vague middle ground, toward indifference and cynicism. Left to itself, politics seeks the easy, painless way. High principles make for difficult political choices, for it is painful to confront higher things, to acknowledge the possibility of something better and to accept the discipline necessary to reach it. Religion in public life can teach politics about the higher things and stimulate, even embarrass, politicians and citizens to discover them.

The tension produced by these conflicting natural tendencies defines their relationship as both competitive and cooperative. The danger of misunderstanding the relationship between religion and politics comes when we forget that it must include *both* cooperation and competition. When the tension is lost, the two either fly apart or, worse, collapse together. The latter is the world's too frequent condition.

PARTICULAR ISSUES

Central to religious identity are the matters of life and death considered above; that is, questions of war and peace, abortion, and capital punishment. Abortion is a good example of border tension regarding life and death. Religion plays a creative role in political discourse when it points out that abortion is about more than tissue and choice. It is about life and the right to take life. Although I recognize the dangers of the politics of abortion, I also believe that it is vital for American society's health that abortion be seriously debated among citizens. That is happening now, thanks in large measure to religious voices. The problem, of course, is that abortion politics has become polarized. The creative role of *politics* to the debate now must be to seek middle ground, for such seeking is difficult for both religious or ideological groups.

The historic parallel is the slavery controversy in the nineteenth century, which was built on the impossibility of considering the slave as simply a piece of private property. Religious arguments played a key role on both sides of the slavery debate, as they do on abortion today (Strout 1975, pp. 140-172). Millennial, apocalyptic, and revolutionary language was as important then (Nat Turner, Harriet Beecher Stowe, and John Brown) as now. Moreover, the pro-life dilemma of how to care for children and mothers, should abortion be banned or severely restricted, is paralleled by the abolitionist dilemma of what to do about the freed slaves (Strout 1975, pp. 199ff).

War and capital punishment are similar issues. Each involves the taking of life. Religious voices have been prominent in debates on both issues. Religious groups and actors were leaders in the anti-Vietnam War Movement and in opposition to capital punishment today. When public opinion can swing rapidly between pro- and anti- on war and the death penalty, it is important that religion remind us of the morally troubling and tragic consequences of the positions we adopt.

Life and death issues are certainly central to the relationship between religion and politics, but so too are other prominent public debates. It would be impossible to consider all key issues, so here follows just a sampling of how religion's voice must and should contribute to the public debates.

"Family values" was one of the catchwords of the 1992 presidential campaign. Both Democrats and Republicans attempted to claim the high ground. Family touches on many of the most important policy issues of our time—teen pregnancy, welfare, support for the elderly, crime and its causes, homosexual rights, and race, just for starters. Teen child-bearing, for example, seems to be a private matter for the pregnant girl and her family, but it is also a civic matter as it relates to public assistance spending and the feminization of poverty. Welfare reform today deeply evokes questions of individual responsibility that might legitimately be expected of public assistance recipients. The realm of kinship, tied as it is to so much of culture, cannot be isolated from politics (Walzer 1983). Yet religion always has been deeply embedded in the whole range of family life. It "hatches, matches, and dispatches." So it would seem impossible to isolate religious values and institutions from public policy approaches to the family and connected policy issues. Indeed, as Strout (1975, pp. 126-139, 242ff) points out, theologians, preachers, and social reformers from colonial times to the present, and from different sides of the political spectrum, have looked to the family and home as key institutions for personal redemption and for public order. Many of the contentious issues of the nineteenth century focused on the family values of minority religious groups, for example, Catholics and Mormons.[10]

Today, in many respects, America is becoming a two-tiered society, the gaps between rich and poor within different population groups becoming wider, affecting the life-chances of all citizens. Gaps grow between black and white, but also between the black middle-class and the black underclass, between the elderly with pensions and those living only on Social Security, and between married couples and single-parent families. Each of these areas of society (race, care of the aged, and family) are areas in which churches traditionally have been important.

Similarly, cost, access, and quality of health care are fundamental public policy issues of the last decade of the twentieth century. Churches must enter the debate because of their historic role in providing health care. Therefore, they should be able to work creatively to devise policies that ensure universal access to care, provide long-term care to the elderly, and develop alternatives to institutionalization.

Finally, there are a host of pressing issues with a strong moral component and with traditional religious prescriptions, teachings, and institutions. I am thinking of rising levels of anomic violence, of crime and the need to find alternatives to incarceration, of drug and alcohol addiction, of sexually transmitted diseases, and of pornography, rape, and other crimes against women. Implicitly or explicitly, the issues demand quality of life judgments, which are (willy-nilly) religious judgments. They involve, in Hunter's (1991, pp. 52-54) terms, questions of the source of moral authority in society, of who will dominate culture. Even more, churches are able to speak on these issues in a direct way because often their ministries bring them face-to-face with the harsh realities represented by this list of problems. Hence, there is a place for religious advocacy in the public policy arena and for implementation of public policies through church-related agencies.

THE VOICE OF RELIGION IN DEMOCRATIC DISCOURSE

Political theorists recently have been recovering and extending the civic republican tradition in the history of political thought. That tradition has its own roots in the American experience, but has recently been overshadowed by the notion of liberal democracy (see, for example, Taylor 1990). In the liberal tradition, democracy and freedom are viewed in protective terms; that is, the institutions of a democratic society protect individual interests and the rights of citizens against both tyrannical government and majority domination. The civic republican tradition, though not denying importance to these protections, also views freedom and democracy in participatory and developmental terms. Democratic institutions promote freedom because they require an active citizenry, which in its political labor develops and tests skills of moral reasoning, public discussion, and prudential judgment.

In contemporary terms, the civic republican tradition can be conceived in terms of a democratic polity that encloses various communities of discourse, a model particularly appropriate to a pluralistic political, social, and religious culture (Spragens 1990).[11] Democracy is not finding and promoting self-interest through voting and interest groups, but it is rather the public conversation of representatives of different moral and political perspectives, who seek common ground on which to build policies that best promote the public good. Anyone may enter the conversation, but those who enter fully must take the time and effort to become informed on the issues. Their reward is the development of special talents of understanding, reason, debate, and personal broadening through encounter with others from different traditions of discourse.

It must be recognized, then, that democracy as participation in a conversation about justice and the common good explicitly recognizes, indeed depends on, different conversational voices. The significance of religion is this: because religious communities are significant traditions of discourse, furnishing many persons their own voice and their most important idiom for expressing public concerns, these communities cannot be excluded from the conversation without loss of democratic legitimacy. Within the strictly liberal tradition of freedom as protection and individual choice, privatized religion is acceptable, for public discourse is secondary to interest protection. In the civic republican or discourse theory of democracy, however, such exclusion produces only a distorted conversation (Taylor 1990, pp. 105-112). In a democracy dependent upon what Hunter calls "communities of moral conversation" exclusion of some communities is the height of intolerance (Hunter 1992, pp. 18-19). Moreover, exclusion is impossible in light of research on political behavior showing the basic connection between images of the sacred and policy positions (e.g., Benson and Williams 1986).

The key issue in the normative theory of religion and politics is to understand how to describe the proper voice of religion(s) in the civil discourse of a secular, pluralistic society with both a need for public philosophy and a plethora of public issues of clear moral content (see above). Much theoretical effort has recently gone into this task (Hunter and Guinness 1990; Greenawalt 1988; Perry 1991; Cochran 1990; Hunter 1991, pp. 295-325). To describe religion as quasi-political or politics as quasi-religious distorts democratic discourse, which is best served by clear voices in all parts of the conversation.

Separationists might object that religion should be allowed a role in democratic discourse only where shared secular premises do not settle an issue. Secular argument takes pride of place. This objection, however, must fail. Political language does have its own dimensions, value, and validity. Therefore, it must possess a very wide scope, and this scope properly includes politics and public policy. Political argument, however, must not play the only role in settling political issues. This priority keeps the voice of religion muted in political debate, taming its dangerous political tendencies. For political effectiveness, religion must always seek political links between general principles and particular policies.

Nevertheless, despite the fact that political argument may be primary, the border area between religion and politics will be the scene of very lively discussion and debate. But that discussion and debate should be conducted at the border, not at the political center; that is, the religious voice must enter *policy* debate, not the central *political* experiences of candidate endorsement and interest-group lobbying. To conceive of religion in this case as quasi-political, or of politics so conducted as quasi-religious, would be to obscure this vital distinction between center and periphery. Precisely because of its distance from the center, religious belief will have the opportunity to challenge conventional, secular perspectives and to present alternatives not otherwise available.[12]

A tensional model of religion and politics, such as the one advocated here, provides a way that liberal democracy can achieve tolerance, protection of individual freedom, and the public freedom of political participation. As the different participants seek common ground, they begin to discover the participatory virtues of the public realm in a new way. All will not be sweetness and light. Not all religious persons will adhere to civil discourse. Not all political actors will adhere to civility. Yet the value of the preceding argument is to show not only that religious and political language can properly interact, but also that there are some kinds of issues on which religious language gives a perspective unavailable to purely public reason. Moreover, there is a way in which religion, as part of our cultural heritage, may become a repository of principles and traditions from that heritage that otherwise might be neglected. Sometimes those principles are needed to call politics to account when it might ride roughshod over important principles. There is, in short, a proper way for religious language to become the language that challenges dominant political forces. When that happens, religious language may look like an invader from across the public-private border. Yet it invades speaking a language neglected, but not forgotten, in the political realm. And it must be willing to learn political ways of speaking, even as it challenges dominant political forces.

NOTES

1. The ideas expressed below are developed more fully in Cochran (1990, 1994) on which the argument here draws.

2. I am indebted to John E. Hare of the Philosophy Department at Calvin College for this metaphor.

3. Religions have more than didactic teachings on these subjects. The exemplary lives of saints in many religious traditions provide models of outstanding lives, often in tension with ordinary cultural norms and expectations (see Haley 1987). John A. Coleman, S.J. (Hawley 1987, p. 221) points out how saints represent religion as a whole in being liminal figures, pointing "beyond the threshold they occupy to a larger, transcendent whole. They represent the primary locus for the human experience of the religious."

4. It is precisely the tension between religion and public life that draws the prophet to the public realm to challenge its complacency. This same tension frightens the priest away or drives him to collapse the two realms together.

5. Although, we try in many subtle ways (see Becker 1973). Becker's account of how repression of the knowledge of death distorts individual life suggests the necessity of considering how the public denial of death distorts public life.

6. Philosophy, of course, may do so. Nothing in my discussion rules out philosophy, and I explicitly do not assimilate philosophy to religion. Although politics could itself never perform the special functions of religion considered in this paper, philosophy might; hence, the tension between Athens and Jerusalem. Nevertheless, historically speaking, philosophy, though it motivated individuals such as Socrates and Seneca to die, seems unlikely to play a significant public role in regard to death. Ideology is another matter, and I address it below.

7. For a different historical perspective on these developments, see Marty (1976).

8. I owe this insight to Graham Howes.

9. Note the central idea of Martin Luther King, Jr.'s "Letter from Birmingham City Jail" (1964): the goal of nonviolent resistance is to set up the creative tension necessary for growth.

10. America in this respect is not radically different from the Third World, in which family law has been most closely tied to religion and most resistant to change (Smith 1971, pp. 67-91; Mortimer 1982).

11. The text can only hint at the features of a discourse theory of democracy. For a richly descriptive account of the difference between rights-based, liberal politics and participatory, communal politics in the governance of local water rights, see Crawford (1988).

12. The position that I have articulated seems to opt for religion's "witness" over its possible political "effectiveness." See the excellent discussion of this issue in Hertzke (1988). It is indeed the role of religion to witness, to call issues and forgotten perspectives to attention. Yet religion can only be effective in civil discourse if its themes are picked up by ordinary actors and

appropriately translated into political language, and then tried in the furnace of interest groups, PACs, electoral politics, and legislative compromise.

REFERENCES

Anthony, D., and T. Robbins. 1992. "Law, Social Science and the 'Brainwashing' Exception to the First Amendment." *Behavioral Sciences and the Law* 10: 5-29.

Becker, E. 1973. *The Denial of Death.* New York: Free Press.

Benson, P.L., and D.L. Williams. 1986. *Religion on Capitol Hill: Myths and Realities.* New York: Oxford University Press.

Berger, P. 1988. "Religious Liberty and the Paradox of Relevance." *The Religion and Society Report* 5: 1-2.

Cochran, C.E. 1990. *Religion in Public and Private Life.* New York: Routledge.

————. 1994. "Politics and Eternity: The Voice of Religion in Political Discourse." In *Religion, Public Life, and the American Polity,* edited by L.E. Lugo. Knoxville: University of Tennessee Press.

Cochran, C.E., J.D. Perkins, and M.C. Havens. 1987. "Public Policy and the Emergence of Religious Politics." *Polity* 19: 595-612.

Crawford, S. 1988. *Mayordomo: Chronicle of an Acequia in Northern New Mexico.* Albuquerque: University of New Mexico Press.

Doerr, E., and A.J. Menendez. 1991. *Church Schools and Public Money: The Politics of Parochiaid.* Buffalo, NY: Prometheus.

Glendon, M.A. 1991. *Rights Talk: The Impoverishment of Political Discourse.* New York: Free Press.

Greenawalt, K. 1988. *Religious Convictions and Moral Choice.* New York: Oxford University Press.

Hammond, P.E. 1991. "How to Think about the Sacred in a Secular Age." Pp. 115-127 in *Religion and the Social Order,* Vol. 1: *New Developments in Theory and Research,* edited by D.G. Bromley. Greenwich, CT: JAI Press.

Hawley, J.S., ed. 1987. *Saints and Virtues.* Berkeley: University of California Press.

Hertzke, A.D. 1988. *Representing God in Washington: The Role of Religious Lobbies in the American Polity.* Knoxville: University of Tennessee Press.

Hunter, J.D. 1991. *Culture Wars: The Struggle to Define America.* New York: Basic.

————. 1992. "What Americans Really Think about Abortion." *First Things* 24: 13-21.

Hunter, J.D., and O. Guinness, eds., 1990. *Articles of Faith, Articles of Peace: The Religious Liberty Clauses and the American Public Philosophy.* Washington, DC: Brookings.

King, M.L., Jr., ed. 1964. "Letter from Birmingham City Jail." Pp. 77-99 in *Why We Can't Wait.* New York: Harper and Row.

Lowi, T.J. 1988. "Forward: New Dimensions in Policy and Politics." Pp. x-xxi in *Social Regulatory Policy: Moral Controversies in American Politics,* edited by R. Tatalovich and B.W. Daynes. Boulder, CO: Westview.

Marty, M.E. 1976. *A Nation of Behavers.* Chicago: University of Chicago Press.

McWilliams, W.C. 1984. "The Bible in the American Political Tradition." Pp. 11-45 in *Political Anthropology, III: Religion and Politics,* edited by M. Aronoff. New Brunswick, NJ: Transaction.

Mead, S. 1975. *The Nation with the Soul of a Church.* New York: Harper and Row.

Mortimer, E. 1982. *Faith and Power: The Politics of Islam.* New York: Vintage.

Niebuhr, R. 1932. *Moral Man and Immoral Society: A Study in Ethics and Politics.* New York: Scribner's.

Oakeshott, M., ed. 1946. "Introduction." Pp. vii-lxvi in *Leviathan*, by T. Hobbes. Oxford: Basil Blackwell.

———. 1962. *Rationalism in Politics*. New York: Basic.

Perry, M.J. 1991. *Love and Power: The Role of Religion and Morality in American Politics*. New York: Oxford University Press.

Quade, Q.L., ed. 1982. *The Pope and Revolution: John Paul II Confronts Liberation Theology*. Washington, DC: Ethics and Public Policy Center.

Rieff, P. 1968. *The Triumph of the Therapeutic*. New York: Harper.

Robbins, T., and R. Robertson. 1991. "Studying Religion Today: Controversiality and 'Objectivity' in the Sociology of Religion." *Religion* 21: 319-337.

Smith, D.E., ed. 1971. *Religion, Politics, and Social Change in the Third World: A Sourcebook*. New York: Free Press.

Spragens, T.A., Jr. 1990. *Reason and Democracy*. Durham, NC: Duke University Press.

Strout, C. 1975. *The New Heavens and New Earth: Political Religion in America*. New York: Harper Torchbooks.

Tatalovich, R., and B.W. Daynes, eds. 1988. *Social Regulatory Policy: Moral Controversies in American Politics*. Boulder, CO: Westview.

Taylor, C. 1990. "Religion in a Free Society." Pp. 93-113 in *Articles of Faith, Articles of Peace*, edited by J.D. Hunter and O. Guinness. Washington, DC: Brookings.

Walzer, M. 1983. *Spheres of Justice: A Defense of Pluralism and Equality*. New York: Basic.

Wuthnow, R. 1988. *The Restructuring of American Religion: Society and Faith Since World War II*. Princeton, NJ: Princeton University Press.

A NEW RELIGIOUS MOVEMENT AND SPIRITUAL HEALING PSYCHOLOGY BASED ON *A COURSE IN MIRACLES*

Arnold S. Weiss

ABSTRACT

A new unique religious movement has been generated through a set of spiritual and psychological teachings titled, *A Course in Miracles,* purportedly channelled by Jesus to a psychology professor at a major university medical center over a 7-year period ending in 1972. With 800,000 *Course* volumes published, and popularized by a best seller nonfiction book with 750,000 copies as well as a leading talk show TV personality, the *Course* has grown internationally. Although the *Course* is Christian in terminology, it differs radically from contemporary Christian teachings. Some of these principal differences in theology are explained. The *Course's* status as a "religion" and as a "church" from both sociological and legal perspectives is examined. The *Course's* distinctive perspectives on "miracles," prayer, and worship are discussed. The *Course* teaches that psychotherapy is the only form of therapy there is and that all healing is of the mind, because only the mind can be sick. The body is regarded as a neutral communication device controlled by the mind. The world is taught to be a dream, an illusion from which all its inhabitants, without exclusion, will someday awaken by changing their

Religion and the Social Order, Volume 4, pages 197-215.
ISBN: 1-55938-763-7

minds and returning to their natural state of heaven. Jesus and the Holy Spirit are assigned by God to be in charge of this earthly transformation through the teaching of the Atonement Principle of forgiveness.

A COURSE IN MIRACLES: ORIGIN AND DESCRIPTION

A new, unique, religious movement based on a system of spiritual philosophy and teachings that purports to be able to heal the mind and the world, has been generated by a 3-volume, 1,188 page set of writings purportedly channeled from Jesus called, *A Course in Miracles.* Originally published anonymously in 1976, its source was revealed in 1984 to be an Associate Professor of Medical Psychology at the Columbia-Presbyterian Medical Center in New York City named Helen Schucman, who had died in 1981. Helen was a research scientist and a self-styled atheist who privately and fervently tried to find God. For some time, she had heard an inner soundless *voice* claiming to be Jesus with whom she had an on-going dialogue in which she participated with apprehension. In 1965, this *voice* urged, "This is a course in miracles, please take notes" (Wapnick 1989, p. 199). Sensing this to be a demand for a deeper commitment and frightened about her state of mind, she called her immediate supervisor, a full professor named William (Bill) Thetford, director of the Psychology Department, with whom she had had a close but conflicted relationship. Bill, who was aware that for some time Helen had had "psychic" experiences, asked her to take the notes and to read them to him. Fascinated with the first dictation, he urged Helen to continue to take notes for he saw unusual value in the material and believed that this might be an answer to problems they were experiencing at work. A routine became established in which Helen would read her shorthand notes aloud or channel directly and Bill would type them.

This collaboration continued for seven years until the books were completed. The *voice* instructed that the books would eventually be published but did not explain any means for this to happen. After a 300 copy anonymous off-set printing in 1975, a series of uncanny circumstances led to publication in 1976. Schucman and Thetford were told by the *voice* that the books were not to be publicly promoted or given media exposure, and that they were to be given without charge to those who could not afford to pay. Knowledge of the books was to propagate through personal associations and actions of interested persons.

Helen and Bill both refused to have their roles in this drama revealed for several reasons, including fear of losing their jobs, being ridiculed by the scientific community, and being made into gurus or cult figures. After Helen's death and Bill's retirement, the story behind *A Course in Miracles* (*ACIM*) was first told in a book by Skutch (1984) and later, after Bill's death in 1988, in greater documented detail by clinical psychologist Wapnick (1991, p. 373), a close personal friend of Helen's who functioned informally as her therapist.

The three volumes were intended as a self-study course and comprise: a large *Text,* which provides theory, a one-year *Workbook for Students* with 365 daily lessons utilizing sophisticated thought modification techniques, and a smaller *Manual for Teachers.* There are also two pamphlets channelled later, *Psychotherapy: Purpose, Process and Practice* (Anonymous 1976) begun in 1973 and finished in 1975, and *The Song of Prayer* (Anonymous 1978), channelled in 1977. The language is predominantly Shakespearean in form, and much of it is written in iambic pentameter and blank verse. The material is profoundly psychologically sophisticated, and for many very difficult to read as well as to understand. Consequently, study groups and classes have become popular.

The *Course* is Christian in language, using such terms as Christ, Son of God, and Holy Spirit, but the definition and usage of these terms differs markedly from prevalent Christian teachings (see the Appendix). There are similarities to both Western and Eastern religions, and parallels with Gnosticism, particularly the Valentinian form, although the *Course* differs critically with regard to the psychological aspects that it emphasizes. Wapnick teaches that the *Course* is not "just like" other spiritualities and is unique in its own right (1989, p. 546). (For a more complete discussion, see Wapnick 1989 and his summary starting on p. 405.)

ACIM's focus is on healing the mind through universal forgiveness, rather then healing the body. The body, a consequence of mind, is only a device which may be used in this world to help bring about the healing of the mind. Some of the material is written in the first person, purportedly by Jesus. The spiritual center for the *Course* is God, but there is no call for worship, ritual, tithing, a formal church, conventional prayer, priesthood, hierarchy, or even a congregation. *ACIM* specifically advocates religion and church, but not in the conventional sense as will be discussed below.

ACIM STUDENTS AND TEACHERS OF GOD

Everyone qualifies to be a student of the *Course,* and upon self-completion without formal certification, qualifies as a "teacher of God" who is to teach this philosophy to others in the course of normal daily activities and through any formal means that may be organized. These ways for most are simply their way of "being" in this world as loving, forgiving persons. Adherents tend to be from the more educated, white-collar, higher socioeconomic groups. This belief system, which promises self-healing, has also attracted the severely and terminally ill, many of whom have tried and rejected other religious or spiritual philosophies. The *Course* calls itself a course in spiritual psychotherapy and teaches that each person's own mind alone determines his or her destiny.

ACIM ORGANIZATIONS AND ACTIVITIES

A Course in Miracles and associated pamphlets are published, distributed, and translated by the Foundation for Inner Peace of Glen Ellen, California, a nonprofit foundation organized for these sole purposes. As of this writing (June 1992), 800,000 volumes have been printed and distributed in over 50 countries. Three translations, German, Spanish, and Portuguese, were to be ready by 1993 with French and Hebrew following in late 1994. Nine other translations are in various states of progress. The *Course* will soon be available on a computer disk which may be scanned to find specific words and phrases (Robert Skutch, Director, Foundation for Inner Peace, personal communication, June 1992).

The *Course* has been popularized by Marianne Williamson's book, *A Return to Love: Reflections on the Principles of A Course in Miracles* (1992), which for seventeen weeks (as of June 1992) has been the nation's number one nonfiction best seller with 750,000 printed copies (Marianne Williamson, personal communication, June 1992). Williamson was featured in February 1992, for a full hour on "The Oprah Winfrey Show," TV's number one daytime talk show (*TV Guide,* May 16, 1992), with Winfrey announcing that she had been so impressed with the book that she had purchased 1,000 copies to give to her friends and staff. In June 1992, Williamson was again featured on the show with Winfrey announcing that Williamson's February appearance had received the most response of any of her show's telecasts. Winfrey, who professed her belief in the *Course,* also admitted that she prayed publicly for the first time on her show when Williamson led the audience in prayer.

Williamson, a layperson, found her personal life markedly changed by the *Course* and wanted to share it with others. Lectures, tapes, and an international following ensued, drawing audiences of over 1,000 to her regular weekly talks. Williamson, who is currently writing two more books related to the *Course,* has also become a minister in California; this enabled her to officiate at the 1992 marriage of actress Elizabeth Taylor. She has also been featured on other nationally syndicated TV talk shows and in magazines such as *Time, Vogue,* and *People.*

The Foundation for *A Course in Miracles* at Roscoe, New York, is the largest *ACIM* activity center with 18 full-time employees. Founded in 1983 by Kenneth Wapnick and his wife, Gloria, it is a nonprofit religious organization with a Conference and Retreat Center situated on 95 acres in the Catskill Mountains, the former site of a resort hotel. Wapnick is the leading exponent of *ACIM* education and has self-published many scholarly and pedagogic books and tapes through his foundation which are available by mail order. The foundation's primary purpose is to help students to "be more effective instruments of the Holy Spirit's teaching in their own particular lives." It also serves to correct or reinterpret traditional Christian principles such as sin, suffering, forgiveness, the meaning of the Crucifixion, and the Atonement using *ACIM* ideology. Emphasis on experience and practical application are taught at the many workshops and seminars offered throughout the year and attended by between 1,000-2,000 persons. A newsletter is sent to 5,000 subscribers four times a year. Telephone contact plays a minimal role, and spiritual counseling is not offered (Elizabeth Schmit, secretary to Kenneth Wapnick, personal communication, June 1992).

Perhaps the second largest activity center for *ACIM* in the United States is the Miracle Distribution Center (MDC) in Fullerton, California, a nonprofit organization begun in 1978. MDC, according to Beverly Hutchinson McNeff, Director and Founder, fosters the teaching and practice of *A Course in Miracles* through classes, workshops, a 24-hour recorded lesson phone line, and a mail order catalogue for books, tapes, and videos. A newsletter, *The Holy Encounter,* is published every two months to a mailing list of 10,000. MDC maintains a current list of *ACIM* study groups which number 1,550 in the United States and 265 in 21 other countries, and furnishes these to students. The average size of a group is estimated at six.

MDC provides *ACIM* spiritual counseling by telephone as its major ministerial activity and has a counselor referral service which includes 280 counselors in 36 states and 4 foreign countries. Although, California based, only 25 percent of MDC's callers are from within the state, with 75 percent from around the United States. McNeff conceives of MDC as a church in the sense in which *ACIM* defines the term (as delineated below), rather than as a conventional church. MDC's present form is that of an educational organization which McNeff is considering changing to that of a church, without changing the content of its *ACIM* activities (Beverly Hutchinson McNeff, personal communication, June 1992).

MDC, as such, is a broad-based, rather than a community-based, church serving spiritual needs primarily through the telephone system and the mails. This modern image of a church, also common to many radio and TV ministries, was clearly not envisioned by the founders of early churches whose ideas still form part of the traditional definition of "church" as a structure serving and supported by a local population.

In San Francisco, Reverend Tony Ponticello is the Minister and founder of the California Miracles Center, which he calls a "legally chartered" church begun in 1987 to teach *ACIM*. Oddly enough, this "charter" is from the Internal Revenue Service and the California Franchise Board which is responsible for the collection of California state taxes (Tony Ponticello, personal communication, June 1992). Legally, separation of church and state precludes the state from chartering any church or endorsing any religion although IRS recognition of church status permits tax privileges.

Ponticello's church has an ordination program and about twelve ministers had been ordained by the summer of 1992. An informal membership of 300 to 400 persons is claimed with Sunday service attendance said to be about 30 to 40. The main thrust, as well as the main source of revenue, is to teach *ACIM* classes. Books and tapes are also sold. A monthly newsletter is provided free to about 1,300 national subscribers. Healing circles, prayer requests, and retreats are part of the church's program.

Ponticello says that no special interpretation of *ACIM* is promoted, leaving that for each individual's own decision. He acknowledges that having a church is controversial because the *ACIM* community does not generally agree with the conventional image of a church with formal structure and hierarchy. In fact, *A Course in Miracles* specifically teaches that *formal* religion and conventional church structure have no real place in religion (Anonymous 1976, p. 5; Wapnick 1989, p. 488). Ponticello does not see his church as a conventional church but as "a spiritual family following the same path together, helping each other."

A Course in Miracles has also become part of the curriculum taught at many Science of Mind and Religious Science churches, and many books and tapes by diverse authors and professionals, as well as periodical magazines, have been produced to advance its teachings.

IS *ACIM* A RELIGION? THE WORLD AND EXISTENCE ACCORDING TO *A COURSE IN MIRACLES*

The definitions of religion are as varied and complex as their application in any given situation. Definitions of religion may be sociological, folk (or common-place), theological, or legal. Whether a particular organization or worldview qualifies as a religion will depend on what type of definition is employed. A religion seen as truth from one perspective may be blasphemy, myth, or absurdity from another. Religion appears to exist, as does beauty, in the "eye of the beholder" and is a perception rather than a calculation that follows logically from the application of a set of precise technical criteria to a set of empirical data. We now consider the status of *ACIM* from a number of perspectives.

ACIM As Related to Sociological Definitions of Religion

Sociologically, functional definitions of religion require the crucial provision of an "encompassing system of meaning" or the ability "to relate man to the ultimate conditions of his existence," while substantive definitions of religion insist on a reference to the supernatural or sacred (Greil and Rudy 1990). *ACIM*, it will be shown, meets both sociological sets of criteria as it has a clearly defined and encompassing system of belief that relates humans to the ultimate conditions of their existence which depend wholly upon a supernatural being, God, the Giver and Supporter of life.

According to *ACIM*, God created each and everyone as part of Himself, at once, in a spiritual world as the act of love. That world, called heaven, is a state of being without time or space. It contains no forms or bodies, only *beings*. Everyone is unified into One. Happiness and joy prevail; there is nothing else.

Time began when some of these beings decided to try a new concept, called separation or individuality which they, not God, made up. As separation was in fact impossible, this was an illusory state—a dream. Space and time seemed to be made by these beings for without space (and its inseparable corollary, time) separation between any two beings was impossible. The earth and the cosmos were made by these beings so that there would be an illusory dimension of being called consciousness, where separation could seem possible.

Because time and space were not created by God, their seeming existence is limited. When the illusion of time and space end, the cosmos will vanish and all beings will return to their former state of undifferentiated unity in heaven as if the cosmos and their lives in it had never existed. This ending is guaranteed by God's Will which cannot be changed for everything is in or of Him.[1] God is perfect and never makes a mistake, and this includes never changing His mind. He even supplies the energy for the dreaming of this world in which the separated beings express their separation by believing that they are bodies that are spaced apart. Because God's unalterable will is for unity, the separation cannot occur in truth or reality, but only in a dream, a fantasy, or an illusion, much as children may play pretend games under the watchful and protective eyes of their parent until it is time to quit and come to dinner. The games of separation entail all that we experience in this world, including pleasure and pain. This world is neither evil nor good, but a dream of no consequence once we awaken from it.

Death is an illusion in this game. The body expires because it can exist only in time, and hence must be temporary, while the being that was associated with the body is eternal. The same being may continue in the illusion, perhaps dreaming himself to be another body. The dream can only end for a being when she gives up all desire for separation. This entails a plan of forgiveness of all past wrongs, not by God, but by the being for himself and for all others. God knows nothing of these dreams because He is not dreaming and therefore has nothing to forgive. A lack of forgiveness in the dream is synonymous with separation because it makes one being or person seem different than another. Difference is the foundation of separation and its corollary, judgment. God does not judge. Hence, forgiveness—the relinquishment of judgment—is the key to ending the illusion and returning to heaven.

ACIM teaches that forgiveness is one's only function in this dream world and that unconditional love for all living things and the remembrance of God's love comes from this act. When beings accomplish total forgiveness, their dream will end as God takes the final step to ensure their return to heaven. Eventually, all beings will realize this is best for them, and they will voluntarily forgive all and return to God. The realization will occur because love will eventually be seen as preferable to separation which leads to loss and pain, and the memory of God and heaven will begin to be re-established. No one will be left behind for all are equally loved by God. When time ends, eternity will continue as a state of unending bliss and unity, and beings will never again decide to experiment with the dream of separation because they, of their own free will, have decided to surrender and forget/forgive the experiment.

To accomplish the goal of forgiveness, God has not simply allowed His children to dream endlessly, for they have the power to dream as long as they wish, and to incur as much pain and death as they choose. Time does not have a fixed end, but can continue until its makers, we beings, decide that it is needed no more. Having all eternity, which is a concept of infinity, in which to dream, time could continue indefinitely except that it is the will of God that all awake and return to Him.

To ensure our eventual return, God created a formless spiritual entity as His Voice to serve as His Ambassador to the separated ones. This voice for God is called the Holy Spirit and may be heard in the mind of everyone who desires to hear Him. The Holy Spirit is not dreaming as is the separated being, but can be in the dream to advise the being. He straddles between heaven and earth, so to speak, because these are not in truth *places,* to help guide those who are open to, or pray for guidance. His mission is to aid beings to return home through their individual acts of forgiveness. This is called the Atonement Principle.

ACIM teaches that one being who listened to the Holy Spirit was the first of the separated to awaken and return to heaven. Since his return, there have been others. This first being, in his[2] final dream, dreamt that he was Jesus of Nazareth. By his life and teachings he attempted to show the way back to God. Because he was the first among the separated to return, he was put in charge of teaching others how to return. He does that today in spirit, without form except that his voice may be heard. Jesus purportedly characterizes himself in the *ACIM Text* as a loving older and wiser brother helping his siblings, along with the Holy Spirit who first taught him. Both he and the Holy Spirit serve identical goals and are literally of one mind, the Mind of God which all the created share. They are also free of time and space, and this permits them to be with anyone and everyone simultaneously. The books, *A Course in Miracles,* and the accompanying pamphlets—according to *ACIM*, were all dictated by this being, who formerly dreamt that he was a man named Jesus, to a being dreaming that she was a psychology professor named Helen Schucman.

ACIM As Related to Folk or Common Sense and Theological Definitions of Religion

According to folk or commonsense definitions, *ACIM*'s concepts of a transcendent deity, God, the Creator of All, the Holy Spirit, and Jesus as the being in charge of the plan of forgiveness and return, all unmistakably evince a sense of traditional religion. The similarities and parallels of the *ACIM* account to contemporary Christian, Eastern, and earlier religions such as Gnosticism are very clear as are the theological differences.[3] It is the theological differences expressed in the logical and cohesive psychological *ACIM* structure, though, that give *ACIM* its uniqueness and enables it to be classified as a religion in its own right.

ACIM As Related to Legal Definitions of Religion

Although a belief system may qualify as a religion under sociological, folk, or commonsense definitions, it may not be legally classifiable as a religion under law, for law in fact prohibits a precise definition of religion. Under the First Amendment to the Constitution, separation of religion and government has long been established by the courts, even though there has been much litigation about how this separation is to be maintained. Although both federal and state income tax laws provide exemptions for "religious organizations," there are no statutory or regulatory definitions of the terms "religious" or "religion" for tax purposes (Hopkins 1983, p. 168). However, if everything qualified as a religion, taxes would never be collected. Hence, a working concept of "not religion" had to be defined by the courts without defining its opposite, religion. This problem defies ordinary logic which would dictate that defining something simultaneously defines things that are not that something. As Hopkins (1983, p. 178) states, "[t]here is no question but that the current state of law on this subject poses perplexing and probably unbearable burdens on regulatory officials and judges. These difficulties are exacerbated as new religions emerge."

Courts have generally accorded the status "religion" to beliefs that are within the mainstream and can be described by buzzwords such as, "traditional" and "orthodox," but they have also recognized nontheistic beliefs as religion. Hopkins (1983, p. 177) provides what he considers to be the most expansive, yet definitional statement of religion, from a 1957 California case (*Fellowship of Humanity v. County of Alameda* 1957). This includes: a belief, not necessarily referring to supernatural powers; a gregarious association or cult openly expressing the beliefs; a system of moral practice directly resulting from adherence to the belief; and an organization within the cult designed to observe the tenets of belief. The beliefs of *ACIM* can be seen to fit within the realm of traditional-appearing orthodox religions, while the history, proliferation, and current state of the *ACIM* community as a newly emergent religion are seemingly nontraditional, but meet or exceed the criteria for definition as a religion cited by Hopkins.

Clearly, traditional religions at their inception were nontraditional. Early Christians, for example, were not well received by the then established religions. Only with the passage of considerable time and widespread acceptance did they become "traditional." At birth, it appears impossible for any candidate religion that differs markedly from the established religious norms to receive much of a welcome from those content with other beliefs. *ACIM*'s success appears to be due to both its similarity to and differences with Christianity and Christianity's foundation, Judaism. *ACIM* is traditional in its theological format, but sufficiently different in major definitions and concepts that those discontented with traditional Christian or Judaic offerings have a close alternate choice without radically changing to such religions as Hinduism or Islam.

THE QUESTION OF "CHURCH" AND FORMAL RELIGION IN *ACIM*

The definition of "church" is perhaps a more knotty and frustrating legal problem than a sociological one, because for tax purposes courts must decide whether an organization is a church without infringing on its constitutional right to be one. The U.S. Internal Revenue Service (IRS) requires that a "church" (Hopkins 1983, p. 180) meet some of 13 criteria. No fixed number is specified, nor is there a relative weighting assigned to each. This is explained further in Publication 557, *Tax-Exempt Status for Your Organization* (1988, p. 14), where the IRS states, "[b]ecause beliefs and practices vary so widely, there is no single definition of the word 'church' for tax purposes. The Internal Revenue Service considers the facts and circumstances of each organization applying for church status." Effectively, the IRS defines "church" in the United States though it is *only* for tax purposes, because failure to be recognized as a church by the IRS can have far-reaching implications in terms of fund-raising and taxes, as well as community and national respect. Thus, our very concept of how we perceive a "church" is strongly, and perhaps unduly, influenced by the conceptions of the IRS which determines which religious organizations are entitled to be a "church." An organization unrecognized by the IRS as a church still may call itself by that name under the separation of church and state as long as it claims no tax privileges accorded only to churches. This, however, would appear to reduce its legitimacy and usefulness in the eyes of the public.

An historic reason for tax exemption of religious groups was to protect religions not favored by the taxing agencies from being taxed into oblivion. Fear of governmental interference in religion precluded the idea of a uniform tax policy and resulted in separation to protect church from the state. Today, an unfavorable IRS decision can effectively overtax an organization that is indeed a church "in the true sense" but is not an "IRS church." An improved tax definition of "church" is sorely needed.

The U.S. Tax Court in 1980 has gone so far as to enunciate eight criteria for a church in addition to a "religious-type function" (Hopkins 1983, p. 181). These are: holds services or meetings on a regular basis, performs marriages or other ceremonies, has ministers or other representatives, has a place of worship, ordains ministers, receives financial support from members, has a form of "formal operation," and satisfies all the other requirements of the federal tax law rules for religious organizations.

The U.S. Claims Court endorsed these criteria in 1983 and concluded that a "new religious organization should not be held to a standard only an established church can satisfy." The U.S. Supreme Court in 1981 in a partial definition held that the word "church" must "refer to the congregation or the hierarchy itself, that is the church authorities who conduct the business of hiring, discharging, and directing church employees" rather than "the actual house of worship used by a congregation" (Hopkins 1983, p. 182).

Simply applying these criteria may not be sufficient. Hopkins (1983, p. 185) summarizes the situation, "[t]hus, just as the law cannot formulate an appropriate tax definition of the term 'religion', it seems incapable of formulating an appropriate definition of the term 'church'. Probably the entanglement doctrine [separation of church and state] precludes the application of such definitions in any event."

Generally speaking, the tenets and practices of a religion are what constitutes its "churchly" activities. These are the *content* of the religion. The formal structure or organization in which they appear is the form. The definition of "church" by the IRS and the courts appears to be based strictly on form, assuming that the content is a "religious-type function." Thus content not packaged in an IRS-approved wrapper may fail to meet its criteria for a church. But what happens in the unique case of *ACIM* when the tenets and practices of a religion specifically proscribe such forms, not for any legal or secular reasons, but because of earnest fundamental beliefs that if violated would constitute violation of the religion?

As Wapnick (1989) explains, "participation in the sacraments, or any formal means of worship or ritual, is directly antithetical to the study and practice of the *Course*—if one believes that the form of the ritual is salvific—for by affirming that spirit can exist in form, one makes real the error of believing in the reality of the world" (p. 484). Also, a "church too is redefined in the *Course* in terms of its purpose, having nothing at all to do with a formal structure" (p. 488). Moreover, the "*Course* fosters an *a*morality, emphasizing that it is not our behavior that is important, but rather the purpose that our minds impute to the behavior. In other words, it is the content (purpose) that is essential, not the form (behavior). Religious sacraments and rituals thus are not essential to reach God" (p. 407).

The church of *ACIM* carries out the "churchly activities" or content of *ACIM*. This *church* according to *A Course in Miracles* is built on the very people who carry out these activities (*ACIM, Text*, p. 86). It is not a structure of earthly materials (*ACIM, Text,* p. 18) or prescribed rituals, but a spiritual joining of brethren who harken to Jesus's calling to join to practice forgiveness: "God's Teacher [the Holy Spirit] speaks to any two who join together for learning purposes.[4] The relationship is holy because of that purpose, and God has promised to send His Spirit into any holy relationship" (*ACIM, Manual,* p. 5). "The Holy Spirit's temple is not a body, but a relationship" (*ACIM, Text,* p. 407). Form as such is not required and besides the point. If form is used, it cannot serve any religious purpose. This formless quality clearly sets *ACIM* apart from other religions. Formlessness and spirit are equated, as are form and separation. For example, the concept of an everlasting, pure spiritual body, found in some religions, is unacceptable in *ACIM* for it still permits separation of beings with bodies as specific boundaries or limits on them.

In Bible-based religions, the Bible is often considered to be "holy" or sacred in itself as the Word of God. Other written religious teachings such as the Torah or Koran are also considered as sacred objects or forms and religious laws pertaining to the use, handling, preservation, and destruction of such holy books, as well as the use of certain words from these, are carefully prescribed by some religions. The formlessness prescription of *ACIM* precludes consideration of *A Course in Miracles,* in any form, including any parts or words, to be considered as holy or sacred. The *Course* states, "Forget this world, forget this course, and come with wholly empty hands unto your God" (*ACIM, Workbook,* p. 350).

WHAT ARE THE "MIRACLES" IN *A COURSE IN MIRACLES?*

An understanding of *ACIM* requires an explanation of its concept of miracles. The *Course* begins by listing 50 principles of miracles. Miracles here are not the classical miracles or spectacles sometimes used to induce belief that involve mystical, religious, or unexplainable physical or psychological phenomena such as spontaneous physical healing, visions of religious beings, weeping figures, magical appearances, and so forth. Miracles are said to lead to healing of the mind for only the mind is real and, therefore, only the mind can be sick. They are defined, for example, as "expressions of love among equals", "natural...habits..., involuntary..., not under conscious control," "everyone's right," and "thoughts," "natural signs of forgiveness." Miracles as taught by the *Course* are shifts in psychological perception that enable the perceiver to view something from a totally new perspective without otherwise altering what is being viewed. An example would be viewing the same glass as half empty rather than half full, a classical illustration of the difference between a pessimist and an optimist. The *Course,* however, focuses on the perceptual difference between love and fear. Viewing experiences or events, past or present, in the light of love results in forgiveness, the major theme of *ACIM.* According to *ACIM,* everyone is entitled to love and forgiveness from each other, for there is in fact no sin or grievance because God is wholly nonjudgmental and loving. The miracle, then, is a psychological shift or change of one's mind that releases fear and hate and allows love, which the *Course* contends is always present, to be made manifest. As the *Course* states, "The holiest of all spots on earth is where an ancient hatred has become a present love" (*ACIM, Text,* p. 522). The concept of "holy" in *ACIM* can be taken to mean "in accordance with God's Laws."

Miracles in *ACIM* theory are a choice to shift one's perception momentarily from the dream state to the state of nonjudgmental love. Miracles are the means of healing the part of our mind that is dreaming the separation. All disease, illness, pain, or discomfort is said to represent a state of mind based on the dream of separation. When the mind awakens, illness vanishes and joy returns. Jesus is purported to be in charge of miracles and the physical laws of time and space are adjusted by him in order to work miracles. He guides us in working miracles if we request his help. Help or guidance is never thrust upon one; it must be sincerely requested as a prayer of the heart preserving each being's free will to choose her or his own perception.

PRAYER IN *A COURSE IN MIRACLES*

Prayer, considered to be a traditional religious function, takes on an altogether different meaning in *ACIM*. Rather than a request to God for something, *ACIM* teaches that true prayer asks for nothing because in truth we have everything. In this illusory world, the only request should be to receive help in accepting this truth so that we can recognize and forgive the illusion that we have needs. "But the only meaningful prayer is for forgiveness, because those who have accepted forgiveness have everything. Once forgiveness has been accepted, prayer in the usual sense becomes utterly meaningless" (*ACIM, Text,* p. 40). Upon transcending this world, prayer becomes what God originally intended it to be, a song of endless love sung between God and His creations. The love they share *is* the prayer (Anonymous 1978, p. 1). Moreover, "The secret of true prayer is to forget the things you think you need .... Prayer is ... a letting go, a quiet time of listening and loving. It should not be confused with supplication of any kind" (p. 2).

Ultimately, *ACIM* considers prayer as formless. "Prayer has no beginning and no end. It is a part of life. But it does change in form, and grow with learning until it reaches its formless state, and fuses into total communication with God" (Anonymous 1978, p. 3). This growth and change in form is described as a series of rungs of a "ladder of prayer ... reaching up to Heaven" (p. 4), with each rung corresponding to a level attained along an upward spiritual path.

WORSHIP IN *A COURSE IN MIRACLES*

Traditional worship of deities generally entails prayer or requests to a powerful being to satisfy perceived needs in a manner that may (1) in return for favors requested prepay divine honors; (2) express reverence, respect, or veneration; and (3) express intense love and admiration. The latter two expressions often tacitly involve the belief that the superior being will significantly alter the worshipper's life if the petition is made with abundant quantities of these attributes. Major goals are usually the avoidance of pain and illness, salvation from death, and the granting of a "good" life. In some religions it is believed that the deity(s) demand such adoration and recognition of their superiority in return for favors, while in others the human being's loyalty, faith, obedience, love, and so on must be demonstrated or tested through a variety of means ranging from severe suffering to ecstasy in order to receive these favors. These concepts are anthropomorphic and the superior being(s) are often symbolized by or given the form of idols, images, or statues. Traditional religions generally have rituals, sacraments, or rules governing the conduct of worship.

In *ACIM* there is no requirement for worship of its only deity, God. Hence, there are no rituals, sacraments, or rules of worship. It is said that God does not have an ego and, therefore, does not need to be told of His wonderfulness, love, or kindness. Such worship could only result from a misunderstanding of the God of *ACIM* who always gives unconditionally, without expecting anything in return. God expresses His love by eternal causeless giving. That is, to give without the giving being earned, deserved, or used as a manipulation. A striking difference from other religions is that in *ACIM* God is completely unaware of our world and our problems because it is an illusory dream that He had no part in making. Thus, the prayers and worship that would befit a deity that did take an active role in interfacing with the world would be meaningless to *ACIM*'s deity.

Worship of God in any manner is mentioned only once in *ACIM* (*Text,* p. 5), and occurs only as a state of awe when individuality is transcended and one becomes united with God. Such awe cannot occur in the daily world of the "miracles" of *ACIM*. Miracles are said to be a sign of love among equals, and equals should not be in awe of one another for that implies inequality. Hence, Jesus, the purported author of the *Course,* asks to be seen as an equal, albeit wiser, elder brother who in his role of devotedly and lovingly guiding others to salvation is entitled to love and respect but not to awe or worship. Jesus purportedly writes about himself, "There is nothing about me that you cannot attain. I have nothing that does not come from God. The difference between us now is that I have nothing else. This leaves me in a state which is only potential for you" (*ACIM, Text,* p. 5).

PSYCHOTHERAPY ACCORDING TO *ACIM*: HEALING OF THE BODY

The pamphlet *Psychotherapy* (Anonymous 1976) states, "Psychotherapy is the only form of therapy there is. Since only the mind can be sick, only the mind can be healed. Only the mind is in need of healing" (p. 1). This is the belief that the mind is real while the body is not and that psychotherapy is necessary so that an individual can begin to question the manifestations of the world that seem real and eventually learn the truth as expressed in *ACIM*. "Its [psychotherapy's] aim is to aid the patient in abandoning his fixed delusional system and to begin to reconsider the spurious relationships on which it rests" (p. 1). The mind, a nonphysical, active part of spirit, is considered to be independent of the physical brain which acts upon this unlimited mind as a restricting device or filter passing a greatly diminished and altered version of it into the physical world.

Healing of the body may follow healing of the mind, but this is not a necessary or even desired consequence. The body is seen as a neutral thing, a learning device whose sole purpose is to communicate between separated beings who dream that they are bodies. The ultimate purpose of communication is to learn that this world is a dream and to help awaken others (the teacher of God concept). Once this is accomplished, the body is no longer necessary and it is simply set aside as the being awakens in heaven. If healing of the body does occur, it is only for the purpose of continuing education toward the ultimate goal. Physical death involves parting with a body that has served as a temporary learning device. If additional learning is required other such communication devices will be manifest until learning is complete.

LACK OF EFFECT OF *ACIM* ON ITS FIRST ADVOCATES, THE SCRIBES, HELEN AND BILL

It might be expected from our knowledge of others who were the first to "receive" a religion from a high spiritual source, that Helen Schucman, who purportedly directly heard Jesus dictating *A Course in Miracles* to her, would have undergone a beneficial transformation. Further, we would expect that the conflicted relationship between her and Bill Thetford would have been blissfully resolved using the philosophy of the *Course* and the forgiveness they were taught, and that they would "live happily ever after." Strangely, nothing could be further from the truth.

The story of Helen Schucman told by Kenneth Wapnick, the person who knew her best, is appropriately titled *Absence from Felicity* (1991). It is a highly detailed analysis by her closest friend and de facto therapist of a conflicted woman whose rage against Jesus could be nearly as powerful as her love for him. She seemed not to have found peace. As Wapnick (1991) writes, "However, the fact remained that Helen's life, at least from the vantage point of her own ego experience, did not change for the better as a result of her relationship with Jesus" (p. 439). With regard to her and Bill, Wapnick (1991) writes, "Moreover, her relationship with Bill, the immediate stimulus for the

Course's scribing, was from all external indications unhealed by Jesus' message" (p. 385).

Neither Helen nor Bill assumed any leadership role in propagating the message of *ACIM*. As Wapnick (1991, p. 380) explains, "Helen's and Bill's inability to forgive each other, let alone identify with *A Course in Miracles,* made such a leadership role impossible. And this despite repeated assurances from Jesus of the important roles they each would play, above and beyond the scribing of the *Course*." In essence, these two professors appeared unable to pass the course they needed to learn the most.

CONCLUSION

The theory and philosophy of *A Course in Miracles* can be recognized to have factors in common with many traditional Western, Eastern, and Gnostic religious beliefs. Yet, it stands apart as a psychological system with a unique view of the individual as a mind dreaming this world of physical existence in a harmless dream from which it can awaken by forgiving itself and others for literally nothing but dreaming! As a whole, the *Course* is persistently logical and psychological, forcefully expounding its teachings in a highly persuasive intellectual manner. It is a religion that has a church that is as formless, yet as spiritual, as it believes God's heaven to be. Its temple is the holy relationship in which the Holy Spirit enters "where two or three meet in my name." It promises freedom from doubt, fear, disease, and death, and even assures heaven eventually for everyone.

The price of our freedom from the dream of this world is no more than unconditional love and a gentle forgetful-forgiveness of all perceived wrongs, no matter how serious they may appear to be in our dream. For so little a cost heaven may be had according to *A Course in Miracles.*

APPENDIX: SOME KEY TERMS IN *ACIM* THEOLOGY THAT DIFFER IN USE FROM CHRISTIANITY

Christ or the Son of God

Whereas in traditional Christianity terms like Christ or the Son of God refer exclusively to Jesus, the *Course* asserts that we are all equal parts of God's creation called the Christ or equivalently the Son of God, presently dreaming that we are separate beings.

God has innumerable creations all created perfect. Each is an extension of Him in the sense of attributes, and not in the sense of physical space. Each, called a Son[5] of God, is created perfect and identical in all ways to God, and hence to all others. The sum of these creations, called the Sonship, comprise

God Himself, there being nothing else but God. As this sum is limitless, it is unbounded because God is unlimited. As each Son of God is identical, each is treated equally by God and each of God's communications always affect each Son identically. Thus there is only one communication whenever there is a communication, and this is the same for all. Hence, in the metaphorical eyes of God, He sees or has only One metaphorical Son. This explains the use of the term "Son of God" as singular although it encompasses the entire Sonship, an unlimited or infinite set of beings.

Heaven

Heaven is the original state of communication between God and His creations. It is a state of union in love. Because everything God created is perfect, nothing need or will ever change. Perfection can no more be altered than God can be rendered imperfect. Because we are literally part of God, we cannot be rendered imperfect. Thus we all continue to exist in heaven despite the illusion that we are presently living in a physical world. Heaven is not a place. It is formless as are God and His creations, these being Thoughts in the Mind of God.

The Holy Spirit

The Holy Spirit is an eternal spirit created by God as His Answer to our dream of the separation. Because we chose the dream of separation, we also chose not to communicate with God. Because communication with God is Heaven, we dream that we are no longer there. Out of His infinite love God honored our request for the separation by suspending communication with us. Because we have the power to shut off His intended direct communication to us, he created the Holy Spirit as His Ambassador to us, to be received by us only when we are willing to hear Him, as the Voice that speaks for God. The Holy Spirit abides in our minds in order to eventually guide us out of the dream and back to God, but only if we use our free will to hear His guidance. God realized that we needed such a Guide for without Him we would never find our own way back to heaven for the power of our minds to dream is equivalent to that of God's because we are part of Him. However, there are limits on our free will for God's Will to have us return supersedes ours to dream. In truth, as part of God our true will is really the same as His and thus our desired destination must be to return to heaven by allowing us to be guided by the Holy Spirit.

Jesus

Jesus is the name used by a being whose life as a man was recorded in history. He eventually learned to listen to the Holy Spirit's guidance and awaken from the dream to return to heaven. It is not made explicit whether this happened during his life as Jesus, or before. Because he was the first being that awakened from the dream by learning the path of return to God, he was placed in charge of the Atonement process by the Holy Spirit. This being, who can be called by his earth name[6] Jesus, is thus a fully awakened being, simultaneously able to perceive both the dreams of others and their awakened reality in order to guide them along the path of return. This being took limited form as a *voice* to dictate the *Course* to Helen Schucman. He acts as an older, wiser brother to guide anyone who asks for his help and he is available through our minds to help us perform miracles and achieve the Atonement. Jesus as such is entitled to respect and love. He along with us is a Son of God. Jesus and the Holy Spirit share the Mind of God and are thus literally of one mind. God's creations likewise share the same Mind, but those who dream of separation have forgotten this and need to be "re-minded."

Salvation and the Atonement

Salvation means to awaken from the dream and return the mind to its natural state of communication with God. Salvation is achieved through the Atonement Principle which was put into operation by God at the instant of the separation, and is taught by the Holy Spirit. The Atonement occurs when we forgive or undo the past as if it really never occurred (which in fact it never really did because this world is a dream).

For example, our minds will insist that we continue the dream if we hold a grievance against anyone, for the mind believes that only if the dream continues can this conflict be resolved. The mind also believes that there are some permanent unresolvable issues such as the existence of someone that can never be forgiven for a heinous crime or injury. This unforgiven circumstance would continue time without limit, against God's Will for our return, which is impossible. The Atonement is the recognition that the past never really occurred and that there is nothing to really forgive. The injury never really was, and the perpetrator of the harm to us was really ourselves in believing that it actually happened. Thus our dreaming is responsible for our discomfort. Once our dreaming is recognized, we give up all grievances and forgive the world and ourselves. Then we are ready to surrender the dream of this world which is no longer of use to us and happily return to heaven.

ACKNOWLEDGMENT

Portions reprinted from *A Course in Miracles* (1975), *Psychotherapy: Purpose, Process and Practice* (1976), and *The Song of Prayer* (1978) by permission of the Foundation for Inner Peace, Inc.

NOTES

1.   The *Course* uses the masculine gender exclusively to describe everyone including females, the point being that in truth gender does not matter or truly exist. The male choice simply agrees with the tradition that the illusory world is more used to seeing the masculine gender in print to stand for both genders.

2.   All pronouns referring to Jesus are not capitalized in *ACIM* because he is not considered a deity and this is a reference to a man that walked the earth. The spirit that is the life force of that man has no name as names are given only to the illusion of separated beings. This spirit that dictated the *Course* is referred to for convenience by the man's name.

3.   An excellent historical comparison may be found in Wapnick (1989).

4.   This is similar to Matthew 18:20, "For where two or three meet in my name, I am there among you." In *ACIM*, Jesus and the Holy Spirit share the same mind. Hence, "Jesus is the manifestation of the Holy Spirit" (*ACIM, Manual*, p. 85).

5.   With respect to gender, see note 1 above.

6.   The concept of a "name" to identify a being implies uniqueness or difference between things. In the case of true equality and simultaneous unity, a name is useless for it no longer serves a purpose. The name "Jesus" helps us to focus on a particular being that once appeared to be a separate body. It is only our state of separation that makes it necessary for us to use a name.

REFERENCES

Anonymous. 1975. *A Course in Miracles.* Tiburon, CA: Foundation for Inner Peace.

————. 1976. *Psychotherapy: Purpose, Process and Practice.* Tiburon, CA: Foundation for Inner Peace.

————. 1978. *The Song of Prayer: Prayer, Forgiveness, Healing.* Tiburon, CA: Foundation for Inner Peace.

Fellowship of Humanity v. County of Alameda. 1957. 315 P. 2d 394 District Court of Appeal, 1st Division, California.

Greil, A.L., and D.R. Rudy. 1990. "On the Margins of the Sacred: Quasi-Religion in Contemporary America." Pp. 219-232 in *In Gods We Trust: New Patterns of Religious Pluralism in America,* edited by T. Robbins and D. Anthony. 2nd ed. New Brunswick, NJ: Transaction.

Hopkins, B.R. 1983. *The Law of Tax-Exempt Organizations.* 4th ed. New York: Wiley.

Skutch, R. 1984. *Journey Without Distance.* Berkeley, CA: Celestial Arts.

Wapnick, K. 1989. *Love Does Not Condemn.* Roscoe, NY: Foundation for *A Course in Miracles.*

————. 1991. *Absence from Felicity.* Roscoe, NY: Foundation for *A Course in Miracles.*

THE MARKET FOR GODS AND SERVICES:
RELIGION, COMMERCE, AND DEVIANCE

Nikos Passas

ABSTRACT

This paper applies the market analogy to the analysis of New Religious Movements (NRMs), quasi-religions and mainstream religions. I contrast business-like and questionable practices of the Church of Scientology (CoS) with those of other religions to argue that commercial activities and even unlawful practices engaged in by representatives of NRMs are insufficient grounds to deprive them of their religious status. I also argue that the NRMs' for-profit activities are prominent due to disadvantages they face as new competitors in the markets for spiritual goods and services, hostile societal responses, regulatory actions by state authorities, and vulnerability to law suits from former members and "anti-cult" activists. The NRMs' success and the demand for their services highlight structural contradictions inherent to the U.S. culture of competitive individualism. Therefore, while regulation and law enforcement are necessary to minimize the crime-facilitative nature of this demand, they are no panacea and must be used in moderation and with fairness.

Religion and the Social Order, Volume 4, pages 217-240.
Copyright © 1994 by JAI Press Inc.
All rights of reproduction in any form reserved.
ISBN: 1-55938-763-7

INTRODUCTION

Commercial activities of new religious movements (NRMs) have drawn a great deal of attention (Bromley 1985; Bromley and Shupe 1980; Richardson 1988a). By pointing to profit-making practices, critics have raised the question of whether some NRMs are mere fronts, lucrative enterprises hiding behind the shield of religion, or even massive scams taking advantage of gullible or "brainwashed" members and followers (Behar 1986, 1991; Bromley 1985, p. 265; Wallis 1975). At the very least, the economic activities of NRMs appear to instill serious doubts as to whether their tax-exempt status is justifiable (Bird and Westley 1988; Moore 1980; Robbins 1988).

Among the questions that may be posed are the following: why would commercial enterprises want to be regarded as a religion? Why would religious organizations' practices involve business-like financing and self-presentation? Does this constitute sufficient cause to place them on the fence between the sacred and the secular? Do economic activities cause legal difficulties or cause the religious status to be called into question? What is the relation between religion and business?

These issues are more central when it comes to quasi-religions. According to Greil and Rudy (1990, p. 221), quasi-religions are "collectivities in which organizational and ideological tension and ambiguity regarding the group's worldview, perspective and regimen are profitably used to facilitate affiliation as well as commitment. Quasi-religious organizations (often intentionally) ride the fence between the sacred and the secular." These authors examined the Church of Scientology (CoS) as one illustration of quasi-religious groups because of its peculiar history, inherent ambiguity, and its battles with conventional organizations, authorities, and individuals.

It has been argued that the CoS can be analyzed as a commercial business which has occasionally adopted unlawful methods in the pursuit of its goals and that its deviance and tension with its environment is a key to its success (Passas and Escamilla 1992). In this paper, I argue that the market analogy can be applied to the analysis of other NRMs and mainstream religions, to the economic practices of NRMs, their appeal, and deviance.

I also argue that the resort to profitable endeavors and even illegal methods of financing do not ipso facto justify the rejection of religious status for any group whose representatives engage in such activities. Were this not so, we would be left with virtually no religion. Engaging in commercial practices is consistent both with NRMs' dogma and with conventional values. Of course, this may be seen as an invitation to commit fraud against vulnerable believers. By no means do I purport to defend sophisticated offenders who set up a self-proclaimed "religion" simply to flout the law. Whenever good faith can be shown to be absent, religious and other types of fraud ought to be prosecuted. Bad faith must be shown, however, and not assumed to exist when a religious group makes a lot of money.

My thesis develops through several interrelated arguments. First, all religious organizations require resources for their survival and success, and may be analyzed as corporations. At one level, rather than sharply distinguishing commercial from religious organizations, I suggest that a better approach is to regard them as ideal types occupying the opposite ends of a continuum, depending on the prominence of economic versus purely religious activities and organizational goals. At another level, the market analogy may apply to all religions. When the market of spiritual and religious goods is protected, monopolies are likely to develop or be perpetuated. When a measure of free trade is introduced, oligopolies and pluralism may develop, as more competition is allowed. Second, NRMs do not have the same pool of resources as mainstream religions. They often need additional resources for their survival and growth, in line with their professed goals, so they may appear to be more profit-oriented than conventional religions. Third, NRMs are likely to attract negative publicity because of the salience of for-profit operations, their newness and their deviant practices. In this sense, they are at a competitive disadvantage relative to other religions or professional bodies catering to the same audience/clientele. Fourth, the negative societal response may provoke more deviance (i.e., profit-making branches or even law violations). Collisions with mainstream society generate a more acute need for financial resources and commercial activities, which serve as support for the argument that they are businesses and not religions. Finally, this argument alone is insufficient to deprive them of their religious status, because their practices find parallels in early as well as present stages of conventional religions.

I first outline the CoS's economic practices and deviant/criminal activities (or those of its members) that have been used by critics and regulators to discredit it. Then, I compare the CoS's economic activities and illegalities with those of other religions. Finally, I turn to factors that fuel the ambiguity of NRMs and render their economic aspects more prominent.

The method I employ to examine the interrelation of religious and commercial activities in quasi-religions and NRMs is qualitative case study analysis. I use the findings on the CoS as a springboard to generalize on other NRMs to the extent allowed by theoretical arguments and information provided by other researchers. My data include CoS and other NRM-related court cases decided in the United States and Europe. Secondary data include a lengthy interview with the current head of the CoS aired on *Nightline* in 1992, published accounts of former Scientologists, critiques of the CoS, and scholarly work focused on CoS, other NRMs, and religious movements in general. For my analysis, I drew on concepts and theories developed in the sociology of religion, deviance, and organizations. The primary objective was not to generate new data, but to try and make sense of existing data.

THE COS: ITS FINANCIAL AND UNLAWFUL ACTIVITIES

"Why Scientology is a religion? Religion is about the spirit, and Scientology deals with the spirit. We are in the tradition of the much older religions, Buddhism, Hinduism, helping the person as a spiritual being improve himself. That is what religion is about. That is why this is a religion. It doesn't fall into any other field."
—David Miscavige (Interview for *Nightline* 1992)

L. Ron Hubbard began as a science-fiction writer. His *Dianetics,* published in 1950, contained the philosophical background of psychotherapeutic techniques aiming to help people get "clear," to clear away aberrations in a process similar to repairing a faulty calculator. Professional "auditors" assisted "pre-clears" at Dianetic Foundations to get rid of "engrams" that had been recorded in their minds in the past and were interfering with their mental and bodily functions. The auditing sessions contained elements of confession, counseling, and psychotherapy. An "e-meter," a sort of lie-detector, was used to "disclose truth to the individual who is being processed and thus free him spiritually" (Malko 1970, pp. 75-76). According to Dianetics, Clears have gained full access to their inherent mental ability and imagination. Their physical health improves and all psychosomatic illnesses disappear for good (Wallis 1977, p. 27).

For some time, Dianetics flourished and expanded beyond the United States. However, Dianetic therapies were not as effective as advertised, they encountered active opposition from medical, psychological, and psychiatric professions, and internal divisions occurred as some broke away and attempted to improve Hubbard's methods. At this point, in 1953, Hubbard's ideas moved into the realm of religion, and he founded the CoS. As control and self-determination became even more central, the ultimate objective in CoS became attaining the state of "Operating Thetan," to become "aware of one's awareness." The CoS addressed the needs of people looking for practical solutions to everyday problems (Beckford 1986, p. 53). Auditors were turned into "ministers," franchises into "missions," payments and fees into "fixed donations." Even though not all followers approved of the shift to religion—they thought it would be just a "legal cloak over the group's activities" (Senn 1990)—the CoS grew into a rational organization consistent with the principles of a market economy (Straus 1986). Each stage of this development effectively helped avoid some problems and appeal to new audiences.

Irrespective of Hubbard's motives, these initiatives were profitable, which raised many eyebrows and questions. Is the CoS a business that needs religious claims to safeguard its commercial viability or is the reverse true? Has CoS used religion as a resource to facilitate or create wealth and profit? Has it used the First Amendment to shield itself from attacks from professionals, other critics, and the state?

Behar's (1986, 1991) articles, which provoked strong responses from the CoS (Behar 1991, p. 57; Donaton 1991; Levin 1991), referred to CoS's business practices, public-influence activities, and its troubles with the law to argue that "[i]n reality the church is a hugely profitable global racket that survives by intimidating members and critics in a Mafia-like manner" (Behar 1991, p. 50). Among the items he presented are the following: the CoS engages in book publishing, charges excessively high fees for auditing, and invents all sorts of goods and services, such as tape-recorded speeches and Hubbard books in collector's editions, that may be obtained by donations. The CoS has had television advertisements for its books and full-page advertisements in publications like *Newsweek* and *Business Week* which portray it as a philosophy. CoS members manage the HealthMed chain of clinics that promotes saunas, exercise, and Hubbard-designed vitamins to purify the body.

The concerned Businessmen's Association of America is allegedly a CoS front that seeks to recruit students and gain educators' favor by organizing anti-drug contests and offering $5,000 grants to schools. Behar described Narconon and Criminon, CoS-sponsored drug rehabilitation centers, as "a classic vehicle for drawing addicts into the cult" (Behar 1991, p. 55). The Association for Better Living and Education gave Narconon a gift of $200,000 and praised its work, but turned out to be controlled by the CoS. The CoS recruits well-to-do individuals through a number of consultancy firms with secret ties to it. Stirling Management Systems, for example, allegedly targets health-care professionals with the promise to help them dramatically increase their income, offers seminars and courses priced at $10,000, and lures them to the CoS.

The CoS seeks to exercise public influence in various ways: the Way to Happiness Foundation distributed 3.5 million copies of a Hubbard book on morality; Applied Scholastics aims to gain access in public schools for Hubbard's tutorial program and to train educators to teach Hubbard's methods; the Citizens Commission on Human Rights (CCHR) supports CoS in its war against psychiatry by issuing damaging reports on individual psychiatrists and on the field as a whole; CCHR also attacked Eli Lilly regarding the anti-depressant drug Prozac. The CoS retained the public relations firm of Hill and Knowlton (which later severed its ties with the CoS and denied that this had to do with Lilly being their client as well; Levin 1991), and sponsored Ted Turner's Goodwill Games along with Sony and Pepsi.

Finally, Behar (1991) alleged that the CoS bought its own books to artificially create best-sellers, that Hubbard laundered money deposited in Switzerland through dummy corporations in Panama, and that CoS members have been involved in financial crimes and money laundering, while others have been charged with theft of government documents in Canada. In fact, Scientologists have been convicted for similar offenses in the United States (*United States v. Heldt* 1981) and government agencies have raided CoS premises in several other countries, too.

Former Scientologists have accused the CoS of defrauding them by overcharging for auditing, falsely promising to improve their lives (Moore 1980; *Van Schaick v. Church of Scientology* 1982), and inflicting emotional injury upon them as a result of its "fair game" practices against perceived enemies (*Wollersheim v. Church of Scientology of California* 1989, 1992).

The economic activities of the CoS, transfers of profits to private individuals, and illegal conduct by its members have been advanced as reasons either to cast doubt on its religious status altogether or to justify increased regulatory control and taxation (*Founding Church of Scientology v. United States* 1968; *Church of Scientology of California v. Commissioner of Internal Revenue* 1987). In *Church of Scientology v. City of Clearwater* (1991, p. 1510), Clearwater claimed that the CoS "has not proven that it is a religion"; more to my point, the argument was that "[e]ven if Scientology is a religion, the actions at issue here are commercial, and sometimes criminal in nature." The CoS has been also accused of tax evasion and of avoiding public scrutiny by hiding behind the veil of religion (Moore 1980; Robbins 1988).

THE THIN LINE BETWEEN COMMERCIAL
AND RELIGIOUS ORGANIZATIONS

The development from science-fiction to Dianetics and to the CoS, now described by CoS members as an "applied religious philosophy" and a science (Greil and Rudy 1990, p. 224), has invited much skepticism over the sincerity of its religious beliefs. Functionalists would use this to argue that this is why the CoS was created and organized in this particular way. Some would point to the sequence of events in the life of Hubbard and argue that he sought First Amendment protection when the e-meter could no longer be used as part of scientific treatment (Behar 1991, p. 51). Others may require additional evidence to back up this suggestion, arguing that consequences should not be confused with intent. Whether actual outcomes and intentions coincide in the case of the CoS is beyond our scope here. It should be noted, however, that the CoS is not alone in having religious traditions influenced by or originated from secular psychotherapies (Whitehead 1987, pp. 27-28).

There is certainly ambiguity in the way the CoS presents itself. For instance, the organization that manages the CoS and Dianetics is called the Religious Technology Center and the chairman of its board is David Miscavige. Such self-created ambiguity is typical of quasi-religions (Greil and Rudy 1990). Yet, do the above business practices and misconduct suffice to conclude that the CoS is not a religion? If other organizations also engage in similar activities without losing their religious status, the answer must be "no." Much evidence strongly suggests that wealth and religion are not necessarily incompatible, as illustrated by the following sample of secular investments, other business activities, and even crimes by church-associated people or organizations.

The total income of the Papal See in the thirteenth century was estimated to be higher than the combined revenues of all the secular sovereigns of Europe, giving rise to heresy and critical commentary assailing the venality and corruption of church officials located both low and high in the church hierarchy (Durant 1950, pp. 767-768). Fund-raisers for the church occasionally kept a part for themselves, while others misrepresented human and animal bones as those of saints or even "offered purgatorial bargains for a maximum of coin and a minimum of prayer" (Durant 1950, p. 740).

Protestantism, which was born during the passage from feudalism to capitalism, has never had objections to material success. Among the main reasons Max Weber explored the origins of the spirit of capitalism in the religious principles of the Reformation was that certain Protestant groups "like the Quakers and the Baptists had been as 'proverbial' for their wealth as for their piety" (Bendix 1966, p. 56).

The estimated value of church-owned and tax-exempt property in the United States was valued at about $1 trillion in the mid-1970s (Larson and Lowell 1976, p. 204). The same authors suggested that at least 40 percent of all U.S. real estate was under church ownership, and church annual income was about $20 billion. One can only guess exactly how much income is generated by contemporary television evangelists, who have demonstrated that NRMs are not alone in pointing out that "finding God and getting rich are not necessarily polar opposites" (Harris 1981, p. 151; see also 157 ff. on the born-again movement, the personal "gospel of wealth," and a number of video evangelists' business, legitimate and fraudulent).

In this light, David Miscavige may have exaggerated, but not too much, when he stated: "As a matter of fact, the officials in the [CoS] are paid far less and live far more frugal existences than any other church leader" (Nightline 1992, p. 10). At any rate, the constitutionally appropriate salary of religious leaders can hardly be determined (Dershowitz 1988, p. 272).

Further, the CoS is not the only religious organization receiving money for concrete services. The Supreme Court ruled that auditing fees paid by Scientologists involve a quid pro quo, even if of religious or spiritual nature, and could not therefore be considered as tax-deductible donations (*Hernandez v. Commissioner of Internal Revenue* 1989). Dissenting justices, however, observed that there are similar connections between payments to conventional religious organizations and services rendered. Catholic mass stipends, Mormon tithes, Jews buying tickets to enter High Holy Day services, Protestants obtaining a pew through a rental fee, Orthodox Christians paying fees for services such as weddings,[1] and other exchanges can technically come under fixed fees for services traditional religions offer. They also involve a quid pro quo as did, at earlier times, the practice of indulgences—exemptions from purgatorial punishment for sins which were granted in exchange for constructing bridges, roads, churches, hospitals, clearing forests, draining swamps, or contributing to a crusade.

A related parallel to contemporary allegations that converts to NRMs "disconnect" from their families and offer everything they have to a "cult" can be found among European landowners who sold or mortgaged their property to churches or monasteries in order to finance their crusade. This happened to such an extent that, after the failure of crusades, the state became envious of church property (Durant 1950, pp. 611-612). In addition, donations entailing sacrifice are not unknown among born-again Christians (Harris 1981).

Today, the Church of Jesus Christ of Latter-Day Saints may be the wealthiest religious organization in the United States after the Roman Catholic Church. Its financial diversification is reminiscent of that of the CoS. In addition to religious facilities and buildings, "the church owns television and radio stations, a daily newspaper, insurance companies, more than 800,000 acres of working farmland, a company that develops industrial parks, several food-processing plants, department stores, office buildings, and a portfolio of stocks and bonds said to be worth hundreds of millions of dollars" (Norgren and Nanda 1988, pp. 81-82).

In 1929, Mussolini signed the Lateran Treaty and Concordat and gave the Vatican a financial settlement of several million dollars which were invested through the Amministrazione del Patrimonio della Sede Apostolica. Some investments in the 1960s caused embarrassment following revelations that the Vatican and other Catholic entities owned shares in companies manufacturing arms, pornography, and even birth-control pills. Later, the Istituto per le Opere di Religione (IOR), the Vatican Bank, was found to have strong ties to Banco Ambrosiano, interests in Italcementi, investments in bluechip companies (e.g., Fiat); it was fined in the United States for improper documentation in acquiring stock in Vetco Industries, and funneled flight capital from Italy (Cornwell 1984, pp. 57, 228). The collapse of Banco Ambrosiano shook the international banking system and exposed the Vatican's reckless financial affairs, political intrigues, secret societies, and more mundane crimes (e.g., blackmail and murder). While the church was trying in vain to distance itself from this international scandal, the chairman of IOR stated, "But can you live in this world without worrying about money? Even the Church has to see to the financial needs of its dependencies ... *You can't run the Church on Hail Marys*" (Cornwell 1984, p. 58; emphasis added).

Religious frauds of significant magnitude committed by three major U.S. televangelists were documented by the investigative journalists of ABC's *Prime Time Live* on July 9, 1992. Their deceptive practices included the collection of donations for the sponsoring of a Haitian orphanage which only received a token amount per month representing an insignificant fraction of the amounts collected; soliciting money for the construction of a church at the site of a German concentration camp, but only contributing a tiny proportion of the donations; and pretending to heal sick members of the congregation in front of a wide audience, but staging deceptive "magician's" tricks (see many additional examples and lengthy quotations from televangelists in Harris 1981).

The close association between contemporary religion and entertainment and leisure is highlighted by the success of the "Electronic Church," Jim Bakker's conviction notwithstanding (Robbins and Bromley 1992, p. 16). In fact, Bakker's conviction taught a lesson to others, and care was subsequently taken by other televangelists to avoid his mistake of keeping records of whose donations went to which charity, according to the *Prime Time Live* report.

Finally, public relations are not neglected by mainstream religions, which engage in lobbying and seek to shape public policy. Podus' analysis of such activities concluded that all "religious organizations can indeed be viewed as corporate actors and that their actions both reflect and influence the social organization of religion in society" (1991, p. 197). Podus also argued that "contemporary patterns of tax/religion policy participation more closely resemble that of conventional interest group politics, and coalition formation has varied across issue areas" (1991, p. 191). As different religions compete among themselves, the separation of church and state is designed to ensure that none of them gains unfair advantages over others. Yet, their diverse lobbying ability and popularity may render state authorities more sympathetic to their views than those of NRMs.

No one would seriously suggest that the above questionable activities of representatives of mainstream religions undermine their religious status or that "genuine religions" must abstain from business. It appears that there is no clear-cut distinction separating religious organizations from commercial ones and the two are best conceived as the ideal-type ends of a continuum. In the middle of this continuum, where quasi-religions are situated, the distinction is fuzzier. Spiritual, philosophical, social, and commercial concerns on the part of new religious leaders and followers are likely to be intermingled. As this ambiguity is noted, the religious status of a group or movement becomes contested. Ironically, what is essential for a group's survival and success (Khalsa 1988) gives rise to legal difficulties that add to the costs of running its organization. It is, thus, a delicate balance that NRMs have to achieve. If they overdo their commercial part, they may draw additional attention from the authorities or may alienate their followers. If they do too little, their very existence is at risk.

Odd practices and incredible ideas of NRMs are stigmatized and ridiculed by critics in the same way those labeled "heretics" were ridiculed centuries ago. Does it follow that because some practices and beliefs are longer-standing, they must be treated differently from contemporary ones?[2] Are we to negate religious status to the Roman Catholic Church because of the Ambrosiano and other related financial scandals? If we are to use the same criteria to protect the public and consumers against misrepresentations, we would similarly regulate, tax, and restrict all religions. Because this is unrealistic, the only constitutionally consistent policy is to treat NRMs and other religious groups in the same way and prosecute them only when their conduct clashes with the criminal law.

UNDERSTANDING NRM'S SPECIAL NEEDS FOR RESOURCES AND AMBIGUITY

The organization of religious institutions and the way they conduct their activities are influenced by the social environment and the prevailing economic conditions. In the Middle Ages, the Church was a powerful political, military, economic, and religious institution that shared in feudal revenues and received land from the nobles. Just as "[f]eudalism feudalized the Church" (Durant 1950, p. 564), capitalism and new technologies have shaped the practices of contemporary religions. In a social landscape "dominated by advanced mass media technology and corporate style organization on an international scale," NRMs inevitably "articulate with economic components of contemporary society" (Bromley 1985, p. 272). While Bromley refers to groups such as the Unificationist Movement, the New Christian Right, Transcendental Meditation, and the CoS, television Evangelism is an equally good illustration.

NRMs, however, spend a disproportionate fraction of their time on economic activities and devious practices (Harris 1981, pp. 148, 150; Robbins 1988, pp. 72-73; Passas and Escamilla 1992). Is this because they seek only material wealth? What social conditions are conducive to heightened financial activities and to the mixed features that characterize NRMs and quasi-religions? To a large extent, the answer lies in the NRMs' comparatively high cost of doing business and strained resources. Many NRMs do not have very high expenditures, partly because of their small size and partly due to labor donated by followers (a matter that also stirs controversy). On the other hand, a number of factors limit their access to resources available to conventional religions and/or increase their operational costs.

Disadvantages of New Competitors

The size of NRMs places them at a disadvantage in their competition with mainstream religions for a niche in the spiritual market. Because NRMs tend to have smaller population bases than established religions, they finance themselves differently. As we have seen, traditional religions engage in financial activities similar to those critics of the CoS mention as "unreligious." Nonetheless, mainline religious institutions have easier access to traditional religious charity-type resources, which do not appear as secular. Not being able to rely on small pledges from many followers, NRMs turn to heavier contributions from fewer people, free labor, begging, or the sale of goods and services to the larger public (nonmembers and marginally committed "clients"). While mainline religious organizations receive bequests and donations, many NRMs meet their financial needs and achieve success through purposeful investments, which makes them appear as profit-making corporations (Bird and Westley 1988, p. 58; Grafstein 1984; Robbins 1988). So, although smaller size may keep their operational costs low in some respects, it also contributes to the ambiguity surrounding NRMs.

The higher operational cost of NRMs is also due to their need to make their presence, their "gods and services," known. Proselytizing is not as easy as for churches whose members routinely follow family or ethnic/cultural tradition. Recruiting for NRMs thus may take place in the streets, near church buildings and schools, and on university campuses. In the face of concrete, useful services that are offered and promises of a better life (or, less often, after-life), the potential recruits' indifference, reluctance, and hesitation may diminish. Such practices, however, appear less typical of a genuine religion and cast doubt on the ultimate objectives of NRM leaders and their followers.

Hostile Social Environment

Unlike established religions, NRMs of all types frequently face unfriendly social environments; this creates NRM-specific needs for funds. World-transforming NRMs often generate outright hostility from the wider society or particular segments that come under their critique (Bromley and Breschel 1992; Bromley and Schupe 1980, p. 229). World-affirming NRMs are more accommodative, but clash with conventional (religious and nonreligious) forces because they are in effect competing for a share of their clientele or audience. The CoS's battles with government agencies, psychiatrists, the American Medical Association, and other professional bodies in the United States and many countries overseas are notorious (Passas and Escamilla 1992; Wallis 1975, 1977). As Miscavige put it on his 1992 *Nightline* appearance, "there are a group of people on this planet who find us to be a threat to their existence, and they will do everything in their power to stop us. And that is the mental health field." Regardless of whether this is a precise representation of the motives of the mental health field and of whether they fight the CoS for good or bad reasons, the statement reflects a competitive relationship that strains the resources of the CoS.

It is not only today's religious movements that trigger negative societal responses as they emerge. Pointing to the lack of universally accepted criteria establishing the point at which a "cult" becomes a "religion," Ogloff and Pfeifer (1992, pp. 117-118) noted how today's mainstream religions struggled against "antipathy and harassment" in the past (see also McCloskey and Brill 1983; Richardson 1992; Richardson and van Driel 1984; Shupe et al. 1984).

Not only are there organized "anti-cult" popular movements, but juries may also be prejudiced against NRMs. This is reflected in the disproportionate punitive damages awarded to former Scientologists, which were later reversed on appeal (*Allard v. Church of Scientology* 1976; *Wollersheim v. Church of Scientology* 1992). To some extent, such initiatives and negative attitudes may be reinforced by the authorities' activities.

In view of such adversity, the entrepreneurial aspects of the CoS and many other NRMs (Bird and Westley 1988; Bromley 1985; Khalsa 1988) are essential for organizational survival. In addition, as the case of the CoS indicates, business structures have the potential to survive the death of the founder of a movement or the decline of a religiously oriented group (Robbins and Bromley 1992, p. 20).

Protectionism and Free Trade

Because they lack an age-honored tradition, NRMs are less able to mobilize the resources that are necessary to influence policy and law making. Whenever religions enjoy state protectionism (e.g., in European or Third World countries where one religion is declared "official"), monopolies are promoted or perpetuated. When the market for gods and services approximates free trade arrangements, oligopolies or pluralism are the likely outcome. American society promotes the latter at several levels. As religions vie among themselves, the separation between Church and State serves to ensure that there is no competitive advantage of one over the other. Their diverse lobbying ability and popularity, however, may render state authorities more sympathetic to the views of conventional religions than those of NRMs. Despite the principle of formal neutrality, some religions are practically treated more favorably than others in terms of exemptions from taxation and regulation (*Corporation of the Presiding Bishop v. Amos* 1987; *Staples v. Commissioner of Internal Revenue 1987, p. 1327; Jimmy Swaggart Ministries v. Board of Equalization of California* 1990). The U.S. Supreme Court itself has recognized that the differential treatment of religions by law enforcement and legislative authorities "will place at a relative disadvantage those religious practices that are not widely engaged in" (*Employment Division v. Smith* 1990, p. 1606; discussed in more detail in Laycock 1991).

So, NRMs are at a competitive disadvantage even in relative free-market conditions, where they are allowed to lobby and engage in activities consonant with their commercial pursuits. Thus, the growing pressure for government regulation is accentuated when it comes to NRMs (Beckford 1986; Richardson 1985; Robbins 1985a, 1985b; Stark 1987).[3] As in cases involving the CoS, the tax evasion trial of Rev. Moon raises issues as to who decides whether financial investments and "donations" from the faithful are for religious or nonreligious purposes and how a church ought to be structured (Robbins 1985a, 1985b). It is instructive to note how the U.S. government attempted to reassure conventional religions that what happened to Rev. Moon would not affect them: "Contrary to the fears expressed by the numerous religious individuals and groups appearing in the amici curiae..., informal financial arrangements maintained by churches in good faith are not in jeopardy" (Richardson 1992, p. 62).

Such attacks may reduce NRMs' clientele somewhat, although they add credibility to arguments that NRMs are unfairly treated, which tends to strengthen the followers' beliefs and allegiance to the group. The CoS's "clear" business, for instance, has not been damaged severely. This may well be because the religious claim of the CoS has not been renounced by U.S. courts, despite sarcastic comments made by judges (*Barr v. Weise* 1969, p. 341; Passas and Escamilla 1992, p. 110; *Wollersheim v. Church of Scientology* 1989, pp. 887-888). Court rulings have rejected only specific practices and did not extend to the overall activities of the group.

The CoS's religious claim was denied altogether in Spain, however, in a way that breaks from the European consumer protection approach and a "managerial" view of NRM problems that entails ad hoc pragmatism instead of constitutional principles (Robbins and Beckford, in press, p. 35). Given the domination of traditional religions in Europe, the market for religious goods is cornered. Despite recent changes, there is still a good deal of protectionism. The CoS was not allowed to register as a religion because of a cited lack of religious aims[4] and concerns relative to public order issues. When religious freedom is formally institutionalized,[5] then the status of NRMs is scrutinized as such and may be denied. Attacks on NRMs are unlikely to threaten interests of dominant religions, which might otherwise form alliances (and amicus curiae), as they do in the United States. In short, to the extent that they stress their religious character, NRMs are less likely to be successful in Europe.

On the other hand, the European political market is more open than in the United States, where institutions are based on and support a two-party system. World-transforming messages of NRMs may thus be quite appealing in the Old World. An hypothesis to be explored is that NRMs are more successful in Europe when they emphasize the political/ideological aspects of their theology, alternative worldviews, and life-styles. Europeans may be more inclined, for historical/cultural reasons, to search for new meanings and join NRMs as they get alienated from other institutions or movements.[6] More marketable than the utilitarian approach (message of success within current social arrangements) is the provision of alternative moral meanings. The same NRM may be successful in both markets (the United States and Europe), if the marketing strategy is different and the most appealing aspects are stressed in each market, while the rest are comparatively toned down.

Deviance and Social Control: A Self-fulfilling Prophecy

Strained resources, blocked legitimate opportunities to attain culturally approved objectives, and overemphasis on goal attainment make for organizational misconduct (Passas 1990; Vaughan 1983). This applies to religious institutions reaching for goals consistent with First Amendment rights. In view of strains caused by the above factors, not only are the financial needs of NRMs multiplied, making them appear more profit-oriented, but other forms of deviance can be expected (i.e., other activities instrumental to goal attainment, such as false advertising, other forms of deception, harassment, tax evasion, etc.).

Authorities should and usually do respond to such deviance and crimes. In many instances, however, societal overreaction not only compounds NRMs' problems by increasing organizational needs, but also escalates or amplifies their deviance. This irony of social control has been noted long ago: societal responses to mild forms of deviance may become self-fulfilling prophecies by unwittingly producing more deviance (Becker 1963; Lemert 1951; Wilkins 1964).

The case of the CoS illustrates this process that may render NRMs more deviant and bring them closer to the commercial end of the religion-commerce continuum, where state regulation is more likely. Moral panics and multiple attacks directed against the CoS in several countries (Wallis 1975, 1977) did not go unanswered. The CoS fought back, even by illegitimate and criminal means (Wallis 1975; *United States v. Heldt* 1981), and has been reported to pay "an estimated $20 million annually to more than a hundred lawyers"(Behar. 1991, p. 56).

Processes of escalation and amplification of deviance after societal interventions are not unique to the CoS. More spectacular and costly confrontations include the 1978 killings and suicides by members of People's Temple in Guyana, the 1985 bombing of the MOVE house killing 11 members and destroying a whole block of houses in Philadelphia, and the 1993 tragedy in Waco, Texas, where dozens of Branch Davidians and four federal agents lost their lives in fire or shoot-outs. What caused the authorities to clash with these groups? Alleged mistreatment of members in People's Temple, city health code violations and alleged threats of violence by MOVE, and alleged illegal possession of firearms by Branch Davidians. The comparison between the initial causes for concern with the final outcomes demonstrates how control efforts may have disastrous unintended effects.

The point is that external social forces often strain NRMs' resources, induce further deviance as NRMs defend themselves, or "deform" them in unanticipated or undesirable ways beyond the control of NRM leaders. The CoS, the Unification Church, the Bhagwan Rajneesh would probably have evolved into different organizations, had social control agencies responded in a different way. These interactions have an impact also on NRMs' finances: "Some organizations have had to change the ways in which they support themselves because of the pressure that has been brought to bear on them by legal authorities and by public opinion" (Richardson 1985, p. 168). Further, NRMs are comparatively flexible in the initial phases of organizational and dogma formation and may adjust their practices to state regulation to exploit whatever benefits may be gained (Richardson 1985, 1988b).[7]

THE NATURE OF THE DEMAND FOR GODS AND SERVICES

The survival and success of the CoS is a remarkable feat given the long aggressive attacks it has encountered over the years and the costly legal and public relations battles it has waged.[8] What does this tell us about the United States and other societies where the CoS operates? Even if the CoS and other NRMs are frauds as alleged, why are hundreds of thousands of people taken in? What kind of demand is there and how is it fulfilled?

Although the conflicts of the CoS with authorities, former members, and professional organizations suggest at first sight that it is a marginal organization, many important aspects of it are mainstream. The CoS's success reflects conventional Western values (Passas and Escamilla 1992) and a contemporary trend toward holism that brings together science, health, spiritual healing, and religion (Chagnon 1986). The CoS exploits a need for spiritual support and economic success, in a context of competitive individualism (see also Chagnon 1986, pp. 505-506). It is successful because its goods and services are consonant with, not antithetical to, a society which has shifted toward this-worldliness. The CoS focuses explicitly on self-improvement and problem-solving according to Miscavige's 1992 *Nightline* interview: "most [religions] in the Judeo-Christian society ... say if you have faith and you live your life that you'll achieve spiritual salvation in the afterlife. We believe in spiritual salvation, but in the *here and now*" (emphasis added). The CoS's welcoming of individualism and competitiveness contrasts with traditional religions, such as the Church of England.[9] As Hubbard wrote in 1970:

> The average man is up against problems. He's asking himself, how can I make more money? How can I make my wife faithful to me? How can I help my children grow up? ... in Scientology processing he resolves these questions, he understands what he's doing, and he turns from a man who is simply a puzzled static being into somebody who is more than that.

Jazz musician Chick Corea stated on *Nightline* in 1992, that CoS's technology of the mind "really directly affects my relationship with people, with individuals around me, with my loved ones, and also with audiences."

Interestingly, a study has found that there may indeed be certain benefits for long-term Scientologists (Ross 1988). Effective or not, however, the help offered by the CoS is not unique in that it holds the promise of taking care of mundane problems, very much like a large number of NRMs (Bird and Westley 1988; Harris 1981; Richardson 1988a; Zaretsky and Leone 1974), and exhibits an association between religion and entrepreneurial innovation. This association, the emergence of "do-it-yourself" theologies and middlemen as religious leaders, is quite American (Robbins and Bromley 1992, p. 13; Zaretsky and Leone 1974, p. xxxiv). Among all new ideas that are marketed, most successful are those that capture the pulse of a significant part of the society. Of course, those monitoring what is and what is not successful could then try to create a new "theology" or "dogma" strictly for profit, preaching whatever the market will bear.

NRMs gained prominence and flourished in the 1960s, a time of sociocultural turmoil.[10] At that time, the liberalization of values and norms, an emphasis on individual autonomy and education, the decline of traditional structures that mediate between individuals and larger institutions, the exploration of ideas beyond the Judeo-Christian tradition, privatization trends, the appeal of science, all combined to create a market for new religions by generating disillusionment with traditional lines of authority and a search for new means of control and new meanings (Beckford 1986; Greil and Rudy 1990, p. 231; Robbins 1981, pp. 214ff.).

The U.S. utilitarian culture has been very important in shaping the new spiritual market: the "what works" approach became a common denominator of quasi-religions (Greil and Rudy 1990, p. 226). It is hardly surprising that service-oriented religious movements surface and succeed in a service-oriented economy. Traditional religions may have been more instrumental to making life bearable to the faithful (e.g., by promising after-life rewards), a fact that drew criticism from Marxian and conflict theorists. It is true that many of their elements have concrete benefits for this life, albeit not always framed in such terms. For example, confession may also help one's self-esteem and social integration. To the extent that there is a trend toward secularization, however, the appeal and worldly functions of such rituals are undermined.

Traditional religions may have lost some of their attractiveness in the context of widespread questioning of authority, especially as their influence in policy-making could be viewed as support for the status quo. The appeal of NRMs thus lies in their newness, their offer to help bring out the human potential and a promise to solve worldly problems, social and individual. Their dogmas are pragmatic and consistent with individualism. In short, NRMs often offer a new means to reach for the American Dream (Harris 1981) or cope with pressures that accompany the strong emphasis on competition.

Since opportunities for culturally defined success are structurally limited, the ceaseless race after the American Dream and material wealth produces failures and frustrations (Merton 1968; Passas, forthcoming a). Many services offered by NRMs and quasi-religions meet needs arising out of this pursuit. Some help redefine success in more realistic terms or stress other goals/values as more rewarding (e.g., Nichiren Bouddhists, Transcendental Meditation, Integral Yoga, Milarepa Dharma, and Sri Chinmoy followers; Bird and Westley 1988, pp. 59-60). While some NRMs reduce their members' strain by toning down chimeric parts of the dominant culture, many others effectively take advantage of the cultural theme of success and promote self-enhancement. The CoS belongs to the latter category, as the titles of Hubbard's books make clear: *The Problems of Work: Your Guide to Personal Job Satisfaction, How to Live Though an Executive* (this book's cover suggests that "You can learn to effectively run your company and live to tell about it"), and *Self-Analysis.* On the cover of all these books, it is claimed that Hubbard is the "#1 Best-selling Self-Improvement Author."

The NRMs and quasi-religions, some of which are also called New Age groups, that operate in the market of intuition, human potential, personal experience, and spirituality are quite profitable enterprises. As business publications have reported, Werner Erhard—the founder of Erhard Seminars Training (EST; see Tipton 1988)—"is selling franchises in his business-focused program of Zen, Scientology and Gestalt through an organization called Tranformational Technologies, Inc. Those franchises allegedly are going like hotcakes.... Called 'The Forum' [Erhard's new] program takes up two weekends and promises 'a decisive edge in your ability to achieve'—for $525 a head" (Zemke 1987, p. 27). Even NASA and former USSR managers have sought Erhard's services. The *Economist* (1993, p. 70) observed that the

> New Age has crept into some unlikely areas of life, including management training courses, where surprised executives can find themselves criticized for failing to use the right side of their brain... The ability of many of these movements lies in their ability to tap a thirst for spirituality... Most areas of religious growth are more to do with the spiritual than the dogmatic—they offer to fill some hole people perceive in themselves, rather than giving a set of rules to live by.

In the "land of opportunity" in particular, failure is more likely to be linked to oneself (or bad luck/fate) than to the social structure. Whenever a competitive edge may be gained, it is worth trying; no one likes being accused of not trying. This is well illustrated by the words of someone who called the editor of *Training* "to ask if it wouldn't be a good idea for his company to run a pilot or something—just in case there's some competitive advantage to be gained" (Zemke 1987, p. 27).

Producing results and delivering the goods thus becomes a more prominent objective. Given the competition among NRMs for a share in this market, it is not surprising to find that the populations effectively targeted by various

NRMs are not always the same. The People's Temple, for instance, attracted the weak and underprivileged, whereas the CoS appeals to relatively educated and successful people. In 1992, to Ted Koppel's question "What about those fools 'down there'?" Miscavige replied "we don't ignore them, but my point is this, *Scientology is there to help the able become more able*" (emphasis added). He went on to explain that the market of CoS is upscale, "in Scientology...we want to bring the individual up to a higher level ability so that he's more intelligent, he has better reaction time, he's more able and intelligent so that he can handle his life better." One of the reasons we find a remarkable degree of religious diversification (Beckford 1986, p. 9) is that there are an equivalent diversity of audiences in the general population.

This demand has also influenced mainstream religions and the way they interact with their followers. Televangelists may be regarded as significant competitors in the healing, consolation, and "God-will-fix-it" market. The worldly emphasis of the gods and services offered by NRMs helps explain their antagonism with professional bodies in the areas of mental and physical health, social work, etc. It also renders them highly vulnerable to lawsuits (which adds to the problems mentioned earlier). This is due to the consumer protection approach that anti-cult movements and state agencies have adopted (Beckford 1986; Richardson 1985, 1988b). If NRMs fail to deliver, the customer is there to complain. In contrast, traditional religions that focus on after-life rewards are shielded against such complaints.

THE BENEFITS OF AMBIGUITY

Being on the border between the sacred and the secular brings certain benefits to NRMs and quasi-religions. Being recognized as a religion provides financial and regulatory advantages. They are able to instill loyalty among people who feel their experiences are religious. In addition, religions enjoy legitimacy and respectability in their communities (Greil and Rudy 1990, pp. 228-229). The disadvantages of being a religion are that they have a narrower base for recruitment and that they receive less services from the government, protectionism notwithstanding. Not being a religion, on the other hand, may bring another kind of legitimacy and some business advantages, as it will be easier to sign contracts with companies (Greil and Rudy 1990, pp. 229-230). Sitting on the fence allows many NRMs to transcend the two worlds and derive benefits from both sides.

Whatever the original intent of CoS leaders and members, the ambiguity surrounding their organization serves them well. It is instrumental in that it enables CoS to keep its clientele, including the market share it has absorbed from therapeutic-psychological organizations, without having to demonstrate scientificity. At the same time, it is possible to employ the religious status for tax or other purposes. The potential market of the CoS would be reduced were it not conceptualized as a religion. In this sense, the battles it has fought in courts around the world have operated as a means to defend and preserve its market.

For example, the CoS sued a group of former members for the theft and dissemination of its teachings under a trade secrets law. Yet, it lost the case because it only argued that the teachings could cause harm if received without proper CoS training and did not claim any economic damages (Robbins 1988, pp. 81-82). In a later case, when a former member sued the CoS for severe emotional injury as a result of auditing, "disconnect" and "fair game" practices, the CoS paid a large amount of punitive damages because it did not request a "corporate responsibility" instruction (arguing that its employees acted without authorization). The judge noted that this was "[p]erhaps because [it] wanted the jurors to think of it as a religious 'church' and not a secular corporation" (*Wollersheim v. Church of Scientology* 1992, p. 538). Its claim to being a religion is a type of resource CoS requires to establish an important difference from its clearly secular competitors.[11]

CONCLUSION

The foregoing analysis suggests that there is no sharp line distinguishing religious from secular institutions, which constitute rather the two ends of a continuum. The ambivalence is more obvious with quasi-religions and NRMs whose finances and deviance, although qualitatively similar to those of mainstream religions, are closely scrutinized. As newcomers in the market for gods and services who dispose limited resources while facing hostile societal reactions and state authorities favoring established religions, NRMs resort to purely commercial or deviant practices for funding. Institutions (perceived to be) located closer to the religious end are more likely to be granted the full benefits of religion; they can also afford more conservative economic strategies. Those approaching the secular end, are more likely to see certain activities ruled out of the realm of religion or strictly regulated. In this sense, state regulation increases NRMs' need for financial resources and may inadvertently contribute increasingly serious deviance.

Despite appearances, however, NRMs reflect and often support conventional values. Their emergence owes much to social changes and crises. NRMs' proliferation and success reveals structural contradictions inherent to a culture stressing competitive individualism. These conditions give rise to the demand for services provided by NRMs. The market analogy applied here suggests that, whenever there is a demand for something, suppliers will be found. To a large extent, NRMs that offer what other institutions are unable to deliver are successful. Recognizing the structural sources of this demand also entails skepticism toward psychological reductionist accounts of NRMs, whereby "mind control" practices and personal pathologies of followers are overemphasized.

Further, commercial activities and deviance or unlawful conduct by NRM representatives are insufficient to deny them bona fide religious status. Existing laws can be used to ferret out criminal and fraudulent intent to prevent or punish unlawful acts. However, current practice appears to contain seeds for discrimination and persecution (Laycock 1991). Indeed, those concerned with the activities of NRMs and the spreading of their teachings may find a more effective way of control by officially recognizing them as religions. Transcendental Meditation is a case in point, as it argues that it is not a religion, so that it can be taught in schools (Greil and Rudy 1990).

In any event, in the same way Catholicism does not cease to be a religion following the exposure of shady economic transactions, the CoS and other NRMs should not cease to be recognized as religions either. Criminality and other unlawful conduct must be dealt with, but even-handedly. The very exposure of financial malpractice harms the interests of a given religious group and may lead to decreased appeal. This, again, is not very different from embarrassing disclosures about a secular company's misdeeds: Many potential customers may be driven away, at least for a period of time.

Any attempt to tax or otherwise regulate the quid pro quo or other activities of mainstream religions would be met with extreme resistance. It would also clash with Constitutional principles. The choice appears to be either freedom of religion and exercise, or equal repression. The latter is unacceptable and goes against the founding principles of the United States (a country initially populated largely by Europeans persecuted for their religious beliefs). The former carries with it the opportunity for religious fraud. But, this is the price we must pay for consistency and faithfulness to the First Amendment. Wall Street also gives rise to opportunities for inside trading and fraud; yet, no one suggests it should be closed down. The solution to the threat of religious fraud and the risks of theocracy does not lie solely in regulation. The underlying causes of the success of most NRMs cannot be legislated away. Solutions may be found only by addressing the structural and cultural features which create the demands NRMs meet, render the population susceptible to fraud, and make deceptive religious practices possible.

Moreover, too much focus on the practices now in the limelight may decrease the resources and attention directed to their international financial practices (not only of NRMS, but all groups, religious and nonreligious, with economic branches). The CoS claims significant success by producing figures showing its growth and increased number of followers in more than 70 countries. If it was possible to classify it as a "religious multinational" in 1981 (along with the Unification Church and the International Society for Krishna Consciousness, Beckford 1981); this classification may be even more fitting in the 1990s. The globalization of trade has seen its parallel in the internationalization of NRMs. Lessons we are learning from the regulation of cross-border transactions must be applied to NRMs as well. While current laws may adequately cover NRMs' misbehavior, the regulation of international financial transactions remains fragmented, inconsistent, occasionally contradictory, and often ineffective.[12] That is a far more important area upon which to focus, if our concern is not with what these groups preach and offer, but with their concrete practices that violate existing law (Ogloff and Pfeifer 1992).

ACKNOWLEDGMENTS

This paper draws on a joint project I have been conducting with Manuel Escamilla Castillo. I am grateful to him for his valuable comments, information on Spain, and the warm and stimulating atmosphere that he created. I am also indebted to Tom Robbins and Larry Greil for their constructive criticism, suggestions, and support.

NOTES

1. Even the contemporary Greek Orthodox Church maintains that it is unsafe for a mother to leave her house at night in the 40 days immediately after she gives birth, because she is vulnerable to demons who could harm her health. At the end of the 40-day period a priest offers special wishes, at a price. Interestingly, the period may be cut in half, if the priest visits her home to provide this service, again at a price.

2. The CoS's "fair game" practices of retribution or threatened retribution against perceived enemies and deserters find their parallels in the Inquisition, excommunication in Christian denominations, and "shunning" in the Mennonite Church (see *Bear v. Reformed Mennonite Church* 1975) or in the Jehovah's Witnesses Church (see *Paul v. Watchtower Bible & Tract Soc. of New York* 1987). Nikos Kazantzakis, the author of *Zorba the Greek* was excommunicated by the Greek Orthodox Church for his "blasphemous" book *Christ Recrucified* and died in poverty. A contemporary example is the death threat against Salman Rushdie for his *Satanic Verses*.

3. On the targetting of the CoS by the FDA, IRS, and other agencies overseas, see Wallis (1975, 1977; also Passas and Escamilla 1992, p. 113 on dissenting view in *Hernandez v. Commissioner of Internal Revenue* 1989). Much evidence is also produced in the U.S. Ministerial Conference of Scientology Ministers (1977).

4. Ruling that no specific relation between human beings and God can be traced through the CoS's practices and rituals, the Spanish Supreme Court found that the CoS is a scheme of purely human philosophy (*S.T.S.* 1990).

5. This was the case in post-Franco Spain.

6. Support for this hypothesis is provided by the fact that many former U.S. activists in the highly politicized early 1970s turned to NRMs (Kent 1988, pp. 105-106).

7. In a case coming close to religious fraud, for example, the Basic Bible Church of America's constitution was written in a way that the church was shielded from taxation and did not recognize the authority of state courts to rule on the tax dispute (*Waushara County v. Graf* 1992). Seven pages of a statement of its "fundamental beliefs and philosophy" were devoted to its tax-exempt status.

8. In its campaign against the *Time* article (Behar 1991), the CoS spent $3 million in advertisements in *USA Today*.

9. The Archbishop of York, for example, criticized the British government for emphasizing competitive success so much that it "feeds the notion that in our society ... we are against each other" (*Economist* 1993, p. 65).

10. Originating and thriving in a period of social crisis or transition is not peculiar to NRMS, but a feature shared by all religions (Harris 1981, p. 143).

11. Some would deduce motives out of consequences; however, I do not subscribe to this type of functionalist causal explanation. Rather, I employ the functional analysis heuristically, to raise questions about intended or unintended consequences of social action. On the distinction between functionalism as a form of causal explanation and functional analysis as a meta-method, see Passas (forthcoming a).

12. Plenty of evidence of this was furnished by the 1991 scandal around the failed Bank of Credit and Commerce International (BCCI), which has also been called a "cult" due to the philosophy of its Pakistani founder and the loyalty he inspired (Truell and Gurwin 1992).

REFERENCES

Allard v. Church of Scientology, 58 Cal.App.3d 439, 463 [129 Cal.Rptr. 797] (1976).

Barr v. Weise, 412 F.2d 338 (1969).

Bear v. Reformed Mennonite Church, 462 Pa. 330 [341 A.2d 105] (1975).

Beckford, J.A. 1981. "Cults, Controversy and Control." *Sociological Analysis* 43: 249-264.

_____. 1986. *New Religious Movements and Rapid Social Change*. Beverly Hills, CA: Sage.

Behar, R. 1986. "The Prophet and Profits of Scientology." *Forbes* 138(9): 314-322.

_____. 1991. "The Thriving Cult of Greed and Power." *Time* (May 6): 50-57.

Bendix, R. 1966. *Max Weber: An Intellectual Portrait*. London: Methuen.

Bird, F., and F. Westley. 1988. "The Economic Strategies of New Religious Movements." Pp. 45-68 in *Money and Power in the New Religions*, edited by J.T. Richardson. Lewiston/ Queenston: Edwin Mellen Press.

Bromley, D.G. 1985. "Financing the Millenium." *Journal for the Scientific Study of Religion* 24(3): 253-274.

Bromley, D.G., and E.F. Breschel. 1992. "General Population and Institutional Elite Support for Social Control of New Religious Movements: Evidence from National Survey Data." *Behavioral Sciences and the Law* 10(1): 39-52.

Bromley, D.G., and A. Shupe. 1980. "Financing the New Religions: A Resource Mobilization Approach." *Journal for the Scientific Study of Religion* 19(3): 227-239.

Chagnon, R. 1986. "Religion et Santé: Le Cas de l'Eglise de Scientologie." *Social Compass* 34(4): 495-507.

Church of Scientology v. City of Clearwater, 756 F.Supp. 1498 (M.D.Fla. 1991).

Church of Scientology of California v. Commissioner of Internal Revenue, 823 F.2d 1310 (9th Cir. 1987).

Cornwell, R. 1984. *God's Banker*. New York: Dodd, Mead.

Corporation of the Presiding Bishop v. Amos, 483 U.S. 327 (1987).

Dershowitz, A.M. 1988. *Taking Liberties*. Chicago: Contemporary Books.

Donaton, S. 1991. "Scientology Fires Ad Barrage at 'Time'." *Advertising Age* (June 3): 50.

Durant, W. 1950. *The Story of Civilization*, Vol. 4. New York: Simon and Schuster.

Economist. 1993. "Worship Moves in Mysterious Ways." (March 13): 65, 70.

Employment Division v. Smith, 110 S.Ct. 1595 (1990).

Founding Church of Scientology of Washington D.C. v. United States, 7CCH 7927 Stand. Fed. Tax Rep. (1968).

Grafstein, L. 1984. "Messianic Capitalism." *New Republic* 190(7): 14-16.

Greil, A.L., and D.R. Rudy. 1990. "On the Margins of the Sacred." Pp. 219-232 in *In Gods We Trust: New Patterns of Religious Pluralism*, edited by T. Robbins and D. Anthony. New Brunswick, NJ: Transaction.

Harris, M. 1981. *America Now*. New York: Simon and Schuster.

Hernandez v. Commissioner of Internal Revenue, 109 S.Ct. 2136 (1989).

Jimmy Swaggart Ministries v. Board of Equalization of California, 110 S.Ct. 688 (1990).

Kent, S.A. 1988. "Slogan Chanters to Mantra Chanters: A Mertonian Deviance Analysis of Conversion ro Religiously Ideological Organizations in the Earky 1970s." *Sociological Analysis* 49(2): 104-118.

Khalsa, K.S. 1988. "New Religious Movements Turn to Wordly Success." Pp. 117-140 in *Money and Power in the New Religions*, edited by J.T. Richardson, ed. Lewiston/Queenston: Edwin Mellen Press.

Larson, M., and S.C. Lowell. 1976. *The Religious Experience: The Growth and Danger of Tax-Exempt Property in the United States*. Washington, DC: Robert B. Luce.

Laycock, D. 1991. "The Remnants of Free Exercise." Pp. 1-68 in *1990 Supreme Court Review*, edited by G. Casper, D.J. Hutchinson, and D.A. Strauss. Chicago: University of Chicago Press.

Levin, G. 1991. "'Time' Squabble: Scientology Adds WPP Units to Attack." *Advertising Age* (June 17): 4, 47.

Malko, G. 1970. *Scientology: The Now Religion*. New York: Delacorte Press.

McCloskey, H.B., and A. Brill. 1983. *Dimensions of Tolerance: What Americans Believe about Civil Liberties*. New York: Russell Sage.

Merton, R.K. 1968. *Social Theory and Social Structure*. New York: The Free Press.

Moore, J.P. 1980. "Piercing the Religious Veil of the So-called Cults." *Pepperdine Law Review* 7: 655-710.

Norgren, J., and S. Nanda. 1988. *American Culture Pluralism and Law*. New York: Praeger.

Ogloff, J.R.P., and J.E. Pfeifer. 1992. "Cults and the Law: A Discussion of the Legality of Alleged Cult Activities." *Behavioral Sciences and the Law* 10(1): 117-140.

Passas, N. 1990. "Anomie and Corporate Deviance." *Contemporary Crises* 14(3): 157-178.

_____. forthcoming a. "Continuities in the Anomie Tradition." *Advances in Criminological Theory* 6.

_____. forthcoming b. *Advancing Criminological Theory: An Exercise in Middle-Range Theorizing*. Albany, NY: SUNY Press.

Passas, N., and M. Escamilla. 1992. "Scientology and its 'Clear' Business." *Behavioral Sciences and the Law* 10: 103-116.

Paul v. Watchtower Bible & Tract Soc. of New York, 819 F.2d 875, 880 (9th Cir. 1987).

Podus, D. 1991. "Churches, Tax Exemption, and the Social Organization of Religion." Pp. 179-202 in *Comparative Social Research*, Vol. 13, edited by C. Calhoun. Greenwich, CT: JAI Press.

Richardson, J.T. 1985. "The "Deformation" of New Religions: Impact of Societal and Organizational Factors." Pp. 163-175 in *Cults, Culture, and the Law*, edited by T. Robbins, W.C. Shepherd, and J. McBride. Chico, CA: Scholars Press.

_____. ed. 1988a. *Money and Power in the New Religions*. Lewiston/Queenston: Edwin Mellen Press.

_____. 1988b. "Changing Times: Religion, Economics and the Law in Contemporary America." *Sociological Analysis* 49: 1-14.

_____. 1992. "Public Opinion and the Tax Evasion Trial of Reverend Moon." *Behavioral Sciences and the Law* 10(1): 53-63.

Richardson, J.T., and B. van Driel. 1984. "Public Support for Anti-Cult Legislation." *Journal for the Scientific Study of Religion* 23(4): 412-418.

Robbins, T. 1981. "Church, State and Cult." *Sociological Analysis* 42(3): 209-226.
_____. 1985a. "Government Regulatory Powers Over Religious Movements." *Journal for the Scientific Study of Religion* 24(3): 237-251.
_____. 1985b. "New Religious Movements on the Frontier of Church and State." Pp. 7-30 in *Cults, Culture, and the Law,* edited by T. Robbins, W.C. Shepherd, and J. McBride. Chico, CA: Scholars Press.
_____. 1988. "Profit for Prophets: Legitimate and Illegitimate Economic Practices in New Religious Movements." Pp. 69-116 in *Money and Power in the New Religions,* edited by J.T. Richardson, ed. Lewiston/Queenston: Edwin Mellen Press.
Robbins, T., and J.A. Beckford. In press. "Religious Movements and Church-State Issues." Unpublished manuscript.
Robbins, T., and D. Bromley. 1992. "Social Experimentation and the Significance of American New Religions: A Focused Review Essay." Pp. 1-28 in *Research in the Social Scientific Study of Religion,* Vo. 4, edited by M.L. Lynn and D.O. Moberg. Greenwich, CT: JAI Press.
Ross, M.W. 1988. "Effects of Membership in Scientology on Personality: An Exploratory Study." *Journal for the Scientific Study of Religion* 27(4): 630-636.
S.T.S. (Sentencia del Tribunal Supremo)—Sala 3a, Sección 5a—June 25, 1990.
Senn, S. 1990. "The Prosecution of Religious Fraud." *Florida State University Law Review* 17: 325-352.
Shupe, A.D., D.G. Bromley, and D.L. Oliver. 1984. *The Anti-Cult Movement in America: A Bibliography and Historical Survey.* New York: Garland.
Staples v. Commissioner of Internal Revenue, 821 F.2d 1324 (8th Cir. 1987).
Stark, R. 1987. "How New Religions Succeed: A Theoretical Model." Pp. 11-29 in *The Future of New Religious Movements,* edited by D.G. Bromley and P.E. Hammond. Macon: Mercer University Press.
Straus, R. 1986. "Scientology 'Ethics': Deviance, Identity and Social Control in a Cult-like Social World." *Symbolic Interaction* 9(1): 67-82.
Tipton, S.M. 1988. "Rationalizing Religion as a Corporate Enterprise: The Case of est." Pp. 223-240 in *Money and Power in the New Religions,* edited by J.T. Richardson. Lewiston/Queenston: Edwin Mellen Press.
Truell, P., and L. Gurwin. 1992. *False Profits.* Boston: Houghton Mifflin.
United States v. Heldt, 668 F.2d 1238 (1981).
Van Schaick v. Church of Scientology, 535 F.Supp. 1125 (D. Mass. 1982).
Vaughan, D. 1983. *Controlling Unlawful Organizational Behavior.* Chicago: Chicago University Press.
Wallis, R. 1975. "Societal Reaction to Scientology: A Study in the Sociology of Deviant Religion." Pp. 86-116 in *Sectarianism,* edited by R. Wallis. New York: John Wiley & Sons.
_____. 1977. *The Road to Total Freedom: A Sociological Analysis of Scientology.* New York: Columbia University Press.
Waushara County v. Graf, 480 N.W.2d 16 (Wis. 1992).
Whitehead, H. 1987. *Renunciation and Reformulation: A Study of Conversion in an American Sect.* Ithaca: Cornell University Press.
Wollersheim v. Church of Scientology of California, 212 Cal.App.3d 872; 260 Cal.Retr. 331 [July 1989].
_____, 6 Cal.Rptr.2d 532 (Cal.App. 2 Dist. 1992).
Zaretsky, I., and M. Leone. 1974. "The Common Foundation of Religious Diversity." Pp. xvii-xxxvi in *Religious Movements in Contemporary America,* edited by I. Zaretsky and M. Leone. Princeton: Princeton University Press.
Zemke, R. 1987. "What's New in the New Age?" *Training* 24(9): 25-33.

THE PROBLEM OF AUTHENTICITY IN
THE STUDY OF RELIGIOUS TRADITIONS

Lewis F. Carter

ABSTRACT

This paper urges systematic scholarly examination of the "criteria-in-use" by religious and secular groups for deciding about the "authenticity" of religious beliefs, experiences, and practices. The discussion notes that these criteria differ greatly across the major world religious traditions and that the notion of "authenticity" itself should be seen as an "essentially contested construct" which takes on very different meanings depending on whether one refers to judgments made by (and about) individuals, groups, or larger institutionalized collectives. Although the paper acknowledges the risk of inquiries into the bases of authenticity devolving into partisan doctrinal disputes, it is argued that ignoring such issues of authenticity involves the greater risk of being unable to fathom the unique nature of the strength of religiously grounded commitments and the tenacity with which beliefs, judged by their holders to be "authentically religious," may be held.

Secular American scholarship displays reluctance to address issues of the "authenticity" of religious experiences, practices, and institutions. This reticence is understandable given normative caveats about "objectivity" and

Religion and the Social Order, Volume 4, pages 241-249.
Copyright © 1994 by JAI Press Inc.
All rights of reproduction in any form reserved.
ISBN: 1-55938-763-7

about multiple frames-of-reference implicit in "cultural relativism," and the reluctance is further reinforced in the United States by generalized commitments to poly-culturalism implied by the legal and ideological content of the "establishment clause." Nevertheless, answers for certain important questions at the level of individual adherents, as well as issues for religious leadership and yet other concerns at the institutional-collective level, may require broaching "authenticity" issues. Minimally, we need to know more about how adherents and critics of specific traditions develop their own "authenticity judgments"—what logics and evidentiary bases they use in making authenticity claims and in defending these claims among themselves, as well as in defenses to outside individuals and agencies. This paper notes a range of traditional approaches to addressing authenticity issues in established religions—schism, religious authority, Canon Law, as well as secular law (although we should remain cognizant of the fact that sacred and secular law are distinguished in only some cultures). The paper raises a set of questions concerning how secular scholars might develop approaches to "authenticity" criteria to aid our interpretation of individual commitments and beliefs, as well as of collective claims and actions. These issues lead to speculations that those religious traditions which are transmitted primarily through an oral tradition, based on direct individual experience, representing colonial and other syncretisms, and certain New Religious Movements raise special problems for "authenticity" assessments, whether at individual or institutional levels. The paper is intended to open "conversations" among scholars about a variety of strategies for addressing "authenticity."

First, let us be very clear that I do not even pretend to have identified the criteria for authenticity in any very large or powerful sense, and certainly in no sense claiming absolute validity. Although the theme of this volume is "quasi-religions," I would not even imagine trying to specify how to distinguish between what we might call "real religions," "quasi-religions," and (for the sake of categorical closure) "false religions." Although adherents and leaders of many traditions do make such judgments in everyday practice, I am persuaded that authenticity is an *essentially contested concept* which enters the discourse of different religious traditions very differently. Further, both within and across a number of religious traditions, the meaning of the term authenticity (and how judgments about what is and what is not "authentic" are made) will vary considerably depending on whether we are discussing the level of individual, a circle of peers and intimates, a small cultural group, a congregation, a larger collective, an elaborately developed set of religious institutions, or a poly-cultural social system.

The authenticity concept may be fairly manageable within a single tradition and at a single level of aggregation, but the notion becomes very troublesome if we attempt to apply it across time, traditions, or level of aggregation (e.g., individual, collective, and institutional).

LARGE INSTITUTIONALIZED COLLECTIVES

In large, organized religions (or perhaps more properly stated, "institutional-ized" religious traditions), the criteria for authenticity of a teaching, a text, or a practice will ordinarily be addressed through some form of faith in the authority of a scripture (or written code), and usually also subordination to the interpretive authority of church leaders or other interpretive figures or to organized bodies of such leaders. The scriptures and written codes are taken in a number of these traditions as inspired writings, and the authenticity of these writings is assumed within the tradition (although there may even here be internal conflicts concerning competing versions and interpretations). The various versions of the Christian bibles and associated interpretations, the Talmudic discourses, and the Sharia tradition of Islam are well known examples of such texts and associated collections of interpretations.

Internal disputes and more external socio-historical contexts have given rise to the numerous well-known competing variations within these traditions. The various splits have often centered around specific historical conflicts— sometimes with apparently doctrinal motivations and at other times apparently motivated by political, economic, and even the personal agendas of powerful historical figures. Doctrinal differences range from issues which appear, even from a secular orientation, to be quite basic to other issues which outsiders might see as trivial. Instances of the former include the dualism of Christian and Islamic traditions (locating the divine outside the human) versus the monism of Hindu and Buddhist traditions, monotheism versus polytheism, and reliance on priesthoods for authentication versus written texts or individual experience; instances of less basic differences which have nevertheless been the subject focusing bitter division have included such seemingly superficial matters as whether the sign of the cross should be made with two or three fingers. The consequences for English religious history of Henry VIII's personal stake in a church permitting divorce are well documented.

As we all know, authenticity of text, teaching, or practice is usually not assumed or acknowledged across major traditions (Christianity, Buddhism, or Islam), and authenticity frequently is not assumed across the schisms within these traditions. Ecumenism, and to some extent agreed upon syncretisms, represent sociopolitical attempts to broaden the domains across which authenticity will be granted—in a sense, a softening of conflict between competing traditions and interpretations, which usually involves blurring some doctrinal boundaries or agreements to be pluralistic in terms of institutions, practices, and beliefs. Splits, schisms, and in extreme cases, active persecution (or even holy wars) represent the opposite extreme of adaptation in the direction of declaring a single tradition (interpretation or institution) to be authentic to the exclusion of all or some defined set of others. While many of these histories are well known and meticulously researched as doctrinal matters, there has been little detached sociological speculation, much less systematic theorizing about the conditions which might produce accommodation versus those leading to exclusive claims of authenticity. In some cultures and some traditions such speculation and research would itself be seen as heretical and utterly improper—a forbidden research. However, in pluralistic secular legal climates such as are now found in a number of regions of the world, such investigations would be both permissible and illuminating. The United States may be such a context. It is something of an irony that the very legal and cultural settings which are most permissive in terms of allowing discussion of such questions may be the very settings in which scholars are most reluctant to address these issues, as in the United States.

These issues of authenticity become yet more problematic when one moves to the Hindu and Buddhist traditions in which there has been less primacy given to a single set of writings and less dominance given to exclusive interpretive institutions. Indeed, some extreme variants of these traditions would deny the relevance or meaningfulness of "authentic/inauthentic" judgments, although even here there is a considerable history of sometimes bitter competition in these traditions, both between different schools of thought or practice and between different teachers or proponents of these schools. These traditions have not generally developed the extremely close linkages with secular institutions and power bases as may be found in the Islamic state or as has been found historically in a number of Christian-based states. While there has at times been conflict among adherents of variations of the Hindu and Buddhist traditions, the traditions have not been as prone to push exclusive authenticity claims to the same extremes found in the Christian and Islamic histories, although wars and warlike actions can be noted where differences within these traditions are also connected with denial 'of allegiance to the surrounding secular authority or state. (The Sikh dilemma in India is illustrative of the problems encountered by separate religions denying secular authority in otherwise poly-cultural states.)

INDIVIDUAL TRANSFORMATION

Authenticity judgments take on a very different character when we move to examine the small groups characteristic of the splits common in Christian congregations as well as the so-called "new religions" and also perhaps the level of individual adherents of these traditions. Often these splits are based on some disagreement about doctrine or practice. In a sense, these may be seen as situations where faith in, or subordination to, some established religious authority has failed (or at least been replaced by an alternative authority). Interpretive differences about doctrine or practice, while still acknowledging basic texts or histories, may be seen as more minor challenges, although even these have led to major splits of great historical significance. The assorted Protestant splits within Christianity represented a major challenge in changing the locus for determining authenticity.

The various traditions which have emerged that emphasize direct personal experience as the criterion (or a major criterion) for authenticity of religious experience represent an even more fundamental shift. These include the various Gnostic Christian traditions as well as some of the Sufi outgrowths of Islam. These variants have in common with a number of Hindu, Buddhist, and Animist traditions that the test of authenticity may be seen as lying in individual experience rather than in written scripture or in a priesthood or institutionalized religious bodies. To be sure, these traditions may emphasize the importance of adepts, or guides, to show proper paths (or surer paths or safer paths) to the religious goal which is usually some form of "transcendence." Further, there may be debates and competitions among adepts for followers, but the test of the outcome is seen as occurring within the individual. In a sense, some "born again" Christian movements also emphasize an individual transformative element, but these will usually have "external tests" of the transformation, tests which are more or less visible to the religious collective. For example, internal change or transformation is commonly assumed to have occurred only if there is some "reform" exhibited in individual behavior as prescribed by collective rules of conduct.

We have little systematic research of the differences between groups with strongly collective religious prescriptions and those which give strong emphasis to direct individual experience. Nor is there systematic examination of conditions seeming to facilitate or deter the development and preservation of systems which vary in these terms. It likely makes considerable difference whether the criteria for the occurrence and authenticity of such personal transformations are totally individual judgments, judgments of peers or mentors as opposed to being tested against some formal body of belief and practice (or, more extremely, tested by a group of judges or a form of court or, in the most extreme cases, tested by inquisitional processes).

CHARISMATIC AND ORAL TRADITIONS

Between traditions relying most completely on "direct personal knowing" and those which are most elaborately institutionalized, it is useful to distinguish two other forms of religious tradition which may pose special problems in addressing the notion of authenticity—charismatic movements and oral religious traditions. I am using the term "charismatic" in the particularly narrow sense of movements relying on the rather arbitrary authority of a central figure who is seen as having special powers to determine the authenticity of any matters of belief and practice. Most particularly, I refer to those movements without a substantial body of written code or with a written code which is attributed to a living leader who has the authority to change elements of that code without justification. The Rajneesh movement, which I studied for a number of years, and Elizabeth Claire Prophet's Church Universal and Triumphant represent two such cases among the so-called "New Religious Movements." These differ in terms of Rajneesh's having been seen as simply having special enlightenment and insight, whereas Prophet's special knowledge is attributed to her function as a "channel" for communication from "ascended masters." However, any group in which the living leader is seen as sufficiently "special" in terms of enlightenment or in terms of contact with spiritual powers as to be unaccountable to written code or to constraint by some collective body poses unusual problems in terms of authenticity criteria. Pronouncements cannot be tested, either against relatively invariant writings or against organized collective judgments.

In a sense, the doctrine of Papal infallibility, if taken literally and out of its institutional and historical context, might have qualified the Catholic church for this category, but of course Popes were virtually never utterly without constraint by historical codes and by the Vatican as well as by more distant institutional structures. In the sense that I use the term "charismatic" here, the leader (and his or her personal connection to something powerful) is seen as the primary or exclusive criterion for authenticity of beliefs and practices for the group. The most controversial characteristic of such groups is the extent to which practice and belief is subordinated to the will and judgment of a single person. This characteristic generates concern partly because for such groups "authenticity" lies in the person rather than in any historical continuity, whether written code, collective lore, or communal body.

Considerable research has been devoted to such movements partly because of the extreme variation possible under such conditions and partly because of a societal anxiety about potential for abuse under such conditions (though I need not remind scholars of religion that even our most institutionalized religions have had their own violent histories). Some of this research on charismatic groups has taken the unfortunate turn of treating authenticity as it is treated within a competing external religious frame, and thus the research becomes part of an attempt to further the authenticity claims of the alternative.

External criteria for authenticity are sometimes imposed, albeit implicitly, by observers of these movements when they focus on exotic practices, apparently extreme or coercive control, or on inconsistency. Some of these movements explicitly deny the relevance of consistency, either among religious components at any time, or from one period of time to another, and this very denial may be seen by critics from the other tradition as implying "inauthenticity." It is probably unnecessary to point out to religious scholars that very few among us would claim to have found the perfectly consistent tradition.

At a superficial level, many of the world's oral religious traditions might appear similar to the charismatic "New Religions." By definition, religions relying on oral transmission through story and song have no written codes or written histories (or at least not complete or definitive ones which are seen as controlling or constraining innovation). However, many if not perhaps all (at least most) of these oral traditions will rely on some collective form of "corrective" for defining appropriate and inappropriate deviations from acceptable doctrine and practice. Collective oral traditions vary in terms of their degree of "fixity," but even in the most flexible of these we will find groups of people who are seen as having the authority to decide whether new additions are within the "character" of the tradition—that is, whether changes represent some continuity with some more or less consistent body of belief and practice. The preservers of tradition may be a group of elders or a group of specialists (in some cases even the whole collective), but their deliberations about authenticity will be characterized by some appeals either to continuity of past belief and practice or by appeals to some notion of consistency with the character or principles of that past.

CONCLUSIONS

The limited attention given to "authenticity" questions in sociological and other secular scholarly discourse has sometimes been justified by a kind of misguided relativism which holds that to examine such issues moves from "objective" discourse into the arena of religious advocacy. While crude and unself-conscious examination of authenticity questions can indeed become such an advocacy, there is nothing intrinsic in these questions which precludes their examination from some intentionally uncommitted external frame of reference.

We can examine the arguments, evidential bases, and criteria used in courts, ecclesiastical bodies, and other groups to make decisions about what is authentic and do so without ourselves necessarily sharing those conclusions or taking an advocate's posture. Many interesting and important insights could be developed into the power of religion in culture by the study of where jurisdiction for such judgments is seen to lie in different religious traditions and in different secular contexts. We can determine how practitioners, religious leaders and critics, and secular authorities make authenticity judgments as well as what criteria they use to determine and defend authenticity claims in specific domains. We can study variation in these claims, in their correspondence to other criteria, in their internal consistency, and in the consequences of those choices without ourselves necessarily advancing independent or exclusive authenticity claims. We can attempt to develop appropriate analytic categories to allow analysis of important variations in "authentication" systems and criteria.

If we develop more systematic comparative studies of the criteria-in-use by people of many faiths in different cultural contexts for making authenticity judgments, we are likely to learn that there are strong and interesting commonalties (though I doubt wholly "universal" ones across all of those diverse things claiming the status of religions). For example, the consistency criteria is widely appealed to in Christian, Islamic, and Judaic traditions but seems to be less of an issue in others. Why, and what are the consequences of this? The transformative criterion is widely shared among Christian "born again" groups as well as within the Gnostic versions of Islam and several versions of Hinduism and Buddhism. The devices and pathways to "transformation" are notably different, and perhaps so are the criteria for deciding who has been transformed (as well as the importance placed on making such judgments).

While our tendency as sociologists to avoid studying how authenticity is defined and/or determined may be understandable, it can also be seen as itself an appropriate subject of study. We seem to have forgotten that these are the important, perhaps the fundamental, judgments made about what teachings are "proper," what behaviors are desirable, and who is included (and excluded) from the "elect." The avoidance may keep us from being obvious zealots, proselytizers, and bigots, but it may also prevent our studying some of the fundamental dimensions of conflict between religious traditions as well as some of the devices used to process those conflicts.

I recall a discussion some years ago with a Tlingit Indian who was also the Chairman of the Board of the Sea Alaska Corporation in southeastern Alaska. I had been invited to lunch with him and the corporation's director of economic research after I had requested access to some information about forest and fish resources, and he wanted some gauge of me, of my intentions and orientation. In the middle of a course of sashimi, this man turned to me and said, "I have heard that sociologists are reluctant to study things that are politically controversial. How do you feel about this?" I replied that this was true of some, but that I believed that avoiding such topics would prevent our study of some of the things which people cared most about and which were most powerful in the shaping of behavior. He turned immediately to his director and said, "Let this sociologist use any of our library resources."

Similarly, the fact that it is controversial to study issues related to authenticity can as easily be argued to indicate that these are important topics of study, central to religious commitment and to the power of religious traditions. It is always risky to study sources of the legitimacy and power of institutions as well as areas of deep individual commitment. Personal risks may range from collegial suspicion about motives, detachment, hidden agendas or advocacy to the extreme of death in some cultures and some historical eras (for example, the European Inquisition in the distant past and the Islamic Fundamentalism of Iran in the not so distant past). Yet one seems intrigued by the question, "If the study of authenticity is so suspect (even taboo), might this very fact not suggest that the related issues are fundamental enough for people to care enough about as to suggest that excluding authenticity from the domain of discourse can be done only at the peril of a greater risk—the risk of a superficial discourse with little chance of illuminating why religions are sometimes so powerful and their adherents so committed?"

I should reiterate the demurrer that I would not presume to claim definitive criteria for distinguishing "real religions, quasi-religions, and false religions," but I am convinced that systematic examination of how people and institutions do make such judgments and how they defend such claims is of fundamental importance. To exclude authenticity issues from the domain of secular scholarly discourse would likely prevent that discourse from understanding the "sound and fury" of religious conflicts, understanding the bases for accommodation of competing traditions, or examining some of the mechanisms by which social and moral order are grounded in human systems.

ACKNOWLEDGMENTS

I wish to thank Walfred H. Peterson and Erik T. Carter for their meticulous reading of a draft manuscript and their suggestions for clarifying some of the ambiguities in that draft. I wish also to thank Thomas Robbins for his advice and encouragement, and to acknowledge Benton Johnson (1987) for broaching some distinct, but related concerns, about the restricted domain of discourse in the sociological analysis of religion in his thoughtful essay, "Faith, Facts and Values in the Sociology of Religion." While I remain responsible for all interpretations and judgments made here, the conversations ("real-time" in the case of Robbins, and "virtual" and long-term through the published word in the case of Johnson) have been invaluable in developing the ideas in this paper.

REFERENCE

Johnson, B. 1987. "Faith, Facts and Values in the Sociology of Religion." Pp. 1-13 in *Religious Sociology: Interfaces and Boundaries,* edited by W.H. Swatos, Jr. Westport, CT: Greenwood Press.

PART IV

INTERPRETING QUASI-RELIGIONS
AND PARA-RELIGIONS

THE QUASI-SACRED:

A THEORETICAL INTRODUCTION

Richard K. Fenn

ABSTRACT

In this paper I develop the notion of the quasi-sacred as belonging along a continuum. At the outset, the quasi-sacred takes the form of a state of mind in which the individual is virtually entranced by the larger society and regards it as sacred. The individual may then develop a set of qualifications of this mentality, in which the larger society seems to be progressively incomplete or artificial, and in which the individual develops competitive or imitative forms of the sacred. Toward the further end of the continuum, the quasi-sacred develops as the individual regards the larger society as virtually demonic and in need of radical purification. In the extreme case of the quasi-sacred, the individual simply denies the existence of the sacred "other" as there is nothing left to oppose. The sacred is no longer contested or demonic, simply because it has been assigned to a secular world—a world that is passing away.

Why choose to investigate the "quasi-sacred?" It is always possible that the selection of a topic says more about the researchers than about the problem

Religion and the Social Order, Volume 4, pages 253-271.
Copyright © 1994 by JAI Press Inc.
All rights of reproduction in any form reserved.
ISBN: 1-55938-763-7

at hand; in any event, a "reflexive" comment is always in order, especially at the beginning of a project such as this.

A clue toward finding an answer to this question can perhaps be found in an unlikely source; Turner's *The Ritual Process* (1966) comments on his initial studies of ritual among the Ndembu. The source is "unlikely," if only because Turner is studying religion in a context where boundaries between the sacred and the profane are relatively strong—as strong as the boundaries, say, between the genders and the generations, or between the living and the dead, or between the Ndembu and outsiders. There is little about the sacred in such a context that one would want to call "quasi-." Turner's comment on why he trusted the rites he observed is instructive:

> In all this time we never asked for a ritual to be performed solely for our anthropological benefit; we held no brief for such artificial play-acting (p. 10).

This is a comment, mind you, from someone who admits that he had to overcome his prejudice toward ritual (p. 7).

Here the point is simply that his rather stern view of ritual may make the quasi-sacred problematic in a way that would not pose a problem to someone with a more benign and relaxed view of the matter. Others have noted that there is an element of playacting even in relatively serious rituals, as long as an observer is present. Even in playacting itself, the drama is changed by the presence of an audience. As for the adjective "mere" that precedes "playacting," there are a number of assumptions riding on the use of such a term. Runciman (1983), for instance, disagrees with the notion that a ritual can only be performed in good faith when individuals are not going through the motions but are somehow wholly caught up in the ritual enactment. Such an assumption, he argues, is as unnecessary as it is prejudicial. All that is needed for a rite to be performed properly is that individuals, regardless of their psychological state, honor the purpose of the performance and respect its obligatory nature. This is a more Anglican view of the matter than the more pietistic view of Turner, who may have been revolting from his earlier Catholicism and from what he perceived as the insincerity of ritual performances noted in his youth and childhood.

For some, the sacred is always mixed with an element of contingency. The production and consumption of the sacred can never be total, whole-hearted, universal, and unqualified but is always contingent on the context, on the state of mind of the performers and their beneficiaries, and on the range of relevant social differences among them. What matters is the degree to which the machinery for producing the sacred is conspicuous or relatively unobtrusive, so that those engaged in constructing the sacred can afford to pay little attention to the process of manufacture and can become lost in the performance itself. The meaning of the prefix "quasi" then suggests a sense of the partial and incomplete, the provisional and the ersatz, and the possibility of corruption. I propose to adopt this range of meanings as one semantic and logical spectrum along which to array a hypothetical series of empirical cases of the quasi-sacred.

The sacred, even when performed with the utmost seriousness and according to all the relevant rubrics, is therefore always in danger of becoming the quasi-sacred. Even the neurotics who Freud observed were self-conscious about their performances of their own private rituals. That is how they became patients, of course. The same insight informs the comment of O'Keefe (1982, p. 276) that there is an element of quite self-conscious playacting even in the compulsive rites of obsessives. These suffering souls go through the motions of their private rites with what borders on an extreme self-consciousness—a consciousness of the right way of doing things and a consciousness of what is supposed to happen if they do (or, worse yet, do not) follow the rules.

Thus there is something illicit, illegitimate, and potentially dangerous about the quasi-sacred. In aping the rituals and authority of the family or the larger society, the quasi-sacred rites of the neurotic are stealing the community's magic. No wonder that neurotics perform their rites not only with a strong awareness of what they are doing but with the apprehension that their own rites are a mere "double," a copy, a "fake" (O'Keefe 1982, p. 276). For them a rite is not merely incompletely sacred; it is artificial and counterfeit: "quasi" in the strong sense of the term and potentially seditious.

PSYCHOLOGICAL BASES OF THE QUASI-SACRED

Now, there are reasons for these quasi-sacred rituals, but I agree with O'Keefe that they all boil down to one—the preservation of the self against psychological death or "soul-loss."

> Magic expropriates religious power and uses it against religion, *in order to defend the self against religion, against society, against the superego, which at all times threaten to implode the self and snuff it out* (O'Keefe 1982, p. 277, emphasis in original).

Now, there are threats to the self at each stage of its emergence from the matrix which includes, initially, the mother and her world. The first danger point comes when the baby experiences the frustration and rage that accompany helplessness. The mother's absence is experienced as a mortal threat, and the infant also experiences its own rage as an explosive force capable of overwhelming or dissolving it. Time is literally running out on the infant with every moment that delays the satisfaction of his needs. To fight the sacred fires of the infant's yearning for, attraction to, and rage against the mother, the infant needs to kindle, as it were, the fires of the self. This withdrawal of energy and interest from the mother and its reinvestment in the self is a primitive form of fighting fire with fire—*a sympathetic magic* in the service of defending the fragile and evanescent self. In this way the self becomes quasi-sacred: not partially sacred or pseudo-sacred but a mirror image, a reflection that not only reverses but is opposed to the original image of the sacred.

The withdrawal of affection from the world and the investing of that same affection in the self is experienced as a dangerous act, however, against which the world may retaliate. The punishment for the crime of separating oneself from the world is to be cut off: abandoned, castrated, isolated. There are psychological penalties for the development of a quasi-sacred world. It is never quite the real thing, and its way of protecting the self never really works. The self, as quasi-sacred, is always subject to attacks from the "higher" self for being partial and incomplete, counterfeit, competitive, and contrary. In the same vein conservative sociologists have criticized the more individualistic expressions of religiosity as being inadequate or artificial, competitive with or even opposed to the values on which communities and societies depend for their legitimacy and order.

The individual's quasi-sacred universe is a fortress, however precarious and contingent, against the self's enemies—against the conscience or superego, against social pressures toward conformity or sacrifice, and even against religion itself, against all those pressures which can make the self seem helpless, unworthy, and, in the end, incapable of staying alive. "In a showdown, what magic defends the self against is death" (O'Keefe 1982, p. 277).

It is only later in the essay that O'Keefe goes on to remind us that magic perpetuates the very helplessness from which it is supposed to deliver the fledgling self.

> One feels that magic works for a while, but becomes symptomatic or even iatrogenic if overly indulged, and that it is less adaptive in modern than in primitive societies.... The magician is like a handyman who keeps patching things up, repairing old machines out of the debris of wrecked machines, patching up broken egos with some of the sacred symbols that smashed them—the whole thing barely works and there are never any fresh or permanent solutions; it is all conservative, defensive, just adequate, or an actual botch (1982, p. 317).

With friends like magic, therefore, the self does not need such enemies as an overweening conscience or sociological inquisitions against "individualism."

THE QUASI-SACRED AND MODERN RELIGIOSITY: A CASE OF FAILED MAGIC

In describing various forms of the quasi-sacred, we may therefore find ourselves looking at a sort of mix-and-match religiosity—bits of the old blended with fragments of the new. What passes for a "postmodern" form of religiosity may therefore be quite primitive. "New Age" movements, for instance, or conservative Christian groups resemble what one would expect to find, for instance, in a primitive society overwhelmed by Western institutions. Wherever individuals fear for their own psychic survival, they will patch together a sort of quilt of Western and indigenous, conventional and innovative, forms of expression to preserve what can be saved of their selfhood. This sort of religiosity, however, also comes at a price: continued helplessness, a sense of guilt for withdrawing trust and affection from the larger society or for wearing stolen religious finery, and a sense of dread at having to face a day of reckoning.

There is something complex and burdensome about the play of religious symbols in "postmodern" (read "primitive") religiosity. The way magic works is to give the helpless and inarticulate self words and meanings with which to understand and control a fate that seems oppressive and constraining, or empty and relentless. Quasi-sacred religiosity—incomplete, counterfeit, competitive, and contrary though it may be—is simply a strategy for fighting off the death of the soul. Like the brooms in "The Sorcerer's Apprentice," however, the techniques of magical religiosity begin to proliferate. Simply the range of cultural offerings in the so-called "New Age" reads like a rummage sale of worn-out cultural techniques. O'Keefe's own analysis of these magical-therapeutic offerings would be funny if it were not a bit sad.

Still another implication comes from O'Keefe's position—namely, that individuals and communities can make themselves sick or scare themselves to death by their own magical, quasi-sacred beliefs and practices. Note that this argument goes well beyond the usual arguments about magic and alienation. O'Keefe recognizes the argument, primarily associated with the Frankfort School, that reason has become so complex, so embedded in administrative or scientific organizations and practices, that individuals can hardly know, let alone control, their own societies. As a result, these societies seem strange or uncanny to them, and like anyone faced with the demonic, individuals develop their own magical defenses. This may be true, but O'Keefe is going on to the next stage of the defensive process, the "iatrogenic" stage, in which it becomes apparent that individuals sicken themselves by becoming chronic patients, or frighten themselves by peopling their worlds with strange forces, and literally treat or doctor themselves to death. No wonder that the media are fascinated with cases of Christian Scientists who pray while their children sicken and die or by the young man who repeated his self-help slogan but failed to keep his battery charged and thus missed a crucial job interview (*New York Times* 1992, p. 1)

To put the thesis directly, I would argue that quasi-sacred forms of religiosity, from therapies, spiritual disciplines, and twelve-step programs to the most self-aggrandizing ways to acquire an identity based on gender, ethnicity, education, or money are fated to turn into enemies of the self under certain conditions. O'Keefe stresses this fatal dialectic when he argues, on the one hand, that magic has enabled individuals to "buy time" in their struggle with social systems, and, on the other, that modern social systems engender "voodoo death" or other forms of psychological self-destruction precisely because they make the self superfluous and vulnerable. Bureaucracies can run effectively without any particular individual, and yet when one is forced into social exile through premature retirement or other forms of dismissal, individuals in fact get sick and die (O'Keefe 1982, pp. 296-300).

Quasi-sacred forms of religiosity are therefore likely to be ways of making up for lost time, buying more time, or, for the desperate, a way of speeding up the social clock so that a day of reckoning can "put paid" to all unfinished business between the self and society. Individuals may "buy time" for themselves through magical processes that give the soul a chance to survive and to grow in the face of overwhelming social pressures, but time is already at a premium in modern societies. Individuals constantly feel as if they do not have enough time, that they are running out of time, and that they must have something to show for the time they have already spent. However, to adopt a strategy that requires one to pay in advance, as it were, for buying more time is to burden the soul with an unpayable debt.

Each such effort to manipulate time suggests the presence of trance-like states of consciousness. It is in trances that individuals visit the past and the future by suspending the flow of time in the present. In trances the individual is placed in touch with a world beyond the self—without interruption and discontinuity between the self and society, so to speak. New possibilities—and new dangers—open up, including the threat of the dissolution of the self. Indeed, trance-like states of mind are very common, and they may occur several, maybe dozens, of times a day to the average individual. Only when they are institutionalized in ritual or drama, in meditation, or through the use of hallucinogens, do such states become recognized for what they are. Self-consciousness ends in the trance; playacting ceases, and the individual is placed in touch with a transcendent order that supersedes all the small sources of opposition and contradiction in the soul and in everyday life.

I am arguing that the quasi-sacred occupies the conceptual space between two continua or spectra. One continuum extends horizontally from the proto-sacred to the anti-sacred; the other extends vertically from the proto-sacred to the sacred, as in Figure 1.

The sacred, as I will use the term here, refers to a condition in which attributions of sacredness by individuals to groups, communities, institutions, or societies are supported by a high level of consensus by members of the social unit in question. The anti-sacred refers to a condition in which the individual successfully resists or challenges such attribution of or claims to sacredness by members of the unit in question. At the meeting point of the two continua (or axes of the diagram) lies the proto-sacred, a fledgling form of the anti-sacred and of the sacred. In the conceptual space that opens up between the

FIGURE # 1

Conceptual Possibilities for
the Quasi-sacred

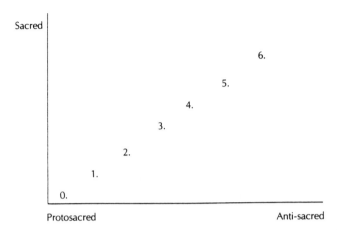

Figure 1.   Conceptual Possibilities for the Quasi-Sacred

two continua will develop a primitive form of the quasi-sacred (point 1). Its hallmark is the transparent nature of the machinery of producing the sacred. Further out in this conceptual space lies a form of the quasi-sacred that I have called counterfeit—slightly more convincing as a facsimile of the sacred but still vulnerable to charges of being contrived and artificial (point 2). Somewhat further along the same continuum lie forms of the quasi-sacred that are more effectively competitive with the sacred—magic that can give the sacred a good run, as it were, for its money (point 3). At this stage in the continuum one finds the clergy, for instance, actively engaged in efforts not merely to neutralize but to eradicate the competing expressions of the sacred, as in current attacks on "individualism." Further along the continuum lie forms of the quasi-sacred that are clearly mirror images of the sacred: beliefs and practices that are capable of effectively opposing institutionalized forms of the sacred. Here rhetorical attacks on individualism give way to more inquisitorial approaches to eliminate the "enemy" (point 4). Paralleling these aspects of the quasi-sacred, I have argued, are experiences of the self that are increasingly fortified by, and dependent on, magical thinking and practices for the defense of the self; by the same argument, the further one goes on this continuum of the quasi-sacred, the more the self is vulnerable to magic.

What lies at the zero-point where the two continua meet? Consider, for example, the individual who is completely enthralled by the larger society, its symbols, institutions, and ways of life. Purely hypothetical, of course, this zero-point can at least be conceptualized as an extreme and continuous form of trance-state, in which the individual is virtually mesmerized by the social order. The individual has not yet begun to withdraw emotional investment, energy, and loyalty from the larger society and its various personifications, not even to the point of acquiring a partial form of selfhood that is at least quasi-sacred. At the other end of the continuum (anti-sacred), of course, lies the individual for whom the larger society is virtually demonic; to stare into its face is an unbearable prospect, and the society must therefore be demonized in some form or another and consigned to an age that is passing away, considered subject to a conspiracy of aliens, or even identified with Satan.

As O'Keefe (1982) repeatedly argues, Western societies have succeeded in adapting magical techniques to capture the imagination of their publics through the use of transcendent symbols, powerful collective gestures, the mass media, advertising, and the proliferation of therapies—all of which serve, more or less successfully, the purpose of keeping the public entranced. Still, it is not known how successful these techniques may be, as opposed to how transparent they are to the individual as mere playacting. To what extent do modern societies, then, succeed in giving individuals the illusion that they are individually and collectively informed by a transcendent principle of order? Some will be merely satisfied rather than entranced, others merely pacified, while some may actually feel that their social order is sufficiently alien and powerful to seem demonic rather than benign.

In the middle of this conceptual space, somewhere along the horizontal axis between entrancement (society experienced as the proto-sacred) and the experience of the demonic (society experienced as the anti-sacred), and also somewhere along the vertical axis between the most public forms of the sacred and those I have designated as the "proto-sacred" (to indicate that they may be fantasy states), are states of mind in which the body politic is experienced alternately as the source of enchantment and of torment. Here the public is relatively difficult to distract from its everyday concerns and is unlikely to suspend its disbelief except on state occasions or in major crises. To the extent that individuals are monitoring their own performances even while they are engaging in them, their performances will be relatively self-conscious and will begin to approach "mere playacting."

The demand for magic, I would argue, increases to the extent that individuals—especially because they are engaged in magical defenses of the self—become increasingly aware of what they are doing, of how and why they are doing it, and of how it may come across to other. As O'Keefe puts it:

> Magic takes over these [religious] abstractions and applies them. But then it quickly develops self-conscious theories of what it is doing and these theories create new abstractions which make further magical applications possible (1982, p. 321).

The extreme cases of this, I have argued, occur at the end of the continuum where the individual seeks the protection of magic against a society perceived as demonic. The conditions under which this self-conscious application of magical technique is least likely to appear occurs at the other end of the continuum, where individuals are relatively entranced by the social order.

Now, we might assume that the incidence of self-conscious *ritual* performances would increase to the extent that individuals are relatively self-conscious performers in everyday life. For instance, the work of Goffman (1959) suggests that in complex societies, where performances are becoming increasingly subject to situational rather than institutional constraints, individuals will be more concerned with the effect they are having than with the performance itself. They are in fact becoming party to social contrivance. Goffman began his work by studying an island culture where the forms of social interaction were relatively constrained: the formal dinner was a serious performance designed to suspend disbelief and to disguise the true state of a family's condition, so that the guest would not know the extent of the family's poverty. Goffman's later work concerned more modernized contexts, that is, public places where more improvisation was in order. Public speeches that seemed to be given only to the immediate audience were in fact carefully calculated efforts to speak to a wider audience through the media. In these contexts, even apparent spontaneity and improvisation were mere playacting. The occasion, then, needs to be investigated in close detail to know how "quasi" is the "sacred."

The incidence of the quasi-sacred may therefore be highest when it is difficult to define the boundaries of the audience. That is the clear implication of Goffman's analysis of forms of talk, and it is the explicit argument in Lasch's (1978) work on narcissism. To the extent that one cannot draw a sharp line between the audience and the actors, he argued, the incidence of disbelief, of awareness of playacting, increases. The incidence would be the highest when individuals are aware that the President of the United States is issuing a "definitive" statement only for the moment; its truth is therefore measured only in terms of the shelf life of something called "credibility."

Others might seek to find the incidence of the quasi-sacred in the characteristics of the rite in question. For instance, in examining the change in liturgies in the Anglican church, I have had occasion to note a number of factors that make the participants more aware of what they are doing while they are doing it. The mere fact of any liturgical change is likely to increase such awareness, of course. In the case of the Anglican *Alternative Service Book,* however, I notice other factors that might heighten such awareness, especially the marked increase in the number of "options" built into the performance of various rites such as Baptism, so that any performance is conditional on a number of factors, such as who is present and for what reason. The rite becomes increasingly a matter of calculated choice and of personal preference in the doing of it—hardly a development likely to enable individuals to suspend their disbelief or to feel that they are caught up in an event that is superior and constraining to themselves (to use Durkheim's metaphors for the sacred).[1]

Whether influenced more by Durkheim or by Weber, sociologists have generally agreed that the sacred is a social force or social fact that confronts the individual as alien, prepossessing, and superior to the self. In the form of charisma, however, sacred authority is somewhat evanescent and contingent on actual performances from one day to the next. Charismatic leaders derive their authority from an agreement with their followers on the nature and truth of leaders' claims to supernatural power or divine mission. That is why I would call this extreme point on the continuum the "proto-sacred" and would reserve the term "sacred" for the public, authoritative, and consensual forms of devotion. I have placed these two positions along a continuum that leads from the unqualified attribution of sacredness by the individual to some "other" (the proto-sacred) to the legitimation of claims to the sacred by an entire public. The proto-sacred also lies at the opposite end of the spectrum from the conscious attack on the very existence of the sacred "other" as being demonic or consigned to the realm of the dead (the anti-sacred).

The extreme case of the quasi-sacred, I would argue, is a point between the two spectra where the individual simply denies the existence of the sacred "other" as there is nothing left to oppose. The sacred is no longer contested or demonic, simply because it has been assigned to a secular world, a world that is passing away. The secular will indeed not stand the test of time and is already marked in advance, as it were, by its temporality; it is destined to pass away. On this view, the emergence of the secular is due either to the individual's total withdrawal of energy, attention, interest, and loyalty from what was initially regarded as sacred, or it is the result of a massive reaction-formation against the existence of such a world.

THE QUASI-SACRED IN MODERNITY

Now, in "primitive" societies the person of the individual is far less institutionalized than in the "modern." Indeed, one of the axioms of sociological commentary on Western societies has been that in modern societies the individual is enshrined in a wide range of institutions that protect the person from invasions of privacy, from magical influences, and from intrusions by neighbors, by religious groups, and by the state itself. Charisma has been dispersed, as Shils once argued, to include the individual, who, as an institution, is at least partially sacralized. Certainly individuals are regarded as defaulting on their social obligations if they do not pursue their individuality and develop their own potential. As De Martino puts it,

[t]his whole complex historical world made up of experiences and moral judgements *presupposes* the singularization of the individual and expresses the establishment, within the conscience, of questions that ask the meaning and value of one's individual being (1988, p. 71, emphasis in original).

Even so, it would be premature to assume that the institutionalization of the individual in contemporary, complex societies renders individuals less likely than in primitive social systems to experience their natural and social environments as alien, superior, and prepossessing. To what extent, in other word, are individuals in modern societies still living in an enchanted universe, even in the relative absence of cultural or social support for attributions of sacredness on the part of the individual? The answer to that question, I will argue, depends on the extent to which the institutionalization of the individual has been accompanied by a corresponding development on the part of the self.

The quasi-sacred in modern societies reflects a lag between the success of modern societies in institutionalizing the individual and a corresponding increase in the individual's confidence in the reality and persistence of the self. If De Martino is correct, the notion that the self is real and persistent is a rather late cultural achievement. It would therefore not be surprising if a wide range of personality-types existed even in modern societies along the continuum from the proto-sacred to the anti-sacred. The further along the continuum one goes, the more likely one is to find the self well-protected from the demands and constraints of the sacred. Contrast those whose experience of themselves and of their societies is infused with magical thinking in the form of the proto-sacred.

In the magic world, the soul may be lost; its existence is not founded on the same principles— it is rather a fragile presence that the world may swallow up or make disappear. In the magic world, the identification of one's soul is not a fact, but a task to be carried out, and one's being within the world is a reality that must be established (De Martino 1988, p. 71).

The question is how widespread this primitive "magic world" may be in modern societies. While De Martino can find primitive tribes that believe that individuals can fuse themselves with others and so gain access to the knowledge or control of another's soul, we now understand that the unconscious is filled with similar identifications and projections that deprive the individual of a sense of his or her own presence and control, as if others could gain access to and control over the person's innermost self. Indeed, the unconscious processes by which such access to another's soul is gained in primitive societies may be very close to those by which individuals fall under one another's influence in a complex society. There is in both cases not only a desire for fusion but a process of mirroring, by which individuals act out what they imagine to be another's wishes. For some primitives this leads to a form of play, but it can also have deadly consequences as individuals punish themselves for violating a taboo or for not preventing a disaster as they internalize what they believe to be the punitive judgments of their comrades.

In modern societies as well, it is no secret that individuals have taken to heart the rejection or indifference of their employers or neighbors or of influential leaders or dominant groups. O'Keefe has made it clear that the sickness and premature death that accompany rejection, retirement, confinement, or other forms of social isolation are due to the same process of mirroring and identification by which individuals internalize and act out the implied judgments of their communities. In both cases, the soul or essential self is placed in jeopardy by what De Martino has found to be a belief in a "controlling presence" (1988, p. 70). That experience lies at the beginning of the continuum along which the quasi-sacred develops.

Such individual and collective phenomena may be far from absent in modernity; on the contrary, they are prevalent not only in crowds, congregations, and audiences but also in smaller groups devoted to problem solving, therapy, policy formation, or other forms of symbolic production (cf. Deikman 1990). The question is: to what extent has the modern world substituted a rational rhetoric based on the individual and his or her assumed rights and capacities, responsibilities and potentials, while individuals still experience, consciously or otherwise, the danger of losing not only their social character and identity but their innermost selves? To what extent does *the danger of losing one's soul and the overcoming of this danger,* so typical of the world of primitive magic, persist, more or less unrecognized as such, in the modern world?

It is entirely possible for individuals to feel as if their innermost selves are in the control of powerful figures, whether these are shamans or the modern corporation, sorcerers or professional rivals, all of whom are assumed to have the power of sealing the individual's fate, of taking away his or her place in the community, and of sapping the powers and energies of the soul. Individuals can—and often do—feel lost or depressed, drained or empty, shamed or stung, simply by investing their colleagues and employers, politicians and governments, friends and neighbors, with (unexamined and putative) magical powers.

ORGANIZATIONS AND THE SURPLUS OF TIME: LOOKING FOR SOUL-LOSS

Whereas in a "primitive" society it was the shaman who announced the appropriate time for various courses of action (and in so doing provided a magical cure for the sense that time was running out on the soul), in modern societies it is the corporation that announces and controls the times of the individual's life. For instance, organizations have intensified their control over time, its allocation for various goals, and the criteria by which the organization's productivity will be assessed. "Just in time" forms of resource management—the setting of quarterly objectives, piece-rate measures of productivity, round-the-clock forms of production, and the shelf life of products and technological innovations—have all intensified the organization's control over time. Indeed, time is both one of the last remaining commodities and one of the scarcest resources in the capitalist system.

Under these conditions, I am arguing, the modern corporation is not only a threat to the individual's sense of being but also provides the magical cure for the threat of soul-loss by adopting an increasingly complex and demanding set of rules for the allocation and disposal of time. The organization represents both the form of the disease and its cure; a vicious circle has been created.

If one is to look for the quasi-sacred in a complex society, then, one would therefore first have to investigate the personal dimensions of organizational life. Just such a tactic has been adopted by Deikman (1990) in his recent survey of cult-like behavior. There he makes it clear that what Freud called the "primal horde" is alive and well; it exists as a potential for submission to authoritarian figures and for abject conformity to exclusive and demanding groups or organizations. Whether surveying major corporations that develop a strong "corporate culture" or examining "group-think" in government, Deikman finds a strongly primitive and child-like dependency at work under the cover of modern and rational forms of organization and self-government.

None of Deikman's ideas will come as a surprise to those who have long since absorbed the findings of social psychologists on obedience and conformity or who have felt that George Orwell got it right a long time ago. What is striking about his analysis is his insistence that childhood dreams and fantasies of being secure, loved, protected, and guided can—and frequently do—undermine even more rational and autonomous individuals, even in organizations or communities that are ostensibly self-determining, democratic, and authentic in their pursuit of clearly stated goals, objectives, and principles. Deikman finds that individuals have great difficulty in disagreeing with one another, in making up their own minds, and in deviating or departing from the organization or community. Saying "no" and "goodbye" seem to pose a mortal threat to individuals who, realistically speaking, have every reason to feel that they have alternatives and can survive such conflict or even a permanent parting of the ways. That is because these organizations and institutions, communities and groups have taken on the aura of the sacred. For Deikman, General Motors and the various professions, like evangelists and the papacy, are able to survive and prosper only by fostering child-like faith and dependency on others in whose presence and good opinion the devotee, the citizen, the employee or client finds a secure foundation for both heart and soul.

By adopting the metaphor and illustration of cult behavior, Deikman makes it clear that he is speaking of the quasi-sacred aspects even of organizations, communities, or nations that have avowedly secular identities and purposes. It would therefore be a mistake to underestimate the depths to which even modern social systems provide foundations for the self. The process of secularization does not go very deep into the psyche, he warns; the self, or in extreme cases even the soul, is therefore continuously in danger of being lost or surrendered to those who promise the individual the security and recognition longed for in childhood. It matters far less whether individuals ever enjoyed these delights of infancy than that everyone was once a child. Every generation therefore brings with it a fresh inheritance of longing for a sacred universe. The quasi-sacred is therefore the rule rather than the exception in modern societies, and—if Deikman is right—the potential for authoritarian social systems, and for personal acquiescence, submission, surrender, or even sacrifice to social systems remains very high. The modern is not very modern, after all.

On this view, the sacred thrives with each new generation because each generation grows into adulthood with undischarged burdens and debts to childhood. No matter how rational the adult, even the most autonomous individual will be susceptible to authoritarian promises and guarantees simply because she or he still harbors, if only in the unconscious, a desire for the omniscient and omnipotent parent that one imagined one had—or longed for—in one's infancy and childhood. The more things change, the more they stay the same.

Indeed, Deikman (1990) has identified a number of social processes that preserve the illusion that one is in the presence of salvation and greatness: strong pressures for conformity, suspicion of outsiders, and a profound willingness on the part of each individual to suspend disbelief and to comply with the group even when one's own conscience or close friends and relatives must suffer the consequences. Deikman suggests that the more insidious forms of the quasi-sacred in fact appear to be therapeutic or bureaucratic; legitimation is based on what is good for the individual or consistent with professional ethics and corporate responsibilities rather than on more abstract beliefs and justifications. The latter would include, if used, such notions as "national security." On closer examination, both sorts of appeals invoke the oppositions familiar to structuralist analyses of the sacred and the profane: an outside world that is in danger, sick, needy, or deserving of correction, and an inner, social world that is full of resources, answers, therapies, solutions, or products for a hungry and endangered world.

BEYOND THE QUASI-SACRED: REASON AND THE SOUL

Freud, like Descartes, argued that the essential self emerges from the analytic process of distinguishing reality from the projections and displacements of the individual's unconscious fantasies and nocturnal dream life. The question now is whether the process of secularization can go still further, far enough to enable individuals to disentangle themselves from the quasi-sacred. That is, will the prevalence of the quasi-sacred intensify and popularize a self-critical awareness that the world itself is partially constituted by often unconscious fantasies and fears? As this form of awareness increases, there is an opportunity for reason (and the reality principle) to intervene. Deikman's analysis of cult-like behavior may therefore be typical of modernity's potential for Cartesian self-consciousness, its awareness that social life is constituted by a reflexive relation of the innermost self to the self's projections and identifications in the world.

I am suggesting that modernity not only blurs the boundaries between the sacred and the non-sacred, but that modernity therefore also fosters the critical sort of self-awareness that in the end allows the individual to separate out his or her innermost self, or soul, from the projections and identifications that it has enjoyed and from which it has suffered in one way or another. That awareness (I would call it reason) is essential if one is to overcome the lag between the institutionalization of the individual and the development of the self.

Indeed, I am arguing that the role of reason is to foster the development of the self, whatever reason's capacities or incapacities may be for ordering social life or for understanding nature. Even if reason in the modern world cannot help us choose among ends or give content to its own will (cf. Cascardi 1992), reason can still monitor the way in which those ends and the human will are shaped by and embody not only "animal spirits" but the dreams and fantasies, the hopes and fears, of the pre-rational self. If reason is still a stranger to unconscious desires and interests, because of repression, reason can nonetheless recognize these aspects of the self when they return in the form of gods and demons which struggle with the autonomous will—or with the state and its institutions—for control. As Deikman pointed out, even those individuals who are encapsulated in cults do break out and come to their senses. That is, they make the distinction between their soul—their essential self—and the spirit that comes into play in social interaction.

It is all the more crucial to maintain this distinction, however, because it has been elided or lost in much contemporary discussion of the psychoanalytic literature. As Bettelheim (1984) has pointed out, Freud had the innermost self, indeed the soul, in mind in his use of the term "psyche," a term that has been unfortunately reduced to quasi-technical or mechanical meanings in the translation of Freud for American popular and professional audiences. It was to reason that Freud looked for the ability of the individual to separate the essential self, the soul, from the aspects of the self that were caught up in people and things, relationships and groups, aspects of the self or spirit that could masquerade for the real self when reason was not along to make the essential distinction between the two.

In the very discontinuities between oneself and the world, in the frustration and the uncertainty of the desires which find their objects in people and things in the world, people come to their own senses. That is to say that alienation breeds self-consciousness. There is a similar Hegelian apologetic for our fate in the modern world in Giddens' (1990) account. Not only does an impersonal world call out efforts to create intimacy even in the abstract and impersonal spaces of bureaucracies and cities; it takes "self-disclosure" in modern societies to create trust and intimacy. Giddens goes on to conclude that:

> Personal trust, therefore, has to be established through the process of self-enquiry: the discovery of oneself becomes a project directly involved with the reflexivity of modernity (1990, p. 122).[2]

What is required is fresh insight into the difference between the true self, which is also mortal, and one's imaginary self, which lays claim through the various forms of religious culture to immortality. The true self, shorn of its cultural protection, faces death squarely, although, as Hobbes pointed out, for many the fear of death may still be assuaged by assurances from priests or witches.[3]

With each added degree of difference between the true self and its personifications in the world, however, there is an added degree of uncertainty about what is truly sacred beyond the self. That is why, for instance, Hobbes is thoroughly skeptical not only of witches and goblins but of the established churches that have exploited such uncertainty and the individual's increased fear of death by offering ecclesiastical guarantees of magical control over fate and death (Cascardi 1992, pp. 446, 220). The most suspect of these forms of the quasi-sacred is found in those churches that, to paraphrase Hobbes, offer a purchase on the future and claim that the Kingdom of God is already realized, if only in part, in the church itself. This advance purchase of the Kingdom was picked up not only by the established churches, however, but in the new United States of America by an evangelical culture that made the advent of the Kingdom contingent on the moment of faith. Secular time was the vestibule, as it were, into sacred time, and the meaning of time was intensified.

For the Enlightenment, time is time—the past over and done with and the future not yet arrived—whereas the suspension of the reality-principle in the churches makes them capable of offering assurances of having transcended time, history, and death itself. It is this same suspension that makes them dangerous to a state that relies only on reason for its policies and justifications. No wonder, then, that Hobbes sought in the State the apotheosis of the sacred, if only to keep its subjects in awe and to monopolize the cultural antidotes to the fear of the loss of one's essential self (cf. Cascardi 1992, p. 227). The state itself became a way of bracketing time and space, of becoming the microcosm and the crucible of the world, and hence a place where one's soul could truly be found. In that microcosm and that crucible, however, the institution of the individual developed. Now that the political bracketing of time and space has broken apart, however, the individual is left with the responsibility for the development of the inner self. It is a responsibility from which, as we have seen, many flee.

In redefining the boundary between the true self and its extensions, the Enlightenment focused particularly on the awareness of dreams. For Hobbes, it was in dreams that individuals imagined a future far more terrifying than any individual could control; thus the imagination, informed by the unconscious, was the source of the need for external guarantees and sanctions for those who could not bear to face their mortality. The sacred had its origins in the unconscious, in the apparitions of the night, and in the daydreams of a soul hungry for recognition and security. The notion that among primitives the sacred originates in a mind incapable of distinguishing dream from reality corresponded to the unenlightened imagination of the average Western soul.[4] These residues of the unconscious would continue to disturb Western polities if they were not safely contained in institutions that, given the scope of reason, could henceforth be understood as at best quasi-sacred. When the church's monopoly on the sacred is broken, however, all other claimants, including the church as well as the state, are understood to be mere pretenders to the throne of God.

For Descartes, dreams were the reminder of an inner essence that was not to be confused with its manifestations, apparitions, projections, and identifications. Hegel, too, understood that behind the desire for the external objects with which the soul identifies is a desire for oneself, for one's "interior essence" (Cascardi 1992, p. 235). Without the self-knowledge of one's dreams and of their difference from reality, the world claims an illicit devotion. Clearly the world can embody only a secondary, provisional, or ersatz form of the sacred in the eyes of the enlightened soul who can distinguish its innermost essence from the expression of that essence in the world.[5]

The more one is aware of the sanctity of one's soul, so to speak, the more questionable is the sanctity offered by the world. No object of individual devotion can sustain the claim to be truly sacred; each is subject to being demythologized by the self and by others, and each is in competition with previous and subsequent objects of devotion. Granted that Hobbes was right about the ideological struggle of professions, institutions, and the state to lay claim to the sacred at the expense of others' claims: still, it is individuals themselves who are continually involved in a process of demystification and re-sacralization. The objects of their temporary devotion may be lovers or spouses, therapies or gurus, disciplines or esoteric knowledge, the church or the state. No claim to the sacred can be unqualified, long lasting, or incontrovertible. As institutions and the state claim increasing control over the private sphere, the demand for sanctuary—for the protection offered to the soul by the sacred—grows in proportion.

What offers hope that modernity will not relapse once more into a fascist revery is the extent to which individuals can separate their innermost selves from the other aspects of the self as well as from a wide range of other persons and objects in the world that may represent or recognize the self. As with Hobbes and Descartes, the turning point is reached in the willingness to examine the extent to which one's experience of the world is informed or even determined by other states of mind like dreams and fantasies, and *vice versa*. The gap between imagination and reality provides the space for the soul. That soul, in modernity, will also have to be understood as emergent and mortal as well as real, giving rise to a secular mysticism.

NOTES

1. I have discussed these issues in Fenn (1987).

2. It is difficult for sociologists to comprehend the absolute or irreducible or essential self, let alone to image a self that is not wholly constituted by social interaction. Trilling (1972) made just such a comment, however, on Rousseau; the problem therefore lies with aspects of the tradition of social theory. Giddens (cf. 1990, pp. 13-124), nonetheless, cannot imagine a self-trust or self-awareness that is not part of a process of mutual self-disclosure in a reflexive world of relationships that are based on abstract social institutions and networks rather than local or kinship relations. The self is a continuous social process.

3. In this passage, as elsewhere in the discussion of modenrity and the Enlightenment, I am heavily indebted to Cascardi. On this aspect of Hobbes, for example, see Cascardi (1992, pp. 45ff.).

4. To speak of modernity in these terms could be deceiving if it meant that the so-called "primitive" world is not familiar with the distinction between the soul and its various appearances or projections. On the contrary, as Levy-Bruhl (1966) has argued, there is ample evidence even among primitives that the soul is distinguished from its "appurtenances" and from its various defenses. Primitives know of a "protective genius" that can help to preserve the individual against bad fortune and enemies, but this is not the same as the soul, and indeed owes its vitality to the soul, rather than vice versa (cf. Levy-Bruhl 1966, p. 234). Indeed, we might say that for the "primitive" it is the soul that is truly sacred, and that the quasi-sacred embodies that extension of the self ad the spirit: the "appurtenances" and expressions of the spirit but not the soul itself.

5. Even for Descartes, however, the soul faces the loss of itself when there is no absolutely perfect and trustworthy other who can give it the recognition for which the soul, incomplete and unsure of itself, continues to long (Cascardi 1992, pp. 235-236).

REFERENCES

Bettelheim, B. 1984. *Freud and Man's Soul.* New York: Knopf.

Cascardi, A.J. 1992. *The Subject of Modernity.* Cambridge: Cambridge University Press.

Deikman, A.J. 1990. *The Wrong Way Home: Uncovering the Patterns of Cult Behavior in American Society.* Boston: Beacon.

De Martino, E. 1988. *Primitive Magic: The Psychic Powers of Shamans and Sorcerers.* Dorset, UK: Prism Press.

Fenn, R.K. 1987. *The Dream of the Perfect Act: An Inquiry into the Fate of Religion in the Secular World.* New York: Tavistock.

Giddens, A. 1990. *The Consequences of Modernity.* Stanford, CA: Stanford University Press.

Goffman, E. 1959. *The Presentation of Self in Everyday Life.* Garden City, NY: Doubleday.

Lasch, C. 1978. *The Culture of Narcissism: American Life in an Age of Diminishing Expectations.* New York: Norton.

Levy-Bruhl, L. 1966. *The Soul of the Primitive,* translated by A. Clare. London: Allen and Unwin.

New York Times. 1992. April 13, p. 1.

O'Keefe, D.L. 1982. *Stolen Lightening: The Social Theory of Magic.* New York: Continuum.

Runciman, W.G. 1983. *A Treatise on Social Theory,* Volume 1: *The Methodology of Social Theory.* Cambridge: Cambridge University Press.

Trilling, L. 1972. *Sincerity and Authenticity.* Cambridge: Harvard University Press.

Turner, V. 1966. *The Ritual Process: Structure and Anti-Structure.* Ithaca: Cornell University Press.

GENDERED SPIRITUALITY AND QUASI-RELIGIOUS RITUAL

Meredith B. McGuire

ABSTRACT

Several recent quasi-religious movements give particular emphasis, in their beliefs and practices, to members' experiences and identities as women or as men. A number of nonmedical healing movements address their healing rituals specifically to gender-specific physical-emotional-spiritual needs of adherents. Some religious or quasi-religious movements have focused exclusively on females' physical-emotional-spiritual experiences and development; others have, more recently, separated to attend to males' experiences and development. This paper examines how religion and religion-like beliefs and practices are used in these movements; historical and cross-cultural parallels are also relevant. These movements raise some interesting interpretive questions about the linkage between religion and gender roles, between religious practice and the socializing of emotions and bodies, and about diverse religious responses to fluid or uncertain societal and cultural definitions of maleness and femaleness.

Religion and the Social Order, Volume 4, pages 273-287.
Copyright © 1994 by JAI Press Inc.
All rights of reproduction in any form reserved.
ISBN: 1-55938-763-7

Gender issues have become a prominent and salient theme for quasi-religious ritual expression. Many religious and quasi-religious groups are addressing adherents' gender concerns by offering new images of what it means to be a man or a woman and by creating rituals and other opportunities for gender identity transformations. At the same time, other religious and quasi-religious groups are adamantly reasserting "traditional" gender role expectations and many of their rituals celebrate and socialize members into thus-defined gender identities. While religion has always indirectly addressed gender issues (e.g., by legitimating gender roles), this paper focuses on those religious and quasi-religious movements which devote specific attention to beliefs and practices that link the gendered self with the spiritual self. *Gendered spirituality* serves to express, produce, or transform the individual's gender identity itself. By means of a gendered spirituality, the individual can interpret and revise his or her biography: "This is who I am (and how I came to be) as a man" (or woman).

These religious and quasi-religious expressions of a "gendered spirituality" are not mere accidental products in contemporary societies' spiritual supermarket; rather, they are closely linked with the changing locations and functions of religion, as a social institution, in modern society. Specifically, I would argue that emerging gender issues are the epitome of contemporary identity concerns. Sociological analysis of gendered spirituality may shed light on new patterns of individual-to-society relationships, the changing nature of identity and autonomy in modern contexts, and how religion (in both traditional and new forms) shapes and reflects these changes. Gendered spirituality may be a prime example of what Hervieu-Léger (1990) has identified as a "new work" for religion to accomplish.

I first began to notice the themes of gender and sexuality in my study of ritual, nonmedical healing among suburban middle-class adults in New Jersey (McGuire 1988). In several of the groups and movements studied, there were rituals addressed to gender-specific physical-emotional-spiritual needs of members. For example, respondents spoke of seeking healing in response to problematic reproductive events (such as miscarriages, stillbirths, hysterectomies, and Caesarian sections). Some respondents made causal connections between their unsatisfactory social roles (as women, daughters, workers, etc.) and specific ills for which they needed healing (e.g., eating disorders, arthritis, anxieties, and stress-related illnesses). Others described rituals and meditations for healing scars of sexual abuse, spousal abuse, or a troubled relationship with a parent.

All of the groups studied were adamant that the emotional, physical, social, and spiritual well-being of the individual could not be separated; the healing process must address all aspects of the person. Women were far more likely to link their healing needs with their relationships and their social roles *as women*; men, by contrast, were more likely to name stressful work situations and rarely identified their troubles with their roles *as men.* Only occasionally did male respondents cite a need for healing relationships; their problematic relationships were usually with their fathers (indeed, typically, deceased fathers). This focus was markedly different from that of women respondents, who emphasized healing relationships and mentioned, as the object of healing, all kinds of relationships: instrumental and affective, present and past, with men and women, children and parents, relatives and nonrelatives, intimates and nonintimates.

Many recent women's and men's spirituality movements appear to be closely related to these healing movements, partly because they, too, use the metaphor of healing. In contrast with healing movements, however, these groups focus directly on the gender identities of participants. They emphasize religious or quasi-religious beliefs, rituals, and symbols to address members' gender identities, either to confirm a traditional image or to transform the self toward some alternative ideal. Thus, like the healing movements, the gendered spirituality movements are connected with larger changes in the self-to-society linkage, whereby individuals have been relatively freed of many external constraints on the self (see McGuire 1988, pp. 252-256). In response to this freedom, some groups proffer a multitude of pathways of self-transformation and new images of roles and opportunities; at the same time, other groups— also using the idiom of well-being and healing—adamantly reaffirm traditional roles and moral constraints.

Both responses are necessarily active, because traditional gender roles and moral constraints can no longer be taken for granted. The core nature of gender identity and its expression has become open, fluid, even voluntary. Individuals have multiple options of what it means to be a man or a woman. This fluidity is part of the larger development of an idea of the emotions and the body, not as givens, but as reflexively malleable parts of one's identity (see Dreitzel 1981; Giddens 1991, p. 217). Gender can, thus, be chosen, shaped, and transformed. Modern individuals are encouraged to consider, choose, and control all the components of gender roles: their emotional expression, patterns of relating to coworkers and friends, postures and gestures, clothing and personal props, fitness, manner of speaking, and so on. There is even the option of whether to physically "change sex." One's identity—including one's gender identity—thus becomes a continuing project to be accomplished. Rather than fading away in a sunset of secularization, religious and quasi-religious groups may become more important, in this situation, as the source of images of ideals and alternatives, as the social setting for self-transformation, and as the mutual support for those identities. In the face of a relatively pluralistic and open set of possibilities, gender identities must be *accomplished,* rather than given. Religious and quasi-religious beliefs and practices appear to be important paths (among others) for doing identity work in modern societies.

SOCIAL CONTEXTS FOR SOCIALIZING GENDER IDENTITIES

Such religious and quasi-religious movements are not the only sources of gender identity. "Therapy"—in its many guises—is probably the foremost "expert" system for addressing gender concerns, so there is often conflict between the interests of those marketing professional therapy and those promoting religious "help" alternatives. In contemporary societies, many nonreligious groups are involved in socializing or resocializing male or female identities. Comparisons and contrasts between the spiritual and non-spiritual movements would be fruitful. How do the "Wildmen" weekend experiences promoted by some men's spirituality leaders compare, for example, with other group experiences of male socialization, such as the Boy Scouts, the military, college fraternities, sports gyms, hunting trips, and high school football?[1] Might other contemporary groups—as diverse as Mary Kay Cosmetics, Society for Creative Anachronism, Christian Patriotism, and Satanism—also be understood as socializing members into gender identities, although defined very differently within each movement?

Religiosity and religious roles are deeply gender-linked. Religion provided a firm legitimation for traditional gender prescriptions, and religious rituals and gatherings served to socialize males and females into gender-appropriate feelings and behaviors. At the same time, however, there have been numerous historical examples of gendered spirituality as a counter-assertion against the mainstream norms. It should be no surprise that these alternatives appear most frequently as nonofficial religious expressions or quasi-religions.

Identifiable historical processes have led to the development of official religion(s), distinguishable from popular religions and other nonofficial religious expressions. The consolidation of official religion(s) was the result of the assertion of social and economic power, whereby official religion came to be connected to the viewpoints and interests of privileged, franchised, and educated social classes, males, colonial powers, and dominant ethnic/racial groups. Those religious expressions representative of the experiences and interests of subordinate groups were relegated to nonofficial religion (e.g., folk healing cults, witchcraft, and spirit possession cults), which was typically marginalized or actively suppressed.

What appears to be different about contemporary religious expressions of alternative gender roles and images is that, not only are definitions of gender roles themselves more fluid and less socially given than ever before, but also the cultural hegemony of both official religion and orthodox gender prescriptions appears to be severely weakened. Individuals in contemporary societies are faced with multiple options—a plurality of both possible religious identities and gender identities. Just as some religious identities are more widely accepted and prestigious than others, so too are some gender identities more approved and successful than their alternatives. Nevertheless, there does not appear to be a firm, single, society-wide definition of masculinity and femininity; nor is there a clear-cut successful pattern for socializing men and women into "appropriate" gender roles.

The particular forms that gendered spirituality takes are linked with the socioeconomic conditions, prevalent modes of individual-to-society relationship, and patterns of socialization in a given period. Comparison and contrast with the gendered spiritualities that emerged in Victorian America suggest how some of these factors are connected.

GENDERED SPIRITUALITIES IN AN EARLIER ERA

The Victorian period in America was a period of dramatic socioeconomic change. The industrial revolution, entrepreneurial expansion of scale and scope of economic control, rapid urbanization, and the proletarianization of large segments of the work force produced profound changes in the nature of work and the role of the family. It was the period in which the sequestered, nuclear family became the dominant middle-class mode, and the work-world became increasingly physically and socially separate from private life, while many middle-class workers experienced considerable bureaucratic constraint and lack of autonomy at work. Some interpreters note that Victorian gender roles became far more monolithic and rigid than had been the case in the early part of the nineteenth century (Griffin 1990), so rigidly separate that even the illnesses by which gender role stresses were expressed were gender-appropriate—hysteria for the women and neurasthenia for the men (Drinka 1984). Interestingly, it was also an era of proliferation of religious and quasi-religious alternatives for men's and women's roles.

Several of the "new" religions emerging in the latter part of the nineteenth century reinterpreted women's roles, often giving women significant leadership positions and ritually expressing women's needs and experiences. For example, in Spiritualism and the various Metaphysical Movements (such as Christian Science, Unity, and Religious Science), women were disproportionately represented among the ranks of authoritative leaders, as well as members (Bednarowski 1983; Braude 1985). These movements' special attention to healing, emotional concerns, relationships with the living and dead, and nonaggressive assertion of power (e.g., using mental powers) made them particularly appealing to women seeking alternative gender identities in a changing society.

Official Christian groups, likewise, responded to these socioeconomic developments with religion-linked gender prescriptions. Many middle-class churches embraced the separation of public and private, and they actively promoted an ideal of evangelical domesticity which portrayed homes and women as the primary vehicles of redemption. The rhetoric of preaching and themes of gospel hymns of this period presented the home as the bastion of tranquility in a turbulent world. Women were to be keepers of these refuges who, though their piety and purity—in opposition to the aggressiveness and competition of the public sphere—would protect and uplift their children and husbands (McDonnell 1986; Ryan 1983; Sizer 1979; Taves 1986; Welter 1976). Women actively embraced and promoted this ideology of domesticity, because it elevated their status in the home, even though it circumscribed their range of influence. One result of this institutional differentiation into public (male) and private (female) spheres was the feminization of the churches and nonelite schools (Carnes 1989). While religion continued to legitimate men's power and status in the public sphere, church-oriented religious practice and experience came to be identified as emotional, nurturing, gentle, and unmanly.

This privatization of religion (and, consequently, its place in gender role socialization) is related to the gradual development of the voluntariness of both religion and gender as sources of identity in contemporary society. All elements of the private sphere—family lifestyle, interpersonal roles (including gender), religious belief and practice, social circle, consumption of arts, sports and other "leisure" activities—became less serious and compelling than the "real" world of work and production; they became matters of individual choice, "opinion," and taste.

Another feature of privatized (and, thereby, feminized) Victorian religion was that it could not adequately socialize men into what the culture defined as "manly." Several religious and quasi-religious movements developed alternative gendered spiritualities to meet this perceived need. Contemporary outgrowths of these movements include the various fraternal orders (e.g., Elks, Odd Fellows, and Masons), Mormonism, and the Ku Klux Klan. Although the eventual ideologies of these men's movements differed dramatically, they shared an emphasis on secret fraternal initiation, which was intended to produce a sense of transcendence and personal transformation—a conversion experience for a new identity which was simultaneously manly, righteous, and upright in the face of a frightening and awesome God, and bonded in fraternal solidarity (Carnes 1989, pp. 69-90).

Membership figures for the churches and fraternal organizations in the second half of the nineteenth century strongly suggest that middle-class "women were in the churches and the men were in the lodges" (Hackett 1991b). By 1897, more than one in four U.S. adult males belonged to such organizations as Odd Fellows, Freemasons, Knights of Pythias, and Red Men: the proportion among urban males was far greater, probably more than one in two. Lodges outnumbered churches in most cities.

Some observers link this widespread attraction to problematic changes in the American family, in which fathers had become increasingly dominant, but emotionally distant and physically absent, while mothers had become increasingly devoted to child-rearing and omnipresent in the home (Carnes

1989).[2] While changes in marriage and family relations, especially patterns of socialization of the young, are undoubtedly related to shifts in gender roles and identities, they are only one factor in a much larger set of changes.

The fact that both the Victorian gendered spiritualities and today's men's and women's spirituality movements arose predominantly among *middle-class* persons suggests that we need also to examine class-linked features of contemporary production and consumption. These movements may be responses to (a) changing patterns of economic production and the place of middle-class workers in the sphere of production, (b) changes in the nature of work itself and changes in the workplace setting, and (c) changes in the modal "self" that is expected or effectively productive in the contemporary work-world. That both the Victorian brotherhoods and many contemporary men's quasi-religious movements emphasized rituals of initiation[3] suggests that we should consider issues of dominance, control, and dependency. As Simmel (1906) noted, secret (or exclusionary) rituals are linked to assertions of status, dominance, autonomy, and boundaries. We might expect organizations engaging in such ritual initiations to be particularly important in periods when those very features are threatened. A special ritual to separate the in-group (i.e., men) from the out-group (i.e., women) may be more salient when men are experiencing less autonomy or control, for example, in the workplace.

Clawson (1989) interprets Victorian fraternalism as part of an ongoing process of class formation in an emerging capitalist social order. By proffering bonds of loyalty ostensibly across class lines—working class, middle class, and some entrepreneurs—fraternalism held out an ideal of solidarity among white men. Accordingly, boundaries of inclusion and exclusion were redrawn or changed emphasis: The "important" distinctions became those of gender and race. Their ideology held that these latter differences were inherent—a matter of essence; whereas, white men of all classes were basically kin—brothers or fathers and sons. Clawson's analysis of fraternal ritual also suggests why contemporary gender-focused rituals point to socioeconomic problems. She observed that these Victorian rituals were effective because they both represented and metaphorically resolved contradictions in social life— particularly those brought on by increasing rationalization of the workplace and its rewards structure. Through these rituals, fraternalism also effectively diminished women's claims to a share of authority, power, and influence.

CONTEMPORARY GENDERED SPIRITUALITIES

The second half of the twentieth century is, likewise, characterized by dramatic socioeconomic changes which have reshaped the nature of work and economic opportunity, patterns of family and childhood socialization, definitions of and pathways to success, and lifestyle options. Throughout the century, but especially since the 1960s, U.S. society has experienced a number of "liberation" movements (notably those of women, ethnic and racial minorities, homosexuals, and persons with handicaps). Although far from fully effective in structurally changing the opportunity structure, these movements do appear to have created greater pluralism of lifestyles and opened a range of new options to many people.

The mass media have, at the same time, made Americans aware of the existence of lifestyle options—religions, occupations, family patterns, recreation, and so on—other than those of their immediate families and communities. U.S. society may have never been as narrowly defined by a single tradition as many other modern societies, but the last three decades saw an unprecedented increase in plausible alternatives to traditional patterns of social life and personal identity. The emergence of many and diverse movements proffering alternative images of gender roles and identities, cast in the framework of spirituality and of healing, is one type of response to this new relative freedom.

Most women's spirituality groups are consciously connected to a broader movement for women's liberation, because the impetus to reshape women's religion derived from evaluation that traditional religions had strong biases against women embedded in their core beliefs and practices. The sheer diversity and aversion to "orthodoxy" within these religious and quasi-religious movements make it very difficult to generalize about them. We may roughly characterize them as consciously articulating alternative spiritual beliefs and practices which envision and celebrate positive images of females, such as female images of a deity, rituals of female empowerment, and moral norms which do not promote female submissiveness. Most appear to promote positive images for women by focusing on nonhierarchical relationships; a few, however, envision inverting male-female power and status relationships.

Power appears to be the foremost common theme among women's spirituality groups, although it is conceptualized and accomplished very differently in each. In many groups, ritual action is focused on symbolizing and using women's power and agency. For women who have been the victims of men's power (e.g., spousal abuse, rape, incest, and emotional abuse), gendered spirituality that accomplishes a sense of empowerment and agency is often effectively therapeutic. For all members, however, these groups pose options—and the means—for transforming their gender identities.

Far more so than in men's groups, women's gendered spirituality movements appear to be challenging the *core* content and underlying assumptions of gender role expectations in this society and its religious traditions. Some of these movements are within existing religious groups in the Christian and Jewish traditions, where they are trying to give practical form to feminist theologies which are increasingly respected in many mainstream religions. Other women's spirituality movements are separate, alternative religions. For example, several variants of witchcraft, neo-paganism, neo-nativism, and spiritual eco-feminism are not contained within any other religious tradition, nor do contemporary members appear to be seriously constrained to adhere strictly to traditional beliefs and practices of any nonofficial religions, but often liberally adapt and combine beliefs and practices (see Albanese 1991; Jacobs 1989, 1990; Melton, Clark, and Kelly 1990; Neitz 1990). This aversion to imposing an orthodoxy is not an incidental feature of many women's spirituality groups. Rather, it is linked with an ideal of nonhierarchical group organization, together with the sense that patterns of decision making and control in those religions with a clear orthodoxy represent male means of dominance for which women's groups should find a better alternative.

The more recent men's spirituality movement does not yet have any clear grass-roots basis. There does appear to be a relatively enthusiastic response to a handful of spokespersons who have received considerable media attention. In practice, so far, the movement has spawned few ongoing men's groups— indeed, many of the enduring men's groups are more like the 1970s support groups and do not accept the approach of the newer movement toward articulating a spiritual/ritual expression of a new masculinity. Thus far, the men's spirituality movement appears to be largely an entrepreneurial effort, in which (for a fee) men are brought together in temporary group settings for an orchestrated spiritual experience. The considerable success of such programs suggests that there exists a sizeable pool of potential recruits, but it remains to be seen whether the one-time weekend or workshop experiences led by movement promoters will develop into any form of commitment, such as to an ongoing, stable group of fellow adherents or to a quasi-religious movement.

The men's spirituality movement appears to be premised on the sense that, although men's statuses and roles may be acceptable, individual men are not functioning well—indeed, may be emotionally and socially crippled—because they have been inadequately socialized into masculinity. According to the leaders/spokespersons, these problems are caused by unsatisfactory role models (especially fathers) and lack of culturally effective initiation into the male role in modern societies.[4] Thus, the movement offers rituals emphasizing catharsis (especially grieving) over painful products of this earlier socialization process, particularly men's problematic experiences with their fathers. The movement also uses extensive initiation rituals, eclectically borrowed from indigenous peoples, New Age, and personal growth movements. Rituals variously emphasize expressing aggression and strength, honoring age and other men's statuses which may be de-emphasized in the larger culture, temporarily relaxing some bodily and emotional constraints, and enhancing the sense that initiation is a step to "something more" in men's realization of their gender role, their masculinity.

Interestingly, several variants of healing groups and some of both the men's and women's spirituality movements emphasize pseudo-anthropological legitimations for their practices. The reasoning appears to be that earlier or "simpler" societies understood truths about healing power, gender, or the environment which modern societies have lost. Thus, some groups borrow myths and legends, adapt rituals and symbols, and liberally synthesize elements of Native American lore with elements of ancient Celtic, Mediterranean, Polynesian, Scandinavian, and other traditions. For example, many adherents of these quasi-religions have sought to study under the tutelage of a Native American shaman—whether in the mountains of South America or a classroom in Manhattan.

These elements are pseudo-anthropological for at least two reasons. First, the accuracy of their interpretation or description of native or ancient people's beliefs and practices is less important to these movements than the usefulness of a myth, ritual or symbol for the group's contemporary purposes. It matters little if, for example, drumming means something specific in a Native American religion; what matters in borrowing drumming as part of a quasi-religious groups' ritual is that it seems elemental, evocative, and desirably "primitive."

It also matters little to some groups whether the pseudo-anthropological elements they choose to celebrate are racist, classist, and sexist. For example, some eco-feminist groups want to believe that women are inherently more closely linked with the earth and its well-being, and they invoke images of other cultures to legitimate this belief, although there is no clear anthropological evidence for their ideological interpretation. Similarly, some men's spirituality groups want to believe that there is some universal and essential masculinity which they are trying to discover or recreate for themselves. Accordingly, they imitate elements of male initiation rites from vastly different cultures and periods despite the anthropological evidence that masculinity is, in large part, culturally defined and highly variable. Although they imitate an eclectic assortment of "primitive" rituals, many of their beliefs and practices embody ethnocentric and even racist assumptions about these peoples. For example, Robert Bly, a prominent writer and speaker in the men's spirituality movement, makes sweeping generalizations about the glorious cultural heritage of the "Indo-European Race" and emphasizes a mythic figure of a golden-haired warrior, even while drawing inconsistent bits and pieces from cultures as diverse as aboriginal Australia, ancient China, and peasant Europe.

This misappropriation of anthropology and history, however, is not a mere coincidence. If one wishes to assert a gendered spirituality which is significantly different from both the gender-relevant and religious traditions of one's culture, one cannot legitimate the alternative gender or religious images by reference primarily to those very traditions. Usually, anthropology and history do not make effective legitimations of "truths," because these disciplines relativize human institutions, showing them to be changeable products of human interaction rather than immutable or transcendent truths.

Some of these movements, however, attempt to link biology or anthropology with gender issues in the context of an essentialist ideology: the idea of some innate "women's nature" or "men's nature" as a legitimation for their beliefs and practices. This line of reasoning argues that all men (or all women)—regardless of culture or historical era—possess a common core nature by virtue of their sex. Presumably, features of modern society have put many people "out of touch" with their essential male or female traits and potentials, whereas people in simpler societies and earlier times implicitly understood, developed, and celebrated these traits. The appeal to pseudo-anthropology is, thus, an attempt to discover such universals of men's and women's "nature" and to borrow cultural practices (abstracted from their social-structural contexts) to resocialize movement members for these traits and potentials.

The alternative spiritualities proffered by some religious or quasi-religious movements, however, are only one kind of response to the modern, pluralistic situation. Another response is that of religious movements that reassert *traditional* gender roles and identities with renewed vigor. Both responses are analogous to how groups organize to react to religious pluralism (see Berger 1967): Some groups embrace the diversity, expand their definitions, but risk losing control over the boundaries of their beliefs/practices, while other groups retrench into sectarian enclaves to protect members from the "bad" influences present in the larger society.

The recent rise of religious movements vigorously reasserting traditional gender roles is closely related to the development of religious (or spiritual) movements promoting alternatives to those roles. For example, Davidman's (1991) study of women who became newly Orthodox Jews suggests that a large part of the appeal for women is the reassertion of traditional gender and family roles in the face of the uncertainty and fluidity of gender roles in the larger society. Similarly, one important function of private fundamentalist schools is the sectarian socialization of children into traditional gender identities and family roles.

A more extreme contemporary quasi-religious movement reasserting gender roles is the Christian Patriot movement, a sometimes violent right-wing movement linking religion, racism, sexism, and patriotism. Aho (1990) describes the dualistic worldview of this movement as causally connecting all of the "evils" of modern society: sex education, birth control, drunkenness, pornography, drug addiction, raucous music, dance, provocative dress, secular humanism in the schools, liberal media, blurring of roles, and the mixing of "distinct" categories of people (such as races, classes, nations, and creeds). Aho notes that these things are not viewed as evil in themselves, but rather they are abhorred because "they represent, among other things, the assertion of the feminine principle and the loss of masculine control, sensibility, creativity, consciousness, aggressiveness, and rationality" (1990, p. 220). Although such sectarianism is an extreme form, it illustrates that—in the context of modern pluralism of both religion and gender roles—asserting a traditional response requires a considerable effort not needed in a traditional society.

CONTEMPORARY SELVES AND SPIRITUALITIES

It is almost a truism to say that gender meanings are, today, uncertain and changing. Although many barriers to women in the workplace, political office, and legal rights have been diminished or demolished, gender boundaries remain an important arena for the assertion of power, authority, and privilege. Gender identity is also a very important feature of individual self-presentation, esteem, and interaction. If the creation, maintenance, and transformation of individuals' gender identities are, indeed, among the foremost identity work to be accomplished, then extensive empirical study of the many contemporary instances of gendered spirituality is very worthwhile.

In particular, we need more data about the beliefs and practices of ordinary adherents of these alternative spiritualities, because we cannot assume that media portrayals and the pronouncements of movement spokespersons (often self-proclaimed) adequately represent the meaning of gendered spiritualities to adherents themselves. We also need an accurate portrait of relevant demographic variables: Are these groups appealing to people in a certain life-stage? Are they drawing people disproportionately from certain social classes, or might there be parallel movements attracting people from other social classes? What part of the work-world is represented? Are adherents drawn disproportionately from white-collar or human service occupations? Are adherents particularly likely to be in or trying to move into nontraditional work roles for men or women? Do recruits experience particular stresses or contradictions of freedom and constraint in their work-lives? Are traditional identity patterns problematic or less successful in these socioeconomic settings? Just how amenable is the modern work-world to diverse identity patterns of its participants?

Another quality of these social developments that needs far more research is the actual organization of gendered spiritualities. While, in principle, these transformations could be accomplished individually, there is considerable sharing of ideas, mutual support, and fervor possible in a group setting. When these quasi-religious groups form, how are they organized, led, and spread? Thus far, these organizational qualities within men's groups appear to be very different from those in women's movements. How is the organization of these movements linked to economic arrangements? Are they extensions of professional expertise (and fee-for-service), commodified packages of consumerism, mutual help and reciprocal care, or denomination-like congregations?

Recent quasi-religious movements suggest several questions for interpreting larger societal changes. What socioeconomic structural factors make gender a salient issue for religion? How are gender roles embedded in and disembedded from institutional (or "official") religion? If modern industrialized societies are becoming "secularized," why are issues of gender and sexuality being expressed in spiritual idioms? What is the social location (e.g., social class, education, political agenda, etc.) of these gendered spiritualities and what does that location imply for their influence and long-term impact? How is gender identity (as well as religious identity, ethnic identity, and so on) chosen and accomplished in nontraditional, pluralistic social contexts? Such data may enable the social sciences of religion to address important theories of the self in modern society.[5]

ACKNOWLEDGMENTS

The author wishes to thank Paula Cooey, Phillip Hammond, and Sheryl Tynes for their helpful comments on earlier drafts of this paper.

NOTES

1. See, for example, Foley's (1990) analysis of how football teams, marching bands, cheerleader and pep squads are engaged in gender-role socialization in a South Texas town. Compare also, Messner's (1990) discussion of the identity processes involved in the gendered institutions of organized sports. Sanday (1990) examines gender roles of college fraternity members and their female companions. She notes how the initiation ritual is linked to images of masculinity and the production of bonds of brotherhood; these same values make gang-rape a plausible expression of being a man and being "one of us." Hantover's (1978) historical analysis observes that the Boy Scouts served both adult men and adolescent boys as an opportunity to develop and prove manliness in an era in which social structural changes—especially reduction of autonomy in the workplace—had restricted the opportunities for many men to enact the culturally recognized symbols of being a man. In a fascinating discussion of the nature and history of rural Southern male culture, Ownby (1990, pp. 27-32) notes that hunting enabled men to leave the restraints of evangelical culture and female notions of propriety. Being a man on the hunt meant "excitement, freedom, and an opportunity for the unrestrained exercise of will," including binge killing and a sense of recklessness, often enhanced by excessive drinking.

2. By locating the central cultural change in the structure of the family, most of these interpretations explicitly or implicitly borrow from psychoanalytic theories, such as Chodorow's, of parent-child relations in socialization. Hackett (1991b) gives a succinct overview of psychoanalytic interpretations of both Victorian women's and men's gender roles constructions.

3. Indeed, in the growth years of fraternal orders, the creation and enactment of initiation ceremonies into ever-increasing levels of membership were the foremost activity of most lodges (Carnes 1989, pp. 27 ff.). Several contemporary men's movements use American culture's lack of ritual initiation into "Manhood" as a legitimation for their activities; they assume that men psychologically require initiation into their male identities. This idea is precisely parallel to fraternal orders' beliefs about their rituals—many of which were patterned after "primitive" male initiations; they explained ritual initiation into Manhood as fulfilling "a 'universal' need among men" (Carnes 1989, p. 104).

4.   Reliable empirical studies of these movements have not yet been published, so this discussion is based on journalistic reports, personal narratives of informants, and the statements of various movement spokespersons. Apparently balanced descriptions are provided by Adler et al. (1991), Gabriel (1990), and Gelman (1990); for a critical report see Tevlin (1989).

5.   See, for example, Robertson's (1977) overview of this theme in the sociology of religion. Luckmann's (1967) thesis addressed precisely these issues of how modern religion is linked with the relative autonomy and constraint of the self, and other contemporary social theorists have developed alternative interpretations. Space does not permit discussion here, but the phenomena discussed here are linked with recent theories of the self-society linkage discussed by Berger, Bourdieu, Dreitzel, Elias, Foucault, Giddens, Goffman, Habermas, Lasch, Luckmann, Riesman, Sennett, among others.

REFERENCES

Adler, J., K. Springen, D. Glick, and J. Gordon. 1991. "Drums, Sweat and Tears." *Newsweek*, June 24, pp. 46-51.

Aho, J. 1990. *The Politics of Righteousness: Idaho Christian Patriotism*. Seattle: University of Washington Press.

Albanese, C. 1991. *America: Religions and Religion*. Belmont, CA: Wadsworth.

Bednarowski, M. 1983. "Women in Occult America." Pp. 177-195 in *The Occult in America: New Historical Perspectives*, edited by H. Kerr and C.L. Crow. Urbana: University of Illinois Press.

Berger, P. 1967. *The Sacred Canopy: Elements of a Sociological Theory of Religion*. Garden City, NY: Doubleday.

Braude, A. 1985. "Spirits Defend the Rights of Women: Spiritualism and Changing Sex Roles in Nineteenth-century America." Pp. 419-431 in *Women, Religion and Social Change*, edited by Y.Y. Haddad and E.B. Findly. Albany: State University of New York Press.

Carnes, M. 1989. *Secret Ritual and Manhood in Victorian America*. New Haven, CT: Yale University Press.

Clawson, M. 1989. *Constructing Brotherhood: Class, Gender, and Fraternalism*. Princeton, NY: Princeton University Press.

Davidman, L. 1991. *Tradition in a Rootless World: Women Turn to Orthodox Judaism*. Berkeley: University of California Press.

Dreitzel, H. 1981. "The Socialization of Nature: Western Attitudes towards Body and Emotions." Pp. 205-223 in *Indigenous Psychologies: The Anthropology of the Self*, edited by P. Heelas and A. Lock. New York: Academic Press.

Drinka, G. 1984. *The Birth of Neurosis: Myth, Malady, and the Victorians*. New York: Simon and Schuster.

Foley, D. 1990. *Learning Capitalist Culture: Deep in the Heart of Tejas*. Philadelphia: University of Pennsylvania Press.

Gabriel, T. 1990. "Call of the Wildmen." *The New York Times Magazine,* October 14, pp. 36-39, 47.

Gelman, D. 1990. "Making It All Feel Better." *Newsweek,* November 26, pp. 66-68.

Giddens, A. 1991. *Modernity and Self-Identity: Self and Society in the Late Modern Age*. Stanford, CA: Stanford University Press.

Griffin, C. 1990. "Reconstructing Masculinity from the Evangelical Revival to the Waning of Progressivism: A Speculative Synthesis." Pp. 183-204 in *Meanings for Manhood: Constructions of Masculinity in Victorian America*, edited by M. Carnes and C. Griffin. Chicago: University of Chicago Press.

Hackett, D. 1991a. "Women and Men in Nineteenth Century American Religious Culture." Paper presented to the International Society for the Sociology of Religion.

————. 1991b. "Gender and Social Class in Late Nineteenth Century American Protestantism." Paper presented to the American Academy of Religion.

Hantover, J. 1978. "The Boy Scouts and the Validation of Masculinity." *Journal of Social Issues* 34: 184-195.

Hervieu-Léger, D. 1990. "Religion and Modernity in the French Context: For a New Approach to Secularization." *Sociological Analysis* 51: S15-S25.

Jacobs, J. 1989. "The Effects of Ritual Healing on Female Victims of Abuse: A Study of Empowerment and Transformation." *Sociological Analysis* 50: 265-279.

————. 1990. "Women-centered Healing Rites." Pp. 373-383 in *In Gods We Trust: New Patterns of Religious Pluralism in America,* edited by T. Robbins and D. Anthony. New Brunswick, NJ: Transaction.

Luckmann, T. 1967. *The Invisible Religion: The Problem of Religion in Modern Society.* New York: Macmillan.

McDonnell, C. 1986. *The Christian Home in Victorian America, 1840-1900.* Bloomington: Indiana University Press.

McGuire, M. 1988. *Ritual Healing in Suburban America.* New Brunswick, NJ: Rutgers University Press.

Melton, J.G., J. Clark, and A. Kelly. 1990. *New Age Encyclopedia.* Detroit: Gale Research.

Messner, M. 1990. "Boyhood, Organized Sports, and the Construction of Masculinities." *Journal of Contemporary Ethnography* 18: 416-444.

Neitz, M.J. 1990. "In Goddess We Trust." Pp. 353-383 in *In Gods We Trust: New Patterns of Religious Pluralism in America,* edited by T. Robbins and D. Anthony. New Brunswick, NJ: Transaction Press.

Ownby, T. 1990. *Subduing Satan: Religion, Recreation, and Manhood in the Rural South, 1865-1920.* Chapel Hill: University of North Carolina Press.

Robertson, R. 1977. "Individualism, Societalism, Worldliness, Universalism: Thematizing Theoretical Sociology of Religion." *Sociological Analysis* 38: 281-308.

Ryan, M. 1983. *Womanhood in America: From Colonial Times to the Present.* New York: Franklin Watts.

Sanday, P. 1990. *Fraternity Gang Rape: Sex, Brotherhood and Privilege on Campus.* New York: New York University Press.

Simmel, G. 1906. "The Sociology of Secrecy and of Secret Societies." *The American Journal of Sociology* 11: 441-498.

Sizer, S. 1979. *Gospel Hymns and Social Religion: The Rhetoric of Nineteenth Century Revivalism.* Philadelphia: Temple University Press.

Taves, A. 1986. *The Household of Faith: Roman Catholic Devotions in Mid-Nineteenth Century America.* Notre Dame, IN: University of Notre Dame Press.

Tevlin, J. 1989. "Of Hawks and Men: A Weekend in the Male Wilderness." *Utne Reader* (November-December): 50-57.

Welter, B. 1976. *Dimity Convictions: The American Woman in the Nineteenth Century.* Athens: Ohio University Press.

OCCULTISM AND PRIVATE SALVATION MOVEMENTS IN ISRAEL

Benjamin Beit-Hallahmi

ABSTRACT

Ideas about the external control of the self are much more prevalent, and much older than ideas of human self-determination. All religions promote the idea of an invisible world, inhabited by various creatures, gods, angels, and devils, which control much of what happens to us. The occult provides answers to the question of individual destiny within a traditional, external-fate framework. The most remarkable thing about occultism in Israel is its very short history, and the historical context in which it has appeared. The events of 1973 and since in Israeli history have been nothing short of cataclysmic in their practical and psychological consequences. Occultism in Israel is the gateway to bigger and better miracles, through the maintenance of a miracle-oriented worldview. Occult involvement is superficial and usually does not entail individual transformation. At the same time, as part of the Israeli mass-culture, it provides a wide ideological base and a climate which makes other, more significant roads to private salvation more easily accessible.

Religion and the Social Order, Volume 4, pages 289-301.
Copyright © 1994 by JAI Press Inc.
All rights of reproduction in any form reserved.
ISBN: 1-55938-763-7

My aim here is to describe one particular occultism complex in a particular historical context, to elucidate this context, and beyond that to offer more general observations on private salvation phenomena. The description provided here is necessarily brief and anecdotal. More detailed analyses are available elsewhere (Beit-Hallahmi 1992a, 1992b; Sobel and Beit-Hallahmi 1991).

PRIVATE SALVATION AND SALVATION IDEOLOGIES

Private salvation is an individual transformation through conscious "enlightenment" and the adoption of a newly acquired belief system. A salvation movement, or a road to salvation, denote here a complex of beliefs that serves as the context for cases of private salvation. In any society there are several roads to self-transformation, which dissatisfied individuals may choose. They stand in contrast to life choices which would not involve a dramatic self-transformation, and to life choices which involve self-destruction, such as drug addiction. When an individual experiences personal distress, which is not directly related to a physical ailment or limitation, there are (at least) five ways of defining the sources of distress, and, accordingly, possible ways of its alleviation. These five ways are presented in Table 1.

In the face of an external crisis, individuals have the choice of attempting to transform their selves or the world around them. Psychotherapy as a response to crisis aims at transforming the self, religion aims at transforming both, and a political reaction aims at changing the real world. Private salvation is possible through humanistic-rational psychotherapy, which emphasizes individual responsibility and self-determination, or through the occult, which emphasizes external forces controlling human destiny. Ideas about the external control of the self are, of course, much more prevalent and much older than ideas of human self-determination. All religions promote the idea of an invisible world, inhabited by various creatures, gods, angels, and devils, which control much of what happens to us.

Religion and mysticism of all kinds emphasize the existence of forces external to the person which have to be dealt with and considered. Secular psychotherapy, on the other hand, emphasizes forces inside the personality and the lonely self in its struggle for autonomy and growth. The occult offers an explanation of personal (and sometimes collective) destiny through references to external, visible, and invisible powers. The occult is the obverse of secular psychotherapy. It provides answers to the same questions of individual destiny as psychotherapy, within a traditional, external-fate framework.

Actually, the occult ideology is halfway between self-control and total helplessness, as it allows us some capacity for affecting those external forces, or at least knowing more about them. Religious beliefs and occult beliefs share

Table 1. Defining Sources of Personal Distress

Organic. Source of distress is to be found in invisible organic disequilibrium. Change will be affected by a change in diet, exercise, medication, surgery, or healing.

Psychological. Source of distress is to be found in invisible psychological disequilibrium. Change will occur through psychotherapy.

Religious. Source of distress is in the individual's alienation from invisible cosmic powers that control the universe. Change will come through creating a psychological tie with those powers.

Occult. Source of distress may be in a variety of visible and invisible forces (e.g., planets and witchcraft). Change will come through knowledge and manipulation of forces.

Political. Source of distress is in the social divisions of power existing around the individual. Change will come through changing these divisions.

---

the quality of offering certainty and completeness, in placing the self within a cosmic order.

A basic assumption and an article of faith for customers and practitioners of occult popular psychology is the ease with which questions regarding personal destiny can be answered. Secrets of the past and the future are uncovered with certainty. Dynamics of personal fortune and misfortune, and the true nature of one's hidden personality become known. The knowledge is there for the asking. There is a body of information that provides this knowledge, and it is retrieved from storage through the personal expertise of practitioners. Personality diagnosis is done through signs (birth dates and lines in palms) and not actual behavior. The whole process is a miracle, but that miracle is readily accessible. External forces, that truly control our lives, can be interpreted for our benefit. If we do not gain control, at least we have gained understanding.

The occultist is a modernized shaman, using charisma and the weakness and vulnerability of his clients to perform mini-miracles. It is the belief in the miraculous which is the main characteristic of the occult and the "alternative" healing subcultures. The atmosphere around the astrologers, the homeopathic healers, the palm-readers, and other miracle workers is thick with the certainty of miracles which would relieve all pains and would deliver us from this vale of tears through physical and mental shortcuts.

While occultist practices only rarely provide a complete metamorphosis, and thus do not lead to private salvation, they do offer clients meaning, if not purpose. Occultism cannot supply relief but a world in which events are interconnected and miracles are possible. The basic miracle in occult divination is in the simplicity and accessibility of answers to complicated questions.

NONSENSOLOGY IN CONTEMPORARY ISRAELI CULTURE

In early 1986, the executive assistant to the Chief of Staff of the Israel Defense Forces (IDF), General Alik Harmatz, went to Jerusalem to visit the home of a civilian and to personally receive a document prepared by that civilian. It does not happen very often that a general is sent personally to collect documents from civilians, but the mission was apparently considered important enough. The civilian was Mr. Elitzur Kdoshi, who makes a living as an astrologer. The document, which General Harmatz received and read, was an astrological birth map for the Israel Defense Forces. The IDF, like human beings, animals, organizations, and structures, has a birth date, and so, according to astrological logic, should have a birth map from which diagnoses and predictions can be drawn. Indeed, such maps have been published quite often in Israel.

This story about a trip by a general from his office in Tel-Aviv to the home of an astrologer in Jerusalem in search of vital information may sound surrealistic, but it is not very deviant in terms of the Israeli mass culture of the 1980s and the 1990s. What may seem to us like an unusual and illogical behavior seemed to General Harmatz like nothing out of the ordinary. This visit by a general to the home of an astrologer is merely one of many indications of triumph of occultism, which has become legitimized and absorbed to an impressive extent. In the Israel of 1986, astrology was simply another way of understanding and predicting people and events. The culture contained a particular Israeli mix of occult practices that appear together and enjoy mass popularity. This mix includes astrology, graphology (which is not really part of the tradition but is used by occult practitioners), palm-reading, and magical healing. The occult in Israel offers individuals a form of pop psychology, providing self-understanding and explanations for private destiny.

Pop psychology, unlike the official, certified kind produced by professionals, uses everyday language, rather than professional jargon, and gives clients what they are looking for: straight answers to pressing questions about personal destiny and personal difficulties. Clients get, for their money, natural language personality descriptions. For many Israelis, demonstrating a knowledge of astrology has become proof of sophistication, intelligence, and breadth of interest. It is indeed perceived as being in the same realm as psychology, except that the latter seemed complicated and imprecise, compared to astrology, seen as an "exact science." Astrological typology, dividing humanity into twelve personality classifications, has become part of everyday language in Israel, and proof of that can be easily found in the many cases in which it is used by individuals for description and explanation, sometimes self-explanations. Thus, when an eighteen-year-old political activist, a follower of Meir Kahane's extremist party, is interviewed about what had led him to his political position, he replies: "I am a Libra. We believe in what we do, and we carry it through to the end." A press portrait of a fourteen-year-old Palestinian, sentenced to five years in prison for producing five Molotov cocktails and using one on an Israeli bus, includes a reference to his birth sign (contributed by the Israeli journalist).

But astrology in Israel is more than pop psychology. Certain occult traditions, particularly astrology, are used as guides for thinking about collective issues, from the stock market to the future of the whole country. A subculture of the occult has been developed, containing beliefs, norms, members, and leaders. It has achieved legitimacy and stability. What is significant about the occult subculture in Israel is the degree to which it is taken seriously by the media and by the elite. While the occult in other countries is treated as declasse, in Israel it is established and legitimized. Those who do not share the faith in the occult feel deviant and excluded.

The Israeli occult subculture is not identical by any means with occult subcultures in Western countries. The occult subculture in Israel does not include such things as witchcraft, exorcism, belief in reincarnation, extraterrestrials, or the cultivation of trance-like states, which are integral parts of the occult subculture in other countries. Certain staples of occultism, such as spiritualism, are totally absent in Israel and have not managed to gain popularity. Ghosts seem to avoid the Israeli population, and the feeling is mutual. Parapsychology, which has its origins in the nineteenth-century spiritualism has shown so far a minimal presence in Israel.

The most remarkable thing about occultism in Israel is its very short history and the historical context in which it has appeared. The uniqueness of the Israeli occult subculture is matched by the uniqueness of the whole Israeli complex of private salvation subculture. Occultism is tied to other cultural changes. Several varieties of religious and secular salvation movements have appeared in Israeli society over a fairly recent period. Four such roads have developed in Israel since 1973. They are:

1. the occult, the most superficial movement, which serves as the broad base for other phenomena;
2. secular psychotherapy, a movement which leads to personal change within a worldview that is radically different from those of all of the other ones;
3. the return to Judaism, which is the most popular road to personal salvation, involving thousands, and constitutes at the same time a radical rebellion (against the secular majority) and a conformist solution; and
4. the new religions in Israel, which have led to hundreds of cases of profound personal transformation and constitute the most radical road in the context of Israeli society.

These social movements can be arranged in a diagram in the form of a pyramid, which would have them in order from bottom to top with number (1) as the wide base and number (4) as the narrow point, according to popularity and impact.

All four roads to salvation discussed here are roads to self-enhancement and ego support. Returning to the Old Religion, joining a new religion, graduating from est, or visiting a fortune teller all lead, in the vast majority of cases, to a better feeling about oneself and to a better functioning in the real world. Our egos cannot function well for long without outside supports and structures, and the roads to salvation lead to new ego supports. Thus, any of these roads, though we may regard them as escapist and illusory, is better than other ways of coping with stress, such as drug addiction, which are clearly self-destructive.

One can point to a similar structure of salvation options in North American or French culture. The Israeli case is different from what can be observed in other societies not in terms of beliefs, practices, or personal experiences, but in its historical context and its particular appearance and growth.

All of these movements, which were almost totally unknown in Israeli culture before 1973, started developing at the exact same point in history and have shown a parallel growth curve since then. There is a new discourse of private salvation which did not exist in Israel in 1970 or 1960 but which was very much in evidence in 1980. Private salvation discourse in Israel represents a startling cultural innovation, and its acceptance is a consequence of some cultural changes. One may speak of a *zeitgeist* which made these developments possible. The same historical situation and the same social forces seem to give rise to different, but parallel, movements.

The major change in the cultural climate is the general openness to magical and religious ideas. While Israelis used to pride themselves on being hard-nosed and practical and thus suspicious of salvation through religious or psychological means, some of them have lost enough of their hard-nosed attitude to start experimenting with the new roads to salvation. Once a basic openness to these alternative views exists, then steps toward "conversion" are possible.

THE TOP OF THE PYRAMID: NEW RELIGIONS

In attempting to assess the existence and growth of new religions in Israel since 1973 we are fortunate to have a survey published in 1972 by two researchers at the Hebrew University (Cohen and Grunau 1972). This detailed survey of ethnic and religious minorities in Israel at the time also included a section on cults. Using informants, official statistics, published research, and media reports it gives us what we can call our baseline. The only groups listed were Theosophy, Anthroposophy, "Yoga according to Vente Kesananda," TM, ISCKON, Subud, "Zen," Krishnamurti, Rosicrucians, and "Spiritualists." The total number of members was estimated to be at almost 250. Most of the groups that became prominent later, such as Scientology and the Divine Light Mission, were simply unknown. The number of TM practitioners was estimated at less than ten.

A census of groups active in Israel since 1972 should also include ISKCON, TM, DLM, Ananda Marga, Rajneesh followers, Subud, Syda Foundation, Sivananda Yoga Vedanta, The Emin Society, Gurdjieff groups, Emissaries of Divine Light, Cafh Spiritual Culture Society, New Acropolis, ECKANKAR, numerous groups of messianic Jews, Jehovah's Witnesses, and Universal Life.

By 1982, a government commission was appointed by the Education Minister, to investigate and report on "Eastern cults." By 1990, there were seven communal settlements in Israel created and maintained by followers of new religious movements, all but one founded after 1980. These included two settlements devoted to the teachings of G.I. Gurdjieff, two devoted to Transcendental Meditation, and one each for messianic Judaism, Emin, and Anthroposophy. In the 1992 Israeli general elections Transcendental Meditation ran a party calling itself the Law of Nature.

THE HISTORICAL CONTEXT

The first question we will have to answer is that of timing. Why did all of these movements appear on the scene at the same time? What is their historical context? While explanations for the appearance of salvation subcultures in modern society emphasize the themes of reactions to rationalism, industrialization, urbanization, and impersonality of social relations, characterizing capitalist society, the Israeli situation is unique and requires unique explanations. Israel is not a "normal" capitalist society. It is a garrison state without any real economic base, founded on a vision of national revival and on a practice of dispossessing the native population. The disenchantment in Israel, leading to private salvation movements, is first a disenchantment with the Zionist dream and with Israeli reality.

The struggle of Zionism in the world arena for almost 100 years focused on obtaining legitimacy for itself and political rights for Jews in Palestine, while denying the same legitimacy and the same rights to the Arab natives of Palestine. This struggle has been eminently successful and culminated in the Partition Resolution of 1947, passed by the United Nations General Assembly, and the creation of the State of Israel in 1948, which eliminated the entity known as "Palestine" from the maps and the world's consciousness (see Beit-Hallahmi 1992a).

The 1967 war seemed to many Israelis a decisive victory that has changed the course of their history. It was to be the last war, because Israeli superiority could not be challenged. Israelis had, after 1967, everything they wanted. Their survival was not in doubt, their living standards were rising rapidly, and they could look forward to a future of security and prosperity. Their enemies may not have recognized their legitimacy, but there was nothing they could do about it. The future belonged to Israel. The air-raid sirens heard by everyone in Israel at 2:00 p.m. on Saturday, October 6, 1973, shattered this dream. In the wake of the war, the search for sources of faith started.

Since the hour of 2:00 p.m. on October 6, 1973, Zionism has been facing its long hour of truth in an encounter with history that it wished very much to escape. Until that hour, Zionism was an amazing success story. Since then it has been coping with late twentieth-century history in which its survival is very much in question. According to Shapira (1983):

> Until 1973 it seemed that Israel's survival was guaranteed. The first three days of battle in 1973 showed this assumption to be fragile. Accepting this reality was hard.... It was joined by the shock of the casualties and the reduced self-confidence of the leadership, and the nation descended into a collective depression.... The leadership, which saw itself charged with the fate of the people, found out that it committed a terrible mistake, that led the nation to the edge of the precipice (p. 17).

The events of 1973 and since in Israeli history have been nothing short of cataclysmic in their practical and psychological consequences. A leading Israeli journalist (Golan 1983, p. 2) described the outcome of the events of October 1973, as follows:

> The Yom Kippur War landed on the State of Israel like an all shattering earthquake.... Possibly the bluntest change following the War is the loss of faith; unhesitating faith in the political and military leadership, that could not see the signs of the approaching quake; the automatic faith in the superiority of the Israel Defense Forces, that this time, only once since 1948, did not win a final, total victory; and above all the faith in the future, the vision that the State of Israel is the safe haven for the Jewish people, and the solution to the "Jewish problem."

The dominant mood in Israel after 1973 has been one of exhaustion and fatigue coming from the experience of past warfare and the prospect of future warfare and crises. The catastrophe of the October 1973 war was the beginning of a continuing crisis, as Israel's fortunes seemed to be going from bad to worse.

For many Israelis the years since 1973 consist of a series of traumas and failures for their society, with its future more and more in doubt. The Lebanon War of 1982-1985 has been considered by most Israelis as an unmitigated disaster, similar in kind to the 1973 catastrophe. What all Israelis are aware of, sometimes only in the back of their minds, is their historical predicament, the ticking clock that reminds them that things are not getting better and their enemies are not getting weaker. The experience of Iraqi missile attacks during the 1991 Gulf War has only reinforced these feelings. Israel's continuing precarious situation in West Asia will ensure a steady demand for private salvation. The real issue in the crisis, and the real question for every Israeli, is not secularization, modernization, or alienation. The real issue is unique to Israel: the survival of the whole state and a whole culture in a future filled with growing threats and difficulties.

Israel before 1973 presented to the world a picture of relative cultural uniformity, great self-confidence, and a hard-nosed attitude toward life. We might say that the high point in the history of Zionism was reached in 1967, but the War of Attrition between Israel and Egypt, between September 1967 and August 1970, marred the feeling of triumph. The period between August 1970 and October 1973 can be seen as the point of triumph of Zionism, because there was almost no fighting anywhere along Israel's expanded borders and economic prosperity reached unprecedented levels. Economic growth during the six years between 1967 and 1973 was the highest of any similar period in Israel's history. Between 1967 and 1973, per capita income went from $1,131 to $2,225, almost doubling itself, and the percentage of Israeli families owning an automobile went from 13.3 percent in 1967 to 22.1 percent in 1973 (Central Bureau of Statistics 1967-1974). Optimism and self-confidence were characteristics of Israelis in the early 1960s, and reached their height after 1967 (Antonovsky and Arian 1972). They were lowest after the 1973 war. Stone (1982) reports on how Israelis responded to the question: "How is your mood these days?" between 1967 and 1979. He shows that the two high points in national mood (based on monthly polls using representative samples) were in 1967, after the June War, and in November 1977 after the historical visit to Israel by President Sadat of Egypt. The lowest level was reached between October 1973 and June 1974. Between August 1970 and October 1973 the mood reflected what Stone calls a period of "[p]rosperity and development, confidence and optimism" (p. 121). The low point of Zionism, reached in 1973, was experienced not in terms of economic hardship, but in terms of the loss of hope about the future.

An Israeli psychoanalyst (Moses 1983) describes the consequences of the 1967 war as "an inflation of the national ego, a narcissistic overevaluation, a tendency to believe in our omnipotence vis-a-vis our neighbors and enemies..., an arrogant and superior attitude, a belief in an omnipotence that did not allow for the idea of a successful thrust by the enemy; therefore the threat did not exist.... After the Yom Kippur War came a deflation, a depression not only in response to the death of near and dear ones, but also because of the required change in self-image" (p. 125).

> The inflated balloon of Israeli grandiosity was painfully and saddeningly punctured. As in the Six Day War, there was utter surprise, although quite a different one.... The depressive reaction that set it was only partially in reaction to the loss of life, the injuries, and the number of soldiers taken prisoner. It was more a response to the seemingly incredible fact that the Israeli Army could have been taken by surprise and

overwhelmed...and that in this way the narcissistic grandiosity and omnipotence of the Israeli army, and therefore of the state, shared so widely by many of its citizens, was painfully shattered and suddenly deflated. Feelings of grandiosity and of omnipotence were replaced by those of vulnerability, helplessness, shame and humiliation (p. 131).

We do not have to share the writer's psychoanalytic terminology to appreciate the dramatic changes he has described.

MAGICAL RELIEFS AND SOCIAL PROTEST

Liebman and Don-Yehiya (1984) described the effects of the 1973 war in terms of "the decline of national morale, the sense of disintegration of Israel as a moral community" (p. 133). Such a shattering blow to optimism and self-confidence, as was dealt Israel by the 1973 war, can be mended by a strong faith, and the basis for such a faith did not seem to be available in reality. When individuals can no longer live under these conditions of siege and collective mission and can no longer be mobilized, they start promoting individual needs and individual dreams.

In the context of Israeli society, salvation movements are more or less deviant solutions, from the point of view of the majority in society to individuals' private difficulties. These movements can, and should also be viewed as a rebellion against the majority, a rebellion and a cry uttered by a minority which feels itself to be oppressed within the majority culture. We, together with the majority, can see members of the minority as deficient, morally or psychologically, but we can also be impressed with the crisis which leads to this rebellion.

The phenomena under discussion in Israel may be compared to cargo cults (Worsley 1968) and ghost dances (La Barre 1972), religions of crisis in other times and places. Like cargo cults and ghost dances, they represent desperate efforts to cope with a terrible reality that cannot be humanly and humanely changed.

Salvation movements in Israeli society can be regarded as an active and passive rebellion against Zionism. The cost of Zionism is getting too steep, and so the reactions range from leaving the field altogether by emigration or by changing the psychological field through individual salvation.

Collective self-doubt is translated into individual insecurity and feelings of subjective worthlessness. Hopelessness and helplessness characterize both society and its members at this stage. The growing acceptability of magical thinking in a group reflects collective anxiety and loss of confidence. The rise of the occult into cultural prominence in Israel since 1973 is the most serious symptom of the historical crisis it faces, for such ideas gain in popularity when a society has lived through "a loss of confidence in established symbols and cognitive models of reality" (Tiryakian 1972, p. 510).

A collective feeling of helplessness in the face of a "curse" may lead to a collective acceptance of fatalism, religion, and the occult. The salvation movements we have described in this paper are not going to take over Israeli culture. They will remain the domain of minorities, but they have become a permanent part of the cultural landscape.

Because private salvation, as intense as it may be, does not transform society in a significant way, all the energy fuelling individual salvation movements has not touched the real causes of despair. Gnawing doubts and nagging questions about the Zionist dream and the Israeli future created the openness to new answers and new ideologies—religious, occult, or secular-individualistic. The doubts and the questions have been there all along, but the trauma of the 1973 war gave them much energy and vitality. The questioning voices within became louder and louder until they drowned the old certainties in their deafening noise.

Private salvation might be seen as a form of individual protest resulting from the lack of any channels for effective political action or expression. The search for the meaning of one's personal destiny, if through psychotherapy or through astrology, reflects an alienation for collective goals and meanings. It is an escape from the national to the human. Astrology is a human answer, not a national one.

If we are asked to define the major cultural change which explains the rise of private salvation in Israel, then we would say that it is the greater readiness to define personal problems in religious or psychological-individualistic terms (cf. Lofland and Stark 1965). Private salvation discourse has been part of the United States culture for a long time (James [1902]1961). In Israel it represents a startling cultural innovation, and its acceptance is a consequence of some cultural changes. For the private salvation discourse to be accepted as legitimate, notions of individualism, romanticism, and psychologism have to prevail. Given the cultural pressures in Israeli society, the resulting changes include a greater readiness to turn to psychotherapy, a return to Orthodox Judaism (cf. Beit-Hallahmi 1992b), and the appearance of new religions as a significant social presence. The greater readiness to define problems in psychological terms and the greater readiness to adopt religious ideas then interact with a variety of social forces including strong opposition to certain worldviews. That is why the greatest number of individuals have had some contact with the occult, the second largest group has engaged in psychotherapy, the third largest has turned to Judaism, and the smallest number have turned to new religions.

The most obvious, and most plausible, general explanation is that the appearance of new forms of faith and salvation indicates that the old ones are no longer satisfactory for the population involved. When there is a crisis in established institutions, individuals will turn to alternative ones.

As objective conditions become more difficult and realistic coping does not lead to any change, humans will turn to imaginary ways of coping. During times of stress and crisis, as during times of individual distress, there is a regression to "artistic," religious or magical ways of thinking (Beit-Hallahmi 1989). When realistic coping seems to be failing or futile, individuals may turn to magical or religious ways of coping. When all hope is lost, these ways of coping do seem worthwhile.

In this particular case, a society that had enjoyed a high degree of cultural integration and uniformity has been undergoing a crisis of disintegration and anomie. This crisis has given rise to a variety of cultural innovations of an individualistic, escapist, and religious nature.

The individual personality is always in need of external support structures, and weaker personalities are in need of stronger supports. When society is in crisis, weaker personalities are the first to sense a deterioration of support structures. Individuals may either crumble, or find new, less traditional sources of succor under pressure. When social structures deteriorate, individual egos suffer the consequences without the buffer of external support.

Thus, we may see the search for, and the discovery of, private salvation as a way for disturbed individuals to avoid collapse and find reintegration for their suffering and dying souls. The individuals involved are indeed more sensitive and vulnerable; they are a minority which reacts with more panic to the collapse of an orderly world around them.

From the seekers' point of view, and in their direct experience, their search is for meaning, human community, and love. From the observers' point of view, it is an attempt at compensation for alienation and personal deprivations. For the seekers who have found their private salvations, the voice of faith is used to silence the inner and outer voices of doubts and despair.

Nonsensology is a collection of small miracles, rather than a dramatic, total salvation. The investment needed by clients is minimal, and the rewards match the cost, but nonsensology in Israel is the gateway to bigger and better miracles through the maintenance of a miracle-oriented worldview. The occult as a road to private salvation in Israel is obviously secondary. Occult involvement is superficial and usually does not entail individual transformation. At the same time, as part of the Israeli mass-culture, it provides a wide ideological base and a climate that makes other, more significant roads to private salvation more easily accessible. Occultism assumes and represents a world in which miracles are not just possible, but common, and these include the miracles of self-transformation.

ACKNOWLEDGMENTS

Preparation of this paper has been made possible through the support of CETSAP, CNRS, Paris. The help offered by Daniel Friedmann and Nicole Lapierre is gratefully acknowledged.

REFERENCES

Antonovsky, A., and A. Arian. 1972. *Hopes and Fears of Israelis.* Jerusalem: Jerusalem Academic Press.

Beit-Hallahmi, B. 1989. *Prolegomena to the Psychological Study of Religion.* Lewisburg, PA: Bucknell University Press.

―――. 1992a. *Original Sins: Reflections on the History of Zionism and Israel.* London: Pluto Press.

―――. 1992b. *Despair and Deliverance: Private Salvation In Contemporary Israel.* Albany, NY: SUNY Press.

Central Bureau of Statistics. 1963-1983. *Statistical Abstracts of Israel.* Jerusalem: Author.

Cohen, E., and H. Grunau, 1972. *Minorities in Israel.* The Hebrew University, The Institute for Asian and African Studies [Hebrew].

Golan, A. 1983. "The Hermon Fortress: The Wound." *Yediot Aharonot,* September 16 [Hebrew].

James, W. 1961[1902]. *The Varieties of Religious Experience.* New York: New American Library.

La Barre, W. 1972. *The Ghost Dance.* New York: Dell.

Liebman, C.S., and E. Don-Yehiya. 1984. "Separation of Religion and State in Israel: A Program or a Slogan?" Pp. 129-153 in *Religion and Politics in Israel,* edited by C.S. Liebman and E. Don-Yehiya. Bloomington: University of Indiana Press.

Lofland, J., and R. Stark. 1965. "Becoming a World Saver: A Theory of Conversion to a Deviant Perspective." *American Sociological Review* 30: 862-875.

Moses, R. 1983. "Emotional Responses to Stress in Israel: A Psychoanalytic Perspective." Pp. 114-137 in *Stress in Israel,* edited by S. Breznitz. New York: Van Nostrand Reinhold.

Shapira, A. 1983. "From Ideology to Performance and Back." *Haaretz,* September 16 [Hebrew].

Sobel, Z., and B. Beit-Hallahmi, eds. 1991. *Tradition, Conflict, and Continuity: Jewishness and Judaism In Israel.* Albany, NY: SUNY Press.

Stone, R.A. 1982. *Social Change in Israel: Attitudes and Events, 1967-1979.* New York: Praeger.

Tiryakian, E.A. 1972. "Toward the Sociology of Esoteric Culture." *American Journal of Sociology* 78: 491-512.

Worsely, P. 1968. *The Trumpet Shall Sound.* New York: Schocken.

EVOLUTION:

THE CENTRAL MYTHOLOGY
OF THE NEW AGE MOVEMENT

Irving Hexham

ABSTRACT

This paper argues that an understanding of myth and its function in society throws important light on the New Age movement. Myths are perhaps best understood as stories with culturally formative power. The success of any myth depends on people accepting it as true. Because Biblical myths are no longer regarded by most as historically true, they have ceased to provide the central mythology of Western society. In their place, a new central mythology, centering around the hope for the evolutionary transformation of humankind, has been gaining ground. This myth of evolution can be seen in such nineteenth-century movements as Mormonism and Theosophy and is currently finding widespread expression in the New Age movement as well as in much popular pseudo-scientific literature. The myth of evolution is only marginally related to the science of evolution and represents, in fact, a return to a magical worldview.

Religion and the Social Order, Volume 4, pages 303-321.
Copyright © 1994 by JAI Press Inc.
All rights of reproduction in any form reserved.
ISBN: 1-55938-763-7

INTRODUCTION

This paper argues that an understanding of myth and its function in society throws important light on the New Age movement which is best understood in terms of its mythological substructure. But, before the argument can be developed it is necessary to define what is meant by "myth" and dispel some misconceptions created by the loose use of the term by many writers. Whenever the word "myth" is mentioned, either people think that it denotes something which is untrue or they see in myth some hidden spiritual truth. The first attitude is demonstrated by the unreconstructed Stalinist who said "Eric Honecker is the only honest man in Germany. Don't believe what you read about former East Germany in the newspapers; it's a myth. It's all untrue."

The second attitude is reflected in the writings of men like Mircea Eliade (1907-1988) and Joseph Campbell (1904-1987), both of whom use the idea of myth to promote their own vague defense of spirituality. In the works of these men, and many others like them, myths convey some indefinable transcendental truth, or literary value, which can be grasped intuitively by spiritual people or folk living in nontechnological societies but which most modern individuals completely fail to understand. (For a good discussion of various literary uses of myth, see Ruthven 1976.) Although works like these impress many people seeking an excuse for religious belief all they really do is weave a web of confusion which sounds profound but which, upon closer analysis, is meaningless.[1] Therefore, because of the problems attached to the use of the term myth, many social scientists simply abandon it to the cranks and attempt to use other more respectable terms.

Defining Myth Meaningfully

Abandoning the use of myth to cranks is understandable, but such a retreat causes social scientists to overlook some important aspects of reality which are best understood as myth once the term is meaningfully defined. The value of using myth as an analytic concept can be seen when we consider the alternatives. Instead of talking about myth we could refer to a weltanchaung (worldview), or we could talk about an ideology, philosophy, or perspective.

The problem with all of these and many other similar terms is that they convey the notion of rational argument. Someone who lives according to his or her religious beliefs is usually assumed to be a person who thinks and acts in a logical manner on the basis of rational arguments. Worldviews are consistent entities, and when their consistency fails or at least is recognized as failing by either an outsider or an insider, a problem is created for the believer who attempts to show why, despite the apparent contradictions, the worldview is believable.

By contrast, mythological thinking lacks propositional form. Some mythologies may form coherent wholes but many consist of isolated fragments which coexist in a person's consciousness without any need being felt to express their meaning propositionally. The fact that myths, as myths, lack propositional expression is often missed because one of the functions of myths is to give coherence to the life of individuals who believe them (Miranda 1972). What then is a myth and how can it be defined without lapsing into the sort of vague nonsense which delights Eliade and his kin? Probably the most useful definition of myth is: *a story with culturally formative power.*

What is meant by this definition is that a myth is essentially a story which affects the way people live.[2] It can be any story. Contrary to the opinions of many who write about myth, a myth is not necessarily unhistorical. In itself a story that becomes a myth need be neither true nor false, historical nor unhistorical, fact nor fiction. What is important is not the story itself but the function which it serves in the life of an individual, a group, or a whole society.

Myths are stories that serve specific social functions. They enable members of different societies and subgroups within societies to understand themselves and their world. As anthropologist John Middleton (1967, p. x) puts it, "a myth is a statement about society and man's place in it and in the surrounding universe... Myths and cosmological notions are concerned with the relationship of people with other people, with nature and with the supernatural."

Thus what makes a story a myth is not its content, as the rationalists thought, but the use to which the story is put. Once accepted, a myth can be used to ennoble the past, explain the present, and hold out hope for the future. It gives individual and social life meaning and direction. This ability to guide action distinguishes myths from legends, folk tales, and other stories. In short, myths have the power to change lives and shape societies.

Three Examples of Stories which Became Myths

The traditional Buddhist story about the Buddha in the deer park who lays down his life to save that of a tigress who has just given birth and is too weak to feed her cubs is a good example of an apparently ahistorical story that became a myth. Here the story appears to be clearly fictitious and we are often told that it was understood by its hearers to be fictitious.[3] Nevertheless, it illustrates the meaning of the Buddhist virtue of compassion and as such functions as a myth because the example it sets molded the lives of individuals and communities which seek to follow the Buddha's example (Zaehner 1971, pp. 297-298).

Another story which has functioned as a myth is that of King Arthur. In Tudor Britain the story of King Arthur functioned to legitimate the Tudor monarchy. The central features of this tale were fictitious although historians now argue that it was based upon dimly remembered historical events. Once again what matters is not its truth or falsity but the use to which the story was put and the way its acceptance affected its hearers (cf. Tudor 1972).

Finally, the story of the Great Trek in South Africa, particularly the murder of Piet Retief and the Battle of Blood River, provide a good example of a story that is historically "true" but which came to function as a myth for the creators of Afrikaner Nationalism after 1908 (cf. Hexham 1981). In this case, the actual history of Boer migration into the interior of Africa and their struggles against various African nations became the basis for the myth of apartheid which sustained a vicious racial ideology and political practice.

These three examples of myths show that an apparently fictitious, a semi-fictitious, and a real historical event can all become myths. Contrary to Eliade and company, what is important is not the story itself but the use which is made of the story by people. When a story acts upon the imagination of an individual or collectivity in such a powerful way that it begins to shape their lives, molding their thoughts and directing their actions, then that story has become a myth.

It is important, however, to recognize that these individual myths derived their power from larger frameworks which we call central mythologies. In the Buddhist case this involves the entire story of the life and work of the Buddha; in the case of King Arthur and the Great Trek, the truth of Christianity was presupposed as a central mythology. Yet today, in the Western world, Christianity has ceased to supply most people with a central mythology that gives them a coherent or semi-coherent understanding of life. Instead, most people hold a rag tag set of beliefs which lack cohesion. These beliefs are best described as mythological fragments.

MYTH AND HISTORICAL TRUTH

So far, the argument has been proposed that any story can function as a myth. What is important, it is argued, is how the story is accepted by its hearers and whether or not they act upon it, regardless of its truth. This argument is attractive and one which is very easy to accept. But is it true?

The success of any myth depends upon people accepting it and acting on what they consider to be its message. But, there is considerable evidence that in actual fact most people who accept a myth do so because they believe it is true. In other words, their acceptance of the story before it becomes a myth, which often affects their lives, depends on their belief that the story is true in the first place. Questions of historic, philosophic, or any other form of verifiable truth are therefore not unimportant in the creation of mythologies. In fact, they precede the creation of myths. What matters is not simply the power of myths to inspire belief and to enable believers to make sense of their experiences but the prior belief that the story is true.

Such a claim contradicts most things written about myth. Nevertheless, years ago in his essay "Myth in Primitive Psychology" Malinowski (1954, pp. 96-

111) pointed out that most Western interpreters of myth go wrong precisely because they do not observe how myths are actually used in social situations where they are important. Thus, while it may be nice for Western interpreters of Buddhism to argue that "the truth" of the story about the Buddha laying down his life for the tiger is to be found in the spiritual message of the story itself, there is considerable evidence that traditional Buddhists actually believe they know where these events took place. It is not the case that the story is simply accepted as a myth because it conveys a "deep truth" about the nature of compassion. Rather the message about compassion is accepted precisely because traditional believers accept that the Buddha actually did lay down his life for that of a tiger and her cubs. Thus, the historical truth of the story underlies its acceptance as a myth.[4]

The truth of this observation can be seen in the use of the Arthur myth by the British monarchy. Although the myth was once a powerful one, which united the nation in Tudor England, today it has no power. Tales about King Arthur and the Knights of the Round Table are stories for children while archaeologists excavate Cadbury Hill to discover evidence about a primitive war lord. No doubt many people love Arthurian legends and take a genuine interest in excavations that might throw light on the "real" Arthur. But today no sane person uses these tales to legitimate the monarchy or justify particular forms of government.

Similarly, when in March 1979, University of Pretoria historian Professor Floris van Jaarsveld gave a public lecture where he questioned certain received opinions about the Great Trek in South Africa, he was tarred and feathered by a group of men led by Eugene Terreblanche (*Sunday Times* 1979a). Afterwards Terreblanche, who became the leader of the neo-Nazi Afrikaans Resistance Movement, told reporters that he refused to allow anyone to "desanctify" Afrikaner history. This comment clearly shows that believers in the myth of apartheid fear historical investigation because the power of the myth can be destroyed by history. In other words stories do not become myths regardless of their historical truth. It is the belief that a story is true that makes it possible for the story to function as a myth. But, once the belief in the historical basis of the story is destroyed, then the ability of the story to continue functioning as a myth is also destroyed (*Sunday Times* 1979b).[5]

THE IMPORTANCE OF A CENTRAL MYTHOLOGY

The validity of individual myths is enhanced when they are incorporated into larger or related myths. In many societies, myths are officially sanctioned through public recognition. Thus, in medieval Christian Europe many myths, such as those about King Arthur and the Holy Grail, were publicly recognized. In Hindu society, myths about Krishna and other deities are given sanction in all areas of life. Christian societies have traditionally given official recognition to Christian mythologies, Islamic societies to Islamic mythologies, Buddhist societies to Buddhist mythologies, and pagan societies to pagan mythologies. In other words, the dominant religion in any given society typically provides its members with a powerful mythology that receives full recognition and social sanction because people in that society believe that the underlying stories upon which their mythology is based are true.

Speaking of the power of myth, Frye (1981, p. 33) has noted that "certain stories seem to have a peculiar significance: they are stories that tell a society what is important for it to know, whether about its gods, its history, its laws, or its class structure." Commenting on modern society, he says, "in Western Europe the Bible stories had a central mythological significance of this kind until at least the eighteenth century." By a "central mythological significance," Frye means the power of certain myths to provide a general mythological framework that incorporates all the other myths to be found in a given society.

From the time of St. Augustine in the fifth century to the Enlightenment in the eighteenth century, biblical stories provided the framework of European mythology. Other myths found in different parts of Europe were Christianized and incorporated into this framework. Stories such as that of Beowulf and Islandic, Norse, and Germanic sagas were reinterpreted and given Christian meanings. The legend of King Arthur and the quest for the Holy Grail is a striking example.[6] The thrust of incorporation may take one of two directions. When Christianity is on the advance, pagan myths are Christianized; when it is in retreat, Bible stories are mythologized, sometimes into foreign myths.

Since the end of the eighteenth century, biblical stories have ceased to provide the central mythology of Western society. Owing to the skepticism of the Enlightenment and nineteenth-century freethinking, most Westerners no longer believe that the Bible is true. Therefore, they fail to find in Christianity the basic imaginative and mythological framework by which they understand their place in the world. True, many people still profess to be Christians. But on the whole, Christian belief has been reduced to the realm of private spirituality. As a result, Western social mythologies lack a strong Christian content at both their popular and official levels.

Certain subgroups within modern society, fundamentalists for example, still retain a strong element of Christian mythology in their understanding of life. It is also true that "Christian values" often inform law and other official elements within different Western societies. But nowhere today do we find biblical mythology providing both the popular and official myths of modern industrial society.

Once we realize that myths play an important role in social life and that modern Western society no longer embraces traditional Christian mythology, we might well ask whether other mythologies have replaced the biblical framework. The answer seems to be that Western democracies are experiencing a mythological vacuum; they do not seem to have any officially sanctioned central mythology. Biblical myths appear to have been replaced by a large number of fragmented myths circulating among different subgroups without the benefit of an integrative central mythology. We make this observation with some caution, however, because we shall argue later that a central mythology does, in fact, exist, although it has not received official sanction outside of the new religions.

EVOLUTION AS MYTH

Talk about evolution as myth runs the risk of being dismissed because it sounds like the ideas of Creationists and anti-scientific cranks. Therefore, it is necessary to state very clearly at the outset that what is being discussed is not the scientific theory of evolution but the way in which the theory of evolution is transformed into a story with cosmic dimensions in popular culture. Although science fiction writers and a host of other people contribute to the creation of the myth of evolution, it is our schools which are its main propagandists.

Those who doubt this statement should visit their local "junior" school (kindergarten through grade 4). There they will find a dazzling array of evolutionary tales which have absolutely nothing to do with science. Instead of being told about fairies and giants, today's children, and this seems to have been the case for at least the last 30 years, are fed a diet of cavemen and dinosaurs. The dragon of old has been replaced by the dinosaur, which, very often, inhabits the world alongside cavemen and other evolutionary creatures. At the other end of this absurd spectrum such things as telepathy and astral travel are talked about as the "next step in our evolutionary development." And all of this is promoted in the name of science.

What is worse is the utter garbage that passes for the teaching of science in lower schools. If anyone doubts this all they have to do is visit a local science fair. Children at such events display a wide range of ingenious creations which are supposed to demonstrate how science works. In fact, despite the use of terms like "theory," "hypothesis," and "experiment" most of these activities are not simply unscientific but actually anti-scientific because they create in young minds a totally false notion of scientific evidence.

For example, at an area science fair in Alberta, Canada, a very neat and well-constructed display demonstrated the "scientific fact" that plants grow better when music is played to them. The evidence for this discovery was based on the growth of two bean sprouts. One, which had been kept in the house next to a radio playing classical music displayed luxurious growth. The other, deprived of music, had been grown in the garage where it was said the plant was unable to hear any music. The result was a shrivelled growth with greenish-white leaves.

The carefully printed explanation of the experiment explained that both plants had been given the same amount of water, thus proving that music stimulates growth. That fact that the garage plant was clearly deprived of heat and light was totally overlooked. Yet this exhibit won first prize as an example of scientific thinking! When such ignorance is combined with extended storytelling about the "mysteries of evolution," a myth is born. For equally disturbing findings, see Adelman and Adelman (1984) and Greenwell (1980).

EVOLUTION AS THE NEW MYTHOLOGY

In many ways the situation we face today in terms of our fragmented collection of disconnected myths is similar to that faced by the inhabitants of New England in the early part of the nineteenth century. Like us, the people of New England experienced rapid social change, including revolutions in transportation and communication. Their society was transient and uprooted. Traditional beliefs were on the wane and new ones vied for acceptance. In the late 1820s Thomas Dick wrote about the possibility of life on other planets in a book titled *Philosophy of a Future State* (1828). Swedenborgians speculated about spiritual "worlds." Ethan Smith pondered the origin of the American Indians in his book *A View of the Hebrews* (1825). People were fascinated with the Indian mounds that dotted the landscape. Stories about the pyramids of Egypt and lost civilizations were common.

Against this confused and confusing background, Joseph Smith, Jr. claimed to have discovered a book that explained the true facts about many of the puzzles that intrigued his contemporaries. In the *Book of Mormon* (1830), Smith laid the basis of a powerful mythology that wove together many diverse myths into an integrated whole. In his later "revelations," Smith elaborated these myths so that the developed mythology of Mormonism not only explained the origin of American Indians but also spoke about the significance of their archaeological sites and speculated about life on other planets.

Brodie (1978, p. 172) contends that Joseph Smith "was groping for a new metaphysics that would somehow take into account the new world of science. In his primitive and egocentric fashion he was trying to resolve the most troublesome philosophic problem of the nineteenth century." O'Dea (1957) has argued that while the *Book of Mormon* leaves much to be desired as literature, in its own terms and the context in which it was written, it was a challenging document "concerned fundamentally with the problem of good and evil."

O'Dea cautions us against simply rejecting the *Book of Mormon* as an unbelievable and therefore unintelligible story. Rather, he maintains, it has an important intellectual element that gives its mythology an appeal far beyond the mere telling of tales. This element consists in the folksy but rational way in which Smith presents different viewpoints and argues for and against them.

An important, but often overlooked, element of Mormon mythology that gives it a continuing appeal is its use of evolutionary ideas. Smith wrote some 30 years before Darwin, but even at this earlier time evolutionary ideas were being hotly debated and widely disseminated in philosophical speculations. The influence of these ideas is especially evident in Smith's later work, *The Book of Abraham* (1842) which, with the *Book of Mormon,* is regarded as divinely inspired scripture by Mormons.

Even more clear in its use of evolution as a mythological device is the book *Key to the Science of Theology* ([1855]1973), written by the Mormon apostle Parley P. Pratt. Pratt speculates about mankind visiting other worlds in the future and places Mormon views of human life within the framework of spiritual evolution (pp. 153-159).

According to Mormon theology, human beings are spiritual beings whose existence predates their physical birth. They believe that our spirit bodies originated in eternity and that we progressed to earth to "gain a body" and undergo a probationary period that determines our future state. This spiritual evolution is covered by the law of eternal progression. As their early leader Lorenzo Snow said, "As man is, God was; as God is man may become" (Madsen 1978, p. 212). Evolution gives Mormon theology its essential unity.

Similar views about eternal progression and spiritual evolution are also found in other religions originating in the nineteenth-century. Although her emphasis differs, Mary Baker Eddy, the founder of Christian Science, also used evolution to unify her creed. In the first edition of her fundamental work, *Science and Health,* she states quite clearly that "Mr. Darwin is right with regard to mortal man or matter, but he should have made a distinction between these and the immortal, whose basis is Spirit" (Peel 1958, p. 91).

Evolution was even more thoroughly adapted to religious needs by Helen P. Blavatsky, the founder of Theosophy. In her book, *The Secret Doctrine* (1888), she speaks of moral development and individual lives in terms of cosmic evolution. Theosophy suggests that the inner, spiritual growth of mankind constitutes the heart and dynamics of the whole evolutionary process. Commenting on this, Campbell (1980, p. 61), a recent historian of Theosophy, says "a core of Theosophical teachings emerged. They are a synthesis of the idea of evolution with religious concepts chiefly from Hinduism and Buddhism."

Thus, nineteenth-century religious movements were developed and systematized by way of an evolutionary mythology. The evolutionary framework has been similarly popular in the twentieth century, for example, in the writings of Roman Catholic scholar Pierre Teilhard de Chardin (1955) and British biologist Julian Huxley (1965). More importantly, it is a common theme in the literature of the new religious movements, as in Timothy Leary's (1970) seminal work, *The Politics of Ecstasy.* Leary repeatedly links the use of LSD, spiritual evolution, the evolution of consciousness, and the development of new religions. He argues that the popular use of LSD heralds the next great evolutionary step for mankind. In his more recent work *Changing My Mind, Among Others,* Leary (1982) develops evolution as a cultural myth by giving the reader a vision of a religious consciousness that will lead to the creation of a new humanity.

Roszak's (1975) *Unfinished Animal: The Aquarian Frontier and Evolutionary Consciousness,* Spangler's (1984) *Emergence*, and Blair's (1976) *Rhythms of Vision* are other general works that reflect "new age spirituality." All are structured by the mythological framework of evolution that binds together other fragmented myths and provides the basis for a new religious consciousness. Ferguson (1980, pp. 157-162) speaks of evolution as "the new paradigm" and expresses faith that mankind is entering a new evolutionary phase during which we will control our evolutionary destinies. Not surprisingly, Ferguson finds in Clarke's (1963), *Childhood's End* an apt "literary metaphor" for what she claims "many serious scientists" actually believe is happening today.

Evolution as myth can be distinguished from evolution as science by the type of question it tries to answer. Scientific evolution explains how; evolutionary myths explain why. The mythology of evolution provides religious answers to ultimate human questions about meaning and purpose, while evolutionary science is simply meant to help us understand natural processes.

The success with which spiritual writers and pseudoscientists have advanced evolutionary myths reflects poorly on the educational system of Western society. With the development of modern education, the general public has come to believe in rather than understand modern science. Our culture is characterized more by a faith in science than by an appreciation of the scientific method and rational thought. What this means in essence is that we have allowed magic to replace science as knowledge and procedure.

In the literature of the new religions, faith in science has been transformed into a faith in a "new science," which is associated with an "emerging evolutionary consciousness." The shift in language reflects both a popular belief in science and a distrust of science as it is actually practiced by scientists. Modern science is distrusted because it has brought us the atomic bomb and ecological crises. But the faith in science remains. Instead of questioning the use of modern science or learning how science works, many people take the easy route of believing in the trouble-free faith of the new science.

The transition from belief in science to faith in a new science is most clearly made in Roszak's now classic work, *The Making of a Counter-Culture* (1969). Roszak attacks modern science because of its "objective consciousness" and control by experts. He then advocates the democratization of science by encouraging a return to a holistic vision based on intuitive feelings, magic, and the way of the shaman.

Spangler (1983) merges popular mysticism and faith in science with new age beliefs in a similar fashion, using evolution to make shamanic conversations with nature spirits and disembodied intelligences appear reasonable. Thompson (1975, pp. ix-x) takes much the same approach, drawing on Freud's concept of the repressiveness of civilization.

> Now that the failure of the Green Revolution has dramatized the failure of the industrialization of agriculture, the underground traditions of animism can surface without any sense of embarrassment... The iron winter of the industrial era is beginning its end... Animism and electronics is the landscape of the New Age... The people of Findhorn understand the place of technology in nature, and if they forget, the elves will soon let them know.

The obvious flaw in this point of view is that the Green Revolution has not failed; to the contrary, it has saved millions of lives and greatly improved living standards throughout the world. Moreover, Thompson ignores the oppressiveness of animistic and magical beliefs and life in kin-based bands and tribes. Perhaps it is only the rich and leisured who can afford to glorify nature, spurn technological advances, and presume to commune with elves and other mythological creatures.

PROPAGATING EVOLUTION AS A MYTHOLOGY

When "Star Trek" first appeared in the 1960s, belief in the occult was at a low ebb. By projecting the story into the far distant future and appealing to evolutionary development, the writers of "Star Trek" were able to introduce disembodied intelligences and other strange happenings in a "scientific" context. If these ideas had been placed within a spiritual framework or made to happen in contemporary society, viewers would have rejected the ideas as ridiculous. But given the futuristic orientation and evolutionary framework, such ideas were legitimated as "scientific" and "possible in time."

Once people accepted such things as possible within the framework of "Star Trek," it was an easy and logical step to utilize similar ideas in other contemporary stories. It also became easy to make the imaginary shift from extraterrestrial intelligences to spirits and demons. Contemporary occultism owes a good deal of its popularity to pseudoscientific ideas.

In science fiction writing proper, the shift from hard science to fantasy took place in the mid-1960s. The futuristic scientific interests of older writers, such as Isaac Asimov, gave way to the cultural and intellectual relativism of younger anthropologists such as Ursula LeGuin. LeGuin and other New Wave authors offer us worlds inhabited by spirit beings motivated by magical spells rather than Martians, spaceships, and ray guns.

The step from science fiction to science fantasy and neo-paganism is a small one. Myths centered on beliefs in earth spirits, plant intelligence, talking animals, hobbits, fairies, and other similar creatures soon began to gain acceptance through groups like the Findhorn Community which claims to have direct contact with nature spirits (Thompson 1975). Absurd as these claims may seem to scientifically educated people, they are made palatable through other pseudoscientific books like Watson's (1989) *Lifetide,* which provides a good example of the ways in which these myths are linked with claims about evolutionary development which generate and maintain faith in pseudoscience.

Watson's world and that of believers in the new mythology quickly develops into a universe populated by sea serpents, the Loch Ness monster, Bigfoot, and other creatures that supposedly hide from human beings. Fantastic as these tales may sound, many people believe in them—including anthropologist Carlos Castenada, whose books about Don Juan have an immediacy that is lacking in Watson's dry speculations. Invoking a magical world soon involves the believer in mystical powers, occult forces, and psychic radiations that are said to provide healing powers far in excess of the techniques of modern medicine, so are stories about the nature and power of clairvoyance, ESP, and related phenomena (de Mille 1976; Frazier 1986; MacDougall 1983).

Other books such as *The Geller Papers* (Penati 1976), which is supposed to contain factual reports about the psychic abilities of Uri Geller, add further credence to these myths by offering what many people take to be tangible evidence that the human race is actually evolving through the development of new extrasensory powers.[7] Counterclaims by competent stage magicians, such as Randi (1980), who insist that Geller has abused his skills as an entertainer, are conveniently overlooked by the press and gullible believers (Emery 1987).

Once again extravagant claims about the psychic powers of human beings are given legitimation by academics such as Eysenck and Sargent (1982), whose book *Explaining the Unexplained* is a partisan tract propagating belief in ESP and related ideas.[8] In these ways the public is prepared to believe in evolution as a myth because "evidence" is presented that transforms the scientific theory into a powerful belief about the spiritual development of the human race.

Stories about UFOs, and lost worlds and civilizations complete the development of evolutionary myths and add additional claims that are presented as "scientific evidence" by its apologists. These myths tell about beings who possess or possessed at some time in the distant past, a technology far in advance of that of the modern world. In their contemporary form, these myths seem to date from the publication of Adamski and Desmons' (1953) best-selling book, *Flying Saucers Have Landed.* All later writings about flying saucers and alien visitors to earth draw heavily on this book for their central ideas. It should be noted that Adamski and Desmons, who told the world that they had actually entered an alien spacecraft, were themselves influenced by theosophical writings.

Theosophically inspired thinking is found in other recent works, of which the most successful is probably von Daniken's (1968) *Chariots of the Gods*. However, Michell's (1967) *The Flying Saucer Vision* (published a year before von Daniken's work) and Steiger's (1976) *Gods of Aquarius* more clearly show the relationship between these tales and the new evolutionary mythology.

Finally, the work of various science fiction writers who wove an evolutionary web in their novels should not be overlooked. "Doc" E.E. Smith, for example, suggested in the 1930s that space visitors had influenced the history of the earth. Thus his early space opera *Triplanetary* (1934) deserves recognition for the way he utilized stories about Atlantis and numerous other ideas popular to create a story which has all the elements found in writers like Michell and von Daniken.

It is little wonder that we see many flying saucer religions such as George King's Autherius Society, which was inspired by his (1961) book *You Are Responsible* in which he claims to have "received" his religious message for our age from space "masters." Similarly, L. Ron Hubbard's successful science fiction stories have become the basis for Scientology by providing it with a rich eclectic, evolutionary mythology that its believers accept as a revelation of true events.

The paradox today is that a profound mistrust of modern science combines with a deep respect for science as mythology to create a new central mythology based on stories about evolution. An important element in these myths are tales about a golden age, which they project either into the past or onto an extraterrestrial civilization. The latter involves a vision of man's future. The former involves a nostalgic vision of the past that allows people to indulge vicariously in thoughts about prehistoric humans who lived in harmony with nature and possessed vast powers because they cooperated with natural forces to build great and enduring civilizations.

Mythologizing science, myth merchants argue that hints of the powers of lost civilizations are found among Filipino psychic healers, South African bushmen, and other native peoples who retain some knowledge of nature spirits and forces. Why humans as a whole lost these wonderful powers and why those who possess them today live in abject poverty is never adequately explained. However, the fall of primal civilizations is typically explained in terms of pride and the misuse of magic.

Proponents of such myths maintain that the failure of orthodox archaeologists to affirm this romanticization of civilizations simply proves how sterile modern science is and how much in need it is of the "creative" investigations of spiritual people. Therefore, spiritualists conjure up visions of Atlantis, Mu, Lemura, and other lost civilizations, embellishing them with complex comparisons and apparent erudition held together by an evolutionary consciousness.

L. Sprague de Camp's (1970) book *Lost Continents* is important, not only because he exposes the absurdity of these beliefs, but because he relates these myths to nineteenth-century religious groups. *The Book of Mormon* is based on the existence of a lost civilization built by North American Indians, and Theosophy appeals to stories about Atlantis. Other groups too invoke the idea of lost or extraterrestrial civilizations to objectify their claims. Hare Krishna believe in the Vedic civilizations of ancient India, while Jehovah's Witnesses have given evidence of a preoccupation with pyramids and sacred measurements. It would seem, in short, that myths of other civilizations perform an apologetic function by weaving observable "evidence," for the myth of evolution with such things as the Mayan ruins, into such a web of beliefs as to cloud the believer's doubts in its very complexity. Once the existence, or possibility of the existence, of these civilizations is accepted by the believer, belief in UFOs is confirmed.

TRANSFORMATION AS EVOLUTIONARY HOPE

Behind all of these stories is the hope for the evolutionary transformation of humankind, which, according to Ferguson (1980, p. 19) is, "an attack on the very foundations of Western thought." This attack, and the search for a new way of seeing, is the work of like-minded people who, in the mid-1970s, formed the "conspiracy" that she is writing about. Normally "conspiracy" suggests something sinister. But Ferguson intends it to mean a breathing together of like-minded individuals in the spirit of the age, which she contends is the Age of Aquarius, characterized by the "symbolic power" of the pervasive dream in our popular culture: that after a dark, violent age, the Piscean, we are entering a millennium of love and light—in the words of the popular song, "The Age of Aquarius," the time of "the mind's true liberation."

Another popularizer of new myths, Blair (1976, p. 234), has suggested that "the first burst of Aquarian enthusiasm experienced by the young in the early 1960s has for many subsided into disenchanted apathy." He goes on to argue, however, that the disenchantment is attributable to the fact that our cultures and individuals are experiencing a metamorphosis that will transform mankind.

The sense of expectancy engendered by a strong belief in the Age of Aquarius is often increased and sustained by talk about a coming saviour figure. For some this hope is to be found in a new religious leader who symbolizes the mission of Jesus and fulfills it in the creation of an ideal world. Such an understanding of Christ's return is found in the Unification Church, which equates the Reverend Sun Myung Moon with Christ through a commonality of purpose. For others, the return of Christ simply means the appearance of a spiritual leader who is Christ-like. Still others talk of Christ's return in terms of a Christ spirit that will permeate the world. Certain fundamentalist Biblical groups hold that Jesus will return bodily and fulfill a number of specific prophecies. Various other groups combine elements of all versions of Christ's return in a confident but vague belief that things will someday get miraculously better.

In addition to beliefs about Christ, there are beliefs about the coming of space lords and other aliens who will liberate mankind and save us from the threat of atomic war. Once again, we should note that science fiction has played a key role in propagating and popularizing such views. Novels such as Clarke's (1963) *Childhood's End* and his more recent works suggest this theme in powerful ways. While science fiction started the trend, science religions quickly developed and promoted beliefs in a variety of salvations brought about by benevolent space beings.

Other saviour figures also feature in the myths of evolution. For many counterculture people in the late 1960s the mythic figure of Gandalf, the white wizard in Tolkien's *Lord of the Rings,* became a symbol of the new age. Others have developed beliefs about King Arthur and similar legendary heroes. We find "Buddhas" and "Krishnas" and such personalized saviours as the "Bhagwans." All are liberators sanctioned by one or another of these major coalescing myths.

Whoever the saviour is to be and whatever the terms in which he or she is described, the mythic structure of beliefs surrounding the central figure is essentially the same. The saviour is to come to transform the world through the next stage of the evolutionary process. Mankind will no longer be alone in a hostile universe but once more live in a personalized context in which human values will ultimately triumph.

The assurance of the final victory of good over evil comes from traditional legends, religious stories, and newly invented myths. But their authenticity within the mythology generally, and in new religions particularly, is always assured by the intervention of what Ferguson calls "human catalysts like the Aquarian Conspirators." More perceptively, we can speak of these agents as shamans or sorcerers who are initiators of evolutionary change.

One such agent of evolutionary consciousness is David Spangler of the Findhorn Community, who is described by many writers as one of the foremost leaders of the new age. In his book *Emergence: The Rebirth of the Sacred,* Spangler (1984; see also 1976) gives a coherent account of the new mythology as it is seen by an insider. A similar and more elaborate development of the many aspects of the mythology discussed here can be found in Blair's (1976) *Rhythms of Vision.* Both of these works, and many similar ones, not only articulate the coherence of the fragmented myths of modern society but bring them together through belief in evolution which becomes the central mythology of our society.

THE DANGER OF EVOLUTIONARY MYTHOLOGIES

Evolutionary mythology has nothing to do with science. It is quite simply a return to magic. The Western world once evangelized the Third World. It would now seem that the Third World has in return shamanized the West. The proponents of many new religions are appealing to pseudoscience in their campaign to repudiate the real gains of modern technology and to embrace magic instead. But, magic is rarely called magic, and—when it is—it is always justified through evolutionary myths. Such a path has an obvious appeal: it offers quick and easy solutions and it entails neither choice nor responsibility on our part. Maintaining a technological society, on the other hand, involves hard work, discipline, and education.

All of these movements and many others sought to integrate science, religion, and popular myth into an overall framework of evolutionary mythology that could fill the void left by the decline of traditional Christian views. But none of these attempts to create a new central mythology out of belief in evolution has succeeded in capturing the imagination and commitment of most Westerners. In some ways German National Socialism and Italian Fascism proved more successful in meeting this goal.[9] These ideologies drew on the idea of evolution in such a way as to produce apparently powerful social mythologies.

This link between evolutionary belief as a mythology and fascism has long been recognized by historians of fascist movements. Fest (1970, pp. 28, 212), for example, has noted that "Hitler was influenced above all by the theories of the nineteenth-century social Darwinist school, whose conception of man as biological material was bound up with impulses towards a planned society." The effect of this on Hitler's actions is equally clear, as Fest points out: "Starting from the maxims of Struggle derived from Social Darwinism, Hitler could see nothing in law or the institutions of justice but instruments for combating political foes" (1970, p. 212; see also Rhodes 1980, pp. 106-123).

Reacting not only to the mythologization and politicization of evolution, but more generally to the associated dangers of reductionism, Koestler has devoted considerable scholarly effort to questioning Darwinian evolution. Reductionism, he says, is "the philosophic belief that all human activities can be 'reduced' to, i.e., explained by, the behaviourial responses of lower animals ... and that these responses in turn can be reduced to the physical laws which govern inanimate matter" (1978, p. 19). Koestler considers such reductionism to be dangerous because it leads to the denial of all values. "By its persistent denial of a place for values, meaning and purpose in the interplay of blind forces, the reductionist attitude has cast its shadow beyond the confines of science, affecting our whole culture and even political attitudes" (p. 25).

Lewis (1971) offers a timely critique of the mythologization of evolution when, in his provocative essay, "The Funeral of a Great Myth," he says, "we must sharply distinguish between Evolution as a biological theorem and popular Evolution or Developmentalism which is certainly a Myth... In the science, Evolution is a theory about changes: in the Myth it is a fact about improvements" (pp. 83, 85). The problem with accepting myths of improvement or transformation has to do with where they lead society. Who is to decide what is an improvement and how are improvements to be made? For the Nazi elite the elimination of Jews was an improvement which they felt fully justified in promoting. Should the mythology of evolution ever gain such power again, what horrors might our rulers decide were necessary to transform mankind into a better race?

Once traditional moralities are declared obsolete on the basis of evolutionary development, the "higher" ideals of the party, whether fascist or communist, can be promoted regardless of human suffering and cost. The devotion of fascists, communists, and other totalitarians to evolution as a central mythology explains why it is suspect in the political arena of the West. While it is not politically sanctioned, the myth of evolution nevertheless titillates the imagination. One could even argue that evolution has, in fact, attained the status of an official mythology in much of the public education of the West. It is taught not only in biology classes but as an heuristic framework in history and social studies. This development is both dangerous and little understood. Therefore, the study of myth ought to concern social scientists because myth destroys science just as science, particularly history, can destroy myth.

NOTES

1. The late Walter Kaufman (1958, p. 44) made an apt comment on the followers of the like of Wittgenstein, Jaspers, and Heidegger, which can easily be applied to most writers about myth: "The adherent of a philosopher is often a man who at first did not understand him at all and then staked several years on a tireless attempt to prove to himself that he did not lack the ability to gain an understanding."

2. This is essentially the way the term myth is used in Samuel and Thompson (1990), although their actual definition is far more complex and less clear.

3. As an undergraduate student I was taught at the University of Lancaster in England by Edward Conze and Adrian Cunningham that this story was a good example of a fictitious story which, because it contained "spiritual" truth, was an important myth in Buddhism. The argument was that Buddhists knew it was a story and did not expect it to be historical in the Western sense of history. Thus it demonstrated how the idea of historical truth is foreign to Buddhist thought.

4. Information on this matter came from my colleagues Leslie Kawamura and Anthony Barber based on their contact with traditional Buddhists in Asia.

5. While studying charismatic Christians in South Africa in August 1987 I encountered two fanatical members of the Afrikaans Resistance Movement (AWB) who very clearly believed in traditional apartheid because the myth of apartheid was in their view solidly based on "historical facts." During the same visit I also interviewed Afrikaners who had rejected apartheid because they had realized that the myth was historically false. These encounters convince me that myth does depend on history for its acceptance and power. As a result of these and other interviews,

as well as considerable reflection on the issue, I now reject the position I argued for in Hexham and Poewe (1986, pp. 25-26).

6. Treharne (1971) shows how this body of pre-Christian stories was successfully incorporated into a Christian framework to produce a powerful medieval mythology.

7. For an insightful review, see *The Zetetic* [1(1, Fall/Winter 1976), pp. 73-80]. *The Zetetic* has been renamed *The Skeptical Inquirier.*

8. For a critique of such claims, see Blackmore (1987).

9. Talk about National Socialism is often exaggerated, but in this case it seems justifiable when one studies the occult roots and practices of the movement (Bramwell 1985, p. 60; Goodrick-Clark 1985,pp. 22-23; Mosse 1981, pp. 41, 88-92, 103). In the case of Goodrick-Clarke, the reader should not allow the publisher to distract them. The book is actually a revision of Goodrick-Clarke's Oxford University Ph.D. thesis.

REFERENCES

Adamski, G., and L. Demons. 1953. *Flying Saucers Have Landed.* London: T. Warner Laurie.

Adelman, A.S., and S.J. Adelman. 1984. "Pseudoscientific Beliefs of Sixth-Grade Students in the Charleston, S.C., Area." *The Skeptical Inquirer* 9: 71-74.

Blair, L. 1976. *Rhythms of Vision: The Changing Patterns of Belief.* New York: Schocken Books.

Blackmore, S. 1987. "The Elusive Open Mind: Ten Years of Research in Parapsychology." *The Skeptical Inquirer* 11: 244-255.

Bramwell, A. 1985. *Blood and Soil.* Bourne End: Kensal Press.

Brodie, F. 1978. *No Man Knows My History*, 2nd rev. ed. New York: Knopf.

Campbell, B.F. 1980. *Ancient Wisdom Revived: A History of the Theosophical Movement.* Berkeley: University of California Press.

Clarke, A.C. 1963. *Childhood's End.* New York: Harcourt Brace Jovanovich.

de Camp, L.S. 1970. *Lost Continents: The Atlantis Theme in History, Science and Literature.* New York: Dover Publications.

de Mille, R. 1976. *Casteneda's Journey: The Power and the Allegory.* Santa Barbara: Capra Press.

Emery, C.E., Jr. 1987. "Catching Geller in the Act." *The Skeptical Inquirer* 12: 75-80.

Eysenck, H.J., and C. Sargent. 1982. *Explaining the Unexplained: Mysteries of the Paranormal.* London: Weidenfeld and Nicholson.

Ferguson, M. 1980. *The Aquarian Conspiracy.* Los Angeles: J.P. Tarcher.

Fest, J.C. 1970. *The Face of the Third Reich: Portraits of the Nazi Leadership,* translated by M. Bullock. New York: Pantheon.

Frazier, K., ed. 1986. *Science Confronts the Paranormal.* Buffalo: Prometheus.

Frye, N. 1981. *The Great Code: The Bible and Literature.* New York: Harcourt, Brace, Jovanovich.

Goodrick-Clarke, N. 1985. *The Occult Roots of Nazism.* Wellingborough: The Aquarian Press.

Greenwell, J.R. 1980. "Academia and the Occult: An Experience at Arizona." *The Skeptical Inquirer* 5: 39-46.

Hexham, I. 1981. *The Irony of Apartheid.* Lewiston: Edwin Mellen Press.

Hexham, I., and Poewe, K. 1986. *Understanding Cults and New Religions.* Grand Rapids: Eerdmans.

Huxley, J. 1965. *Essays of a Humanist.* London: Chatto and Windus.

Kaufmann, W. 1958. *Critique of Religion and Philosophy.* London: Faber and Faber.

King, G. 1961. *You Are Responsible.* London: Atherius.

Koestler, A.C. 1978. *Janus: A Summing Up.* New York: London House.

Leary, T. 1970. *The Politics of Ecstasy.* London: Paladin.

————. 1982. *Changing My Mind, Among Others: Lifetime Writings.* Englewood Cliffs, NJ: Prentice-Hall.

Lewis, C.S. 1971. *Christian Reflections,* edited by W. Hooper. Grand Rapids: Eerdmans.

MacDougall, C. 1983. *Superstition and the Press.* Buffalo: Prometheus.

Madsen, T.G., ed. 1978. *Reflections on Mormonism.* Provo, UT: Brigham Young University.

Malinowski, B. 1954. *Magic, Science and Religion.* New York: Anchor Books.

Michell, J. 1967. *The Flying Saucer Vision: The Holy Grail Restored.* London: Sphere Books.

Middleton, J., ed. 1967. *Myth and Cosmos.* New York: Natural History Press.

Miranda, P., ed. 1972. *Mythology.* Harmondsworth: Penguin Books.

Mosse, G.L. 1981. *The Crisis of the German Ideology.* New York: Schocken Books.

O'Dea, T.F. 1957. *The Mormons.* Chicago: University of Chicago Press.

Peel, R. 1958. *Christian Science: Its Encounter with American Culture.* New York: Henry Holt.

Penati, C., ed. 1976. *The Geller Papers.* Boston: Houghton Mifflin.

Pratt, P.P. [1855] 1973. *Key to the Science of Theology,* 10th ed. Salt Lake City: Deseret Books.

Randi, J. 1980. *Flim-Flam! the Truth About Unicorns, Parapsychology and Other Delusions.* New York: Lippincott and Crowell.

Rhodes, J.M. 1980. *The Hitler Movement.* Stanford: Hoover Institution.

————. 1982. *The Truth About Uri Geller.* Buffalo: Prometheus.

Roszak, T. 1969. *The Making of a Counter-Culture.* Garden City, NY: Doubleday.

————. 1975. *Unfinished Animal: The Aquarian Frontier and Evolutionary Consciousness.* London: Faber and Faber.

Ruthven, K.K. 1976. *Myth: The Critical Idiom.* London: Methuen.

Samuel, R., and P. Thompson, eds. 1990. *The Myths We Live By.* London: Routledge.

Smith, E.E. 1934. *Triplanetary.* London: W.H. Allen.

Spangler, D. 1983. *Revelation: The Birth of a New Age.* Middleton: Lorian Press.

————. 1984. *Emergence: The Rebirth of the Sacred.* New York: Delta.

Steiger, B. 1976. *Gods of Aquarius.* New York: Harcourt Brace Jovanovich.

Sunday Times. 1979a. "Johannesburg," April 1.

————. 1979b. "Johannesburg," April 8.

Teilhard de Chardin, P. 1955. *The Phenomenon of Man.* New York: Harper and Row.

Thompson, W.I. 1975. *The Findhorn Garden.* New York: Harper and Row.

Treharne, R.F. 1971. *The Glastonbury Legends.* London: Sphere Books.

Tudor, H. 1972. *Political Myth.* London: Hutchinson, 1972.

von Daniken, E. 1968. *Chariots of the Gods.* London: Souvenir Press.

Watson, L. 1989. *Lifetide.* New York: Simon and Schuster.

Zaehner, R.C., ed. 1971. *The Concise Encyclopedia of Living Faiths.* London: Hutchinson.

Religion and the Social Order

Edited by **David G. Bromley,** *Department of Sociology and Anthropology, Virginia Commonwealth University*

Religion and the Social Order explorers seminal issues being addressed by social scientists studying religious institutions and religious behavior. The organization of each volume is thematic, with several contributors preparing theoretical statements or empirical research results on the same issue. A wide range of theoretical approaches, substantive issues, historical and cross-cultural analyses give the series both intellectual depth and breadth of perspective.

J A I

P R E S S

Revitalization Movement, *Helen Rose Ebaugh.* **The Church and Modernization,** *Gregory Baum and Jean-Gay Vaillancourt.* **PART TWO: CHANGES IN THE INTERNAL DYNAMICS OF THE U.S. CHURCH. The Demographics of American Catholics: 1965-1990,** *Andrew M. Greeley.* **Catholic Youth in the Modern Church,** *Patrick H. McNamara.* **Changes in the Priesthood and Seminaries,** *Dean R. Hoge.* **Full Pews and Empty Altars: Demographics of U.S. Diocesan Priests, 1966-2005,** *Richard A. Schoenherr and Lawrence A. Young.* **American Sisters: Organizational and Value Changes,** *Marie Augusta Neal, S.N.D.* **New Roles for Women in the Catholic Church: 1965-1990,** *Ruth A. Wallace.* **PART THREE: THE CHURCH AND SOCIAL ISSUES: INSTITUTIONAL COMMITMENTS AND SHIFTING ATTITUDES OF CATHOLICS. Catholic Sexual Ethics Since Vatican II,** *James R. Kelly.* **The Church and Social Issues:Institutional Commitments,** *Joseph Fitzpatrick, S.J.* **The Church and New Immigrants,** *Kevin J. Christiano. The Social Movement for Change Within the Catholic Church, Katherine Meyer.* **PART FOUR: CATHOLICISM IN WORLD PERSPECTIVE. Western European Catholicism Since Vatican II,** *Karel Dobbelaere and Liliane Voye.* **The Post— Vatican II Church in Latin America,** *Madeleine Adriance.* **PART FIVE: LOOKING TO THE FUTURE OF THE CATHOLIC CHURCH IN THE UNITED STATES. U.S. Catholicism: The Now and Future Church,** *Joseph H. Fichter, S.J.* **Vatican II and the Reconceptualization of the Church,** *Helen Rose Ebaugh.*

Volume 3: The Handbook on Cults and Sects in America
1993, 2 Volume Set $146.50
ISBN 1-55938-477-8

Edited by **David G. Bromley,** *Virginia Commonwealth University* and **Jeffrey K. Hadden** *University of Virginia*

PART A - CONTENTS: Preface. Introduction. Exploring the Significance of Cults and Sects in America: Perspectives, Issues and Agendas, *David G. Bromley and Jeffrey K. Hadden.* **PART I. EMERGENCE AND DEVELOPMENT OF CULTS AND SECTS. A. Maturing Inquiries. Historical Lessons in the Study of Cults and Sects,** *Bryan Wilson.* **Charisma and Leadership in New Religious Movements,** *Frederick Bird.* **Organizational Development of Cults and Sects,** *Phillp E. Hammond and David. W. Machacek.* **B. Emerging Issues. A Rational Approach to the History of American Cults and Sects,** *Rodney Stark and Roger Finke.* **Research in Social Movements and New Religious Movements: Prospects for Convergence,** *Armand L. Mauss.* **Explorations Along the Sacred Frontier: Notes on Para-Religions, Quasi-Religions, and Other Boundary Phenomena,** *Arthur L. Greil.* **PART II. THE SOCIOCULTURAL ENVIRONMENT OF CULTS AND SECTS. A. Maturing Inquiries. The Organization of Oppoistion to New**

J A I P R E S S

J A I   P R E S S

Religious Movements, *David G. Bromley and Anson Shupe.*
Religious Movements and Church-State Relations, *Thomas
Robbins and James A. Beckford.* New Religions and the
Family, *Stuart Wright and William V. D'Antonio.* B. Emerging
Issues. Rational Choice Propositions About Religious
Movements, *Rodney Stark and Laurence R. Iannaccone.* New
Religions and the Political Order, *Theodore E. Long.* New
Religions, Science and Secularization, *William Sims
Bainbridge.*

PART B - CONTENTS: Preface. Introduction. Exploring the
Significance of Cults and Sects in America: Perspectives,
Issues and Agendas, *David G. Bromley and Jeffrey K. Hadden.*
PART III. CULTS, SECTS AND THE INDIVIDUAL. A. Maturing
Inquiries. Conversion to New Religious Movements, *Richard
Machalek and David Snow.* A Social Psychological Critique
of "Brainwashing" Claims About Recruitment to New
Religions, *James T. Richardson.* The New Religions and
Mental Health, *John Saliba.* B. Emerging Isues. Leaving New
Religions, *Stuart Wright and Helen Rose Ebaugh.* Health and
Healing, *Meredith McGuire.* Life Cycle, Generation, and
Particiaption in Religious Groups, *Wade Clark Roof and Karen
Walsh.* Feminist Perspectives on New Religious Movements,
Lynn Davidman and Janet Jacobs. PART IV. THE ROAD TO
MATURITY FROM EPISTEMOLOGY TO A COMPREHENSIVE
RESEARCH AGENDA. Will the Real Cult Please Stand Up?
A Comparative Analysis of Social Constructions of New
Religious Movements, *Eileen Barker.* Problems of Research
and Data in the Study of New Religions, *James T. Richardson,
Robert Balch and J. Gordon Melton.*

JAI PRESS INC.

55 Old Post Road # 2 - P.O. Box 1678
Greenwich, Connecticut 06836-1678
Tel: (203) 661-7602   Fax:(203) 661-0792

Research in the Social Scientific Study of Religion

Edited by **Monty L. Lynn,** *Department of Management Sciences, Abilene Christian University* and **David O. Moberg,** *Department of Social and Cultural Sciences, Marquette University.*

Research in the Social Scientific Study of Religion functions as an outlet for major research reports, review articles, and theoretical papers in the social-scientific study of religion. This annual publication is interdisciplinary in nature including contributions from such fields as sociology, psychology, anthropology, communication, organizational behavior and theory, economics, and the human service professions.

Research in the Social Scientific Study of Religion allows the publication of longer manuscripts than journals permit. Thus, significant research-oriented theoretical studies, state-of-the-art surveys, and reviews of literature in the field can be accommodated in addition to briefer articles. Invited papers form the bulk of each volume but other articles making a significant contribution to the field are also considered.

Volume 1, 1989, 260 pp. $73.25
ISBN 0-89232-882-7

JAI PRESS

J
A
I

P
R
E
S
S

James Guth and John C. Green. **Beyond the Panopticon: Religion, Technology, and the State in Africa,** *Bennetta Jules-Rosette.* **Civil Religion in Finland,** *Harri Palmu.* **Contributors. Author Index. Subject Index.**

Volume 6, In preparation, Fall 1994
ISBN 1-55938-762-9   Aprox. $73.25

CONTENTS: Introduction, *Monty L. Lynn and David O. Moberg.* **Sects and Churches, Conservatives and Liberals: Shades of Max Weber in the Sociology of Religion, 1904-1994,** *Matthew P. Lawson.* **That They All May Be One: Can Denomination-alism Die?,** *Andre Nauta.* **The Politics of Elite Disunity in the Southern Baptist Convention, 1946-1992,** *C. Kirk Hadaway and Penny Long Marler.* **Catholic Feminist Spirituality and Justice Actions,** *Adair Lummis and Allison Stokes.* **Non-Glossolalic Catholic Charismatics: Psychological and Religious Characteristics and their Interpretation,** *Augustine Meier.* **Religious Identification and Family Attitudes: An International Comparison,** *Bernadette C. Hayes and Michael P. Hornsby-Smith.* **The Contextual Effects of Secular Norms on Religiosity as a Moderator of Student Alcohol and Other Drug Use,** *H. Wesley Perkins.* **The Moralization of Illness: The Role of Moral Values in the Religious Framing of the Aids Programs,** *John K. Cochran, Jeffry A. Will, and Jill Garner.* **Contributors. Referees. Name Index. Subject Index.**

Volume 7, In preparation, Summer 1995
ISBN 1-55938-893-5   Approx. $73.25

FACULTY/PROFESSIONAL *discounts are available in the U.S. and Canada at a rate of 40% off the list price when prepaid by personal check or credit card and ordered directly from the publisher.*

JAI PRESS INC.

55 Old Post Road # 2 - P.O. Box 1678
Greenwich, Connecticut 06836-1678

Tel: (203) 661-7602   Fax:(203) 661-0792